Counterpoints of Ecstasy

Counterpoints of Ecstasy

Music, Mysticism, and the Enchantment of Modern America

LYTTON N. McDONNELL

Published by State University of New York Press, Albany

EU GPSR Authorised Representative:
Logos Europe, 9 rue Nicolas Poussin, 17000, La Rochelle, France
contact@logoseurope.eu

For information, contact State University of New York Press, Albany, NY
www.sunypress.edu

Library of Congress Cataloging-in-Publication Data

Name: McDonnell, Lytton N., 1983– author.
Title: Counterpoints of ecstasy : music, mysticism, and the enchantment of modern America / Lytton N. McDonnell.
Description: Albany : State University of New York Press, [2026]. | Series: SUNY series in religious studies | Includes bibliographical references and index.
Identifiers: LCCN 2025023442 | ISBN 9798855805260 (hardcover : alk. paper) | ISBN 9798855805284 (epub) | ISBN 9798855806847 (PDF) | ISBN 9798855805277 (pbk. : alk. paper)
Subjects: LCSH: Trance music—United States—History. | Altered states of consciousness—United States—History. | Music—United States—History and criticism. | Music—Religious aspects.
Classification: LCC BF1045.A48 M37 2025
LC record available at https://lccn.loc.gov/2025023442

Contents

Illustrations

Acknowledgments

Writing a book requires much more than good sources, and there are many people who have nurtured my research and writing process during the years it took to complete this project. I would like to thank all the faculty, staff, and graduate students who helped foster a rich and welcoming academic environment in the Department of History at Rutgers University, where my research began. While there, I came to feel part of a unique community of peers and professionals who supported me in many ways, and it was a privilege to share part of my academic journey with them. Special gratitude goes to Jackson Lears. Not only has his extensive scholarship provided a crucial foundation for this project, but his encouragement and guidance throughout my time at Rutgers was a centerpiece of my own intellectual development. I am also indebted to the members of my dissertation committee: Ann Fabian, Ginny Yans, and David Suisman. They assiduously read various drafts and outlines of the project and provided me with shrewd advice that shaped and focused every chapter. In doing so, they provided me with excellent models of what it means to think and write as a scholar.

When I arrived at the University of Victoria after completing my degree, I was fortunate to find another vibrant and supportive community in the Centre for Studies in Religion and Society. As an associate fellow there, I have had access to a wide network of curious and insightful minds. The centre has provided a crucial space for me to remain focused and motivated on this project amid all my other professional responsibilities.

While my mentors and peers have been integral to this book, my progress has also relied on financial support. This includes the funding I received from the Rutgers Department of History and Graduate School–New Brunswick, the Mellon Foundation, and the Social Sciences and Humanities Research Council of Canada.

I must also give special thanks to my parents, Roger McDonnell and Barbara Naegele, my sister, Lillooet, and my closest friends. Without their moral, emotional, and intellectual support, this project—along with all the others—would simply never have been possible. Like many of the phenomena discussed in this book, my gratitude to them can hardly be expressed in words.

Perhaps most importantly, my wife, Jenny Weston, deserves special mention. She knew me long before I started this book, and she has given me the gift of enduring patience, positivity, support, and companionship—not to mention vital technical and historical expertise—throughout the entire process, even as our responsibilities have grown with the birth of our two children.

Lastly, I would like to thank you, the reader. If you are here, then we occupy the same intellectual landscape and are animated by a common set of interests. By reading and engaging with the following pages, you therefore participate in the co-creation of this book. I can think of no greater honor.

Introduction

This book is a history of self-transcendent experience and music in America, covering the period from the 1620s to the 1920s. It investigates the historically contingent ways in which Americans—namely those people associated with the cultural and geographic regions closely linked to the United States and its political precursors[1]—used music to find meaning in experiences that drastically transformed their senses of subjectivity.[2] In the modern era, these experiences are often associated with terms such as "ecstasy," "trance," or "unitive" or "mystical" experiences, as well as other related words, all of which are used interchangeably here.[3] Despite their differences, what they all share is the experience of transcending, expanding, dissolving, or otherwise overwhelming normative Western notions of the self.

The thesis of *Counterpoints of Ecstasy* is twofold and intertwined. First, it argues that throughout the period covered, Americans regularly, widely, and meaningfully integrated music into the changing ways they interpreted and represented trance. Second, it contends that through this process, musical Americans of varying backgrounds and outlooks helped develop four distinct, yet interrelated, interpretations, or "modes," of unitive experience.

Americans who underwent, thought, or wrote about ecstatic experiences spanned an array of cultures, classes, races, ethnicities, and genders. They encountered self-transcendence in churches, camp meetings, concert halls, city squares, saloons, living rooms, hospitals, movie theaters, and dozens of other public and private settings. In different places and among different people, the experiences could take on decidedly, sometimes drastically, different forms, but everywhere music was regularly featured. In many cases, nonmusical activities were also involved, but music—defined here as the human-generated melodic, harmonic, and rhythmic arrangement of sounds and words[4]—proved especially important to the extent that, throughout history, Americans of so many different backgrounds, and in so many different contexts, employed it toward profound and often varying ecstatic ends.

Close relationships between music and self-transcendent experience were not, of course, exclusive to Americans or to the modern era. In so many cultural settings, music has long been implicated in the process of articulating and sometimes collapsing the relationship between the experiencing subject and the experienced object, howsoever those entities might be defined.[5] The historical record reveals that this understanding has existed for millennia, including throughout the history of so-called Western civilization(s). As early as the Mycenaean period (1600–1100 BCE) the peoples of ancient Greece employed musical instruments during religious ceremonies, including those related to the *enthousiasmos* of Dionysus. Classical Greek philosophers also suggested the possibility of a comparable phenomenon, which they called *ekstasis*. They applied this phenomenon to the Music of the Spheres, a theory that had been developed and discussed by the likes of Pythagoras and Plato and held that metaphysical harmonies existed between instrumental sounds, the human soul and body, and the cosmos at large.[6] In ancient Rome, music continued to be tied to ecstasy. It was in this era that the Latin term *incantare*—root of the English word "enchantment"—came to refer to the singing of a magical spell that is meant "to enrapture, to overpower with delight, so as to *stun* the faculties of the mind, and deprive them of their power of action."[7] Ancient Romans also used the term *carmen*, root of the English word "charm," which originally meant a song or "sung spell."[8] Meanwhile, the prophets of ancient Israel incorporated music into their ecstatic rites. The Torah makes several references to prophets playing music while entranced or as a means of conveying their ecstatic prophecies to others.[9] All of these traditions would come to influence the roles of music and mystical experience as they evolved in European Christianity during late antiquity and into the medieval era.[10]

A History of Inattention

Moderns have similarly expressed what the philosopher Roger Scruton calls a "hunger for the transcendent" and have often turned to music as a way of capturing its experience.[11] Research on the history of American music and trance, however, is still in its infancy; scholars in the humanities have written relatively little on the topic. There are undoubtedly several reasons for this paucity. Cultural assumptions about the difficulty (or even impossibility) of undergoing self-transcendent experiences have certainly played a role. These assumptions are grounded in a deeply entrenched model, common within modern Western societies, which frames selfhood as largely based around a circumscribed personal mind and body or soul. (Many people have debated how best to define the constituent features of the self, but most have not challenged the circumscribed character of the model itself.) The philosopher Charles Taylor has succinctly described this model as a "buffered self" and pointed to the ways in which it has historically been framed as relatively inviolable and separated from the outside world.[12] The "buffered self" concept aligns with another term that is much more widely used: individual. According to the cultural critic Raymond Williams, the individual has always been thought of as "indivisible"—a distinct and self-enclosed entity.[13] Scholars have located antecedents to the bounded individual in premodernity, but most consider it to have coalesced and gained prominence in the early modern West, namely during the Italian Renaissance, before flourishing across Europe in the centuries that followed.[14] Part of its popularity was engendered by influential thinkers such as Galileo, Thomas Hobbes, and John Locke, whose new scientific methodologies assumed the existence of sovereign personal subjectivities that were disengaged from their material and social worlds enough to study them objectively.[15] Religious movements, including the Protestant Reformation, similarly elevated the role of the individual in determining one's understanding and relationship to God.[16] Social and economic relations reinforced the paradigm of bounded individuality all the more: class anxieties of European aristocrats encouraged a culture of individual self-discipline and genteel manners;[17] capitalism encouraged individual self-interest in the form of greed and ambition;[18] and the division of labor—integral to the growth of industrialization and bureaucratic organizations—entrenched notions of individuality by encouraging specialized occupations and loosening the mutual bonds of reliance that existed between people.[19] Eventually, the political philosophy of liberalism would ensure the ascendency and stability of the individual by guaranteeing it rights. In America, as the historian Joyce Appleby has demonstrated, the liberal concept of individuality gained wide currency in the revolutionary era and the early republic of the United States, when it became enshrined as a cultural and political commonplace.[20] Americans' distinctly strong faith in individuality, therefore, did much to fortify the notion of the buffered self.

Throughout its rise, the circumscribed nature of the individual was not only something to be understood conceptually, it was also to be experienced consciously, as the subjective feeling of being unconnected to others. According to Taylor, the buffered self is "essentially the self which is aware of the possibility of disengagement. And disengagement is frequently carried out in relation to one's whole surroundings, natural and social."[21] To the extent that it is understood as a relatively impervious phenomenon, the buffer around the self would seem to inhibit the possibility of self-transcendent experience.

In the modern West, the general individualizing impulse that effectively buffered notions of selfhood was also applied to the world beyond the self. Max Weber found it within the drive toward rationalization, a process he described as atomizing the world into its component parts in order to make them more calculable, predictable, and manipulable, often with the goal of enhancing maximum output and achievement. Rationalization, according to Weber, informed a cultural disposition that sought to demystify what might otherwise have been labeled religious, spiritual, and magical phenomena. Weber (or more accurately his translators) famously described this process as the "disenchantment of the world."[22] He also saw trance experience, or what he called "mystical contemplation," as susceptible to this rationalizing process of disenchantment.[23]

The larger disenchantment narrative and the trends that Weber identified have continued to interest scholars into the twenty-first century. These include Taylor, who has traced the rise in the West of a rational, natural, secular "immanent frame," which can be contrasted "over against a possible 'transcendent' one."[24] The two concepts of the "immanent frame" and "buffered self" readily serve a historical narrative of ecstatic decline. Indeed, in an "immanent frame," divine transcendent entities contract or disappear; and with a "buffered self," the boundaries around selfhood become too strong to transcend. Together, they created what Taylor calls a "hegemony of atomist pictures of agency in modern culture [that] militates against" the notion of "communion" with a deity or similar transcendent entity.[25] Humanities scholars' general lack of attention to topics of ecstasy, therefore, seems to be rooted in a tacit acceptance of this paradigm of the buffered self and the disenchanted, immanent frame. *Counterpoints of Ecstasy*, by contrast, focuses on the temporary and often profound moments when subjective experience broke through the buffer of the individual. During these events, the experience of self was not bounded but rather divisible and porous in its relation to others; it was what scholars have increasingly started to describe as "dividual."[26]

Research on topics relevant to this book is further encumbered by a relative lack of attention to music in the academic study of religion, spirituality, and transcendence in the modern West. The scholar Guy L. Beck has observed a persistent "neglect of music in the field of religious studies" including in its teaching and theorizing.[27] The academic discipline of history has not fared much better in this respect. The historian Matt Karush has recently queried why "despite their enthusiasm for borrowing from other fields and incorporating new types of source material, many historians remain reluctant to analyze music."[28] Moreover, the scholarship that does exist on the relationship between music and ecstatic experience typically focuses on non-Western contexts. The reasons for this focus are undoubtedly complex, but they almost certainly relate to the enduring individualizing and disenchanting trends in Western culture and scholarship described above.

It would seem that scholars have avoided the study of both music and ecstasy, in part, for the same reason—namely, the challenge of expressing them in precise terms. Many luminary thinkers have regularly characterized trance as communicating meaning that exceeds the capacity of words to describe. Even those who were interested in it, including both Ralph Waldo Emerson and William James, to name only some of the well-known historical intellectuals who commented on the topic during the period covered by this book, acknowledged as much; both described self-transcendent phenomena as "ineffable."[29] Commentators in North America and Europe have also long described musical experience in similar terms.[30] In the nineteenth century, the German composer Robert Schumann famously gestured toward music's inarticulability when, after being asked by an audience member to explain the meaning behind a challenging piano étude, he responded simply by sitting down and playing the piece a second time without verbal explanation.[31]

Some notable thinkers have further recognized the shared ineffable quality of music and trance. In describing the value of a symphony, William James directly compared it with mystical experience, where "no adequate report of its contents can be given in words."[32] Rudolf Otto, the German theologian and scholar of comparative religion, wrote of a mental state that is "wholly other" and "outside the self." He labeled the self-transcendent state as "numinous" and compared it directly to musical experience, the content of which he claimed was "in no way merely a second language, alongside the usual one."[33] This propensity to describe both trance and musical experience as beyond articulation has continued throughout the twentieth century and up until the present day.[34]

Existing Literature

Despite these persistent challenges, several scholars have been undeterred in studying musically inflected ecstatic experiences and have produced publications that give crucial attention to many aspects of the topic. Together, they have been invaluable in opening up the intellectual space that *Counterpoints of Ecstasy* is intended to occupy.

One existing set of literature focuses on music in popular culture, and some of its publications include astute sections on transcendent experience in the Western context.[35] In this case, most research has focused on the era of popular music following the Second World War. Some publications have discussed the phenomenon of fanatical audiences, especially teenage girls, erupting in frenzied excitement while attending rock and roll performances by the likes of Elvis Presley and the Beatles. Even more work has focused on the periods that followed, after the 1960s counterculture movement began to embrace music as a tool for spiritual exploration. During this time, rock musicians began to accelerate the spread of an ecstatic ethos within popular culture. The Beatles, the Doors, the Grateful Dead, and Pink Floyd, along with countless other bands, regularly rhapsodized that the nature of the self was vaster than the conventional conception of the individual. Their views were often impelled by a fascination with psychedelic drugs and the philosophies of Eastern mysticism.[36] Such connotations helped entrench the vocabulary of self-transcendence in popular culture, where it continued to be celebrated (perhaps most manifestly in electronic dance music culture, where "trance" and "ecstasy" have remained descriptors of both music and psychoactive drugs, respectively).

Counterpoints of Ecstasy complements this more contemporary minded body of literature by establishing that the relationship between popular music and self-transcendence had deep cultural roots that go back centuries. It explores how American music (popular or otherwise) became entangled with self-transcendent experience in the first place, how it evolved over time, and to what effect. In this way, it contributes a stronger historical lens to the topic and demonstrates what researchers of popular music have sparingly alluded to—that long before Beatlemania or the "psychedelic sixties," a variety of musical traditions had already been established in America that provided conditions for ecstatic experiences to flourish.

Other scholarship—largely from historians of religion, theologians, and scholars of religious and cultural studies—has focused considerably less on music but explored the culture of trance in the United States in greater historical depth than most popular music studies.[37] This body of work focuses on ecstatic traditions within a larger category of what might be called orthodox enchantment. Within the American context, the orthodox perspective has incorporated conventional beliefs and practices associated with mystical experiences that persisted, and in some cases flourished, under the auspices of organized religion, especially (although by no means exclusively) through Protestant evangelicalism.[38] Many publications provide tightly focused studies of their topics by concentrating on certain decades in the nineteenth century, for example, or focusing exclusively on specific religious, ethnic, or racial groups. Much of the work has provided astute research on African American religious forms that praised divine spirit possession as a peak religious experience.

The work of musicological and liturgical historians, and hymnologists, such as Stephen Marini, David Music, and John Ogasapian, among others, has paired careful attention to music with historically attuned analysis in ways that are lacking in much of the other scholarship. These authors have been foundational in identifying the historical importance of music to religious life and experience among Americans from the colonial era onwards.[39] They have also initiated some preliminary investigations of the specific relationship between music and ecstatic experience, at least within the confines of orthodox religion in American history. Their work, therefore, begins the process of filling important gaps in the relevant literature on American music and ecstasy.

Another relevant body of scholarship is associated with the process of re-enchantment—a philosophical and spiritual disposition that remains open to the possibilities of transcendence (and spirit, magic, and so forth) even in the context of thoroughly secularized and rationalized modern settings. According to the authors Joshua Landy and Michael Saler, the project of re-enchantment strives to demonstrate the existence of "forms of enchantment entirely compatible with, and indeed at times *dependent* upon, those features of modernity usually seen as disenchanting the world."[40] It rests on the premise that the rationalization process has obfuscated more than eradicated beliefs in supernatural or numinous entities. When trained on the topic of trance, the theory of re-enchantment contends that modern, secularized cultures have maintained beliefs in the possibility of ecstatic experience outside of orthodox, religious contexts. Only a few authors have undertaken thorough investigations of re-enchanted mystical experiences in the American historical context—among them Anne Braude, Marianna Torgovnick, and Barbara Goldsmith, all of whom study trance and other unusual experiences in the nineteenth and early twentieth centuries.[41] While these authors do not focus a great deal on music, they provide a fascinating portrait of how impulses toward ecstasy populated many unexpected corners of secular society throughout the modern era. In doing so, they contribute to an estimable lineage of scholars (including Charles Taylor)[42] who study the history of re-enchantment, even if some do not always use that term to label their own work.[43] The scholarship on re-enchantment represents some of the most innovative research coming out of the humanities at present.

A few noteworthy works do particularly well at integrating the different narratives of orthodox enchantment, re-enchantment, and disenchantment into a single study and providing broad and inclusive coverage of relevant time periods, social groups, and perspectives toward trance experiences. Ann Taves's 1999 publication, *Fits, Trances, and Visions: Experiencing Religion and Explaining Experience from Wesley to James*, is a rigorous and groundbreaking work in this respect and should be foundational reading for anyone study-ing the history of religious experience in America.[44] More recently, June McDaniel's *Lost Ecstasy: Its Decline and Transformation in Religion* provides an excellent survey of many of the often competing interpretations of ecstasy that have evolved among academic scholars of religion and the societies in which they live(d).[45] These publications contribute valuable perspectives even as they leave room for further exploration—particularly regarding music's role in shaping self-transcendent experiences. Their broadly integrative approach to the history of religious experience resonates most closely with that of the present study.

Counterpoints of Ecstasy brings together the different bodies of lit-erature outlined above. It argues that the cultural history of trance in America cannot properly be told without emphasizing the role of music, and likewise the relationship between music and trance in America cannot be properly understood without understanding its complex history. Not only did Americans of diverse backgrounds and identities regularly employ music to facilitate and represent self-transcendent experiences, but—just as importantly—they used it to develop new and diverse ways to understand these phenomena over time.

In establishing these points, the present work relies on a wide variety of historical sources and numerous written accounts of musical ecstatic experiences. These sources include song lyrics, diaries and personal notes, published autobiographical accounts, research studies, philosophical trea-tises, novels, poems, and more. Their sheer presence, let alone abundance, helps undermine the assumption that music and trance are beyond verbal expression. Indeed, it would seem that the practice of "effing the ineffable," to use Scruton's words, was always more common than many contemporary scholars have assumed.[46]

The historical record reveals that Americans regularly pursued diverse experiences that divided the individual and (re)enchanted the world. These self-transcendent experiences also transcended identities, from the plebeian to the patrician, from the amateur to the professional, from the margins to the mainstream, and across the array of faiths, creed, races, ethnicities, and genders. Depending on context, the words used to refer to such experiences varied widely. They involved not only terms associated with ecstasy, trance, mysticism, and self-transcendence but also words like "rapture," "spirit possession," "enthusiasm," "sublime," "hypnosis," "hysteria," and "transpersonality," not to mention an array of longer descriptive phrases. What all these terms offered in common was an understanding that their referent phenomena exceeded conventional experiences of selfhood.

Modes of Self-Transcendence

The musical cultures that developed around these experiences can be categorized into four relatively distinguishable "modes." This study contends that, just as a musical mode (or the related concept "scale") provides a set of tonal possibilities and parameters for creating sonic patterns, cultural modes of meaning provided a set of phenomenological possibilities and cultural beliefs for interpreting self-transcendent experience. One was the supernatural mode, which cast ecstasy as a mystical experience with a divine force whose power originated exclusively from beyond the boundaries of the natural world, such as the Christian God or the Holy Spirit. Another was the natural mode, which framed ecstasy as a unitive experience with entities that were at least partly grounded in the natural, physical realm. The internal mode, by contrast, interpreted similar experiences as an interaction with objects that existed exclusively within the individual, typically within the hard-to-reach areas of the mind (e.g., the subconscious). Finally, the equivocal mode took on attributes of the other three interpretations and embraced their sometimes-contradictory possibilities.[47]

Each of these modes established a unique framework for experiencing trance, yet within those boundaries, they also allowed for significant flexibility in expression. Just as a musical mode can be subjected to specific melodic, rhythmic, and harmonic choices to create many different styles and genres, so too could the cultural modes studied here be expressed in a variety of different ways, informed by any number of different factors, not least demographic ones like religion, race, denomination, class, ethnicity, region, and gender.

The perspectives associated with a given mode will likely not come as a surprise to specialists in the respective (sub)disciplines that study them.

Indeed, a novel contribution of *Counterpoints of Ecstasy* is not in revealing the existence of any given mode. It is in assembling all of the four perspectives together into one volume, elaborating how each came to (co)exist and evolve in parallel, comparing their respective features, and demonstrating how, together, they grew to touch every corner of American musical culture by the 1920s.

The Concept of Counterpoint

The concept of a cultural mode is one example of this book's theoretical approach, which models how musically derived concepts can inform and clarify theories of culture and historical change. While music's technical terminology might seem an unusual wellspring for the study of culture and history, at a certain level of comparison the pairing becomes entirely logical. Like music, the historian's craft addresses patterns that change over time, often evolving in complex and unpredictable ways. Moreover, because of their highly technical nature, musical concepts are also finely calibrated to capture dynamic processes of pattern-making and temporal change. For these reasons, they should be of interest to historians of all stripes.

"Counterpoint" is one musical term employed and adapted in this book that is particularly useful to historical theory. In music, the term refers to simultaneous musical lines running parallel to each other, containing both independent features (e.g., rhythm and contour) and interdependent features (e.g., harmony) that create moments of both consonance and dissonance (e.g., harmonic, rhythmic) as they progress. In the cultural settings examined in this book, counterpoint is correspondingly treated as an amalgam of separate social voices or "lines" (or traditions) unfolding together in time, both sharing with and diverging from each other in their constituent characteristics. Moreover, this contrapuntal movement often occurs in an extemporaneous manner, with simultaneous modes and their corresponding voices responding to their circumstances in ways that lead to sometimes unpredictable developments and consequences. This kind of contrapuntal improvisation is perhaps modeled best by the collective improvisation that characterized early jazz, whereby all instruments extemporized in concert with each other.[48]

In this study, the counterpoints of ecstasy created moments of cultural consonance and dissonance, and these can be described as having existed at two levels. One level occurred *within* a specific mode. Indeed, the separate contrapuntal cultural lines within a given mode harmonized consonantly around a general interpretation of ecstasy but differed dissonantly in more precise ways. These dissonances could include, among other things, the specific properties that historical voices attributed to trance objects, the ways they described music's relationship to ecstasy, the moral valence they assigned to it, and the forms of communication they employed to express such beliefs. Often, these differences served to privilege certain social groups and identities over others. The counterpoint of experience, therefore, made consensus within a mode historically possible, but only in broad terms. Dissonance and difference remained inevitable.

Another, deeper level of consonance and dissonance might be said to have existed *between* modes, whereby the different sets of supernatural, natural, internal, and equivocal traditions both aligned with each other in very basic ways and also diverged from each other, often drastically, in other ways. Indeed, as this study reveals, individual modes did not disappear in the presence of others, but rather, once established, coexisted, competed, and evolved alongside each other during the same historical period, both in tension and accord.

The Legacy of the Iron Cage

The concept of counterpoint provides a useful model for historical change that leans away from a persistent teleological tendency within the humanities, which often portrays the arc of history bending inextricably toward a singular end, or at the very least provides tacit support for such a narrative. This trend can be identified in some of the existing literature on trance in America, which often instantiates one of two teleological narratives. One narrative is based on the concept of disenchantment, and it describes modern history as involving the gradual but inevitable loss of mystical, spiritual, or magical ways of understanding the world, replaced by rationalization, scientific thinking, and bureaucratic control. Certain elements of Weber's writings gestured strongly toward this view, especially his famous metaphor of the "iron cage," which he used to describe the increasing degree of order, control, and rigidity that accompanied the growing influence of rationalization on all aspects of life in Western culture, including on its orthodox traditions of enchantment and mystical experience. Weber's analogy of the iron cage lent an all-encompassing and inescapable quality to the theory of disenchantment that proved exceedingly popular to subsequent scholars.

A detailed reading of Weber's writings suggests that his understanding of the history of modernity more generally and the history of trance specifically was never as monistic as the iron cage metaphor suggested.[49] And only recently have Weber's scholarly disciples begun to elaborate this more nuanced interpretation of his work. For much of the last century, though, the oversimplified interpretation gained far too much purchase among the academicians who followed Weber. The result has been that too few scholars have given careful consideration to so-called enchanted phenomena, deeming them instead moribund or obsolete.

Another teleological narrative is grounded in the theory of re-enchantment, which describes the expansion of mystical and spiritual possibilities in modern secular contexts that are untethered to formal religious or conventional doctrines. While proponents of the re-enchantment narrative have done much to challenge disenchantment teleology, some of them have nevertheless succumbed to similar iron-cage thinking. For them, the arc of modern Western history still progresses inexorably away from orthodox enchantment and the conventional beliefs and practices associated with organized religion. This interpretation is apparent within some influential contributions to re-enchantment scholarship, including Landy and Saler's *The Re-Enchantment of the World*, which condemns orthodox enchantment, including formal religion, for being motivated by "atavistic yearnings."[50] Leaving aside the pejorative connotations of the term, Saler and Landy's word choice here is problematic for historical reasons: Like the disenchantment narrative, it marks older forms of enchantment as anachronistic vestiges within the modern context on account of the fact that they have not undergone a sufficient amount of rationalization or secularization to be deemed, in this case, "re-enchanted."

Such teleological perspectives impact the study of history to the degree that they encourage obviously partial portrayals of the past. Not only does the re-enchantment teleology contradict a disenchantment teleology, but both of them belie one of the fundamental contentions of the orthodox enchantment narrative—that organized religion has continued to remain integral to modernity despite the undeniable growth of secularity.[51]

By focusing on the American musical context in particular, *Counterpoints of Ecstasy* aims to remediate these teleological tendencies by demonstrating how the modern history of trance is more accurately understood as lacking a single tonal or modal center. The aim here is to provide a more comprehensive account that treats different modes of experience (and their related lines of interpretation) as entangled threads, evolving in tandem rather than simply rivals pitted against each other in a zero-sum game. As such, it seeks to portray the history of ecstasy in America as profoundly multifaceted and contingent. In synthesizing and elaborating the existing narratives, then, *Counterpoints of Ecstasy* endeavors to galvanize, if not exactly inaugurate, a more unified field of what might be called "enchantment studies"—one that recognizes the coexistence of disenchantment, re-enchantment, and orthodox enchantment traditions without fixating on any one of them. In doing so, it also seeks to help redefine our understanding of secular modernity in America.

Chapter Outline

Counterpoints of Ecstasy provides a historical account of the distinct and changing interpretations of musical mystical experience that gained widespread popularity in America across the boundaries of traditional communities and demographic groups. To make sense of what could easily become a cacophony of different voices and traditions, the chapters in this book prioritize clarity above chronology. Most focus on a single mode of ecstasy and the traditions associated therein. Moreover, the chapters and their sections often circle back on earlier ones, focusing repeatedly on different cultural contexts within the same time period.

Chapter 1 addresses the supernatural mode of musical ecstasy as it was framed by formal religious doctrines upheld and debated by Anglo-Protestants from America's colonial era up until the early twentieth century. Although adherents of different denominations, sects, and traditions took seriously the features of their faith that were distinct from others, what all of them shared was a belief that self-transcendence could be explained as a unitive experience with the Holy Spirit or some other spiritual entity whose power originated exclusively from beyond the boundaries of the natural world. Numerous purveyors of evangelical Protestantism—including "New Lights" such as Jonathan Edwards and George Whitefield as well as many participants in the Second Great Awakening—endorsed this mode and advocated for music's integral role in it. At every stage, internal debate arose as many middle-class American Protestants continued to doubt either the veracity or the value of religious ecstasy. Despite these challenges, Christian Americans would never fully relinquish the yearning for self-transcendent release. By the turn of the twentieth century, devotees of the Holiness movement and Pentecostalism would elevate such experiences as the highest form of religious experience.

Chapter 2 investigates the natural mode. It explores American traditions of belief that framed musical ecstasy as a unitive experience with spirits, forces, and other entities that were either entirely or partly grounded in the natural, physical world. This mode became associated with the soft secularizing impulse that informed the mystical traditions that venerated sentimentality and sublimity, both of which pivoted away from purely supernatural explanations. This mode also became associated with the nineteenth-century spiritualist movement, which its advocates described as facilitating close metaphysical contact with the dead. While each of the traditions in this mode maintained certain elements of supernatural faith, they also reframed ecstasy (at least partly) as a self-transcendent experience with other earthly entities that bound together nature and humanity. As in orthodox Christianity, nineteenth-century bourgeois concerns about propriety and control also subjected these naturalized traditions to ongoing debate. But, here too, the mode persisted and flourished into the twentieth century, even as other modes gained cultural resonance within American society.

Chapter 3 focuses on the often-unique ways that musical ecstasy evolved among Americans of African descent up until the early twentieth century. Black Americans had long cultivated rich and complex traditions of trance ritual, many of which were bound up in musical expression and related practices. For numerous reasons, however, these were not identical to the supernatural and natural interpretations advanced by European Americans, nor did they always fit easily within the distinct modal categories addressed in previous chapters. This difference arose partly as a legacy of the distinct nature of African rituals and cosmologies that survived the Middle Passage in fragments and informed the development of new variants in America under slavery. It also resulted from the syncretization process that blended these retentions with Euro-American Christianity. This admixture of influences led to the development of ring shouts, spirituals, the vernacular religious rituals associated with Voudou and its cognates, and other related practices cultivated by free and enslaved African American communities across the American South both before and after the Civil War. Despite the richness of these traditions of entrancement, white observers usually saw in Black ecstasy either the threat of resistance and rebellion to white supremacy or an indulgent pursuit of frivolous entertainment. For all these reasons and others, African American ecstasy had a distinct musical and cultural history that warrants its own, separate consideration.

Chapter 4 explores the internal mode, which expressed doubt over the sheer possibility of unitive experiences with any entities (whether natural or supernatural) outside of the individual. The notion was fostered by medical theorists as well as theological opinions within American evangelical sects during the eighteenth century. During the latter decades of the nineteenth century, it grew more formidable with the popularization of evolutionary theory as well as the professionalization of psychology and the influence of Sigmund Freud. Social scientists and medical professionals who did not fully embrace such views, even influential ones like the psychologist and philosopher William James, never gained a strong enough foothold within their fields to challenge the authority of the internal mode. All of these factors together provided Americans with an increasing number of opportunities to downplay the legitimacy of musical, mystical experience, favoring instead a thoroughly immanent explanation that confined trance and transcendence to the workings of the individual mind or body, or both.

Chapter 5 follows the rise of an equivocal mode of musical ecstasy that simultaneously pursued and blended the seemingly contradictory impulses engaged by supernatural, natural, and internal interpretations. This mode was derived from the early modern Carnival tradition and was encouraged by market capitalism. It came to inform early commercial forms of music, including blackface minstrelsy, and it even influenced the Romantic movement in America. People from all social strata embraced this mode, including those from wealthy backgrounds who increasingly began to seek out intense experiences in reaction to what they perceived to be the softening of society. Such contributions helped create this alternative mode of musical self-transcendence, which (re)attached qualities of sincerity and authenticity onto self-transcendent experiences even as it simultaneously imbued such phenomena with trivial and artificial qualities.

Chapter 6 continues to investigate the evolution of the equivocal mode of musical ecstasy as it became entrenched in the commercial popular music and entertainment industry of the late nineteenth and early twentieth centuries. In this context, music audiences, entrepreneurs, journalists, and researchers all came to embrace the more ambiguous forms of ecstatic experience. Such changes revolved around famous performers and composers, including Enrico Caruso, John Philip Sousa, Irving Berlin, and Cole Porter, to name a few. Focusing predominantly on the 1910s and 1920s, this chapter traces the rise of certain subtypes of equivocal ecstasy, including those oriented toward spirits, other individuals, races, and spaces—all of which became increasingly mediated through recently invented forms of technology.

To argue for a contrapuntal history of trance is not to say that all modes were given equal weight in every historical era or context. Indeed, various interpretations certainly became more pervasive than others at certain times. However, more than this, what *Counterpoints of Ecstasy* demonstrates is that while some forms of ecstasy gained prevalence, none entirely disappeared. Instead, the cultural and musical landscape of trance became increasingly crowded by the early twentieth century. The central purpose of the chapters that follow is to explain why, how, in what contexts, and to what ends these various interpretations of ecstasy gained traction in America.

Chapter 1

The Spiritualization of Self-Transcendence

In 1834, Andrew Reed, an esteemed minister in the Congregational Union of England and Wales, embarked from London on a journey with his fellow clergyman James Matheson to America to observe and build ties with churches there. The practice of religious revivalism was of specific interest to them. This is what drew Reed and Matheson to camp meetings—outdoor gatherings hosted by itinerant American preachers in regions too remote or sparsely populated to support permanent resident ministers. Located mainly in the frontier territories and remote rural regions of the states, these meetings required attendees to travel long distances and camp out over the course of several days to worship. Devotional exercises often included praying, listening to sermons, and issuing exhortations. With tremendous frequency, they also involved the singing of spiritual songs associated with divine salvation.

One day, while tramping through some pine barrens in the Northern Neck region of Virginia, Reed happened upon a camp meeting erected in a clearing of trees. Arriving just as morning worship was commencing, Reed was welcomed by the worshipers and immediately joined them in a hymn of praise. Having never previously engaged in this kind of worship,[1] he was confounded as to what had compelled him to join in so readily. "I could scarcely tell what sensations possessed me," he later declared.[2] Yet it was impossible to deny that he was "filled for the moment with . . . [sensations] of wonder." Upon looking around the scene that morning, he felt that everything was "so novel, so striking, and so interesting, as to appear like the work of enchantment, and to require time full to realize." The singing was soon followed by prayer, a sermon, and religious exhortations from the preacher, after which the singing resumed. The afternoon service followed a similar pattern.

The nighttime events, according to Reed, were particularly impressive. At this time, hundreds of worshipers flocked to the main stand. Behind the pulpit, "stems of trees laid down as seats for the negroes" were occupied by some three hundred enslaved people.[3] In front of the pulpit assembled a "full-sized congregation" presumably white. Although racial divisions obviously remained stark in this setting, all the attendees shared a passion for religious expression. During this gathering, the singing, which had persisted all day, took on a fuller power. Many in attendance, especially the women, collapsed with exhilaration. As Reed observed, "Two or three young women were fainting under the exhaustion and excitement; and one, who was reported to . . . [be] a Methodist, was in hysterical ecstasy, raising her hands, rolling her eyes, and smiling and muttering."[4]

During the several days he stayed at the camp meeting, Andrew Reed remained determined to keep an open attitude toward the worship practices of those in attendance. Only sparingly did he register any judgment or hesitation toward the activities. Once, after uniting in a hymn of praise for the first time and feeling overwhelmed with sensations and wonder, he briefly worried whether his experience was immoral: "I hope I was not void of those [sensations] which are devotional."[5] He also opined that morning and afternoon services were sometimes ineffective or uninteresting, and therefore he was happy to "stroll away into the forest" to contemplate in silence the uproarious activities he had recently witnessed.[6] A more subdued atmosphere seemed to suit Reed well, because when he eventually agreed to preach to the camp, he decided to refrain from "any thing [*sic*] noisy and exclamatory."[7] This method, he observed, made those in attendance quieter themselves. Throughout his discourse, "there was a growing attention and stillness over the people. . . . Many rose from their seats; and many, stirred with grief, sank down . . . but all was perfectly still. Silently the tear fell; and silently the sinner shuddered."[8] Even after he stopped preaching, nobody moved—"the silence, the stillness, became more solemn and overpowering."[9] Only later did the stillness erupt into a "universal wail" from the people and ministers alike, as they all sank down to their knees in solemn recognition of the "divine truth."[10]

Andrew Reed's encounter in Virginia represented a cultural mode of ecstasy that had become pervasive in the United States at the time. It framed mystical experiences as true unions with supernatural entities such as the Christian Holy Spirit, and it employed music to help elicit such experiences. Beliefs in these deeply transcendent experiences had been underscored in Christianity from its earliest days. The sacrament of Communion, for instance, which dated back to biblical times, required churchgoers to ingest the holy body and blood of Jesus in order to join in a life of "common union" with the Holy Spirit. The practice of speaking in tongues, or glossolalia, also dated back at least this far and was believed to signal the loss of ordinary sensations of self or possession by the Holy Spirit. While such ecstasies could be achieved through contemplation or meditation on God, they were also thought to occur through songful expression. The Bible itself twinned the in-dwelling of the Holy Spirit with the performances of psalms, hymns, and spiritual songs.[11] This penchant for musical ecstasy persisted in medieval Christianity too, pursued as it was in the singing and dancing celebrations that took place inside the church.[12]

Yet Reed's description also registered a degree of insecurity over the morality of such ecstatic experiences. Instead of unreservedly acknowledging the mysterious "sensations" that possessed him as a divine presence, he described them as only "appear[ing] like" enchantment and worried whether they were indeed "devotional." Likewise, he was more comfortable contemplating silently and alone in the forest surrounding the camp meeting. Such ambivalence also had important precedents. Indeed, since the early days of the Reformation, Reed's Calvinist forebears had adhered to the doctrine of cessationism, which stated that the possibility for supernatural encounters with the Holy Spirit, along with other "spiritual gifts," had all but ended with the Apostolic Age during the first century of Christianity. Calvinists and other Protestant reformers complemented their cessationist beliefs with a strong affirmation of the paradigm of rational self-control. This formulation was similarly inscribed in the philosophy of René Descartes, who promoted a strong, discerning mind capable of exercising rational control, or "will," that could not be "carried away by present passions."[13] It also informed the writings of thinkers such as Galileo, Thomas Hobbes, and John Locke, whose new scientific methodologies assumed the existence of sovereign personal subjectivities that were disengaged from their material and social worlds enough to study them objectively.[14]

The present chapter investigates the different, often divergent lines of tradition that informed and altered attitudes toward ecstasy among Christians in America from the earliest days of colonialism up until the 1900s. During this period, members of different denominations—including Puritans, Quakers, Anglicans, Baptists, and Methodists—generally agreed on the supernatural character of trance but also diverged in their interpretations of when and how such experiences should occur. So too did the sectarian factions that sometimes emerged within certain denominations, such as the Old Lights and New Lights during the Great Awakening. This chapter contends that, during this period, music became an integral medium through which these different traditions interacted and unfolded. Indeed, Christians of all stripes employed music (in both its sung and instrumental forms) to initiate, represent, comment on, and debate the features of self-transcendent experience. By the nineteenth century, musical expression had become indispendable in entrenching a supernatural mode of trance in America that increasingly shrugged off the constraints of cessationism in favor of a "continuationist" theology, which insisted that spiritual gifts continued into the present day, and with them a more malleable sense of selfhood that remained open to spiritual mergers with other entities.

Music and Self-Discipline in Early Protestant America

The radical Protestants who colonized British territory from New England to Pennsylvania during the seventeenth century were not known as ardent ecstatics. Rather, they gained reputations as vehement supporters of emotional regulation and the integrity of the individual.[15] Their advocacy for a stable and autonomous selfhood may be traced back to the rise of nominalism in European Christianity during the High Middle Ages. Christian nominalism at this time rejected the theory of "universalism," which suggested any foundational entity, including God, could be present in all things. By extracting universal essences from the world, nominalism was intended to salvage the ascendancy and autonomy of the Divine.[16] What it also did was disentangle human action from divine intervention. Thus, an autonomous God also yielded an autonomous subject. Such a formulation proved exceedingly influential to the leaders of the Reformation. Martin Luther and his counterparts, for example, endorsed a nominalist view of individual autonomy by calling for members of the laity to circumvent the hierarchy of the church and focus on their individual relationship with the Divine. Calvinists became especially interested in how personal practice might relate to the will of God. Their doctrine rejected the idea of divine intervention, but it conceded that one's closeness to God could possibly be ascertained by carefully looking for God's divine attributes in one's own life. Systematic self-control, rational planning of one's entire life, and other manifestations of self-sufficient individuality were all deemed Godly characteristics, and therefore potentially indirect indicators of one's predestined election into heaven. For those Protestants who drew inspiration from Lutheran or Calvinist thought, such characteristics became integral features of a pious life.

The Puritan leaders of the early American colonies expressed nothing less than disgust when confronted with the ecstatic tendencies of their compatriots. This much became clear as early as the 1630s, when the leading officials of the Massachusetts Bay Colony condemned as "antinomian"—incompatible with religious law—the views of clergyman John Cotton and his supporter Anne Hutchinson, who claimed that true spiritual knowledge was gained only through sudden raptures brought on by the mystical "inspiration" of God's grace. The era of mysticism and miracles was over, the officials concurred. True revelations of grace would not come freely and suddenly, as an illumination of an "inner light." Rather, they would come gradually and rationally, through empirical observation of external events, clerical preaching, or other means determined by God.[17] In other words, intense experiences of transcendence did not transport one along a scale of religious piety; instead, misguided self-loss could actually stall spiritual uplift and lead one to wallow in a soup of ignoble emotion, or worse.

With this disinclination toward ecstatic experience, New England's orthodox Puritans were not known to use music for purposes of self-transcendence. Indeed, some Puritans set forth with calculated conviction to discredit the reputations of so-called "singing Quakers" (also known as "Ranters"), a radical sect of Quakers that upheld the antinomian notion that divinity penetrated all human beings and employed singing, vocalizing, and dancing to facilitate such spiritual possession. Of particular notoriety within this sect were the "three mad Quakers," also known as "Thomas Case's Crew," consisting of a man from Plymouth, a married woman who was following him against her husband's consent, and the leader, Mary Ross from Boston.[18] Sometime in 1681, the troupe teamed up with others of like mind and set to work converting the soul of Thomas Harris, a young Boston merchant on business in Long Island. Harris's experience was recorded by the famous Puritan minister, Increase Mather: "They all got about him, and fell a Dancing and Singing, according to their Diabolical manner. After some time, the said Harris began to act like them, and to Dance, and sing, and to speak of extraordinary raptures of joy."[19] Mather spared no scorn in describing this "diabolical" deed as morally corrupt, intending to record it "so that others may fear and do no more so wickedly."[20]

Most mainline Quakers, known formally as members of the Religious Society of Friends, had little in common with Thomas Case's Crew. Their movement, founded in the mid-seventeenth century in England by George Fox, did uphold Christian antinomian beliefs in the possibility of direct, personal experiences of God. However, most "Friends," as they called themselves colloquially, preferred silent worship and contemplation, believing it paired well with their rejection of formal sacraments and clergy and their proclivity toward pacifism, equality, and simplicity. Conservative defenders of the Religious Society of Friends thus agreed with the Puritan strictures against singing Quakers and sought to expel them from the fold of Quaker orthodoxy. The Scottish missionary George Keith, for instance, advocated for passion control in Quaker worship and rebuffed the assumption that Thomas Case's Crew should be labeled Quaker at all.[21] Instead, he believed the culprits should be ostracized as a deviant ensemble of dissenters. Although some of Keith's views would become extreme enough to eventually marginalize his influence within the Society of Friends and lead to his transition back to Anglicanism, William Penn and many moderate Quakers shared Keith's disdain for exuberant musical outbursts under the false guise of religious worship. They believed the universalist "inner light" that permeated true Quakers actually led to "Sobriety and Gravity in all things, but into none of these mad Gestures, and ungodly Singings and Dancings, under the pretense of Raptures of Heavenly Joy."[22] By the eighteenth century, sober, orderly behavior became enshrined in the Quaker philosophy of Quietism, which endorsed inward contemplation over unruly outbursts of emotion.

Back in England, Protestant moralists of various stripes issued direct rhetorical attacks on the notion of self-transcendent experience. In 1632, for instance, George Sandys, an English poet and early colonist to Virginia, challenged the veracity of musical entrancement by rejecting as presumptuous the belief that "the Soule, . . . consisting of harmony, & rapt with the sphearicall musick before it descended from Heaven to inhabit the body, affects it with the like desire."[23] Similar condemnations can be found in a 1698 inquiry commissioned by Britain's Royal Society to study "the strange effects reported of musick in former times."[24] The inquiry's chief investigator, John Wallis, concluded that traditional claims about the entrancing effects of song were "highly Hyperbolical and next door to Fabulous."[25] As the historian Gretchen L. Finney attests, other rhetorical tactics were more subtle and involved reducing the concept of musical ecstasy to mere metaphor. This, Finney argues, was probably what John Milton did in *Paradise Lost* with his references to "raptures" evoked by a "charming symphonie."[26] According to poet John Hollander, English poets similarly reduced the Music (or Harmony) of the Spheres theory, a mainstay of Western philosophy for over two millennia with its own ecstatic connotations, to a mere figure of speech.[27] These efforts, while not pervasive in their influence, would have almost certainly helped diminish the perceived veracity of self-transcendent experience.

The early British inhabitants of colonial Virginia shared what, during the seventeenth century at least, was apparently a common English reticence toward self-transcendence. This stance was perhaps assisted by the fact that settlers in Virginia, who were officially required to register as Anglican, also absorbed a significant Puritan influence.[28] In matters of religion, colonial Anglicans in Virginia exhibited an enduring "liturgical piety [that] was staid and habitual."[29] According to the historian Edward L. Bond, theirs was a "low-key piety . . . given to order rather than passion or ecstasy."[30] They did not value any earth-shattering rapture, but instead pursued a "well-ordered journey to God." One was meant to express devotion through an organized life consisting of prayer, the reading of devotional literature, and a practical obedience to God's laws. Expression through intense displays of emotion was never appropriate. According to John Page, a Virginia merchant and colonial council member, all forms of emotional excess—particularly those associated with presumption and despair—had the power to act as "destructive rocks, upon . . . which, if the ship of the soul dash, it is split in pieces."[31] Put another way, Page determined that any feelings that shattered the soul were not only distasteful, but sinful, leading one "head-long into hell." Sermons were accordingly constructed ideally to resemble "balanced, ordered, dispassionate, and polished" essays.[32] Virginia parishes, therefore, were not known to be particularly musical. Although they had no formal restrictions on worship music (as there occasionally were in New England), some Southern churches were even known to do away with psalmody altogether. Instrumental music was even less popular: only three churches had organs and organists prior to 1750.[33]

Overtones of Ecstasy in Early America

While a cessationist theology generally prevented Puritans from ardently embracing the possibility of ecstatic mergers with the divine spirit, the experience of self-transcendence was nevertheless not entirely foreign to them. Notably, cessationism did not preclude the possibility of demonic possession. Elites not only associated evil entrancement with reputedly dissolute groups like the "singing Quakers;" they also recognized that such dangerous experiences could befall even those whom they considered devout and dignified.

Cotton Mather, New England's renowned Puritan minister, and grandson of John Cotton, would become a key popularizer of such beliefs across New England. In 1689, he published a bestselling book on the subject, *Memorable Providences, Relating to Witchcrafts and Possessions*, which detailed episodes of supposed demonic affiliation and possession, including among women and children.[34] The publication is thought to have helped incite the famous Salem witch trials soon thereafter. In the midst of those trials, Mather—at the request of local officials—wrote another book, *The Wonders of the Invisible World*, in which he more deeply explored satanic influence. Demonic possession, he asserted, was an unfortunately common feature of his own society:

> Such is the descent of the Devil at this day upon our selves, that I may truly tell you, *The Walls of the whole World are broken down*! The usual *Walls* of defence about mankind have such a Gap made in them that the very *Devils* are broken in upon us, to seduce the *Souls*, torment the *Bodies*, sully the *Credits*, and consume the *Estates* of our Neighbours, with Impressions both as *real* and as *furious*, as if the *Invisible* World were becoming *Incarnate*, on purpose for the vexing of us.[35]

This passage validated a widespread view among Puritans that Satan could insinuate himself into the souls and bodies of human beings and compel them to commit evil deeds. Mather, for his part, questioned how or whether courts should assess proof and culpability in cases of soul possession. Contrary to many of his legal contemporaries, he doubted that anyone should be convicted as a witch based primarily on "spectral evidence"—that is, the testimony of someone who had a dream or vision of the accused committing unholy acts or criminal deeds. Evidence from the invisible world, Mather maintained, was not sufficient to condemn someone. This debate, however, did nothing to inhibit the belief—widespread across colonial Massachusetts and shared readily by Mather himself—regarding the validity of demonic possession in general. The existence of satanic soul possession was never in question.

Witches were not the only ones who could be possessed. Puritans believed that virtually anyone was potentially capable of succumbing to a demonic influence of one form or another. Under mundane circumstances, it was thought, soul possession could be precipitated by or paired with the illness of melancholy, which could descend on individuals for many reasons, but perhaps most saliently in association with "immense agonies of self-doubt" over one's own predestination, or the fear of damnation.[36] The English Puritan Richard Baxter acknowledged this propensity by noting the many devout believers afflicted with melancholy who "are oft apt to be confident that they are possessed by the devil, or at least bewitched."[37] Cotton Mather recapitulated this same point using the medical discourse associated with bodily humors that was popular during his day. Melancholic people, he argued, had "vitiated humours . . . whereinto Satan does insinuate himself, till he has gained a sort of possession in them, or at least, an opportunity to shoot into the mind, as many fiery darts, as may cause a sad life unto them."[38] It was in this way that Mather described his own identity as able to feel "overwhelmed . . . with melancholy Apprehensions."[39] Although the body was ideally meant to be contained by the rational will, therefore, humoral imbalances within it could leave the individual soul melancholic and vulnerable to the self-dispossessing threat of the devil.

In cases of melancholic spirit possession, Puritans were known to turn to music as an antidote. Indeed, some intellectuals and medical practitioners accentuated music's capacity to exorcise insidious forces that seized control of the body and soul. In 1676, for example, the English musician and theorist Thomas Mace reminded his readers of the biblical story of "how the *Evil Spirit* departed from *Saul, when David played upon his Harp*."[40] Robert Burton, his fellow countryman, reported that physicians in France harnessed the power of music to treat patients "troubled with St. Vitus bedlam dance" or "the phrensy."[41] As a "sovereign remedy against despair and melancholy," music, he wrote, was enough to "drive away the devil himself."[42] From Calabria on the Italian Peninsula came other dramatic stories. It was here that musicians performed "solemn Songs and Tunes" to counteract the frenzy-inducing venom of local tarantulas after they bit unsuspecting victims.[43]

Soul possession by the devil or his proxies may not have been the only form of self-transcendent experience available to American Calvinists. Indeed, despite the prevalence of the cessationist doctrine, divinely inspired transcendent experiences may have also accompanied the Puritan conversion—a process that was thought to involve the spiritual transformation of true believers, and which was typically accompanied by repentance for past sins and a sincere commitment to lead a pious life in accordance with God's grace and the teachings of Jesus. In the Puritan context, the process was often described as involving a pedantic series of stages, much anxiety and uncertainty, and ongoing reading of the Bible.[44] While the process could certainly result in an intellectual recognition of one's spiritual elevation, it did not so easily lend itself to a more mystical experience of the presence of the Holy Spirit.

Nevertheless, it seems that some Puritans, under some circumstances, experienced their conversion in self-transcendent terms. According to Perry Miller, "ecstasy and vision" came legitimately to the Puritan in the moment of his or her vocation (the particular occupation or task to which God determined a person was best suited).[45] Engagement in such an activity was thought to reveal one's election for salvation by God and therefore may have provided a profound and extraordinary release from one's ordinary, anxiety-ridden consciousness. Cotton Mather—having ostensibly absorbed the antinomian inclinations of his grandfather John Cotton—wrote of his conversion as nothing short of an ecstatic release from anxiety that descended upon him one day while he was in prayer: "Being prostrate, in the Dust on my Study-floor, after many Fears of a sad, heavy, woful [*sic*] Heart, that the Holy Spirit of the Lord Jesus Christ, grieved by my Miscarriages, would forsake mee [*sic*] utterly, that Spirit of the Lord made an inexpressible Descent upon mee. A Stream of Tears gushed out of my Eyes, upon my Floor, while I had my Soul inexpressibly irradiated with Assurances, of especially two or three Things, bore in upon mee."[46] Mather was no stranger to such episodes. They occurred regularly and sometimes lasted for days at a time.

Mather also wrote vividly about the ecstatic potential of music in particular, imploring his fellow worshipers to seek out a soulful transport when contemplating the lyrics of spiritual songs: "Let us be Inquisitive after those *Motions of Piety*, which are discernible in the Verse now before us. . . . Let us with a Soul flying away to God try whether we cannot fly *with* them . . . till we feel our selves come into an Holy *Symphony* with the Saints who had their *Hearts burning* within them, when they *sang* these things unto the Lord."[47] This was hardly a condemnation of transcendent experience. Instead, it wholeheartedly embraced the lofty pursuit of soulful flight that he believed could overcome worshipers as they harmonized in symphonic rapture with the heavenly saints. These words seemed to elaborate the thoughts of the English Calvinist poet and satirist George Wither, who wrote a century earlier of the power of song not only to "dispossesse us of evil affections, and such like" but also to induce "divine raptures, that allure and dispose the soule unto heavenly meditations, and to the high supernaturall apprehension of spiritual things."[48] Some forms of music, he averred, could in actuality "raise the spirits to that excessive height, as the soule is almost ravished, and in an extasie." Whereas Wither's mention of "almost" suggested that music could approximate the ravishing of the soul in ecstasy, Mather's words went further by proposing that the rapture could be fully attained.

Puritans were not the only Protestants in the American colonies who understood the ecstatic power of song over the individual soul. Despite their disdain for Ranters and their proclivity toward Quietism, orthodox Quakers had always been open to the possibility of rapturous experience and music's role in facilitating it.[49] Their faith centered on a belief in an inner light, a divine essence that permeated the souls of all true followers of God. This divine force transcended the individual soul even as it illuminated it, and therefore any experience of the inner light could lead to ecstatic experience.

Although music performance was highly regulated by Quaker doctrine, one of the few times it was deemed permissible was during those moments when the individual was spontaneously inspired by the profundity of the inner light. On these occasions, it was deemed perfectly acceptable to have individuals "sing in the spirit"—a term Quakers used to label the spontaneous singing that ushered from the mouths of individuals who were truly motivated by the "Divine Influence."[50] All other forms of music-making were prohibited, including any perfunctory performances of psalms or other formal religious songs. Equally condemned was the performance of any profane song that was motivated by nonreligious feelings. Such music, which was often associated with fiddling and dancing and linked to the sinful antics of the singing Quakers, was considered a form of devilish debauchery.

Admittedly, truly spiritual music, absent of both profanity and formality, was relatively rare among Quakers, but it remained a highly desirable phenomenon from the earliest days of the movement. George Fox wrote fondly of a religious musical experience in his journal. One episode he recounted took place during a stint of imprisonment for his religious and political views. At that time, a cruel jailer who knew of Fox's aversion to secular melodies sent a fiddler to his cell. Instead of being vexed by this insult, however, Fox quite suddenly found himself "moved in the everlasting power of the Lord God to sing" and thereby overwhelm his adversary with the power of a truly sacred song.[51] His voice "drowned the noise of the fiddle, and made the fiddler sigh and give over fiddling and pass away with shame." In Quaker terms, the deep sensation that "moved" Fox to sing would have been motivated by the sudden awareness of the transcendent inner light within him. Despite the profundity of this event, which Fox seemed to experience as ecstasy, it did not appear to encourage widespread musical practice among his followers. The scarcity of accounts, however, probably speaks more to the Quakers' specific moral requirements of musical expression rather than to an outright aversion to musical ecstasy per se. And in this regard, Quakers and Puritans shared a reluctance to endorse the widespread and regular pursuit of musical ecstasy, even if they recognized the value of such experiences under certain circumstances.

Musical Rapture and the Great Awakening

Starting around the 1730s, the Puritan congregations' latent acceptance of ecstatic experience would blossom with newfound credibility in Anglo-Protestantism, as many theologians and laypeople on both sides of the Atlantic grew frustrated with what they believed to be misguided conventions within contemporary Protestantism. Their concerns were multiple (and sometimes at odds with each other): a stagnation of conviction in worship; the dilution of congregational membership through the enactment of the "Half-Way Covenant" in 1662, which granted nonconverts partial membership in the Puritan church; a growing perspective, formally acknowledged within the theology of Arminianism, which deemphasized the doctrine of predestination and preached in favor of individual free will as the determining factor of salvation; a related tendency to interpret the accumulation of material wealth and earthly accomplishments as sufficient for ultimate salvation; and a growing belief in the general moral decay of religious communities as demonstrated by increased drunkenness, swearing, and the like.[52] It was in appealing to these concerns that various theologians and preachers sought to reinvigorate a new era of piety within both the Northern and Southern American colonies—an impulse that developed into a movement of religious revivalism later known as the Great Awakening.

Despite their diverse opinions, what the various Awakening revivalists had in common was a newfound emphasis on acts of emotional devotion. Jonathan Edwards, one of the earliest American revivalists, extemporaneously delivered sermons loaded with passion that warned his congregants of their utter corruption and the suffering that awaited them as "Sinners in the Hands of an Angry God."[53] From England came George Whitefield, a minister from Oxford who was heavily invested in the reform of the Anglican Church. He was also an indefatigable preacher, "fervent in spirit," who traveled endlessly throughout the American colonies and the British Isles converting tens of thousands along the way.[54] Collectively, the supporters of Edwards, Whitefield, and many of their Congregationalist and Baptist counterparts became known as the "New Lights" for their shared rejection of an emotionally desiccated, radically disengaged ideal of religious selfhood. By touring throughout the Northern and Southern colonies of America, they would come to gain a fervent following throughout the continent.

Central to the New Lights' faith was the evangelical belief that true spiritual salvation could be ascertained through an ecstatic experience of religious conversion. Unlike the somewhat plodding process of conversion inherited from the Calvinists, evangelical conversion almost always involved sudden and deeply felt experiences that occurred or recurred over a matter of days, hours, or minutes. So striking and transformative was the experience that the subject felt "born again." Unlike Puritan conversion, the process almost always involved intense emotions and self-transcendence, typically beginning with an acknowledgment of one's abject sinfulness followed by an immeasurable joy that ensued after the revelation of God's grace at the moment of salvation. Even if the long-term consequences of conversion were sometimes a calm demeanor—often the result of a newly expanded faith—moments of rapture were often anything but tranquil.

Music frequently accompanied these moments of ecstatic epiphany. Sometimes singing was prescribed for such purposes, as by the influential English devotionalist William Law, whose 1728 tract *Serious Call to a Devout and Holy Life* encouraged devotees to imagine the music of angels singing the glories of God and to "think upon this till your imagination has carried you above the clouds, till it has plac'd you amongst those heavenly beings, and made you long to bear a part in their eternal musick."[55] Furthermore, Law advised his readers that, before and during the performance of psalms and songs of praise, each should imagine this music and "your self amongst those heavenly companions, that your voice is added to theirs" or to the voice of "our blessed Saviour." Moreover, "think how your heart would have been *inflamed*, what *ecstasies* of joy you would have then felt, when *singing* with the Son of God." Spiritual singing, for Law, was nothing if not the mystical union with the Divine. Law's theological and mystical writings would go on to have an outsized impact on the development of evangelical practice throughout the Anglo-American sphere.

Although many of Jonathan Edwards's conversion experiences did not start with Law's contemplation of a heavenly chorus, a number of them were nonetheless expressed in the form of song. They included one of Edwards's very earliest conversion experiences, which occurred upon reading a passage from the Bible:

> The first instance that I remember of that sort of inward, sweet delight in God and divine things that I have lived much in since, was on reading those words, I Tim. 1:17. *Now unto the King eternal, immortal, invisible, the only wise God, be honour and glory for ever and ever, Amen.* As I read the words, there came into my soul, and was as it were diffused through it, a sense of the glory of the Divine Being; a new sense, quite different from any thing I ever experienced before. Never any words of scripture seemed to me as these words did. I thought with myself, how excellent a Being that was, and how happy I should be, if I might enjoy that God, and be rapt up to him in heaven, and be as it were swallowed up in him for ever! I kept saying, and as it were singing over these words of scripture to myself.[56]

Edwards never forgot the profound feeling of being "rapt up" and "swallowed up" in God or his song-like recitation of scripture that accompanied it. From then on, he found that "it always seemed natural to me to sing, or chant for my meditations; or, to speak my thoughts in soliloquies with a singing voice."[57]

George Whitefield also supported religious singing for the purposes of spiritual uplift through ecstasy. He recounted one experience from Christmas Eve of 1739, in Newborn Town, Georgia, while on a preaching tour throughout the American Southern colonies. On this occasion, after arriving at the inn where he would stay the night, Whitefield had a "sweet Communion in Spirit" while singing hymns and religious songs to usher in the festival of nativity.[58] The experience was one of many profound religious experiences he would have on that tour.

The inclination toward rapture was reinforced by musical revivalists from across the Atlantic, especially the contributions of a few prolific hymn writers who purposely sought to exceed Calvinism's conventional strictures on public musical worship. One of the earliest leaders of this movement was Isaac Watts, an English dissenter who wrote and published hundreds of hymns during the first half of the eighteenth century. In his tract titled "Thoughts on Poetry and Musick," passages of which were reproduced in many American-published songbooks, Watts contended that if songs of devotion were properly approached, they could transport the participant to divine realms: "If the Memory be well stored with devout Songs . . . We may . . . feel our Souls borne up, as on the Wings of Angels, far about this dusky Globe of Earth."[59]

As the historian Karen L. Shadle demonstrates, New Lights frequently reinforced the links between self-transcendent experience and devotional music over the course of the eighteenth century. From the 1770s to the 1790s in particular, New England Congregationalists and Presbyterians published several treatises endorsing this connection. One minister, for instance, used the language of rapture in describing the effects of introducing "regular singing" to a worship community in Connecticut: "Our souls are wafted on the wings of sublime devotion; and with extatic [*sic*] rapture carried even to the third heavens, where nothing else but the exactest [*sic*] harmony, and most melodious, heavenly songs fill the place."[60] This was only one of numerous statements sermonized or published throughout the Northeastern colonies and states that spoke to the same enchanting effect. As Shadle argues, some of the more adept writers of religious songs reflected music's capacity for self-transcendent experience within the form and structure of the song itself. The words to Isaac Watts's Psalm 126, for example, reflected the sudden transition from a "mournful state" to "rapture" that accompanied the revivalist experience of conversion:

> My God reveal'd his gracious name,
> And chang'd our mournful state,
> My rapture seem'd a pleasing dream,
> The grace appear'd so great.

And composer Daniel Read's musical setting to these lyrics, written in 1785, reflected this soul transition by using highly contrasting musical styles to accompany the lyrics. In Shadle's analysis, the first "mournful state" was characterized by "slow-moving notes, mostly step-wise motion, and a homophonic texture in a triple meter." The rapture, by comparison, changed starkly to "a sprightlier duple meter, a frolicking imitative texture, and an abundance of leaping thirds and fourths."[61] The change in musical styles seemed to mimic the onset of ecstasy.

Despite its popularity, the Great Awakening's growing emphasis on emotional soul transport was hardly without its detractors. For a substantial set of "Old Light" Congregationalists and Baptists who remained strictly dedicated to the doctrine of cessationism and to principles of autonomous individuality, the so-called ecstasies of the New Lights were nothing more than a debased indulgence in "enthusiasm," a pejorative term of the day that was associated with nondevotional trance and emotion pursued for its own sake. During the eighteenth century, enthusiasm was regularly defined as an egregious miscalculation: "To equal the *imaginations of men* to the *holy scripture of God,* and think them as much the *inspiration of God,* as what was dictated as such, to the *holy prophets* and apostles, is strictly and properly *Enthusiasm.*"[62] The Boston clergyman Charles Chauncy, who was perhaps the most vocal of the Old Light condemners, suggested the dynamics of enthusiasm were, at their best, mere flights of fancy propelled by an overactive personal imagination, and, at their worst, linked more to "the *Suggestions* of *Satan*" than to any indwelling of the Holy Spirit.[63]

For Chauncy and other Old Lights, all bodily manifestations of so-called ecstatic experience implied a profane origin and were therefore intolerable. And bodily sounds, including many of those linked to music, were considered among the most repellant of all. Chauncy lambasted exuberant congregations not only for the "*Screamings* and *Shriekings* of the People, but their *talking,* and *praying,* and *exhorting,* and *singing,* and *laughing.*"[64]

New Lights typically took a softer approach to religious experiences that abounded with rapturous physicality. "When . . . the affections are so strong, and the whole soul so engaged and ravished and swallowed up," Jonathan Edwards claimed, it was no wonder that "all other parts of the body are so affected as to be deprived of their strength, and the whole frame ready to dissolve."[65] Yet this did not mean Edwards was indiscriminate in his endorsements of self-transcendence and bodily emotion; he too worried about the hazards of over-expressivity, even when people practiced in the name of religious devotion: "There are many exercises of the affections that are very flashy, and little to be depended on; and oftentimes there is a great deal that appertains to them, or rather that is the effect of them, that has its seat in animal nature, and is very much owing to the constitution and frame of the body."[66] Likewise, Edwards warned that bodily gestures such as crying, dancing, feasting, fainting, and tremoring were potentially deceptive in that, while they could accompany truly holy experiences, they could also be manifestations of false religion and satanic delusion.[67] For Edwards, holy practice required not "the Motion of a Body, that knows not how, nor when, nor wherefore it moves," but instead primarily "holy Acts of the Mind, directed and governing the Motions of the Body."[68] Determining the true source of effusive experience was no easy task. Edwards concluded that the act of distinguishing between genuine expressions of God's grace and unholy indulgences in profane affections must be left to "the skill of the observer."[69]

The Wesley Brothers

Into this religious tumult waded John and Charles Wesley, brothers and Anglican theologians from Oxford, England and far and away the most musical of the Great Awakening revivalists. Steeped in the ideology of dispassionate selfhood that permeated most Protestant denominations during the eighteenth century, the Wesleys were raised to be studious and disciplined—an ethic that served them well during their years as students at the University of Oxford in the 1720s. Never lacking commitment in their pursuit of piety, the brothers began a Holy Club at the university that required members to fast two times a week, preach to others, and meet daily for three hours of prayer, psalms, and biblical reading.[70]

Although they endorsed in broad terms the Calvinist emphasis on self-control and self-denial as inextricable from personal salvation, the Wesleys also diverged from Puritan teachings in several important ways. They rejected the Calvinist doctrine of predestination, believing instead in the Arminian principle that individual will can augment one's inner holiness. They also willingly conceded that something like a deep emotional impulse drove all devotional acts, including those of rigid self-regulation. As early as 1726, John wrote of the importance of an "inward . . . religion of the heart" composed of "simplicity of intention and purity of affection . . . one desire ruling all our tempers."[71] And when he spoke of the necessity of giving "all my heart, to [God],"[72] he implied that this emotional brand of devotion involved aspects of self-transcendence. In validating this tacit acceptance of ecstatic experience, Wesley may also have been compelled by his readings of the Church Fathers while he was at Oxford, particularly those of John Chrysostom on *theosis*, a concept that purported that the mind and body could achieve a likeness or union with God through cathartic acts of purification.[73] Wesley's leanings toward devout transport were duly noted by some of his more conservative colleagues at Oxford, who condemned as "enthusiasm" the practice of his Holy Club.

Dogged by this label on a consistent basis, the Wesleys overtly strove to avoid outright enthusiasm, which prioritized experience over devotion, without succumbing to the pitfalls of "formalism," which elevated religious practice over experience. As the historian W. Stephen Gunter observes, John Wesley was always trying to find a balance between "cold rationalism" and "overheated enthusiasm."[74] In this capacity he was reluctant to concede that his devotional work could culminate in the full relinquishment of his soul. Nevertheless, he remained fascinated with finding the counter to both passionless worship on the one hand and indulgent, nonreligious trance on the other.

For John Wesley, the performance of religious music provided an important opportunity for pursuing this middle path. One particularly poignant event in 1736 occurred on a ship bound for Georgia, where both Wesley brothers were hired to work as spiritual advisors to the founder of the colony, James Oglethorpe. Several months into their transatlantic journey a fierce storm broke the mast of the ship. The English travelers on board panicked, but a group of Moravians who were also there remained calm as they sung psalms, never resorting to the crying, screaming, and trembling of their neighbors.[75] Their music, in Wesley's estimation, had somehow enabled them to channel their fear into an affectionate praise of God that in turn imbued them with equanimity and courage. Essentially, it proved that emotional devotion could be attained without abandoning the integrity of the individual. The group's behavior left a lasting impression on John, who described it at length in his diary. Soon after reaching the American colony, he obtained a Moravian hymnal and spent three to five hours a day translating and adapting it into English.[76] It would not be long before the Wesley brothers together published their own collection of psalms and hymns.

As both Wesley brothers' interest in music grew, however, their valuation of the principle of self-control constantly came up against their desire to augment their own religious experience. Ultimately, they conceded that intense passions were necessary for true conversion, even if they entailed something approaching a sense of self-abandon. Here again, music was integral. Probably the closest John Wesley ever got to acknowledging his own capacity for self-transcendent experience occurred on May 24, 1738 at a meeting room in Aldersgate, London. That evening, he attended a reading of Luther's preface to the Epistle to the Romans. At about a quarter to nine, as the reader was describing how faith in Christ enables God to work in the heart, Wesley was inundated with a religious experience like none he had ever had: "I felt my heart strangely warmed," he later recounted. "I felt I did trust in Christ, Christ alone, for salvation; and an assurance was given me that He had taken away my sins, even mine, and saved me from the law of sin and death."[77] The sensation stayed with Wesley into the following day, when going over Psalm 89, he slipped into a synesthetic state whereby he could "taste the good word of God." The psalm he was reading seemed to echo Wesley's own sentiment. It began: "My song shall be always of the loving-kindness of the Lord: with my mouth will I ever be showing forth thy truth from one generation to another."[78]

During that same week that his brother's heart was "warmed" at Aldersgate, Charles Wesley also had a mystical experience that he later found best expressed through song. While recovering from an illness in the home of some Moravians in England, he suddenly felt his soul undergo a profound transformation. "By degrees the Spirit of God chased away the darkness of my unbelief," he wrote in his diary. "I found myself convinced. . . . I saw that by faith I stood."[79] Soon after, Charles felt compelled to commemorate this event by writing a hymn. Although he never specified which of his many compositions it was, scholars generally agree that "And Can It Be That I Should Gain" is the most likely. The final verse ran as follows:

No condemnation now I dread,
Jesus, and all in Him, is mine:
Alive in Him, my living Head,
And clothed in righteousness Divine,
Bold I approach th' eternal throne,
And claim the crown, through Christ, my own.[80]

Such a description of his "Head" living in Jesus and "all in Him" being "mine" would suggest something like an ecstatic interpenetration of Charles's self with that of the Divine.

The Wesley brothers and their followers would remember these moments as their belated religious conversions and the first time they experienced confirmation of their salvation. In many ways these events marked the brothers' transition into a newly devout period in their lives, setting them on the path to developing, with the help of George Whitefield, the distinct religious movement within Anglo-American Protestantism eventually known as Methodism. From these moments onward, the Wesleys and their Methodist followers became more amenable to considering self-transcendence as an acceptable part of religious experience.

Admittedly, their fear of becoming snared by enthusiasm made them proceed with caution, and for this they rarely endorsed flamboyant self-abandon. For example, in describing his most profound conversion experience, John Wesley was sure to articulate his encounter with God as a "strange" sensation that occurred within him rather than an act of outright spiritual communion. Likewise, he suggested that true spiritual development always involved "meekness, patience, gentleness, and long-suffering," characteristics that may have involved a degree of self-control unconducive to self-transcendence. Nevertheless, the Wesleys' approach, perhaps more than that of any other Great Awakening revivalist, celebrated something like ecstatic experience as the essential feature of a truly Christian life: "No man can be a *true Christian* without such an inspiration of the Holy Ghost as fills his heart with peace and joy and love; which he who perceives not, has it not. . . . And this I take to be the very foundation of Christianity."[81] This emphasis on religious emotion helps explain the brothers' subsequent turn to impassioned sermons, their belief in conversion experiences as essential for salvation, their rejection of the doctrine of cessationism, and their faith in the sustained action of the Holy Spirit upon the believer's soul.

Not coincidentally, Methodists would come to elevate the singing of hymns as central to their worship practices. In the words of the historian Leslie Griffiths, "Singing was the medium by which Methodists learned and gave wing to their theology."[82] Charles Wesley alone wrote several thousand hymns during his lifetime, most of them after his conversion experience. John, while less musically prolific, was equally supportive of song as a method of faithful experience and expression. Hymnody proved integral to the spread of Methodism throughout the English-speaking Atlantic world during the eighteenth and nineteenth centuries, and in this capacity, it complemented a Methodist commitment to extensive missionizing. After the conversion events of 1738, for example, John Wesley would follow in George Whitefield's mold by embarking on extensive open-air preaching tours of Britain and the colonies, attracting crowds that numbered in the tens of thousands, and encouraging participants to develop their own intensely emotional relationship with God. The singing of hymns frequently factored into his meetings and, along with the popularity of other evangelical hymnodists like Isaac Watts, helped challenge the prevalence of Calvinist psalmody, which had long influenced religious music life in the Anglo-American sphere.

Baptists and Anglican Resistance in Virginia

Methodists were not the only leaders of religious revivalism in America. Others included members of the Baptist Church, a denomination founded in the Netherlands by John Smyth, an Englishman who disassociated from the Anglican Church during the early seventeenth century. From its inception, the Baptist Church, which had been present on the American continent since the mid-seventeenth century, asserted that only professing, adult believers in Christianity (as opposed to children and infants) should be eligible for baptism, because such a rite should constitute an outward expression of an individual's internal conversion experience. As such, the Baptist tradition remained relatively open to the possibility of religious ecstasy from its outset.[83] Because theirs was an antinomian denomination that promoted an unadulterated, personal connection between an individual and God, many Baptist preachers tended to forego any prepared, written sermons in favor of spontaneous performances that relied on "the gift of the spirit."[84] Congregants followed suit, both in prayer and song. Some Baptists encouraged these practices more than others, with the result that, by the mid-eighteenth century, a new, emotionally oriented sect cleaved off from the original movement and, with the help of evangelical missionaries, spread quickly throughout the American colonies, especially the South. Members of this new sect—called Separate Baptists—could be counted as part of the New Light movement.

As with other evangelicals, Baptists paired their belief in profound religious experiences with a hearty endorsement of musical praise.[85] The lyrics to some of their songs specifically suggested the possibility of self-transcendence under the relentless power of the Holy Spirit:

> Down from above the blessed Dove
> Is Come into my Breast,
> To witness God's eternal Love;
> This is my heavenly Feast.
> This makes me *Abba Father* cry,
> With Confidence of Soul;
> It makes me cry, My Lord, my God,
> And that without Controul [*sic*].[86]

This kind of song was sung by preachers and congregations alike, including during a baptismal service in Fauquier County, Virginia, in 1771. On this particular occasion, the preacher, Daniel Fristoe, wrote of a service attended by approximately two thousand people. Spectators climbed up trees, filling them sometimes to the point of breaking, in order to see dozens of people being immersed in holy water for the first time. Afterwards, those in attendance moved to a field where the preacher laid hands on the newly baptized. The scene overflowed with emotion and ecstasy:

> The multitude stood round weeping, but when we sang *Come we that love the lord* & they were so affected that they lifted up their hands and faces towards heaven and discovered such chearful

> [*sic*] countenances in the midst of flowing tears as I had never
> seen before. In going away I looked back and saw multitudes,
> some roaring on the ground, some wringing their hands, some
> in extacies [*sic*] . . . and other so outrageous cursing & swearing
> that it was thought they were really possessed of the devil.[87]

The vehemence of the Baptists was palpable. While some rejoiced that they had come to God and were finally "born again," others despaired at their sinfulness and inadequacy in comparison to Christ and therefore took to swearing. For some observers, Fristoe acknowledged, the cursing signaled a step too far, representing the possibility of a spiritual merger with demonic rather than divine sources.

In Virginia, this censorious perspective could easily have been shared by the more reserved and conservative Anglicans, who also tended to be the wealthier landowners in the region. (Separate Baptists, by contrast, typically included middling property owners and the poor.)[88] The obvious differences in class, religion, and emotional style were bound to come to a head, and they did so on many occasions. One such instance occurred during the same year as Fristoe's laying on of hands ceremony, when another Baptist preacher, John Waller, had a violent run-in with Anglican elites in the Tidewater region of Virginia. One Sabbath day, as Waller began to sing to his fellow worshipers, the Anglican "Parson of the Parish" stormed into the congregation with his clerk, the sheriff, and other supporters:

> [The parson began] running the end of his horsewhip in his
> [Waller's] mouth, laying his whip across the hymn book, etc.
> When done singing he [Waller] proceeded to prayer. In it he
> was violently jerked off the stage; they caught him by the back
> part of his neck, beat his head against the ground, sometimes
> up, sometimes down, they carried him through a gate that stood
> some considerable distance, where a gentlemen gave him some-
> thing not much less than twenty lashes with his horse whip.[89]

Baptist faith, it would seem, went against so much of what the Virginia Anglicans stood for that, in the opinion of its most ardent defenders, it deserved aggressive, violent retaliation. Waller, for his part, was known to be unflinching in the face of such hostility. Raised an Anglican from a well-known family, he became a Baptist in adulthood only after a deep crisis in faith. During the second half of the eighteenth century, he would become one of Virginia's most provocative preachers.[90]

This vicious outburst against Waller seems to have been motivated not just by an obvious theological dispute but by an underlying social conflict as well. Indeed, the faith of Separate Baptists could be seen as mounting a direct challenge to the status quo that favored the ascendancy of Anglican elites. In addition to remaining open to intense religious experiences, Baptists also fostered radical egalitarian views that rejected the hierarchal structure of the Church of England just as it derided the higher echelons of the colonial gentry. To make matters more difficult for the Anglican elite, Baptist faith and practice proved exceedingly hard to discourage. Despite Waller's suffering under protracted abuse and derision, immediately after being released he "went back singing praise to God, mounted the stage and preached with a great deal of liberty."[91] When asked if he did not feel stifled by the parson's violent persecution, he answered that "the Lord stood by him of a truth and poured his love into his soul without measure, and the brethren and sisters about him singing praises to Jehovah, so that he could scarcely feel the stripes for the love of God."[92] Evangelicalism, it would appear, was not so easy to beat down. The ecstasy that came from having God's love "poured" into their souls fulfilled Baptists' spiritual needs so thoroughly that they could endure direct insult and physical injury.

The Shakers

Some Quakers were also not immune to the influence and controversy of effusive evangelicalism. Long after the censure and suppression of the "singing Quakers" in the mid-seventeenth century, a new radical sect would emerge in England during the late 1740s, amid the excitement of the Great Awakening. At this time, Jane Wardley, a devout member of the Society of Friends, began to experience profound spiritual visions that communicated Christ's return was imminent and would manifest in female form—a claim she believed was supported by scriptural passages. Wardley convinced her husband, James, of the veracity of that message and then proceeded to spread it in public, where it quickly gained traction. Soon, a prosperous neighbor became a financial supporter of the couple's emerging religious movement. Drawing from their Quaker background, the Wardleys' worship style was initially contemplative, characterized by periods of silent reflection. However, intense physical manifestations would eventually mark their religious experiences: Jane would often shake and rock, and occasionally break into singing and dancing, while experiencing divine visions.[93]

Faithful followers of the Wardleys underwent similar experiences. The following account—excerpted from an official theological statement published years later by the Wardleys' religious descendants—described the kind of devotional practices that proliferated among the group throughout much of the eighteenth century: "In their worship they would sit in silent meditation for a while, when they were taken with a mighty trembling under which they would express the indignation of God against all sin. At other times they were affected, under the power of God, with a mighty shaking; and were occasionally exercised in singing, shouting, or walking the floor under the influence of spiritual signs, or swiftly passing and repassing each other, like clouds agitated by a mighty wind."[94] This dramatic episode outlined a panoply of practices, many of which involved ecstatic moments of being "taken" that were simultaneously accompanied by physical outbursts of mystical faith. Such practices gave rise to a distinctive moniker for the Wardleys and their followers—the "Shaking Quakers." It also demonstrated a core belief among devotees that the physicality, emotionality, sometimes musicality, and sheer intensity of their religious experiences was a clear indication of their divine provenance. Mainline Quakers, along with many other conservative religionists, were not at all convinced of the same and instead found such practices disturbing and potentially blasphemous. They soon severed any affiliation with the dissenting sect, which by then were known simply as "the Shakers." (The term, originally used as an insulting epithet by their critics, was ultimately adopted as an acceptable name by the believers themselves.[95])

In 1758, a young woman named Ann Lee joined the growing Shaker movement and soon proved herself to be its most ardent proselytizer and public advocate. Her conviction persisted even in the face of harsh disparagements from more conventional religionists and even legal persecution, which would land her in prison more than once. By about 1770, the Shakers determined that Lee, or "Mother Ann" as they often called her, was in fact the second coming of Christ in female form that Jane Wardley had prophesied, and they recognized her as the sect's leader.[96]

In 1774, Lee led a group of supporters to America, where they hoped to find more religious freedom to practice their particular brand of mystical faith. Upon arrival, they established a utopian settlement in the township of Watervliet, near Albany, New York, where they upheld the principles of gender equality and pacifism, just as Quakers did, but also celibacy, a feature distinct to the Shakers. (The latter value was likely influenced by the death of all four of Mother Ann's infant children and her conclusion that those traumas were punishment for engaging in sexual relations with her husband.) During the 1780s, the Shakers—who formally called themselves the United Society of Believers in Christ's Second Appearing—embarked on a mission throughout New England that was successful in attracting many converts, including New Light Congregationalists and Baptists.[97] One of these was Joseph Main, who visited Watervliet in 1780, and, by his own account, underwent a profound experience of musically inflected trance upon coming into contact with Lee: "Mother Ann Lee was sitting in a chair, and singing very melodiously, with her hands in motion; and her whole soul and body seemed to be in exercise. I felt, as it were, a stream of divine power and love flow into my soul, and was convinced at once that it came from Heaven, the source and fountain of all good. I immediately acknowledged my faith, and went and confessed my sins."[98] The power of song to direct the flow of "divine power" through Main provided the impetus for his conversion and his commitment to a deepened faith in Shaker principles. A similar ecstatic encounter met another member of the movement who sat beside Mother Ann as she sang a religious song. As this happened, the follower recounted, one of Lee's hands, while in motion, "frequently touched my arm; and at the very touch of her hand, I instantly felt the power of God run through my whole body."[99] In this instance, the stream of divine power seemed to channel first through the charismatic leader before reaching her follower. Another among the scores of converts was Joseph Meacham, who would later become the leader of the Shaker movement after Lee's death in 1784 and a brief tenure by her close associate, James Whittaker. Meacham would oversee the establishment of a Shaker community in New Lebanon, New York that would become the central settlement of the sect's rapidly growing network of communities and supporters.[100]

The ecstasy that characterized songful encounters with Mother Ann also occurred regularly in her absence. During many kinds of formal worship, Shaker devotees underwent all manner of songful, spiritual possession. One observer described a typical scenario in the following way:

> They begin by sitting down and shaking their heads in a violent manner, turning their heads half round, so that their face looks over each shoulder, their eyes being shut; while they are thus shaking, one will begin to sing some odd tune, without words or

> rule; after a while another will strike in; and then another; and
> after a while they all fall in and make a strange charm:—Some
> singing without words, and some with an unknown tongue, or
> mutter, and some with a mixture of English: The mother, so
> called, minds to strike such notes as makes a concord, and so
> form the charm.[101]

Such vocal outbursts of Shakers were very often matched with bodily
expressions, including dances and gesticulations, all of which were apparently
motivated by the immanent power of divine grace.

As the Shaker movement grew, Meacham and his successor, Lucy
Wright, both grappled with how to keep the movement organized and
coordinated. Their challenge was partly a result of the movement's success:
larger numbers of devotees meant more crowded meetings and the potential
for chaos when each individual expressed themselves in spontaneous physical
ways under the power of the Spirit. The Shaker leadership would eventually
respond to this risk of commotion by discouraging extemporaneous dancing
and singing.[102] Meacham instead introduced a coordinated dance, received
by him in spiritual visions, which wrested some sense of order into these
worship practices. That dance became known as the Holy Order (or Square
Order Shuffle), which he helped popularize among his fellow Shakers. It
employed many of the features associated with contemporaneous square
dance traditions, including highly structured and symmetrical choreography.
As they sang one of several different songs, worshipers in the Holy Order
would arrange themselves in precise rows, with men and women separated
and often facing each other, performing synchronized movements characterized
by rhythmic stepping, turning, and shuffling.[103] Gone were the independent,
spontaneous movements practiced by the previous era of worshipers.

Over time, the dance evolved. By 1788, after Meacham appointed
Wright as the new leader, dancing gestures became more deliberate and
slower. These characteristics were typical of the Turning Shuffle, another
Shaker dance that emerged around 1790 and featured subtle, synchronized
bent-knee movements. By 1794, the practice of dance in Shaker worship
had all but ceased, an event that no doubt satisfied conventional onlookers
who perpetually worried and complained about the excesses of physical
worship. The halt in dancing would not endure, however. By the early years
of the nineteenth century, younger people raised as Shakers began leaving
the sect at a rapid pace, a trend that amounted to an existential threat for
a movement that upheld celibacy and was therefore perpetually limited in

its rate of growth. Wright sought to curb this trend by reinvigorating the movement via several efforts, including new and expanded missions and a wholehearted reembrace of liturgical dancing. More lively patterns and gestures were soon performed in worship, inspired by Wright's own holy visions.[104] The repertoire also became more complex, often involving intricate floor movements and actions that directly interpreted song lyrics. Yet, while Shakers made their dances more prevalent and passionate, they never fully abandoned the earlier era's inclination toward order. Indeed, dances continued to be highly coordinated and synchronized. Whereas the Holy Order had required women and men to face each other arranged in precise rows as they sang, now all members moved abreast in the same direction with unified movements and voices.[105]

The entrancing, expressive impulses that had been with Shakers from their earliest days never disappeared (see fig 1.1). In fact, they remained such reliably attractive features of the movement that they were promoted eagerly whenever Shakerism underwent declines in faith and membership. Such an occasion occurred again from the 1830s to the 1850s, during what became known as the "Era of Manifestations," when Shakers renewed their efforts to enable conversion experiences, spiritual possessions, and the creative forms of expression that intersected with them. These included drawings and pantomimes as well as a flood of lyric and tune writing. It was under these circumstances that divinely sourced "gift songs"—songs received by entranced Shakers while under divine possession—became particularly prominent.[106] One devout Shaker's account of an event on Christmas Day, 1837, in Enfield, Connecticut, described the process of ecstatic musical "gifting": "A meeting was held at the west family by the brethren and sisters there. . . . [It] was attended with divine manifestations and great power of God, such as shaking, whirling, clapping of hands, speaking in unknown tongue . . . ; some rolling; some turning, down on the floor, while some had new songs given them, with some beautiful words, which were sung for an hour or more."[107] The passive construction of the last sentence accorded with Shaker beliefs of the time. It suggested not that the devotees created their own songs, but rather that they received them fully formed from God in a manner that overwhelmed their will and compelled them to move and speak in unusual ways. (Those who underwent such experiences were sometimes described by their fellows as "instruments.")[108] In the end, several thousand Shaker songs would be produced during the Era of Manifestations, including many gift songs—an enormous output considering the relative size of the sect's population at the time, which itself was only a few thousand.[109] This outpouring of emotional devotion was eventually pulled back into more structured and organized formations, echoing the efforts at regulation made in previous decades.[110] Despite these fluctuations, however, Shaker worship never lost its original association with effusive, communal, revelatory, and musical devotion.

As time passed, the Shaker movement would grow moribund, reducing steadily during the late nineteenth and early twentieth centuries. There are several established reasons for this decline, including the sect's oath of celibacy, which perpetually curtailed its potential for growth; an increasing allowance for pluralism in Shaker thought and action, which resulted in a loss of cohesion among both communities and their leaders; and the large-scale industrialization of American society following the Civil War, which diminished the market demand for handmade products that had traditionally provided a reliable income for Shaker communities, thereby making it difficult for them to thrive economically.[111] Yet another reason, less explored

Figure 1.1. A Shaker woman falling into a trance under the power of a "gift." *Source:* The Whirling Gift, 1848, wood engraving. Published in David R. Lamson, *Two Years Experience Among the Shakers* (West Boylston, Mass; Published by author, 1848), 85. Public domain.

by the existing literature, was undoubtedly related to the growing number of options that became available to Americans drawn to ecstatic forms of worship. Whereas Shakers might have stood out somewhat for their religious revivalism during the eighteenth century, the same could not be said of the nineteenth century, when Christian denominations much larger than the Shakers began turning to it at unprecedented rates.

Camp Meetings During the Second Great Awakening

Starting in the early decades of the nineteenth century, an explosion in religious fervor spread throughout the United States during what eventually became known as the Second Great Awakening. The importance of intense, ecstatic, musical worship practices cannot be underestimated in explaining its growth. Experience-based faith, particularly that endorsed by large and rapidly growing denominations such as Methodism, proved remarkably attractive to Americans of various backgrounds during this era. While the founders of Methodism and other evangelical denominations exercised the utmost caution in order to avoid profane "enthusiasm" while pursuing religious ecstasy, the proponents of the Second Great Awakening took a bolder stance. They elaborated and exploited the careful work of the Wesley brothers and further sought to bring physical and frequent ecstatic experiences firmly into the fold of acceptable religion.

The movement's elevation of passionate devotion made sense not just to the Shakers but to Americans of many religious inclinations. For some, it provided a way of coalescing people around Christian faith during a period when many were fearful about the spread of secularization, liberal ideas, and other political and economic transformations in American society.[112] The evangelical premium on intense boundary-dissolving experiences and its largely Arminian-based emphasis on self-determination could also be reconciled with the antiauthoritarian, antiorthodox ethos that had fueled the American Revolution and permeated the democratic principles of Protestant theology for generations.[113] As it turned out, appealing to the hearts of the people rather than the intellects of elites proved enormously successful. Starting around 1800, evangelical revivalism began to spread like wildfire through the Southern states and American frontier lands, igniting a religious fervor throughout the country.

Music factored regularly into the Southern and Western revivalism of the Second Great Awakening, even more so than in its eighteenth-century forerunner. Exuberant singing featured prominently in the camp meetings organized by evangelicals throughout the South and West.[114] Very often, music was used as an integral tool in eliciting religious trance, or what evangelicals increasingly called being "slain in the Spirit." And more than ever before, this musical ecstasy was meant to be a nonhierarchal, communal event, in which any number of individuals in attendance could experience self-transcendence in the company of other devotees. At one of the earliest camp meetings, organized in Logan County, Kentucky, in June 1800, John McGee, a Methodist preacher, came to the pulpit singing the following words:

> Come Holy Spirit, heavenly dove,
> With all thy quick'ning powers,
> Kindle a flame of sacred love,
> In these cold hearts of ours.[115]

At this, it was reported, the heavenly spirit descended upon the people, causing some to fall to the ground, others to cry out for mercy, pray, or praise God in resounding voices—much to the shock of some Presbyterian ministers in attendance. John McGee himself nearly crumbled under the power of the Holy Spirit. Later, he recounted, "I . . . was near falling; the power of God was strong upon me. I turned again, and, losing sight of the fear of man, I went through the house shouting and exhorting with all possible ecstasy and energy, and the floor was soon covered with the slain."[10] Several Presbyterian ministers who were present—unfamiliar with the sudden and expressive conversion practices of the Methodists—became confused and wondered if they should intervene.[116]

In 1801, another emotional scene took place nearly two hundred miles away, during a camp meeting that attracted some twenty thousand attendees to the Cane Ridge area northeast of Lexington, Kentucky. Shaker missionaries, seeking to expand their movement, participated actively, but theirs was only one of many religious communities represented at the camp meeting. One description of the revival, a synthesis of several eyewitness accounts, reported a "spectacle . . . of the wildest grandeur."[117] Amid a set of blazing campfires and a range of tents, sounds and movements erupted constantly: "The solemn chanting of hymns swelling and falling on the night wind ; the impassioned exhortations ; the earnest prayers ; the sobs, shrieks, or shouts, bursting from persons under intense agitation of mind ; the sudden spasms which seized upon scores, and unexpectedly dashed them to the ground ;—all conspired to invest the scene with terrific interest, and to work up the feelings to the highest pitch of excitement." This cacophony of "reverent enthusiasm" was matched by the fervency of some resident preachers and the "boiling zeal of the Methodists, who could not refrain from shouting aloud during sermon, and shaking hands all round afterwards."[118] Reverend John Lyle, a Presbyterian minister who attended the revival and kept a diary during this time, reiterated the sheer physicality of devotional acts. He described in detail the activities of one active preacher at the revival, Mr. McNamara, who "speaks & sings with all his powers & . . . sometimes rises to ecstatic joy. It smiles through his face."[119] At one point, Lyle saw McNamara praying along with "many others singing praying and groaning all around[,] some rejoicing and some crying for mercy." This kind of "singing ecstacy [*sic*]," as Lyle called it, was a frequent occurrence, involving "great shaking of hands & praying & exhorting."[120] At one point, McNamara urged the people in attendance "to come & taste the love of God &c. &c. He seem'd much affected. . . . One [of the rejoicers] stood staring like he saw Christ in the air."[121] At another point, he went to the meeting house and found many boys and girls "singing & shaking hands & sort of wagging (?) that appear'd like dancing at a distance. When I came among them they appear'd very loving & joyful almost dizzy with joy."[122] McNamara's petition for attendees to "taste" the love of God and the other devotee's "vision" of Christ in the air all pointed to multisensory experiences of divine presence that at the very least approximated self-transcendent experience.

Reverend Lyle, a skeptic of effusive revivalism, was reluctant to see many redeeming qualities in the whole affair. He considered McNamara a "weak man" and believed the intense outbursts of religious expression created "the greatest sense of confusion." Instead, he wished that the "hot-headed men" who led the spiritual exhortations would "command order & silence & desire the distress'd to be carried out."[123] He worried regularly about the "disorder" and the "danger of enthusiasm" and appealed to the swaying boys and girls to "sing the same hymns & not sing different ones so near together."[124] Even through his admonishments, however, Lyle's descriptions perhaps recognized some element of self-transcendence when he described the revivalists' "singing ecstasy" and the "ecstatic joy . . . [that] smiles through [McNamara's] face."

According to the historian Dickson Bruce, music infused camp meetings from start to finish.[125] The opening service of a meeting, which usually began on a Thursday night, typically started with a preacher singing a spiritual song and the congregation joining in. These practices were followed not by a sermon, but by exhortations and more singing, a pattern that was repeated in subsequent night services. The alternation between exhortation and singing proceeded every night until mourners, called by the Holy Spirit, began to enter the pen (the altar area in front of the congregation). In due course, the power of God came down, causing sinners to fall to the ground, slain by the Holy Spirit. Sometime before midnight, after these exercises had continued for a while, the crowd generally dispersed into smaller tents to continue worship. Often the singing and shouting persisted until dawn, when a trumpet called congregants to prayer. After breakfast, another trumpet signaled the beginning of morning service, at which point a few of the participants moved into the seats and started singing hymns until the preacher moved to the stand and began a sermon. Following testimonials, another sermon was presented by a senior preacher, which was closed with more congregational singing. After lunch, there was still more singing, along with sermons and testimonials. During the break after afternoon services, clergy invited laypeople to private tents to continue singing, praying, and exhorting. After dinner, the evening services began anew.

Particularly during evening exercises, camp participants almost certainly experienced prolonged moments of musical rapture. The episodes recounted above in Kentucky as well as the one described by Andrew Reed at the beginning of this chapter provide a few examples. Another comes from the event depicted by Alexander Rider in a lithograph picture dating from about 1830 (see fig. 1.2). It portrays one preacher leading attendees in some exuberant devotional exercise, while a series of other ministers wait their turn on the pulpit stage. One entranced woman is ushered onto a bench beneath the pulpit, while others dance intensely around the camp, apparently enthused with the Holy Spirit. Almost everyone's mouth is open—probably singing or shouting at the behest of the fervid preacher. At the back of the pulpit, someone sounds a signaling horn to draw in newcomers. Observing the scene from the sidelines are several patrician spectators, perhaps local community members averse to participating in the trance exercise but interested or concerned (or both) all the same.

Of particular note in Rider's lithograph is his depiction of the highly gendered nature of religious self-transcendence. The picture focuses on several women dancing and vocalizing in front of the preacher, presumably in the throes of religious rapture. Andrew Reed provided a similar characterization in describing the several young women who fainted or lapsed into "hysterical ecstasy" while attending the camp meeting he observed in Virginia in 1834. In fact, women's susceptibility to intense emotion and self-transcendence

Figure 1.2. A revivalist camp meeting during the Second Great Awakening in America. *Source:* Alexander Rider and Hugh Bridgeport, Camp Meeting, c. 1832, lithograph. Harry T. Peters "America on Stone" Lithography Collection. Public domain.

was frequently documented and highlighted within the historical literature of the late eighteenth and early nineteenth centuries.

A focus on female trance had long been entrenched within the gendered rhetoric of American Protestantism. During the seventeenth century, Puritan ministers Thomas Shepard and Solomon Stoddard celebrated women's emotionality as something that made them spiritual (if not social) equals of "rational" men. By the 1740s, Jonathan Edwards came to a similar conclusion. In making his case for the morality of impassioned conversion experiences, he argued that women's proclivity for emotionalism made them willing recipients of religion, and he often singled out female worshipers as models of Christian piety.[126]

Detractors of revivalist ecstasy also framed women as emotionally vulnerable, but they touted their emotionalism as a sign of weakness rather than of spiritual fitness. Charles Chauncy, for instance, urged that it is in "*young People* and *Women*, whose Passions are soft and tender, and more easily [than men] thrown into a Commotion, that these Things [proclivities] *chiefly* prevail."[127] Appealing to the physiological theories of science, Chauncy explained that the reason for this female vulnerability was likely due to the "Weakness of . . . [women's] Nerves, and from hence their greater Liableness to be surpris'd, and overcome with Fear."

The rhetoric of gender liability never receded from evangelical discourse during the Second Great Awakening, and it regularly employed the language of weakness popularized by Chauncy and his supporters. Indeed, Andrew Reed disparaged a woman at one of the Virginia camp meetings for the physicality with which she progressed through phases of ecstasy, transitioning from singing to raising of hands, rolling of eyes, smiling, and muttering. He compared the woman's actions disapprovingly to that of a hedonistic drunkard, sneering that "it appeared that she courted this sort of excitement as many do a dram, and was frequent at meetings of this character, for the sake of enjoying it."[128] If Reed remained relatively open to the camp meeting's radical evangelicalism, he obviously thought the woman's physical expressivity was unacceptable.

Figure 1.3. A revivalist camp meeting during the Second Great Awakening in nineteenth-century America. *Source:* J. Maze Burbank, Religious Camp Meeting, c. 1839, watercolor. Original at Old Dartmouth Historical Society–New Bedford Whaling Museum, New Bedford, Massachusetts. Public domain.

Refining Revivalist Rapture

Reed's views were not exceptional. The effort to condemn rapturous expressivity was part of a larger cultural movement proliferating within America's middle class that began to endorse self-control starting during the early decades of the nineteenth century.[129] As many esteemed scholars have demonstrated, the impulse toward self-control resonated strongly with economic changes associated with the growth of industrialization, expanding labor demands, and the opening of new markets during the nineteenth century.[130] In America, the bellwethers of this movement were commercially successful elites who enjoyed disproportionate access to intellectual, material, and social resources, as well as alliances with (other) successful northern capitalists.[131] According to Julia Rosenbaum and Sven Beckert, these individuals secured and sustained their socioeconomic ascendancy in part by developing a shared "bourgeois" culture.[132] Self-control became a hallmark of its value system and was promoted widely throughout the middle class and to those who occupied less-privileged social strata.

Among evangelicals, the physical regulation of religious ecstasy started in the Northern industrialized regions of the country and was led by a relatively small coterie of bourgeois elites who believed strongly in adapting the revivalist interest in expressive devotion to the more tempered tenets of emotional control. One of the earliest nineteenth-century proponents of this movement was John Fanning Watson, a Methodist minister from Philadelphia.[133] In his 1819 treatise titled *Methodist Error; or, Friendly Christian Advice to Those Methodists Who Indulge in Extravagant Emotions and Bodily Exercises*, Watson accepted the precept of religious ecstasy, but condemned its fulsome expression in public settings, such as camp meeting "shouts." Effusive bodily behavior, he explained, was noisy and chaotic in these contexts. Therefore, it best occurred in closeted settings where it would avoid the possibility of offending others.[134]

Even Protestant evangelicals who had wholeheartedly accepted demonstrative ecstasy early on during the Second Great Awakening began to pivot toward emotional and corporeal regulation by the 1830s. No one better epitomized this transition than Charles Finney, during his long tenure as the preeminent revivalist leader in the North. Finney's decision to pursue an ecclesiastical vocation occurred after a musical conversion experience in 1821. On this occasion, he was singing and playing his bass viol alone at his law office one night. When he started to play he was overwhelmed by a mystical sensation unlike any other he had ever felt: "It seemed as if my heart was all liquid, and my feelings were in such a state that I could not hear my own voice in singing without causing my sensibility to overflow. I wondered at this and tried to suppress my tears, but could not. . . . I wondered what ailed me that I felt such a disposition to weep."[135] Unable to control his crying, Finney stopped singing and put away his instrument. Soon thereafter, all his inward feelings began to "rise and flow out," and he felt his heart utter the words "I want to pour my whole soul out to God."[136] In this moment, Finney recalled, the divine spirit "descended upon me in a manner that seemed to go through me, body and soul. I could feel the impression . . . going through and through me. . . . I can recollect distinctly that it seemed to fan me like immense wings; and it seemed to me, as these waves passed over me, that they literally moved my hair like a passing breeze."[137] Finney's conversion experience—which he described as a "mighty baptism of the Holy Ghost"[138]—gave him a deep appreciation for the power of emotional experiences to reveal the true nature of God's grace. Intense emotion soon became central to his devotional style, which often employed grand gestures of sentiment to instill spiritual understanding in his followers.[139] It was a style that he would spread actively through revivals across the country and particularly in the western regions of New York State.

However, by the 1830s and 1840s, the famous revivalist had begun to advocate against excessively effusive physical acts of devotion. Unrestrained bodies and demonstrative emotions did not, in this opinion, represent the pinnacle of worship practices, as some earlier revivalists had supposed. Certainly, he admitted, religious ecstasy could involve a degree of physicality. "In every age of the church," Finney acknowledged, "cases have occurred in which persons have had such clear manifestations of divine truth as to prostrate their physical strength entirely."[140] If such responses were authentically religious, however, Finney believed that they were, by and large, relatively tranquil affairs. Indeed, as he described them, such experiences often had an almost paralyzing effect on the subject's mind and body:

> The mind seems not to be conscious of any unusual excitement of its own sensibility; but on the contrary, seems to itself to be calm and its state seems peculiar only because truth is seen with unusual clearness. Manifestly there is no such effervescence of the sensibility as produces tears, or any of the usual manifestations of an excited imagination or deeply moved feelings. There is not that gush of feeling which distracts the thoughts, but the mind sees truth unveiled, and in such relations as really to take away

all bodily strength, while the mind looks in upon the unveiled glories of the Godhead.[141]

That Finney would favor subdued physical trances, such as the one described here, was not exactly surprising. His ethos of corporeal self-control tended to echo that of his intended audiences, who were typically urban and middle class—a status that was often attended by refined sensibilities regarding physical comportment.[142] This approach obviously differed markedly from both Finney's earlier devotional style and the Methodist revivals that had been popular (especially in the South and West of the country) during the earliest years of nineteenth-century revivalism. Finney condemned the latter using terms such as "recklessness," "fanaticism," and "rash zeal."[143]

Although Finney lectured and wrote little about music, he obviously believed it to be an integral feature of his evangelical revivals as well as conducive to the more specific goal of cultivated emotional uplift. The role he ascribed to music in his earliest conversion experience certainly evinced this attitude. So too did his later encouragement of choral and congregational singing at his revival meetings. Indeed, in 1832, after settling in New York City as minister of the Chatham Street Chapel, Finney quickly hired Thomas Hastings as his music director in order to facilitate the spread of his particular brand of revivalism among the urban congregations. The two men already knew each other well. Hastings had been a choir director in upstate New York when revivals burned through the region where Finney was making a name for himself. Hastings also continued to serve as editor to the *Western Recorder*, an important evangelical newspaper at the time. When he joined Finney, Hastings had already made several influential contributions to the growing repertory of evangelical music, including the hymn "Hail to the Brightness of Zion's Glad Morning" and the melody for "Rock of Ages." With the eminent revivalist's support, Hastings would teach and continue to write music, direct choirs, and compile songbooks.

While Finney spoke generally about the necessity to regulate religious experience, Hastings focused this attitude on musical experience in particular. Many of his views were presented in his *Dissertation on Musical Taste*, the first full-length musical treatise by an American. Here, he averred that true devotional song should "school [the] affections" of worshipers and accord with "the tranquil nature of religious feeling."[144] The performance of a religious song was to be "mild, tender, and subdued," distinct and impressive enough to attract attention and evoke sentiment among audiences but never "frantic."[145] A truly moral model for devotional music, Hastings believed, involved singing with "disciplined hearts and voices" a hymn that subdued listeners to tenderness, "not as by dramatic effort or musical enchantment, but by the force of religious considerations, presented distinctly and solemnly by individuals."[146] The performance should be such, Hastings maintained, that the congregation "retired in silence," encouraged toward a "more earnest contemplation of the truths . . . so solemnly presented" by the hymns.[147] Moreover, like Watson, he believed that these musical experiences were best practiced in private whenever possible. "The inspired Psalmist [of early Christianity] appears often to have been singing alone," Hastings contended, and he believed this model should serve to guide the devotional practices of his contemporaries.[148] While Hastings wrote little on the precise topic of ecstatic experience, his general comments about emotional control seem to have been abundantly applicable to such phenomena.

So too did the writings of Hastings's former teacher Lowell Mason. Far and away the most influential educator and publisher of American church music during the nineteenth century,[149] Mason also frowned upon unmitigated exuberance. Although he advocated for the centrality of music to religious life, his popular songbooks highlighted music's ability to calm the mind, cultivate "habits of order and union," and teach singers to "control . . . the modulations of the voice."[150] The principle of union, in this context, seems to have alluded more to a conformity of practice rather than a merger of identities. As the music historians John Ogasapian and N. Lee Orr observe, Mason "eschewed the emotional, spontaneous ecstasy of the revival song for a more rational hymnody, mildly evangelical in doctrine, and sentimental in tone."[151]

With the guidance and encouragement of Watson, Finney, Hastings, Mason, and other musical leaders, the principles of physical propriety and restraint grew increasingly pronounced in American evangelicalism. In fact, they were integral features of the so-called "businessmen's revival" of 1857–1858[152] and flavored the subsequent period of revivalism spanning to the early 1900s—which some scholars have called the "Third Great Awakening."[153] It was in this tradition of cultivated sentiment that the preacher-musician duo of Dwight Moody and Ira Sankey embarked on a musical mission of popular outreach during the 1870s. Although they represented a younger generation of evangelists, they upheld the earlier valuation of refined and restrained emotional expression. Like Finney's, the duo's spiritual journeys were punctuated early on with personal and profound mystical experiences.

Weeks before setting off on his first tour with Sankey, for instance, Moody found himself "roll[ing] on the floor in the midst of many tears and groans and [crying] to God to be baptized with the Holy Ghost and fire."[154] Later, he described the event as "almost too sacred an experience to name . . . I can only say that God revealed himself to me, and I had such an experience of His love that I had to ask Him to stay His hand."[155] Yet, like Finney, Moody and Sankey believed these demonstrative experiences should occur rarely and in private.

Even so, Moody and Sankey's followers may not have been unfamiliar with ecstatic, musical outbursts. According to one account of the duo's performance in Chicago during the mid-1870s, the audience became "wrapt in ecstatic peace by the music of Mr. Sankey's melodious voice."[156] Sankey also observed music's overwhelming effect on full display at other events. This included one occasion when, after hearing the hymn "The Ninety and Nine," a woman who was "so hardened a moment before burst into tears and falling on her knees began to pray to the Good Shepherd to receive her."[157] The words of the tune also profoundly influenced a young man who had left his family "to rid himself of all home restraint." After hearing the lyrics, the man fell on his knees, and returned home.[158]

Notwithstanding these moments of profound physical release, however, Moody and Sankey preferred their musical performances, and the spiritual experiences that often accompanied them, to be tempered affairs. As Tamara J. Van Dyken, David W. Stowe, and other scholars have claimed, the duo's revivals were typically "well-ordered masses" that evoked tender emotions, usually related to pathos, the music being primarily intended to attract would-be converts and channel their attention to the sermon.[159] Regulated devotion was integral here; physically passionate ecstasy was not. This model helped make Moody and Sankey enormously popular in the United States (and abroad) during the 1870s, where they toured extensively, and frequently attracted sold-out venues. Such appearances included P. T. Barnum's Hippodrome in New York City (one of the largest arenas in the city at the time), the Chicago World's Fair in 1893, and dozens of cities and towns across the United States. By the time Moody died in 1899, he had established Christian colleges and schools and was estimated to have preached to over one hundred million people around the world, according to a Moody organization estimate, with Sankey usually accompanying him.[160] Their work culminated a decades-long evangelical effort to refine religious experience, and ecstasy in particular.

The Holiness Movement and Pentecostalism

Not all musical Americans were willing to embrace the bourgeois-led movement for silent and still religious lives. During the last decades of the nineteenth century, just as Moody and Sankey were gaining popularity, there also emerged a movement to reinvigorate mystical musical experiences in accordance with older prescripts. This new crusade embraced almost everything that bourgeois refinement did not. It doubled down on effusive corporeal expression, and it uplifted the status of women, African Americans, and other social groups conventionally relegated to positions of low authority. Much of its impetus originated in the different denominations and sects that constituted the Holiness Movement.

Born of a growing desire among American Methodists to achieve more enduring conversion experiences and a purer, sanctified Christian life, members of the Holiness Movement were initially divided over the role of ecstatic experience. Some members sanctified only those religious experiences that conformed to the more controlled conduct of the middle class. Others, however, found value in more unrestrained experiences. The tension came to a head at a Midwestern camp meeting in 1881, when a debate erupted over the musical ecstasies of one of the attendees:

> One day right in the midst of a great sermon, a woman from Carrol County, a Holiness professor, sprawled out at full length in the aisle. This was in itself not much to be thought of, for to tumble over now and then was expected. But the unexpected happened in this case. It kept some of the sisters busy to keep her with a measurably decent appearance. Directly she began to compose a jargon of words in rhyme and sing them in a weird tune. She persisted until the service was spoiled and the camp was thrown into a hubbub. Strange to say, the camp was divided thereby. Some said it was a wonderful manifestation of divine power, some said it was a repetition of a speaking in unknown tongues as at Pentecost. But every preacher on the grounds without exception declared it to be of the devil. But the camp was so divided in opinion that it had to be handled with the greatest of care.[161]

Some of the more radical members of the Holiness Movement, particularly in the South and the Midwest, came out adamantly in favor of this demonstrative musical ecstasy. They included most notably Maria Woodworth-Etter. An evangelist from Ohio, Woodworth-Etter preached and led revival meetings in towns and cities across the country from the 1880s to the 1920s, converting tens of thousands along the way. Her meetings were well known for their intense emotional and physical vigor, including prostrations, speaking and singing in tongues, trances and visions, and miracles of healing.

For Woodworth-Etter, singing and hearing music while in religious trance states was an important feature of the conversion process. Indeed, one of her own earliest conversion experiences involved singing the hymn "God Be with You Till We Meet Again" and feeling the spiritual power of singers who "broke down crying, one after another, until nearly everyone in the station was weeping. Strong men wept aloud, and the power came upon us. I came near being overpowered."[162] When she herself became a preacher, Woodworth-Etter frequently marveled at the power of the Holy Spirit to draw "heavenly music" out of those who felt the power of its presence. In her writings, she described one of these occurrences in detail:

> Suddenly there fell upon my ear . . . a song of the most wonderful description. It did not at all appear like human voices, but seemed much more like the tones of some wonderful instrument of music, such as human ears never before heard. It began on the right side of the audience, and rolled from there over the entire company of baptised saints in a volume of sounds resembling in its rising and falling, its rolling and sinking, its swelling and receding character, the rolling waves of the ocean when being acted upon by the wonderful force which produces the tide. . . . Such blending of tones, such perfect harmony of sounds, such musical strains, my ears never before heard. . . . It filled me with such holy awe, worship and praise to the Lord, that before I was able to realise the fact fully, the Holy Ghost led me to join in that heavenly song of praise with the rest.[163]

Woodworth-Etter's ministry style, particularly its focus on direct and physical experience of God through the baptism by the Holy Spirit, presented a substantial challenge to the emotional restraints placed on women throughout the nineteenth century. By both embracing extreme affect and taking responsibility for deciding when and where emotional behavior was acceptable, Woodworth-Etter contradicted expectations that women should be both more emotionally sensitive and more emotionally controlled than men.

In doing so, she, along with other radical female evangelicals who aspired to leadership roles in the Holiness Movement, helped revivify self-transcendent experience and make it accessible and acceptable to more participants than most evangelical movements ever had before.

Woodworth-Etter's actions and beliefs served as a model for the Pentecostalism that grew out of the Holiness Movement during the very early years of the twentieth century.[164] So too did the importance she placed on music. Her love of song was shared by Charles Fox Parham, who would become the leading light of the Pentecostal movement. One of Parham's earliest conversion experiences was linked to music. As a young boy, probably not much older than ten, the young Parham was on his way home from a religious meeting in his hometown of Cheney, Kansas, when he suddenly felt wrought with a "deep and pungent conviction" as he thought of the sinfulness of man and the grace of God.[165] Unable to pray under such weighty circumstances, young Charles turned instead to singing. He began quietly at first, humming the familiar hymn "I am Coming to the Cross," but by the third verse he turned his face heavenward and belted out the lyrics:

> Here, I give my all to Thee,
> Friends, and time and earthly store,
> Soul and body Thine to be;
> Wholly Thine forever more.

As he repeated the word "wholly," suddenly he felt a flash from Heaven that was as brilliant as the sun. As Parham later recalled, "like a stroke of lightening [sic] it penetrated, thrilling every tissue and fiber of my being."[166] In this moment of ecstasy, Parnham knew he had been saved and could live his life as a true Christian. By the age of fifteen, Parham was a preacher and within another ten years he had rejected religious denominations and established an evangelical ministry based on the ideas of the Holiness Movement.

During one of the first Pentecostal revivals, the Azusa Street Revival, which started in Los Angeles in 1906, one participant, A. C. Valdez, provided an eyewitness account, and described a scene of intense religious ecstasy and music:

> Many were slain in the Spirit . . . , buckling to the floor, unconscious, in a beautiful Holy Spirit cloud, and the Lord gave them visions. How I enjoyed shouting and praising God. During the

> tarrying, we used to break out in songs about Jesus and the Holy Spirit, "Fill Me Now," "Joy Unspeakable," and "Love Lifted Me." Praise about the cleansing and precious blood of Jesus would just spring from our mouths. In between choruses, heavenly music would fill the hall, and we would break into tears. Suddenly the crowd seemed to forget how to sing in English. Out of their mouths would come new languages and lovely harmony that no human beings could have learned.[167]

Amid spiritual possession, loss of bodily control, and visions, the participants found that everyday speech fell short of expressing what must have been an array of ineffable experiences. Therefore, they resorted to the emotional power of songs and speaking in tongues.

This enduring propensity for songful self-transcendence was commonly condemned by those who subscribed to more refined and scientific cultures of experience. One journalist onlooker, for instance, described the revivalist activities at Azusa in the following way:

> They cry and make howling noises all day and into the night. They run, jump, shake all over, shout to the top of their voice, spin around in circles, fall out on the sawdust blanketed floor jerking, kicking and rolling all over it. Some of them pass out and do not move for hours as though they were dead. These people appear to be mad, mentally deranged or under a spell. They claim to be filled with the spirit. . . . They repeatedly sing the same song, "The Comforter Has Come."[168]

Beyond providing insight into the activities of the Azusa Street Revival, this description also demonstrated the degree to which Pentecostalism challenged mainstream social sensibilities during both the late nineteenth and early twentieth centuries. Its intense corporeality rejected the refined middle-class comportment of both religious and secular elites, and its apparently indiscriminate openness to people of different social backgrounds similarly depreciated the race, class, and gender hierarchies that also benefited bourgeois culture. (Moreover, its unrelenting faith in a transcendent deity flew in the face of more empirically grounded theories that explained spirituality in purely immanent terms, which, as discussed in chapter 4, were already circulating widely in American culture.) When the journalist described the revivalists as "mad, mentally deranged or under a spell," he effectively summed up the range of possible explanations offered by those groups who felt most threatened by their practices.

∾

Historians sometimes divide American religious history into three distinct eras. The first, extending from the seventeenth into the eighteenth century, was characterized by Puritan Calvinism's rational and stoic perspectives. The second, emerging in the eighteenth century and flourishing in the nineteenth, was marked by the rise of evangelical denominations like the Methodists and Baptists, who emphasized religious experience over intellectual reasoning. The third period, developing during the nineteenth century, evoked a refined respectability oriented toward social reform and civic virtue. In broad terms, this basic narrative captures many of the important changes that occurred in Anglo-American religion during this era.

However, through an examination of musical experience, this chapter has demonstrated that this narrative obscures a more complex situation whereby countervailing interpretations continuously coexisted in American religion. During the starchy era of Puritan ascendancy, overtones of antinomian ecstasy still remained perceptible and sometimes even acceptable. And during the mid-eighteenth century, when leaders and followers of the Great Awakening came to encourage more effusive and social forms of ecstasy, John Wesley and other New Lights continued to worry about how far they could acceptably transgress the boundaries of selfhood prescribed (and proscribed) by the Old Lights. This tension persisted into the nineteenth century, as evinced by Andrew Reed's hesitant fascination with the ecstatic rituals of revivalism. During the middle years of the nineteenth century, an inclination toward proper, private, and restrained comportment gained prominence but was also paralleled by a more effusive, revivalist approach that eventually blossomed into the Holiness Movement and Pentecostalism. It is fruitful, then, to understand the counterpoint of religious consciousness during this period as its own distinct formation that could never be perfectly conflated with specific time periods or religious identities.

While Americans interpreted their experiences of self in diverse ways, it is also important to recognize what they shared in common during this era. Despite their differences, the vast majority of Americans addressed in this chapter approached ecstatic experiences as encounters with supernatural phenomena, usually the Holy Spirit or its cognates, but sometimes satanic forces. And all of them believed these events to reveal or maintain some deep truth about the cosmos and their place in it. Despite some likely discrepancies between many individuals' levels of devotion,[169] the paradigm of sincere spirituality remained relatively unchallenged among Anglo-Americans during the eighteenth century. Between 1700 and 1740, an estimated 75 to 80 percent of American colonists attended churches, which at the time were being built at a rapid rate.[170] With the help of music, many of them found ways to authenticate some form of religious ecstasy. By the nineteenth century, evangelicalism alone had gained the support of some ten million people, or roughly 40 percent of the United States' population, constituting what Richard Carwardine calls "the largest, and most formidable subculture in American society" at the time.[171] It was entirely predictable that music would become implicated in religious Americans' alterations of self-experience throughout this period: until well into the nineteenth century, the most musical place in America remained the church.[172]

Beginning around the late eighteenth century, though, some musical Americans followed their European counterparts in radically revamping how they understood self-transcendence. This process did not constitute an outright challenge to the mystical nature of musical experience, but it did alter other features that had remained pervasive throughout the American colonies and the United States for centuries. By the mid-nineteenth century, Charles Finney would declare that "raptures, or ecstasies, or high flights of feeling . . . can exist in full power where there is no religion."[173] Intended as a warning to faithful Christians, Finney's statement also served as an acknowledgment that orthodox religion was not the only viable framework for understanding self-transcendence in American culture.

Chapter 2

The Naturalization of Numen

On the night of February 5, 1853, John S. Dwight entered the Boston Music Hall for a momentous occasion. The Germania Musical Society, in partnership with the Handel and Haydn Society, the United States' oldest classical music group, was performing Beethoven's Ninth Symphony for the first time in America. Earlier in the day, Dwight's *Journal of Music*—a highly acclaimed musical weekly that was respected by readers across New England and around the country—had predicted that "the glorious intention of the music will not be lost upon the audience."[1] That intention, Dwight would later explain, was to "utter the unutterable, by [producing] music 'so monstrous long and difficult'" that it would create a "sublime whole."[2] During the performance, Dwight later contended, each member of the Germania Musical Society "appear[ed] to be united by a sentiment of genuine fraternity and enthusiasm for Art." For them, "music is religion . . . Their success is a moral triumph," explainable only by "the cordial unanimity, spirit of devotion, the merging of the individual in the common interest."[3] Of the performance, Dwight declared, "*not* to be enthusiastic is not to have heard."[4]

Dwight's journal described the audience's reaction to the music in similar terms. During another performance of the concert in April, one of the middle movements, a Scherzo, provided pure joy: "Not the [kind] that satisfies, but that in which the deeply unsatisfied soul seeks oblivion of its torturing aspiration in the most desperate abandonment to the philosophy which makes the livelong day and life itself a feast."[5] The melody in this movement provided the "inspiring rhythm of nature, in which you feel always something rich and new . . . and that you never exhaust its charm."[6] Another movement, the Adagio, was the product of a "communion . . . sweet and pure." As for the final movement, the audience recognized it as "unspeakably sublime," akin to a religious form of "ecstasy."[7] The energy of the orchestra was enough to let it "[rise] above itself [and] seize the actual form and outline of the human utterance to which all is tending."[8] For Dwight, the symphony provided opportunities for profound self-transcendence and helped render the audience the "most earnest, attentive and appreciating ever seen in Boston."[9]

Dwight's assessment of the power of the music can be both compared and contrasted with those of Jonathan Edwards, the Wesley brothers, Andrew Reed, and others discussed in the previous chapter. On one hand, all of these people recognized musical experience as a potent, somewhat ineffable, and sometimes overwhelming force that exceeded ordinary sense perception and revealed some deep truth about the cosmos. More than this, they also believed in the possibility of self-effacement before some kind of metaphysical entity. The commonality was apparent in Dwight's word choice, including not only "ecstasy" but also "religion," "spirit," "devotion," "soul," and "communion"—all of which were borrowed directly from the Christian tradition.

However, Dwight also differed from the evangelicals in his precise interpretation of the object of musical ecstasy. Absent in his account were Christian appeals to an omniscient God who remained separate and distant from the natural world. Although Dwight sometimes referred to "God" in his writings, the term was only one of many he used to describe the vague, elemental force of the universe that operates through all things. For him, other words could describe such a metaphysical essence equally well, if not more potently. According to the transcendentalist philosophies to which Dwight subscribed, "Nature" was an immanently useful concept, for it actively referred to that raw, relentless impulse that animated the workings of the physical world. For Dwight, however, "Art" was perhaps the most useful term of all, for it reflected both the process and product of manifesting the elemental principles of the cosmos through the faculty of the human imagination.[10] Dwight believed music to be the highest form of Art, and although he compared its creation to "religion," his was not a faith that was amenable to that of most Protestants. Dwight believed that evoking the artistic impulse was not to be achieved through religious conversion, but rather through careful listening to European classical music. And instead of making one aware of the presence of the Holy Spirit, Dwight's experience was of an ineffable and elemental essence that created what he called a "sublime whole."

Dwight's ecstatic understanding of "Nature" and "Art" echoed aspects of the classical Music of the Spheres philosophy, which presumed that the sounds of instruments revealed a deeper principle that resonated through every facet of the world.[11] This interpretation found sacred qualities in the natural world, and therefore it could have been considered un-Christian "enthusiasm" by evangelicals. Perhaps for this reason, it is no coincidence that, when describing audiences' reception to what he considered superlative art music, Dwight's writings regularly and affirmatively used the term "enthusiastic." According to the historian Jon Mee, nonevangelicals imbued the term with both negative and positive connotations, giving it less pejorative punch than it had received in orthodox Christian settings.[12] And in this respect, Dwight was reorienting the object of ecstasy away from that which was supported (and debated) by orthodox Protestants.

Ostensibly, some Americans' interpretation of musical self-transcendence had undergone a transformation. The transition might be best described as a process of naturalization, a term that signifies a secularizing tendency whereby the objects of ecstatic experience shifted away from a supernatural source and toward more natural phenomena. In effect, this process involved moving the horizon of transcendence. It was a refocus that gave less attention to the tenets of orthodox religion, but it was rarely intended to deny the existence of supernatural entities altogether. Indeed, like Dwight, the main proponents of naturalized ecstasy considered their philosophies to be compatible with the existence of a deity or other ethereal agents. Yet their focus remained more on the mysterious, mystical, and magical forces that existed *inside* the natural realm. These forces were still considered metaphysical to the extent that they exceeded the agency of the individual and seemed to bind together separate components of the natural, living, and human worlds, as well as smaller social communities such as a nation or family. Although they deserved a sincere respect much like the supernatural spirit of conventional religion,[13] their natural provenance set them apart from their Christian religious counterparts. For this reason, they might be better associated with the term "numen," a Latin word that referred to a spiritual or divine presence that could reside anywhere, including in nature itself. The concept also gave rise to the term "numinous," which Rudolf Otto and other religious scholars later described as the felt experience of a holy, mysterious, or otherworldly presence, often marked by sensations of reverence, awe, and fear.[14]

This chapter traces the multifarious emergence of a naturalized mode of ecstasy as it originated among Deists, liberal Protestants, mesmerists, spiritualists, and members of unorthodox faiths and quasi-religious philosophies that took shape in America during the late eighteenth and nineteenth centuries. It specifically focuses on three musically inflected lines of naturalized mysticism, which were respectively associated with sentimentality, the sublime, and animal magnetism. Each of these traditions was comparable yet distinct. Sentimentality (or sensibility) involved the elicitation of tender feelings such as sympathy and benevolence toward others that tied together a society. Sublime experience provided an antinomian encounter, not with a distant God, but with the universal, mystical currents that flowed through Art and Nature. Animal magnetism involved the merger of self with an ethereal fluid that could balance one's body and soul or communicate with spirits. All of these (lightly) secularized interpretations of entrancement might be loosely associated with the term Romanticism, which allowed for an array of numinous, metaphysical experiences that were not necessarily tethered to a Christian God or other supernatural deity.[15]

By demonstrating musical phenomena as integral to the evolution of this naturalized mode, this chapter helps expand the focus of much existing scholarship on Romanticism in America. Most of this scholarship links the popularity of naturalized ecstasy to the world of literary publications that were bought and shared far and wide throughout the United States. These publications included thousands of sentimental novels, short stories, and nonfictional or journalistic publications written by the likes of Catharine Sedgwick, Maria Susanna Cummins, and Harriet Beecher Stowe.[16] They also included the poems, essays, journals, sermons, and other published writing of Romantic authors such as Ralph Waldo Emerson, Washington Irving, James Fenimore Cooper, Henry David Thoreau, Margaret Fuller, Nathaniel Hawthorne, and Walt Whitman, to name a few. Not discounting the vast influence these works and writers had on the development of Romanticism in America, it is a mistake to assume the Romantic ethos was based only on writing and reading. Doing so neglects the importance of performing and listening generated by the profusion of sentimental songs and Romantic music that swept through America and the English-speaking world during the late eighteenth and nineteenth centuries. It also neglects the deep appreciation of music held by mesmerists and spiritualists. As this chapter demonstrates, music in the Romantic tradition provided Americans of various stripes with abundant opportunities for emotional self-abandon and compassionate connections to secular numens that were not closely bound to conventional Christian doctrines or clerical control.

Sentimentality and Sensibility

The growth of a naturalized mode of musical ecstasy in America occurred over several centuries. It was tied up in a larger pivot toward secular thought that evolved out of contradictions found within Protestant theology itself, particularly those associated with the tenets of nominalism. Although Christian nominalism originally separated the Divine from the profane in order to maintain God's moral authority, the historian Glenn Olsen contends that this theological position ironically accelerated a cultural pivot away from God altogether.[17] Ultimately, Olsen argues, disentangling the Christian Deity from the profane world effectively made God less knowable, less accessible, and less involved in human affairs. This distance provided earthly subjects with a newfound claim to personal autonomy over the mundane world. Accordingly, it rendered the profane sphere (which was originally imbued with vulgarity) both more interesting and more valuable.[18] Nominalism's separation of the supernatural from the natural was not originally intended to challenge the ascendancy of God. But it did tighten the nexus of nature and experience. During the seventeenth and especially the eighteenth centuries in Europe and America, the theological position called Deism came to capture this new secular attention. Those who supported the position, including many revolutionaries and American Founding Fathers, believed that humans did not experience God through supernatural revelation or divine intervention but more obliquely, through observations of the earth and its activities.[19] Such an orientation was only augmented by the philosophy of liberalism, which enshrined secular authority in the idea of a civil state that was autonomous and unfettered by ecclesiastical doctrine.[20]

The Deists' strict focus on earthly activities distinguished them from their evangelical counterparts, but, as the philosopher Colin Campbell has demonstrated, some doyens of Deism shared the Protestant revivalists' general emphasis on sincere feelings and emotional experience in leading a moral life.[21] By the seventeenth century, this attention to emotion prospered among the members of an informal alliance of English Puritan theologians known as the Cambridge Platonists. Drawing on classical philosophies, they developed a theology based on feelings of benevolence, compassion, and pity—attributes that they believed devout Christians shared with the Divine.[22] This valuation of the mundane world and tender sentiment persisted and blossomed within various philosophical and cultural movements of the eighteenth century.[23]

In the transatlantic Anglophone world of the eighteenth century, members of an emerging middle class appealed to this "profound emotional sensibility"[24] as they began competing for cultural hegemony with the traditional aristocracy. They framed tender feelings—or "sentimentality"—as a sign of the intrinsic virtue and the moral authority of their class culture.[25] The theories of the Moral Sense philosophers only reinforced this disposition, for they too imbued subjective feelings of compassion and benevolence with the utmost moral integrity. This turn toward tender feeling became encoded in what was eventually known in the English-speaking world as the "cult of sensibility,"[26] which for the first time elevated human feelings—based primarily on sensations of pity, sympathy, benevolence, and melancholy—as a key site of moral and aesthetic meaning, at times rivaling traditional religious doctrine. In this way, the middle classes partially turned their attention away from considerations of the Divine and more toward feelings for each other—particularly the sentiments that enabled individuals to feel and understand the suffering of others. By the time the cult of sensibility emerged during the second half of the eighteenth century, it had evolved a long way from orthodox Protestantism. Despite a few notable exceptions,[27] it rarely employed the language of "religion or revelation."[28] Instead, it echoed the numinous character of conventional Christianity by imbuing sentimentality with an abstract sacred quality that could be elevated and set apart from more mundane sensations. Indeed, any advocate of sentimentality—or what the Scottish writer Henry Mackenzie called a Man of Feeling—was expected to praise tender sentiments as possessing a hidden and omniscient power that revealed some universal moral truth about the nature of humanity.[29] In this manner, sentimentality was imbued with such spiritual qualities that several modern scholars have described the cult of sensibility as "almost sacred";[30] "semireligious";[31] echoing with "religious valences"; "a science of the soul"; and "implicitly religious."[32]

Another semireligious feature of sentimentality was what one scholar has called its "mystic" quality.[33] This was the belief that tender feelings were not just shared among individuals; they permeated the social world as emotional currents in much the same way that the Holy Spirit was thought to do in conventionally Christian contexts. While this belief did not exactly revive medieval universalism, it did suggest something akin to a secular "spirit" of humanity. Historians have indicated how this principle was institutionalized in American society. For instance, the historian Sarah Knott demonstrates how sensibility offered revolutionary-era subjects and early republic citizens a means of kindling social cohesion in a country that lacked traditional societal bonds (e.g., a monarch or a state religion).[34] According to Jose Torre, sentimentality also presented opportunities to bind American society together economically.[35] These and other historians demonstrate that sentimental feelings became crucial to the sharing of identities and the formation of communities both large and small.

What the existing historical literature rarely demonstrates, however, is how the "spirit" of sentimentality also provided opportunities for profound self-transcendent experience. Yet early supporters of the cult of sensibility—such as the philosophers Denis Diderot and Adam Smith—suggested the possibility that sentimental feelings could grow strong enough to overflow into an ecstatic union between emotionally attuned people.[36] Sentimental trance, defined this way, has some relation to the concept of *communitas*, developed by the twentieth-century anthropologist Victor Turner, which points to the intense sense of solidarity and shared humanity that emerges during liminal phases of sacred ceremonies and rituals, when social roles and hierarchies are suspended and a collective sense of equality arises.[37] (Turner also found something approximating, if not exactly replicating, these liminal experiences in modern cultural performances—such as concerts, theater, and art exhibitions—albeit in more voluntary and individualistic forms.) Yet, both sentimental trance and its *communitas* character remain less studied, particularly in the scholarship on sentimentality in America. Investigating musical performance and experience reveals that Americans continued to interpret the currents of tender feelings as not only tying communities of individuals together but also eliciting expansive and unusual experiences of self-transcendence.

One of the earliest accounts of sentimental, musical ecstasy in America comes from 1771. It was in this year that future president John Adams, then a lawyer and public figure, recalled hearing a choir in Connecticut. Despite his well-established reputation as a curmudgeon, Adams rhapsodized joyously about the experience: "The finest singing that I ever heard in my life; the front and side galleries were crowded with rows of lads and lasses, who performed all their parts in utmost perfection. I thought I was rapt up; a row of women all standing up and playing their parts with perfect skill and judgment, added a sweetness and sprightliness to the whole which absolutely charmed me."[38] Adams, who sympathized with the principles of Deism and the cult of sensibility,[39] did not employ conventional religious terminology in describing the choral music. Instead, his reception of the performance seemed to echo the tender, virtuous feelings associated with the archetypal Man of Feeling. His experience of being "rapt up" in the music suggested a particularly deep level of identification with the choir, a feeling that was condoned if not celebrated by moral philosophy. Absorption into a larger group remained a key tenet of the nation and state that Adams himself helped found. This much was suggested by the de facto motto of the United States starting around the time of the revolution: *e pluribus unum*—out of many, one.

In contrast to the uniform praise expressed by Adams, other American sentimentalists took a more ambivalent stance toward tender feelings, helping popularize them even as they condemned them. Liberal principles of autonomy and self-determination, enshrined as ideals of the revolution, informed notions of selfhood in America both during and following the Revolutionary War.[40] The consequence was that many Americans discouraged extreme forms of sentimentality for fear that they would lead to rampant loss of self-control. One of the leaders of this reactionary movement was the American author William Hill Brown, who, in 1789, published *The Power of Sympathy*, widely considered the first novel published by an American. In the book, Brown included stories of egregious behavior that resulted from an indulgence in tender feelings, particularly sympathy. This sentiment, Brown suggested, could eradicate an individual's free will and lead to tragic outcomes—licentious thoughts, seductive tendencies, incest, disease, and even suicide. At a crucial point in *The Power of Sympathy*, the character Harriot cried mournfully about the hazards of emotional abandonment: "Why do I rave, and why do I again abandon myself to despair!"[41] Fidelia, another character, also learned how the self-transcendence of sentimentality could yield traumatic consequences. She was "a poor distracted girl [who] was carried off by a ruffian a few days before her intended marriage," which caused her betrothed to drown himself in the river after discovering what happened. Upon realizing the tragedy she had set in motion, Fidelia continued to indulge her impressionable sensibility by wandering through the countryside singing sad songs about lost love.[42] Although the story was ostensibly intended to warn against the dangers of sentimentality and provide a guide for good behavior, scholars of the text and its reception have suggested that the book's lascivious stories actually interested readers more than its moral lessons.[43] Regardless of whether one supported Adams's affirmative judgment or Brown's negative one, sentimentalists agreed that the pursuit of tender feelings could result in ecstatic experiences, and in this respect the naturalization process of entrancement depended little on the moral valences assigned to it.

Well-known songs of the nineteenth century regularly evoked sentimentality, but they tilted more toward Adams's endorsement than toward Brown's apprehension. Rarely, however, did their lyrics come out in full-throated support of sentimental trance; instead, they used selective word choice to gesture obliquely toward its possibility. For example, "I Leave My Heart with Thee," a lachrymose love song composed by James Hook in 1804, had the narrator feeling that he left his "heart" with his lover even though he was forced to stray.[44] Thomas Moore and John Stevenson's tune "Oft in the Stilly Night" from 1818 similarly approached the possibility of ecstasy in a nostalgic yearning for days when sentimental delight could be found not only in "the smiles, the tears, of childhood's years" but also in "the friends, so link'd together."[45] Although they may have always been intended to be interpreted poetically rather than literally, the lyrical references to leaving one's heart with a loved one or linking together friends suggest that musical Americans understood the power of sentimentality to evoke some kind of intense communal experience.

On occasion, indirect gestures toward sentimental trance gave way to explicit description. This much was achieved by a short story published in 1835 in *Godey's Lady's Book*, the preeminent women's monthly magazine during the antebellum period, which frequently lauded the virtues of sentimental song.[46] Written by Mary Macmichael and titled "The School-Fellows," it described a scene of mutual musical entrancement between a woman, Mary, and her male admirer, Eugene. In applying the language of sentimental self-transcendence to a romantic liaison between a young couple, the story seemed to blur the lines between ecstasy and seduction.

> [Mary] seated herself unhesitatingly upon the piano-stool, and after a slight accompaniment, sung with exquisite pathos, a plaintive air. There was a natural beauty in her voice—a profound melancholy in its intense sweetness that could dissolve the soul of the listener. Eugene was entranced; all that was dear to him in the memory of the past; the joys of home and childhood; the tenderness and truth of his first friendship . . . all that he had loved and lost upon earth—his gentle mother, seemed again to live and again to fade, as he listened to the strains.[47]

Even as Mary was able to musically "entrance" and "dissolve the soul" of Eugene, she too felt a surge of ecstatic feelings: "The same spell was felt in the heart of the maiden, veiling the world, and lifting her spirit into vast and immeasurable regions of unexplored delight. One moment their eyes met and glanced upon each other the look of exalted, of eternal love. . . . Rapture swelled their breasts, and swelled their full hearts."[48] The "spell" that lifted her spirit into vast and immeasurable regions created a visceral feeling of "rapture."

While inferences of sweet self-transcendence regularly described the love between two individuals, perhaps even more popular were those that acknowledged the emotional union that could exist between members of larger circles of belonging, such as the home and family. This was especially true following the enormous success of John Howard Payne's 1823 song "Home, Sweet Home," which was set to music by Henry Rowley Bishop. While the original lyrics referred wistfully to the sanctity of the home, additional verses added in 1830 celebrated a properly functioning family as consisting of "a fond Father's smile" and "the cares of a Mother to soothe and beguile."[49] As the piece grew to become the single most popular song of the English-speaking world during the nineteenth century,[50] dozens of other songwriters wrote similar tunes embracing the household and its denizens. The lyrics of all of these pieces were specifically intended to pull at the heartstrings of listeners. That they resonated so strongly in American culture likely speaks to the nineteenth century's massive amount of migration—both into the United States and out toward its less populated regions—all of which would have generated deep yearnings for home among Americans of many backgrounds. This factor cannot be overstated when accounting for the rise of sentimentality and its affiliated ecstasies during this era.

Certain songs were more effective than others at suggesting the possibility of sentimental rapture afforded by home and family. Some lyrics took the idea to almost absurd levels, such as the words Eliza Cook wrote for the 1840 song "The Old Arm Chair." These described something close to an ecstatic communion with a chair—ostensibly meant to symbolize, in this case, the sanctified institutions of home and motherhood:

> I love it, I love it; and who shall dare
> To chide me for loving that old arm chair.
> I've treasured it long as a holy prize,
> I've bedew'd it with tears, and embalmed it with sighs;
> 'Tis bound by a thousand bands to my heart;
> Not a tie will break, not a link will start,

> Would ye learn the spell a mother sat there,
> And a sacred thing is that old arm chair.[51]

Firmly "bound" to the narrator's heart through unbreakable ties, the piece of domestic furniture became a "sacred" reminder of the morality of the family unit.

The traveling vocal groups that became popular around the 1840s, many of which used the word "family" in their name, also excelled at insinuating the possibility of sentimental ecstasy.[52] Perhaps not coincidentally, these groups often consisted of members of the same family. Chief among them was the Hutchinson Family, a large troupe of brothers and sisters who sang in tight four-part harmonies and toured around the country singing sentimental songs. Many of their lyrics advanced an agenda of social activism that supported abolition, workers' rights, women's rights, and alcoholic temperance. Their lyrics also asked listeners to join in sympathetic union with those less fortunate than themselves. As such, many of their most popular ballads honored the family, their region or nation, as well as the social plights of various marginalized subjectivities, including those of enslaved people, workers, and women. "The Old Granite State,"[53] one of the Hutchinson Family's earliest and best-known tunes, expressed many of these themes simultaneously. In it the singers proudly identified themselves as "a band of brothers" and "a band of music," "all real Yankees," and New Hampshirites who "despise oppression" and are "friends of emancipation." In just a few verses, the Hutchinsons employed sentimental lyrics and melodies to connect themselves with a series of overlapping communities: their nuclear family, a musical consortium, an American state, the abolitionist movement, and the free North.

Perhaps more than through their lyrics, the Hutchinsons alluded to unitive experiences by blending their voices together in harmony. Indeed, the group was so well trained and well practiced that they could combine their voices to create the effect of one seamless, sonorous outpouring of mellifluous sentiment. They achieved this so precisely that, according to one description, "an audience found it impossible to distinguish between the four voices."[54] An anonymous daguerreotype of the Hutchinson Singers taken in 1845 seemed to depict the unifying force evoked by their vocal performances (see fig. 2.1). It showed ten brothers (out of thirteen siblings total) sitting close together, most of them clasping hands or leaning affectionately on each other's shoulders. The image evoked an undeniable

Figure 2.1. A portrait of members of the Hutchinson Family Singers. *Source:* Hutchinson Family Singers, 1845, daguerreotype. Metropolitan Museum of Art, Department of Photographs. "The Daguerreian Era and Early American Photography on Paper, 1839–60" in *Heilbrunn Timeline of Art History*. Public domain.

intimacy that, in conjunction with the band's song lyrics and vocal work, became a microcosm of the *e pluribus unum* principle.

No evidence confirms whether the Hutchinson Family members' sympathetic accord with each other prompted unitive experiences, but such outcomes certainly seem possible. Most of the siblings in the family are reported to have become "fully convinced of the truthfulness and genuineness" of the possibility that clairvoyants could extend their consciousness into the spirit world through the power of entrancement; indeed, more than one member of the group reported having profound trances in which they felt surrounded by the spirits of deceased loved ones.[55] These feelings of transport suggested that, if the Hutchinsons did not always experience a sense of sentimental self-transcendence, they nevertheless accepted its possibility and were sometimes capable of it themselves.

If the Hutchinsons believed in ecstatic sentimentality, they probably would not have interpreted it in conventional religious terms. Although the family was affiliated with the Baptist Church,[56] their songs mostly avoided the language of orthodox Christianity, opting instead for a rhetoric that more directly espoused the principles of liberalism as well as the socially progressive causes that aligned with them, just as "The Old Granite State" did. Indeed, at least one of their sentimental songs derided what they called the "sectarian lurches" of religious institutions for inhibiting the full embodiment of "Freedom" and the success of the abolitionist movement.[57]

For all their popularity, the Hutchinsons were only one of many musical acts capable of eliciting sentimental entrancement by invoking the secular sanctity of the home. During the 1870s, some accounts suggested that these sensations were regular occurrences on the concert stage, particularly when executed by accomplished female singers. One example came from British-born Clara Fisher, who immigrated to the United States as a young woman and regaled American audiences for decades. On one occasion in 1873, Fisher took to the stage in New York and, according to a theater critic in the audience, transformed what could have easily been "a ludicrous appeal for sympathy" into a masterful performance that had "a majority of the audience . . . overcome with tears."[58] A few years later, another well-known songstress, Charlotte Cushman, was reported to have sung her sentimental tunes with such "dramatic genius, . . . pathos, sweetness, and vigor" that she "riveted" the "audience's attention."[59] These "overcome" audiences' "riveted" emotions were reminiscent of the feelings described about a century earlier by the likes of John Adams and William Hill Brown. It would seem, then, that to listen to and love sentimental tunes during the nineteenth century was to believe in the possibility of ecstasy.

The Musical Sublime

Sentimentality was by no means the only tool used by Americans to uplift musical ecstasy while emptying it of Christian doctrine. Starting in the late eighteenth century, intellectuals from continental Europe began to formulate a parallel ethos of secular musical entrancement that adapted aspects of sentimentality and Christian ecstasy. This tradition switched out references to heaven, God, or the metaphysical currents of social sympathy with other kinds of secular "spirits," an approach that would have a profound influence on American culture. Among the trailblazers of this cultural movement was the German philosopher Wilhelm Heinrich Wackenroder. In a well-known essay from the 1790s titled "The Marvels of the Musical Art," Wackenroder contended that music had the capacity to transport one to a metaphysical realm free of pain: "O, then I close my eyes to all the strife of the world—and withdraw quietly into the land of music, as into the land of belief, where all our doubts and our sufferings are lost in a resounding sea."[60] While this realm resembled the Christian heaven in some respects, as "the land of music," it also appeared to have a decidedly different character. The German pastor and Romantic poet Ludwig Theobald Kosegarten shared Wackenroder's belief in the bewitching, if not exactly religious, power of music. In a poem he wrote titled "Die Harmonie der Sphaeren" (1797), he revived the imagery and philosophy of the Music of the Spheres and venerated the capacity for the self to "dissolve" as it resonated sympathetically with the essential ratios "intoning the hymn of the cosmos."[61] The lyric would later be set to music by the German composer and violinist Andreas Romberg.[62] Without yet knowing it, Wackenroder and Kosegarten would represent some of the earliest contributors to the long tradition of European Romanticism.

Popularized by philosophers such as Jean-Jacques Rousseau, much of the Romantic ethos countered pure rationality by calling for a new emphasis on intuition, feeling, and passion toward the secular world. For Romantic philosophers on the Continent and their counterparts in Britain, this emotional engagement was most fruitfully directed at larger units of belonging. These could include social communities, such as the nation, but very often they were directed at what were believed to be the deep vital currents that ran through the entirety of the natural world and the inner life of every individual—what were respectively referred to as "Nature" and "Genius." Like sentimentality, these deep essences were also considered sacred in a secular way.[63] They were not supernatural spirits originating from a distant, divine realm. Instead, they constituted more immanent numens that permeated the material world. For philosophers such as Edmund Burke and Immanuel Kant, the perception of these mysterious secular forces did not constitute religious experience but rather *aesthetic* experience.[64] According to the religious scholar Christopher Partridge, the concept of the aesthetic resulted from a growing effort among the philosophical and artistic elites of Europe to "know the truth about the nature of reality without recourse to divinely revealed propositions or to religious authorities."[65]

European Romantics tended to embrace the ecstatic potential of naturalized experience. Indeed, for Kant and other philosophers of his day, rapture resided in perceptions of the sublime—that highest and most vital quality of Nature that, when perceived, elicited subjective responses of both pleasure and unease. For Kant, it was a "negative pleasure," involving competing impulses of horror and awe that demanded feelings of respect and admiration in the face of Nature.[66] This complex array of intense impulses, he claimed, evoked ineffable experiences so powerful that they defied rational understanding.[67] They also overwhelmed rational subjective experiences, leading to the surrender of stable notions of self. Kant claimed that this propensity for drastically altered awareness was what made the sublime the highest form of aesthetic experience.[68]

Imaginative individuals who were able to achieve a deep union with the sublime currents of the universe were thought to be more capable of creating cultural works that elicited this knowledge in others. Their creations were almost invariably related to the concept of "art." It was through art, many agreed, that the self could be sublimely transcended, fused with the deep forces present in the elemental and organic matter of the world, or transported to obscure locations both outside and inside the self. Thus, art and aesthetic experience became twinned.

Before long, German Romantics and intellectual descendants of Burke and Kant would come to hold music in a special place among the arts due to what they believed to be its superlative ability to encourage aesthetic experiences of ecstasy. Although Wackenroder and Kosegarten may be counted among the earliest advocates of music's aesthetic capacity, it would be the German critic E. T. A. Hoffmann who crystallized the interconnection between music, aesthetic experience, and entrancement. In what is still one of the most famous music reviews of the nineteenth century, Hoffmann wrote capaciously of aesthetic experience as it related to Beethoven's Fifth Symphony—a work whose sublime power he believed made it one of the greatest achievements of all time. Hoffman's review effectively equated Beethoven's symphony with sublimity, replete as it was with references to the infinite, the ineffable, awe and horror, and self-transcendent experience.

> Beethoven's instrumental music . . . opens up to us the realm of the monstrous and the immeasurable. Burning flashes of light shoot through the deep night of this realm, and we become aware of giant shadows that surge back and forth, driving us into narrower and narrower confines until they destroy *us*—but not the pain of that endless longing in which each joy that has climbed aloft in jubilant song sinks back and is swallowed up. . . . [It] is only in this pain, which consumes love, hope, and happiness but does not destroy them, which seeks to burst our breasts with a many-voiced consonance of all the passions, that we live on, enchanted beholders of the supernatural! . . . Beethoven's music sets in motion the lever of fear, of awe, of horror, of suffering, and wakens just that infinite longing which is the essence of

> romanticism. . . . [His symphony in C minor], in a climax that
> climbs on and on, leads the listener imperiously forward into
> the spirit world of the infinite! . . . The soul of each thoughtful
> listener is assuredly stirred, deeply and intimately, by a feeling
> that is none other than that unutterable portentous longing,
> and until the final chord . . . he will be powerless to step out
> of that wondrous spirit realm where grief and joy embrace him
> in the form of sound.[69]

With these words, Hoffmann elevated Beethoven's symphony—and all music—to a dignified status within the Romantic art movement.

Soon after Hoffmann's review was published in 1810, the philosopher Arthur Schopenhauer would entrench music's elevated status with his assertion that it, more than any of the other arts, was effective in expressing the Will. For Schopenhauer, that term referred not to the rational will of Descartes, but rather to the deepest metaphysical impulses that motivate all desires and actions in the universe, including "every blind force of nature" and "the preconsidered action of man."[70] Unlike sculpture or painting, which required one to engage in intellectual thought and the formation of mental images before discovering the hidden intentions of nature, music expressed the Will of nature directly and intuitively. Indeed, for Schopenhauer there was no ostensible difference between the two entities: "We might, therefore, just as well call the world embodied music as embodied will."[71]

Romanticism's early advocates were mostly European, and particularly German, but Americans of different backgrounds also adapted aspects of the movement's aesthetic. Chief among them were Ralph Waldo Emerson and the transcendentalists. Steeped in the theology of Unitarianism (itself an outgrowth of eighteenth-century Deism),[72] as well as the counter- and post-Enlightenment philosophies of British and German origin, the transcendentalists privileged imagination, venerated nature, celebrated the individual, and linked all these attributes to emotional experiences of self-transcendence.[73] The name "Transcendentalism" itself was adapted from Kant by Emerson to signify a philosophical orientation that rejected simple material empiricism in favor of an idealist knowledge that intuitively "transcended" the senses.[74] This process was said to elicit ecstasy in the sense that it exceeded the soul's ordinary state. However, the object of transcendentalist ecstasy did not reside entirely beyond the natural world, as conventional Protestantism had insisted. Instead, it was thought to constitute an elemental force or feature of nature itself.

Transcendent knowledge, likewise, could be ascertained only by engaging the imagination and the emotions, and therefore it was readily suited to the sublime. In a well-known passage from his widely circulated essay *Nature*, Emerson described one of his experiences of nature as a sublime admixture of horror and pleasure, or as he described it, gladness and fear: "Crossing a bare common, in snow puddles, at twilight, under a clouded sky . . . I have enjoyed a perfect exhilaration. I am glad to the brink of fear."[75] He elucidated the mystical element of this sublime experience by describing how his sense of selfhood was absorbed into (and through) nature, becoming both its component and conduit: "I become a transparent eye-ball; I am nothing; I see all; the currents of the Universal Being circulate through me."[76] Any understanding of the higher plane of reality, he contended, required some transcendence of the self: "From within or from behind, a light shines through us upon things, and makes us aware that we are nothing, but the light is all."[77] Exposure to the spiritual foundation of the natural world, therefore, also led one to an awareness of one's internal divinity. Nature, under this logic, was present both in the external objective world and the internal subjective one, and both were metaphysically intertwined.

Emerson's memorable reference to an ecstatic eyeball accurately captures transcendentalism's general emphasis on visuality, an attribute that distinguished it from German Romanticism's emphasis on the aural qualities of aesthetic experience. Indeed, the Romantic movement in America was predominantly focused on what the eye could see rather than what the ear could hear, and accordingly it tended to focus on literature and visual art. All the preeminent transcendentalists were prolific writers—Henry David Thoreau, Margaret Fuller, Amos Bronson Alcott, for example. Others who were directly influenced by transcendentalist philosophy used painting as their preferred medium, including Thomas Cole and the Hudson River School of American artists who adapted European styles to depict the sublimity of natural landscapes in upstate New York and across America.

Notwithstanding their inclination toward ocular-centrism, the transcendentalists were nevertheless interested in music and often addressed it obliquely through their writing. In this regard, they followed more closely the literary tradition started by early British Romantics such as William Wordsworth and Samuel Taylor Coleridge,[78] who both conflated poetry with music[79] and regularly wrote of music's uncanny power to facilitate an emotional engagement with the natural world. In an 1806 poem, for instance, Wordsworth wrote of the "Power of Music" to make listeners "happy as Souls in a dream,"[80] while Coleridge provided a now-famous description of an opium-induced dream in which the narrator traveled to Xanadu and envisioned "A damsel with a dulcimer."[81]

The transcendentalists' adaptation of the aesthetic ideals of European Romanticism resembled more the British variety than the German one. Emerson, like Wordsworth and Coleridge, also equated poetry with song,[82] and he was similarly less inclined to write music than to write *about* it. In his journal from 1838, he proclaimed that "music takes us out of the actual and whispers to us dim secrets that startle our wonder as to who we are, and for what, whence, and whereto."[83] Some transcendentalists not only recognized music as a true source of ecstasy but equally as a product that results from it. This included Amos Bronson Alcott, who, while staying at his farm, Fruitlands, during the winter of 1844, regularly found musical ecstasy in his daily ablutions: "On raising my head from the flood, there was heard a melody in the ear, as of a sound of many waters. . . . It was not easy to write prose while thus exalted and transfigured. . . . The brain was haunted with the rhythm of many voiced melodies. I enjoyed this state for a couple of months or more."[84] Emerson and Alcott were not alone in their promotion of rhythm and melody as a vehicle for self-transcendent experience. Periodicals published by transcendentalists between about 1835 and 1850 regularly included articles on music.[85]

American Romantics who were not explicitly affiliated with the transcendentalist movement also wrote passionately about the ecstatic qualities of European concert music. Among them was a music critic for *The Corsair*, a gazette of art and literature, who wrote in 1839 about the sublimity of Beethoven's opera *Fidelio*:

> Oh! may you give your spirit up to him fearlessly! He will transport you to other worlds, and infuse a thousand strange and thrilling sensations—will cradle you in his arms until, in admiration of his strength, you forget how powerful you are, and when he has poured those notes into your ear, and you are filled with tremblings, as of golden wires half conscious of their own thrilling—he leaves you petrified, enchanted—in a silent dream where even the echoes have subsided.[86]

These words, perhaps penned by Nathaniel Parker Willis, a well-known writer and the editor of *The Corsair*, described an incontrovertible power of captivation that resided in Beethoven's music and was capable of enthralling listeners into stunned silence and stillness.

Among the most outspoken supporters of Romantic musical ecstasy in concert settings was George Templeton Strong. The lawyer, music aficionado, and dedicated diarist was no stranger to tuneful trance. Indeed, one entry in his diary from 1843 recounted an anecdote about the power of a Wolfgang Amadeus Mozart piece to prime him for self-transcendent experience: "After church I rushed down to St. Peter's [Church], and I reached it just as a Mozart's 'Number Twelve' was in full blast. . . . I was just in a fit state to go into ecstasies at each individual note."[87] Strong referred to his almost obsessive emotional sensitivity to concert music as his "musical mania," and he wrote regularly and eagerly about it in his diary.[88]

Some of the most avid appraisals of the musical sublime were written by John Sullivan Dwight. Long before his encounter with Beethoven's Ninth Symphony in 1853, this Boston native attended Harvard Divinity School, then affiliated with Unitarianism, but drifted away from formal religion after graduating and eventually landed at the transcendentalist commune at Brook Farm for a short stint in 1841.[89] Although Dwight's philosophical leanings changed notably during his early adult years, his love of music remained constant throughout his life. Early in his career, he wrote resolutely that music provided the language of feeling required to communicate life's deepest mysteries: "Love, striving to amalgamate with all,—devotion, reaching forward to eternity—all that . . . which binds us to one another, to the beauty of the world, to God and to an hereafter."[90] Indeed, Dwight was undeniably the most active advocate of the transcendental power of music. For him, music stimulated "native impulses of the soul, or what are variously called the passions, affections, propensities, desires . . . [all of which are inclined toward] union, harmony . . . binding ties of fitness and conjunction with all spheres. Through these (how else?) are the hearts of the human race to be knit into one mutually conscious, undivided whole, one living temple not too narrow, nor too fragmentary for the reception of the Spirit of God."[91] Dwight's statement employed the language of religion (e.g., "God") to highlight music's role in eliciting an areligious mutual consciousness that transcended any personal perception of the world to create a unity of experience between all humans. In interpreting "the passions, affections, propensities, desires" as inextricable from this process, he worked to counteract earlier Enlightenment era efforts to subordinate emotions to the rational will and sever them from transcendent (and transgressive) experience.

Dwight's idealized notions of the musical sublime would have certainly been shared by some of the scores of German and Austrian Romantics who immigrated to the United States, particularly after Europe's calamitous crop failures and revolutions of the 1840s. Among the newcomers were dozens of professional musicians who, upon arrival in the United States, sought work as performers, orchestral and choral directors, music educators, and publishers.[92] The speed with which they found work in the music sector was partly a product of their own excellent education in Germany and partly a result of a scarcity of classically trained local musicians in the United States. Although bourgeois Americans had long desired to foster homegrown art music and musicians, their country's relative lack of elite and aristocratic traditions made the process more difficult. Therefore, it was not long before the German immigrants permeated the musical professions. Their presence was so apparent that Louis Moreau Gottschalk, a well-known American composer and pianist of the day, would later write with equal parts exasperation and hyperbole that "all the musicians in the United States are Germans."[93] Among the most notable German musicians were those who joined the Germania Musical Society, a classical music group formed in New England by several expatriates, which toured the country and gained considerable renown during the 1840s and 1850s,[94] not least due to the frequent recommendations they received from *Dwight's Journal of Music*.

Dwight and the members of the Germania Musical Society were not the only ones in agreement over the numinous power of Romantic music. Dwight's assessment of the ineffable sublimity of Beethoven's Ninth probably paralleled the intention of the composer himself, for the language of ecstasy was also inscribed in the lyrics of the symphony's final movement. It is here, in the "Ode to Joy," where the chorus sings of the bliss that comes with the "universal love and embrace of all Mankind," and the transmutation of this love into that of "the Creator, the All-Father."[95] The coordinated effort of the symphonic orchestra, which required anywhere from a dozen to over one hundred members to work together to create one vast sound, might have itself symbolized the ecstatic proclamation of brotherhood. Indeed, when the symphony debuted in Boston, Dwight's journal reported that, as the night's performance rose to a climax, the singers themselves seemed to encapsulate that "pitch of enthusiasm and inspiration which are the sentiment and the key to the last [movement]."[96] This particular performance, therefore, blended together the language of sentimentality, sublimity, and orthodox religion. The sentiment of the music itself seemed to permeate each performer, who in turn sang with an inspiration that surrendered their "souls" to the "rhythm of nature" and to "the Creator."

Dwight's assessment of the music's powerful entrancement was paralleled by accounts from other genteel audience members who attended the premiere. One veteran musician in attendance, who had felt largely indifferent to European art music up until that point, abruptly changed his mind. Upon hearing Beethoven's music that night, he suddenly felt himself sublimely possessed and rejuvenated by the sounds emanating from the stage: "From the first bars, the music took the deepest hold upon me. I was agreeably disappointed, delighted beyond measure; forty years were gone from me and I was a young man again."[97] Under the influence of the music, he underwent a profound regeneration. Ostensibly, the psyches of many in attendance at the music hall that night resounded with the sensation and appreciation of something like Schopenhauer's Will.

If another American matched Dwight in his articulation of the Romantic experience of musical transcendence, it was surely Walt Whitman. Though born later and lacking the formal education of the transcendentalists, Whitman as a young man became infatuated with the writings of Emerson. The poet touted him as vital to his development as a writer and published a glowing letter of praise from Emerson in *Leaves of Grass*, his famous compendium of poetry.[98]

Probably just as influential as transcendentalist philosophy to Whitman were the Italian operas and opera singers he heard in New York during the 1840s and 1850s. "But for opera," he once proclaimed, "I could never have written *Leaves of Grass*."[99] And indeed, Whitman's passion for music was honed through years of dedicated attendance at operas performed at the Castle Garden, the Park and Broadway theaters, the Astor Place Opera House, and other concert halls in and around New York City. It was here where he fell in love with the works of famous Italian composers such as Gioachino Rossini, Vincenzo Bellini, and Giuseppe Verdi,[100] as well as the singers who popularized their music in the United States during this time. All of them had mastered the bel canto style, wherein the singer oscillated between simple, flowing melodies and elaborate vocal work in order to create an unpredictable and intensely emotional performance. The result was what Whitman believed to be the highest form of art.

In a letter he published in New York's *Evening Post* in 1851, the poet posed a rhetorical question to his readers regarding the experience of music's ecstatic power:

> Have you not . . . while listening to the well-played music of
> some band . . . felt an overwhelming desire for measureless
> sound—a sublime orchestra of a myriad orchestras—a colossal
> volume of harmony, in which the thunder might roll in its

> proper place; and above it, the vast, pure Tenor,—identity of
> the Creative Power itself—rising through the universe, until
> the boundless and unspeakable capacities of that mystery, the
> human soul, should be filled to the uttermost, and the problem
> of human cravingness be satisfied and destroyed?[101]

The references to a limitless "Creative Power" pervading the universe and penetrating the human soul expressed a naturalized spirituality that would have been familiar to Dwight and Emerson. The singing voice that elicited Whitman's fascination was likely Alessandro Bettini, a singer whose voice was known to bring Whitman to tears.[102]

With such intense passion for Italian opera, it is unsurprising that so many of Whitman's poems referenced voice, singing, carols, chants, hymns, choruses, and musical instruments.[103] Some were also written in a way that mimicked the recitative or aria styles of opera. "Song of Myself," published first in 1855 and one of Whitman's best-loved poems, also alluded to a Romantic form of musical ecstasy by celebrating the special knowledge that arises in the narrator as he listens to an opera and finds his soul merging with entities beyond himself or traveling out beyond his body.

> I hear the chorus, it is a grand opera,
> Ah this indeed is music—this suits me.
> A tenor large and fresh as the creation fills me,
> The orbic flex of his mouth is pouring and filling me full.
> I hear the train'd soprano (what work with hers is this?)
> The orchestra whirls me wider than Uranus flies[104]

The tenor's voice permeates the narrator like an act of soul possession, and the soprano works to transport him out into the cosmos. Ten years later, in his poem "The Singer in Prison," Whitman similarly described the power of a convict's song to make "the hearer's pulses stop for ecstasy and awe."[105]

Despite his decades-long devotion to opera, perhaps Walt Whitman's most sublime experience of music occurred on the night of February 11, 1880, while attending a chamber music concert in the foyer of the opera house in Philadelphia. "Never did music more sink into and soothe and fill me," Whitman later recalled. Upon hearing a small chamber group perform one of Beethoven's septets, Whitman felt profoundly "carried away, seeing, absorbing many wonders. Dainty abandon, sometimes as if Nature laughing on a hillside in the sunshine; serious and firm monotonies, as of winds. . . . I allow'd myself, as I sometimes do, to wander out of myself."[106] In recognizing his own capacity to "allow" himself to "wander out of" himself, Whitman evoked something parallel to an Arminian stance, which embraced individuals' capacity to initiate their own conversion rather than awaiting a higher power to dole out grace. Beyond this basic approach, however, Whitman's ecstatic experience was a secular one, devoid of Christian metaphor and replete with the sublime language of Romanticism.

While Whitman found ecstasy in the opera of Italy, it was in fact German opera that was more widely associated with sublime rapture in America. And no other composer engendered this associative power more readily than Richard Wagner, whose operas proliferated on American concert stages starting in the 1880s. Although he was not yet born at the time E. T. A. Hoffmann published his review of Beethoven's Fifth Symphony, as a young composer Wagner nevertheless became greatly influenced by the critic's writings, as well as those of Schopenhauer. These motivated his efforts to emulate Beethoven in his aesthetic pursuit of numinous feeling, sublime self-transcendence, and exposure to the infinite. As an established composer Wagner would echo some of the early Romantic writers in averring that sympathetic listening to great music would plunge listeners into a

> dreamlike . . . state . . . wherein there dawns on us that other world, that world from whence the musician speaks to us—we recognize at once from an experience at the door of every man: namely that our eyesight is paralysed to such a degree by the effect of music upon us, that with eyes wide open we no longer intensively see. We experience this in every concert-room while listening to any tone-piece that really touches us.[107]

This was, furthermore, a "spellbound . . . state essentially akin to that of hypnotic clairvoyance," and an "ecstasy wherewith no other can compare."[108] Its power came from its capacity to make one conscious of the infinitude of the Will:

> I am convinced that there are universal currents of Divine Thought vibrating the ether everywhere and that anyone who can feel those vibrations is inspired. . . . I believe, first of all, that it is this universal vibrating energy that binds the soul of man to the Almighty Central Power from which emanates the life principle to which we all owe our existence. This energy links us to the

> Supreme Force of the universe, of which we are all a part . . . in that trance-like condition, which is the prerequisite of all true creative effort, I feel that I am one with this vibrating Force, that it is omniscient, and that I can draw upon it to an extent that is limited only by my own capacity to do so.[109]

Throughout his long career, Wagner referenced trance regularly, often by exploiting musical conventions and attitudes that had been present but less prominent in previous centuries. One way Wagner achieved this goal was by having the characters in his operas enter trances themselves. His opera *Tannhäuser*, for instance, included Bacchanalian dancing and singing in honor of the ancient god of wine and intoxication. Likewise, *Tristan und Isolde* portrayed characters entranced by love, whose desire for ecstatic (and erotic) union was consistently stifled by Isolde's betrothal to another man. Union was only achieved in the final act, through the death of Tristan's and Isolde's physical bodies and the extinguishing of their rational consciousness. It was during the last scene of the opera, when Isolde lay dying, that an ethereal music, apparently from her dead lover, seemed to envelop and transfigure her:

> Is it I alone am hearing, strains so tender and endearing? Passion swelling, all things telling, gently bounding from him sounding in me pushes upward rushes trumpet tone that round me gushes. Brighter growing, o'er me flowing, are these breezes airy pillows? . . . Shall I breathe them? Shall I listen? Shall I sip them, dive within them . . . ? In the breezes around, in the harmony sound, in the world's driving whirlwind be drown'd, and, sinking, be drinking—in a kiss, highest bliss![110]

It was with Isolde's death and transfiguration that the souls of the two star-crossed lovers were apparently reunited—if not exactly in a Christian heaven, then certainly in some transcendent realm of absolutes.

The form of Wagner's music, though difficult to connect definitively to any given psychic experience, also alluded to aspects of trance experience. Wagner's intentional use of altered harmonic forms in particular can be connected to self-transcendent awareness, creating both a sonic and psychic liminality throughout the opera. The best-known example of these is, without question, the opening chord of *Tristan und Isolde*—the so-called Tristan chord—that recurred as a leitmotif throughout the opera. It defied compositional conventions of the day by partly resolving and partly augmenting the harmonic tension of the music, thereby encompassing both a sense of consonance and dissonance within the implied key.[111] The opera scholar Burton D. Fisher interprets this harmonic tension as encapsulating Tristan's own inner psychic tension, which developed as he yearned for ecstatic union with his lover but was thwarted by the limits of his own physical body and rational consciousness, not to mention the adverse social circumstances that tore them apart. The harmonic and psychic tensions carried throughout the opera, both resolving only during the final act of the performance, when Tristan died and was at last able to break down the boundaries that prevented the synthesis of his own subjectivity and the object of its desire.[112]

Wagner's ecstatic yearnings were not lost on his American audiences. When his operas were performed in urban centers along the eastern seaboard, those in attendance also found themselves swept up into the sublime. One enthusiastic attendee was M. Carey Thomas, a female doctoral student in linguistics (who would later become the president of Bryn Mawr College), who described a decidedly numinous encounter with the sublime will of Nature during a Wagner performance. Writing to Mary Garrett, her close confidant, Thomas revealed how *Tristan und Isolde* evoked "memories of the splendid things of seas & stars and plains and marble & pictures & poetry until all together are blended into one in the rapture & fire of the music."[113] Ecstatic imagery of the natural cosmos blended here with more conventionally spiritual language when she described the experience of soaring "heavenly high, winging thro. the Empyrean." In a later correspondence Thomas reiterated the destabilizing effect the experience had on her sense of self, revealing how she was "carried away" and "utterly lost to everything else."[114] Similar lyrical descriptions could be found in the poetry of Ella Wheeler Wilcox. After attending a performance of *Tristan und Isolde*, she wrote to *Munsey's* magazine of a deep personal transfiguration using the imagery of a natural universe:

> In the flood of music swelling clear
> And high and strong, all things save love were drowned.
> A clamorous sea of chords swept o'er my soul,
> Submerging reason. Mutinous desire
> Stood at the helm; the stars were in eclipse:
> I heard wild billows beat, and thunders roll;
> And as the universe flamed into fire,
> I swooned upon the reef of coral lips.[115]

A more lavish ode to sacred sublimity could hardly have been penned by Walt Whitman, who had died two years earlier.

Music and Mesmerism: Animal Magnetism and Spiritualism

For some Americans, the "spirit" of Nature was not an abstract and amorphous mystical force but rather a physical substance that could be identified by someone properly attuned to its presence. In the 1770s, the German doctor Franz Anton Mesmer postulated the existence of a mysterious, electrically charged fluid called *gravitas universalis,* more commonly described as "animal magnetism," which permeated the universe and created a psychic bridge between living creatures. He also contended that once one learned to locate and manipulate it, this substance could have therapeutic applications in treating illnesses or imbalances in the human mind and body. The practice he developed toward this end became known as mesmerism and garnered appeal among scientific-minded professionals and laypeople alike. They saw in it a possible antidote to emotional disorders and other physical and mental ailments, as well as a method of inducing anesthesia before surgery.

In order to harness the therapeutic power of animal magnetism, Mesmer and other practitioners often encouraged fits or "crises," trance states that required an individual to relinquish control over many of his or her bodily functions and intellectual faculties in order to harmonize with the magnetic fluid. Mesmerists who claimed to be particularly adept at accessing the power of animal magnetism appeared to be able to induce both somnambulism, a "waking sleep" that allowed one to speak without remembering, and clairvoyance, which gave one sight into an ethereal world.[116] In its basic form, mesmerism's faith in the omnipresent force of animal magnetism bore some general resemblance to Schopenhauer's notion of the Will: these were both holistic theories that blended naturalism with mysticism and sought to explain the elemental nature of existence, life, and the universe without a conventional Christian theology. This complementarity helps explain why mesmerism gained such popularity in America starting in 1836, when the French animal magnetist Charles Poyen St. Sauveur toured throughout New England giving lectures and staging demonstrations that used audience volunteers. Starting around this time, some of the most popular novelists of the era—including Edgar Allan Poe, Nathaniel Hawthorne, and Herman Melville—became fascinated with mesmerism and helped spread its cultural appeal throughout America and the English-speaking world.[117]

In order to achieve the desired crises and somnambulist outcomes, mesmeric practitioners developed a number of ritualized practices to perform on their patients. These included hand passes—slow, sweeping hand movements made over the patient's body—along with prolonged eye contact and sometimes light touch. While some sessions took place one-on-one, others were group sessions. In larger settings, mesmerists sometimes used a device called a baquet, a large tub filled with magnetized water and iron filings. Patients were asked to sit around it holding metal rods or cords that were said to channel magnetic fluid from the baquet into their bodies (see fig. 2.2).[118]

Advocates and practitioners on both sides of the Atlantic lauded music as an enhancing feature of mesmeric activities. Mesmer himself was an amateur musician and friend to Mozart as well as other famous European composers, and he regularly employed musical instruments to facilitate the

Figure 2.2. A demonstration of mesmerism during a session led by Franz Anton Mesmer. *Source:* Claude-Louis Desrais, *Mesmeric Therapy; A Group of Mesmerised French Patients*, 1778/1784, oil on canvas. Wellcome Library, Iconographic Collections, London. Public domain.

trance experiences of his patients. For this purpose he often preferred Benjamin Franklin's glass harmonica, an "incomparably sweet" sounding instrument.[119] The piano and other keyboard instruments were also occasionally used to magnetize patients (as illustrated in fig. 2.2). A 1784 investigation of mesmerism, led by Benjamin Franklin and commissioned by King Louis XVI of France, revealed that "the changing of the key and the time, in the airs played upon the piano forté has an effect upon the patients; so that the quicker motion agitates them more, and renews the vivacity of their convulsions."[120] Despite music's early popularity in mesmerism, Charles Poyen and his American followers largely appear to have abandoned it as part of their practice.[121] This did not dissuade the likes of Herman Melville, however, who inferred the mesmeric power of music in his novel *Pierre*. In one scene, Isabel, the protagonist's love interest (and half sister), entranced him by playing guitar to communicate to him those aspects of her life "for not in words can it be spoken." Before long "a strange wild heat burned upon his brow," and as the music stopped, he enthused to Isabel, "thou hast filled me with such wonderings; I am so distraught with thee," then left her company feeling "bewitched" and "enchanted," as if the world was "steeped a million fathoms in . . . mysteriousness."[122]

The practices of mesmerism would prove remarkably influential, not only in popularizing animal magnetism but also in informing spiritualism, another musically inflected movement that circumvented orthodox Christian theology. This quasi-religious belief system accepted that an individual's soul persisted after the death of the body and that those in the afterlife could continue to communicate with the living. Such beliefs could be partially traced back to the teachings of the eighteenth-century Swedish theologian Emanuel Swedenborg, who practiced an esoteric form of Christian mysticism and claimed to have visited a "world of spirits," where souls went after death before it was determined whether they were more suitable for Heaven or Hell.[123] This intermediary world was supernatural to the extent that it existed beyond conventional notions of time and space. However, it remained separated from the material world by the thinnest of veils and was accessible to mortal humans who exercised the appropriate disposition and techniques. The mesmerist methods for inducing somnambulism and clairvoyance proved exceedingly productive in this respect. Indeed, spiritualism did not cohere into a proper movement until the 1840s and 1850s, when American practitioners like Andrew Jackson Davis began using these methods to enter trance states that allowed them to communicate with souls in the otherworld in order to attain special knowledge or advice.[124] Those who achieved such states were known as "mediums," for, much like the

Shaker "instruments," their minds, voices, and bodies could act as conduits to the spirit world.[125]

Spiritualists in America and Britain found music to be a particularly useful tool for achieving their goals. In the 1850s, they published several songbooks intended to support their entrancement sessions, which they sometimes called séances. These included *The Spirit Minstrel; a Collection of Hymns and Music, for the Use of Spiritualists, in Their Circles and Public Meetings*, and *The Spiritual Harp; a Collection of Vocal Music for the Choir, Congregation, and Social Circle*, to name only two.[126] According to one contemporaneous observation, "the singing of hymns or songs is of no less consequence to spiritual gatherings than to Methodist or Baptist meetings."[127]

Although spiritualists did not seek to adulate or placate the Holy Spirit through their hymns, as the evangelicals did, they did share with their revivalist counterparts a belief that music and especially singing were useful tools for accessing "disembodied spirits." Emma Hardinge Britten, one of the most famous American mediums, described music as facilitating her first trance experience. As Britten herself described it: "My last clear remembrance was of listening to a lovely quartette, beautifully sung by the 'Troy Harmonists' and then I had a dim perception that I was standing outside of myself, by the side of my dear father—dead—when I was only a little child but whose noble form I could plainly see close by me, gesticulating to, and addressing somehow, my second self, which was imitating him, and repeating all the thrilling words he was saying."[128] The spiritualists' valuation of music led many of them to both begin and punctuate their services and séances with songs. Often, these were simply Christian hymns with lyrics adapted or already suited to a spiritualist perspective. For the more staunch opponents of orthodox theology, however, this proximity to Christian doctrine became a source of irritation.[129]

Music proved valuable not only for its ability to facilitate séances and numinous trances but also for its apparent capacity to prove a medium's loss of normative self-possession. Maggie, Kate, and Leah Fox, three sisters from New York who are regularly credited as the first spiritualists in America, themselves attested to the possibility of musical possession. Leah, oldest of the three and last to convert to spiritualism, recounted an anecdote from the early days of the movement, when, while reading the memoirs of the Wesley family one day, she became entranced and had a series of letters dictated to her by some spiritual source. The sequence ran "GAGCBA-GAGEFEFAGFEFGFEDAGGCEDGGCBAGCCDBC," and at first she believed it to be a scrambled message from the ghost of "Johnny Story," a simple boy who was never taught to read. But eventually she received a message that the letters should not be deciphered into words, but instead applied as notes to the piano. When she did so, Leah recognized them as "a sweet and tender melody," which she was then told to set to an existing poem called "Haunted Ground" (see fig. 2.3).[130] As early as 1849, the Fox

Figure 2.3. The piano arrangement for "Haunted Ground." Leah Fox claimed the melody was dictated to her from the spirit-world. *Source:* Leah Fox, "Haunted Ground." Published in Ann Leah (Fox Fish) Underhill, *The Missing Link in Modern Spiritualism* (New York: Thomas R. Knox & Co., 1885), 417. Public domain.

sisters introduced song into their séances, and on at least one occasion they invited the Universalist minister Charles Hammond to sing several pieces of sacred music.[131]

On other occasions, spiritualist trances instigated not only the writing of songs but also their performance. An article in the *Spiritual Telegraph*, the movement's primary publication during the 1850s, relayed the story of Catherine Mettler, a young clairvoyant and medium. Having previously taken only a few lessons on the piano and holding only a rudimentary knowledge of music, the girl found one day that her "arms were apparently seized by an unknown power; which at once compelled her to commence the most astonishing improvisation, evidencing an extraordinary mastery over the instrument and a thorough knowledge of the science of harmony. The medium's hands for some time mechanically obeyed the irresistible impulse of this unseen performer without any volition or mental impression of her own."[132] The possessed girl's mother heard the improvisation from another part of the house and concluded that some highly skilled pianist had visited her daughter. She was amazed to find Catherine alone in the parlor, "fixed and spell-bound." From that day on, the girl was reported to become regularly possessed by musical spirits, including the ghosts of famous composers such as Mozart and Beethoven.

On still other occasions, musical ghosts were reported to visit members of séances and perform for them directly. These included events where singing from invisible sources permeated a room or instruments levitated and were played as if of their own accord.[133] Some of the most notable cases occurred to the Hutchinson Family Singers in 1850. During that year, Jesse Hutchinson Jr., one of the founding members of the singing family, visited one of the Fox sisters in Rochester, New York, who, upon entering a trance, appeared to communicate across the veil of reality to the ghosts of deceased individuals, including members of Jesse's own family. For him, the series of rappings and other communications from the spirit world was "something so mellow and pure, and intelligent . . . like the sweet voice or sound of music."[134] Upon hearing about the presence of his several children who had died during infancy, Jesse became "much overcome." He recalled later that it was as if the "dear little children seemed to be upon my knees, and on my shoulders." At one point, the medium declared "Oh! They [the children] are singing, ALL IS WELL," whereupon she burst forth with a melody, singing along with the "spiritual choir" of youths. With this revelation, Hutchinson declared "O! I never knew such joy before. My soul was filled with ecstatic pleasure," as he too joined the sweet song.

One week later, with Jesse's encouragement, some of his brothers and his sister also met with a medium and partook in an interview of the spirits, at which time they too became believers in the power of trance.[135] As the *Spiritual Philosopher* reported later, the family met with the spirit of their deceased brother Benjamin, who answered their questions and sang "an old and familiar tune" that was immediately recognized by all the attending Hutchinsons, who joined in heartily. After someone asked Benjamin's spirit to perform the song he sung on his own deathbed, the spirit did so, and according to Jesse, it "thrilled our every souls." One brother in particular, Judson, was "overwhelmed with ecstasy almost too much to bear." As the clairvoyant became entranced, Judson too began to lapse into a "deep trance." One observer reported, "I saw his hand go to the top of his head in a manner, apparent to me, that he did not place it there himself," at which point he became "overwhelmed with a burst of affectionate feeling, and sobbed aloud." Upon exiting the trance he exclaimed "Oh, Benjamin, it is you! I saw you! I felt you!" Only after some strong persuasion, he was finally "induced" to come back and dwell in his own body. But he had been so severely affected by the transportive experience that, for a time, he endured severe psychic attacks and hallucinations. These episodes, however, were also matched by some of the most "glorious and happyfying [*sic*]" experiences, many of them musical.

Only a few years later, after Jesse Hutchinson himself had passed away, he too was reported to have appeared during a séance hosted by Leah Fox. It occurred at Barnum's hotel in New York, and several notable politicians were in attendance, including the prominent abolitionist and social reformer William Lloyd Garrison. Upon request, the spirit of Hutchinson "beat a march—it seemed to us Washington's march—in admirable time, and in the most spirited manner: no drummer could have done it more skillfully."[136] He then beat time as the company joined in singing several tunes, including the perennial favorite "The Old Granite State." Garrison, still wanting additional confirmation, asked Hutchinson's spirit to grasp his right hand, which he proceeded to fasten between his legs so as to prevent anyone else from touching it. Nevertheless, he felt the touch of another's hand "with no warmth in it" even as he saw every living person's hands on the table.

For some spiritualist leaders, music itself had a similar character to magnetic fluid in that it constituted a mystical substance that surrounded everything in a joyous aura. According to an early exponent of the movement, Thomas Lake Harris, "The universe moves in music. . . . Every heart in Heaven beats in music."[137] Another prominent proponent, James Peebles, elaborated on these sentiments:

Figure 2.4. A spiritualist séance involving music. "'Spirits' and their Manifestations—An Evening's Séance." *Source:* Published in *Frank Leslie's Illustrated Weekly*, April 2, 1887: 105. Public domain.

Music envelops every surrounding object with Aeolian vibrations. The angels, charmed when sweet melodies rise like ocean ripples from joyous souls cannot help approaching us. As our music quiveringly touches and trembles the finer chords of their souls, we hear an echo far sweeter, and in turn we pause and listen, the auditors now of heavenly choirs. Thus the songs we produce, however, humble, set all the universe ablaze with melodious light, and, ringing through the arches of heaven, bless all hearts with new joy.[138]

If Harris's and Peebles's descriptions of the mystical power of music chimed with the theories of animal magnetism, they also echoed the ideas of Schopenhauer and Dwight and might easily have found a receptive audience among Whitman and Wagner.

Sanctioning Self-Transcendence

Those who supported the naturalization of trance differed from their evangelical compatriots in important ways, but they also shared with them an ongoing impulse to reconcile mystical experience with the principles of self-control. From the revolutionary era onwards, sentimentalists who counted themselves as part of America's political and social elite became interested in pursuing tender emotions and self-transcendence without entirely disposing of their own individual autonomy. As the historian Nicole Eustace describes, inhabitants of the thirteen colonies and early republic were abundantly aware of both the necessity to embrace sentiment and the dangers of taking it too far. They rejected the dispassion exhibited by European civility, but they also tried to sidestep the demonstrative overemotionality they attributed to "savage" Indians. What they developed was a careful balance of sense and sensibility that many Americans interpreted to be a unique feature of their nation.[139] When it came to ecstatic experiences, achieving this equilibrium was an ongoing process, but in general terms it constituted a manner of relating to the world in a way that permitted one to compassionately connect (or merge) with other entities while simultaneously maintaining integral aspects of a "singular, self-conscious individual."[140] One can discern this tension in Brown's *The Power of Sympathy*, where, as already discussed, feelings of self-abandonment elicited anything from angst to death.

As in evangelicalism, gender liability also remained deeply ingrained in the discourse of ecstasy and self-control. Indeed, women were consistently considered ill-equipped to maintain their physical autonomy as they ecstatically connected with others. The explosion of sentimental culture during the nineteenth century reinforced this notion. In America, as in Britain and Continental Europe, the bellwethers of middle-class propriety increasingly worried about the predisposition of mothers, wives, daughters, and sisters to lapse from emotional sensitivity into an excess of compassion and rapturous overexpressivity. These susceptibilities, according to the historian Ute Frevert, were often assumed to translate into indiscretions such as "frenzied feeling" and "abnormal agitation of the senses."[141] Even genteel white women were at risk of unseemly physical displays of emotion. American songs of the early republic that reinforced this stereotype included "Oh! Why Should the Girl of My Soul Be in Tears." A popular piece in the United States starting in 1809, the song portrayed the narrator's female love interest as a lachrymose girl with a "languishing smile" who succumbed (too) easily to a "meeting of rapture" or a "moment of blissful delight."[142] The result was that she became prone to weeping "again and again." Prominent thinkers of the day interpreted this kind of propensity to tears as illustrative of an innate predilection among women toward fragility and passivity. Such attributes could likewise be contrasted with the supposed emotional disposition of men, who were thought to possess a degree of rationality that encouraged more physical control of their bodies.[143]

Men were also expected to share some responsibility for modeling equanimity in the face of ecstasy, but they were assumed to be more adept at self-control and therefore were rarely held to the same standard. In Mary Macmichael's aforementioned story, "The School-Fellows," the musical rapture of both characters, Mary and Eugene, swelled their hearts and breasts but elicited few other visible, physical manifestations. Their experience was simultaneously "mute, blessed, and inexpressible"; it was "a rapture felt but not seen; for, motionless, and in deep silence, as if every outward faculty were absorbed in reverence, they continued, each inwardly knowing, hearing, seeing nothing but the divine influence and attraction of the other."[144] This balance of sentimental sensitivity and physical self-mastery helped prove Mary's "purity and integrity of nature"; Eugene, by contrast, was not subject to such expectations. Mary, of course, was a fictional character who was intended to encapsulate *Godey's* model of the "ideal woman." Her attributes were perfect because the author wished them to be. Real women were rarely seen to fare as well in embodying the ideal balance between self-transcendence and self-control.

The tradition of stern judgment toward ecstatic female corporeality also helps explain George Templeton Strong's complaints that overemotionality was a "feminine shortcoming"—that is to say, an essential, if not always exclusive, attribute of the gender.[145] Outrageous expressions by female performers were doubly dangerous, according to the diarist, because they risked reinforcing audience unruliness. For example, after an 1851 performance of Vincenzo Bellini's opera *Norma* at Castle Garden in New York, Strong described how the overexcited antics of the onstage female singer incited similar behavior among the patrons: "The louder this lady screamed, the more uproariously they applauded, and her solitary windpipe was a fair match for the vociferous bravos of her 5,000 admirers."[146] In this account, the audience's commotion took on decidedly "feminine" shortcomings.

The Romantics' endorsement of corporeal quietude should not be mistaken as a recommendation for dispassion or lack of engagement in the performance. On the contrary, in concert settings, audience silence was known to mask a rich landscape of personal experience shrouded by the etiquette of bodily control.[147] Even musical luminaries such as John S. Dwight acknowledged that stoic comportment could obscure a deep, silent self-transcendence. Describing the American premiere of Beethoven's Ninth Symphony in 1853, Dwight's journal implored its readers to consider the relationship between sublimity and silence: "Think of it! . . . if a certain virtue went not out from the music into the souls of the audience, so long and elaborate a work could not possibly, by any preparations and secondary appliances, have kept the crowd so quiet in their seats."[148] In this manner, audience members may have poured their souls out as they listened to the music, but their bodies never betrayed their experience.

Believing it possible to achieve ecstasy in stillness and silence, American aficionados of Romantic music regularly lauded performers' and audiences' efforts to restrain their expressive behavior. Dwight attributed the success of the Germania Musical Society to such proper comportment. The society, he contended, "won the esteem of the community, by modest self-respect, correct deportment and gentlemanly manners. They number among them some highly cultivated and intelligent men."[149] George Templeton Strong shared this attitude. On November 9, 1859, after he attended a concert by the New York Philharmonic orchestra, which included pieces by Beethoven and Wagner and commemorated the birth of the Romantic poet Friedrich Schiller, Strong wrote approvingly in his diary. He lauded an "admirable orchestra" that presented a "program of the first order,"[150] but he also esteemed the "order" of the audience that evening—"a great, silent, appreciative crowd of Teutons,"[151] he recalled, ostensibly referring to the German ancestry of many attendees.

Strong adored audiences that were silent, or at least tranquil; and opprobrium spewed from his pen whenever he witnessed loud and exuberant displays of intense emotionality. He deplored the "frowzy" patrons of concert music who appeared all too willing to mark their approval with raucous applause and "vociferous bellowings."[152] Similarly, he abhorred "crowded and enthusiastic" concert halls, when the performers "screamed" and the audience responded "uproariously" and clamorously.[153] The enjoyment of music was always vexed, the diarist maintained, when one was confronted by "excessive, ill-bred, obstreperous gabblings."[154] When Strong eventually became president of the New York Philharmonic in the early 1870s, he embarked on a campaign to clean up the boisterous and bodily expressions that he found so repulsive.[155]

Strong's goal of tranquilizing audience behavior was shared by Theodore Thomas, the German-born conductor who rose to prominence from the 1860s to the 1880s and was already a leading light within the world of classical concert music when he took up leadership of the Chicago Symphony Orchestra in the 1890s. As a conductor, Thomas quickly made a reputation for himself as a musical martinet, holding his orchestras to a very high standard of "conduct, appearance and propriety." His string sections were expected to practice uniform bowing, which both polished the phrasing and coordinated the visual presentation of the orchestra. Instrumentalists were expected to tune before they entered the stage, and when they did make an appearance in front of the audience they were prohibited from talking or moving their chairs. Thomas held his audiences almost to the same high standard, and he regularly reminded them of his expectations.[156] The conductor himself strove to be a model for his orchestra and audiences, always arriving at his shows highly prepared and restraining his own onstage movements in the pursuit of an orderly appearance.[157]

It was this kind of tempered comportment that the American journalist George Gladden venerated in the expression of musical ecstasies. His opinion on the matter became evident after he attended a Wagner opera at Bayreuth, the German festival town dedicated solely to the Romantic composer's music. Gladden approvingly declared of the audience's tranquility in the presence of trance:

> And so you sit there for perhaps two hours in silence which is never broken except by the voices from the stage and the hidden orchestra. No matter what your emotions are, you must not betray them by any demonstration whatever. When the curtain has gone down at the end of the act, you arise and walk out into the open air. Has there been a wild storm of hand-clapping when some singer has poured his whole soul into the darkness and silence on the other side of the foot lights? Not a sound. Was there a frantic outburst of cheers and shouts when the curtain descended? Not a whisper. That is Bayreuth; the Ultima Thule of the opera; the Mecca of the musical world.[158]

If the singers themselves seemed to undergo ecstatic experiences, as they "poured" their souls out into the auditorium, the audiences never stirred, never whispered. When audiences did turn raucous, however, Gladden hastened to decry them as "diabolical claquers" or compare them to savages "clad in the skins of wild beasts" as they "clash[ed] together . . . spears and shields and battle axes."[159] It was in this way that cultivated musical elites—performers, critics, moralists, and audience members alike—upheld both quiet and quietude as virtuous attributes of sublime self-transcendence in the concert hall.

$\sim$

Over the course of the nineteenth century, certain cultural frameworks that Americans used to explain musical ecstasy underwent enormous changes. Together they created the naturalized mode, which stood in contrast to its supernatural equivalent in many ways. It challenged orthodox Christian doctrines that explained self-transcendent experience as a purely supernatural communion or transport. It offered instead naturalized philosophies that rebaptized musical ecstasy as a unitive experience with the vital feelings or forces that tied together individuals, societies, and elements of the natural world. Sentimentalists, sublime Romanticists, as well as animal magnetists and spiritualists together pivoted ecstasy and emotional absorption toward a more secular sphere.

The term "naturalization" is therefore appropriate in describing the work of these groups for more than one reason. It describes the shift away from supernatural phenomena, but it also represents another meaning of the word, whereby nonreligious interpretations of trance were popularized and validated as an acceptable (if not always normal) phenomenon in American culture. With the work of people like John S. Dwight, the Hutchinson Family, Walt Whitman, and the Fox sisters, Romantic entrancement became viewed as a mainstay of American society by the mid-nineteenth century. The millions of Americans that supported or admired the cultures of sentimentality, sublimity, animal magnetism, and spiritualism populated many corners of American society.

Yet, for all of its differences, the naturalized mode cannot be considered entirely distinct from its supernatural equivalent. As this chapter has demonstrated, the former partly evolved out of the latter. The process of change, in this context, can be best described as "modulation." In a formal musical context, modulation involves transforming one mode into a new one, usually by changing the key (or in some cases the scale). In a historical context, modulation can similarly be interpreted as converting a cultural formation, in this case an ecstatic mode, into something new. This homologous relationship helps explain why the various naturalized traditions described in this chapter did not deny orthodox Christian notions of spirit, even as they flattened out the hierarchy between supernatural and natural entrancement. Just as musical modulation always involves elements of both change and continuity—such as altering the key of a tune while maintaining its relative scale (or vice versa)—cultural modulation can be understood as simultaneously maintaining and abandoning different aspects of existing formations.

Thus, the traditions of musical mysticism outlined in this chapter did not entirely displace orthodox religious ones, and often grappled with their legacy. The shift away from supernaturalism was hardly comprehensive. The proponents of naturalized ecstasy did not always make clear distinctions between the supernatural and the natural. Emerson, Dwight, and others would occasionally describe natural phenomena using the language of Christianity (e.g., God, Holy Spirit). Likewise, Wagner infused some of his operas (e.g., *Parsifal*) with Christian symbols and themes. Spiritualists in particular maintained beliefs in the supernatural realm of the otherworld, but, in a departure from conventional Christian theology, saw it as intimately entangled with the natural world. In many cases, the secular orientation of naturalized self-transcendence could nest relatively comfortably beside an orthodox religious one.

Moreover, even when Romantics of different stripes avoided the language of religion, they nevertheless treated the objects of their ecstasy much like the divine forces associated with conventional Christianity. Although natural, these objects were considered sacred; they worked in decidedly numinous or magical ways, and they represented some higher (or deeper) power that transcended the mundane and immediate concerns of the individual. For these reasons, Romantics believed they deserved reverence. Whether it was the Romantic "spirit" that united a loving couple, a family, a nation, or more abstract metaphysical formations such as the sentimental bond between all humans or the vital force of nature—the ecstatic merger with these transcendent objects demanded sincere appreciation.

More specific comparisons to orthodox religion could also be made. For instance, as the historian Ian Frederick Finseth demonstrates, certain Romantic traditions shared evangelicalism's philosophical embrace of anti-nomianism, which affirmed an individual's capacity to have an unmediated, intimate relationship with a metaphysical entity, often through intense revelatory experiences.[160] Both traditions, too, were inspired by an increasingly popular Arminian stance, which rejected orthodox Calvinism's doctrines of predestination and innate depravity in favor of an optimistic belief in individual free will as the path to spiritual growth. At certain times, particularly during the middle decades of the nineteenth century, the natural and supernatural modes also paralleled each other in contending with persistent yearnings for self-control and cultivated comportment, and the rhetoric of female fragility that often accompanied them. Middle-class elites led this movement in both the evangelical and Romantic contexts, and in doing so both seemed to serve the rapidly growing demands of capitalist enterprise.

Despite their breadth of coverage, this chapter and the one before it do not fully represent all the constituents of the natural and supernatural modes of musical ecstasy in America up until the twentieth century. There is at least one large segment of the population they mostly overlook: the communities of African Americans who had lived, prayed, and performed music in America from the earliest days of the transatlantic slave trade. These communities inherited and established ritualized traditions of musical ecstasy that were as rich and complex as any that evolved among European Americans. However, their history was decidedly distinct because it proceeded under the constraints of slavery and its aftermaths, and therefore they deserve to be addressed in a separate chapter.

Chapter 3

The Syncretization of Spirit Possession

In 1886, the journalist and novelist George Washington Cable wrote an article describing festivities in Place Congo, later known as Congo Square, the central gathering place of the enslaved community in New Orleans during the first half of the nineteenth century.[1] His account focused specifically on the "bamboula" dance, one of many festive activities that took place there on Sunday afternoons, when enslaved people were permitted to meet for religious activities. Writing in the present tense, Cable's account describes the dance as beginning with some "slow and measured" musical movements, accompanied by a "slow and quiet strain" that is also "dull and repetitious." From the first note, many singers join in, finishing the end of the first line with uplifted voices, and growing in spirit the second time around. A chief singer then "rolls out the song from a mouth and throat like a cavern," exhibiting a "play of restrained enthusiasm" that spreads from one bystander to another. The participants then "swing and bow to right and left in slow time to the piercing treble of the Congo women. Some are responsive; others are competitive." The slap of bare feet can be heard, and the musicians "warm up" at the sound. The women's voices "rise to a tremulous intensity," some of them improvising. "Now the chorus is more piercing than ever." The women clap their hands in time. A fellow has taken "one short, nervy step into the ring, chanting with rising energy. Now he takes another, and stands and sings and looks here and there, rising upon his broad toes and sinking and rising again." Now "the music has got into his feet." He moves to the ring's edge, still singing, and leads a girl into the ring.

Wait! A sudden frenzy seizes the musicians. The measure quickens,
the swaying, attitudinizing crowd starts into extra activity, the

female voices grow sharp and staccato, and suddenly the dance is the furious Bamboula. Now for the frantic leaps! Now for frenzy! Another pair are in the ring! . . . And still another couple enter the circle. What wild—what terrible delight! The ecstasy rises to madness; one—two—three of the dancers fall—*bloucoutoum! boum!*—with foam on their lips and are dragged out by arms and legs from under the tumultuous feet of crowding newcomers. The musicians know no fatigue; still the dance rages on.[2]

Cable's description of the bamboula was hardly without its biases, including a willingness to describe the phenomenon as "madness," and it probably sensationalized some aspects of the event. However, it also outlined some basic characteristics of African American music and dance rituals associated with what is commonly known as the "ring shout."[3]

At the time of Cable's writing, the ring shout was known as a communal ritual that was practiced across America mostly by people of African descent, and likely dating back to their earliest presence on the continent. It could vary somewhat based on context, but it generally involved participants standing and shuffling around in a circle, accompanied by the beating of a rhythm with a stick, as well as antiphonal (call-and-response) singing and vocalizations, handclapping that fell on what European Americans would have

Figure 3.1. An African American dance performed at Congo Square. *Source:* Edward Windsor Kemble, *The Bamboula*, 1886, photomechanical print. Published in George Washington Cable, "The Dance in Place Congo," *Century Illustrated Monthly Magazine* 31, no. 4 (February 1886): 524.

considered the nondominant beats of the music, and repetitive chants—all features that have been attributed, although not without debate, to an African provenance.[4] These features remained typical of ring shout gatherings from the eighteenth century to the twentieth century, at which time the dance itself mostly faded out of African American culture.

Irrespective of issues of origin, it is clear that ring shouts presented regular opportunities for African Americans to become entranced, a process they sometimes called "falling out."[5] While ecstatic experience was not a necessary outcome of the ring shout, it was a frequent one. It was typically achieved by progressing through a series of stages that, despite a priority on spontaneity, tended to follow a familiar arc. Beginning slowly with a repetitive tempo, the shout would gradually rise in intensity, often ending with a frenetic climax as participants screamed, fell to the ground, or dropped out of the circle.[6] Cable's description did not directly address the bamboula participants' internal experiences, and he likely had little reliable knowledge of it. However, the phases he described did roughly fit this pattern of ecstatic ritual. Cable also alluded to the possibility of self-transcendent experience in this process when he referred to "ecstasy" and "madness" as the music reached a heightened pitch.

By focusing on the ring shout and other related rituals of entrancement, this chapter examines the distinct history of ecstatic experience among African Americans from the seventeenth to early twentieth centuries. It stands apart from the other chapters in that it does not focus exclusively on a single mode of ecstatic experience. Instead, it addresses how Black Americans developed and challenged their own supernatural and natural traditions. Their self-transcendent experiences could include possession by a variety of spirits, deities, and ancestors or a merger with the Christian God or the Catholic saints. These unitive experiences certainly had parallels in the religious and Romantic phenomena encountered by musical Americans of European descent, but they also contained different attributes and different histories that make them impossible to conflate with the experiences outlined in previous chapters.[7] At least two shared attributes set them apart in this respect. One was their inheritance of ecstatic cultural practices and beliefs from the African continent. Another was their shaping from the unique (and uniquely challenging) circumstances faced by people of African descent during and after their enslavement and forced migration to America. These shared circumstances speak to the power of race and ethnicity as defining features in American history and warrant the multimodal focus of this chapter.

To acknowledge the unique history of Black ecstatic experience in America is not to suggest that its history was internally uniform. The ethnic backgrounds of enslaved populations, the immixing between different ethnicities and races, the prominence of Christian denominations, the enforcement of social and legal regulations, the eagerness of white proselytizers and the ardency of white denigrators—all of these historical factors and more varied by nature and degree in different times and places. Consequently, they engendered a multitude of different ecstatic cultures, making it difficult to speak of a single, unified history of African American experience.

To the extent that one can speak in generalizations, one might be able to refer loosely to two separate cultural-geographic clusters of Black trance in America during the period in question. One was centered in southern Louisiana, particularly around the city of New Orleans. Here the influence and legacy of French Creole colonial rule allowed the Black population and its religious supporters to develop distinct forms of entrancement that aligned with American "Voudou" (later called Voodoo). The other cluster was located in the more Anglo-dominated regions of America, particularly in the South, where Black Americans usually pursued trance that affiliated more closely with Protestant evangelicalism.

These two clusters of Black entrancement shared a few core characteristics. One was their unique musicality. In most places that African Americans pursued ecstatic release, music was involved, often some variation of the ring shout. Even where the ring shout was not entirely identifiable, certain constituent elements of it could often be discerned, whether it was the call-and-response structure of performance, the handclapping, the vocalizations, the heavy reliance on rhythm, or the pairing with dance and other forms of coordinated physical movement. If music was not always a required component of Black ecstatic experience, it was certainly a regular one.

Another predominant feature of African American trance in each of these clusters was the tendency toward syncretization. This process involved amalgamating beliefs and practices previously held by disparate communities. Especially during the earliest period of slavery in America, it included reconciling the communal ecstatic cultures brought to the continent by enslaved people from a variety of different ethnic backgrounds and geographic regions in Africa. After prolonged contact with European Americans, the syncretic process also began to incorporate compatible features of Christianity—including from Catholicism and evangelical Protestantism, depending on the location.

White criticism represented another common feature of African American ecstasy. Irrespective of where it was pursued and under what circumstances, the trance experiences of Black people were almost invariably condemned by others. Many white observers cast African American ecstasy in racialized, religious terms, as a blasphemy motivated by Satan himself. Others condemned it in vaguer moral terms, as an egregious superstition or a threat to the social status quo. Still others adopted a softer, though still disparaging, attitude, deploring it as a hedonic amusement, pursued for its own sake and with no deeper meaning. Often these negative perspectives prompted the introduction of new laws that served to limit or prohibit African Americans from pursuing trance experiences in the manner of their preference.

Unfortunately, the study of these and other historical features of Black ecstatic experience is riddled with complications. Determining how historical individuals interpreted trance experiences is difficult at the best of times, but in this case the task is made all the more challenging by the fact that, for much of their history, most African Americans were deprived of basic resources required to record their impressions and opinions for posterity. For that reason, there are simply very few first-person records of ecstatic phenomena that can be used for this research. The majority of third-person accounts were written by white Americans and Europeans, most of whom held racial biases that negatively skewed their interpretations. (Even the less derogatory accounts were subject to the inevitable distortions that result when one person's experiences are mediated through the cultural interpretative lens of someone else.) The historical sources recruited for this chapter, therefore, must be read with these limitations in mind, and often against the grain.

African Antecedents

The strongest African influence on African American culture is thought to have come from the cultures of West and Central Africa, the regions from which enslaved people were most commonly extracted and forcibly transported to the American continents.[8] The traditional religious beliefs and practices of these Africans were hardly identical. They came from dozens of city-states, kingdoms, and empires, each with their own rituals, sacred stories, gods, and magical practices. Despite these differences, however, they also shared several basic similarities. Notably, they did not typically make clear distinctions between supernatural and natural spiritual beliefs. Many Africans believed in a high God who created the world and was therefore fundamental to everything in it, but, in deistic fashion, that God let the world's history unfold without intervention. Therefore, believers turned to a set of more accessible, intermediary gods that exercised extraordinary power over everyday life; they manifested through natural forces and beings, including wind, rain, thunder, and animals. These deities sometimes arose independently, but in other cases they could have human origins. West and Central Africans often elevated their ancestors in particular to a sacred status, following intricate burial and mourning ceremonies after their deaths and believing they continued to live on and remain interested in the lives of their descendants. Sometimes, ancestors could themselves transform into gods.[9] These cosmologies, it would seem, did not always abide by the modal distinctions discussed in previous chapters. Some, by blending the supernatural and the natural and the sacred and the profane into a unified belief system, could be considered modally malleable: they did not fit exclusively within any single modal framework.

Another common traditional religious belief upheld by West and Central Africans was that of spirit possession, whereby the gods and ancestors transmigrated into individuals. Devotees considered such possessions desirable under certain circumstances and pursued them eagerly when seeking to contact the deities or wrest more control over the course of their own lives. Spirit possession could be invoked through various techniques, but most often it involved music and dance. Historically, ceremonial possession would involve handclapping, call-and-response (antiphonal) singing, and complex percussive rhythms, usually involving dancing.[10] African spirit possession, claims the music scholar Samuel Floyd Jr., was strongly linked to "rhythmic stimulation," including drumming, chanting, and singing, which would have all mutually reinforced each other as participants tended toward trance.[11] In priming themselves for ecstatic encounters, members of the BaKongo tribe in Central Africa, for instance, are believed to have traced cosmograms on the ground and danced over them to invoke spirits.[12] Farther north, in Yoruba territory, contemporary ethnographic studies have demonstrated a similar ingrained propensity toward rhythm and trance. Here, the possessed subject became known as "the one mounted by the god," and as such became its mouthpiece and gained predictive powers.[13] Beyond these characteristics, the spiritual dynamics surrounding possession were also highly communal, participatory, and musical, with multiple devotees each contributing sonically, physically, and psychically to the trance rituals. Those initiates who eventually entered possessive states temporarily gave up aspects of their own self-identity as a way of serving the interests of their group or nation.

At the same time, the loss of self-awareness and self-control during African trance rituals can risk being overstated. If contemporary ethnographic studies of dance, music, and consciousness in West Africa are representative of past cultural dispositions, it seems possible that enslaved people from West Africa—particularly the music-making ones—were also historically concerned with regulating their sense of selfhood during religious ceremonies, including ones involving spirit possession. Ethnomusicologist John Miller Chernoff locates an impulse for self-control in the performance of polyrhythms, which are so integral to many traditions of West African music. They encapsulate, he explains, contradictory impulses—one toward individuality and the other toward collective values.[14] In their music, drummers layer rhythms atop one another, often each one with markedly different meters. According to Chernoff, the polyrhythmic effect they create requires each drummer to simultaneously protect the integrity of his own rhythm without abandoning the coherence of the overall pattern. They must remain detached from the collective even as they participate in it. If each participant provides the appropriate balance of distance and collaboration, what emerges is a super-rhythm (or "phantom" rhythm), which is the true music of the performance and somehow larger than the sum of its component parts.[15]

Part of a West African religious sensibility, therefore, involves—and perhaps involved—what might be called a "polyrhythmic consciousness" that rejected a stark distinction between self and other, and likewise individuality and self-transcendence. Just as ceremonial musicians in West Africa do not prioritize one rhythm over another in a polyrhythmic performance, so too do they reject the dichotomies between normal and altered consciousness. What they affirm, in the researcher Sam Mickey's words, is "the ongoing alternation or liminal interplay of what are hastily called opposites."[16] And in this, they approach Antje Linkenbach and Martin Mulsow's concept of the "dividual" as well as Morris Berman's notion of a "participatory conscious-ness," a sense of self that, although somewhat contained, extends out and merges with one's surroundings.[17] In musical trance, therefore, participants always emphasize the control and protection of aspects of their own selfhood even as they let a god "ride" or "come up" to them. This balance is valued to such a degree that, as Chernoff observes, a religious figure is frequently present who specializes in "cooling down 'hot' people."[18]

The art historian Robert Farris Thompson elaborates this notion of controlled self-experience, or what he calls "the aesthetic of the cool," and finds it to be an integral element of much African expressive culture, and not just in polyrhythmic settings.[19] (The concept of "cool" itself is prevalent in African languages and cultures.) It is this sensibility that compels trance initiates to value individual composure and social stability, expressed through the ability to be nonchalant or stoic in exciting, passionate, or stressful situations. This cool mind-state, exhibited at the right moment, is considered to be very attractive.[20] Was this balance of self-possession and deity-possession present in the expressive culture of Black diasporic communities in America? Thompson and others certainly think so.[21]

A paucity of historical evidence makes it impossible to know for certain which cultural beliefs and practices Africans retained as they became Americans. Yet, despite the horrors of the Middle Passage and the genocidal logic of chattel slavery, it is apparent that enslaved people managed to smuggle in elements of their spirituality and music even as they were forced to adapt them to their new worlds. The songs and dances that were closely tied to religious rites seem to have fared better than most cultural practices in surviving the transatlantic crossing.[22] Handclapping, call-and-response singing, and chanting all featured regularly in the music produced by enslaved community members.[23] Notably, polyrhythmic gestures also seem to have endured the forced migration, particularly in the form of the "hemiola"—a rhythmic pattern that, in simple terms, involved the simultaneous performance of three-beat rhythms against two-beat rhythms over the same time frame. Common within African musical cultures, hemiola patterns were also regularly performed by enslaved Americans.[24]

There may be several reasons why these musical features persisted. One may have been simply that newly landed Africans in America would have valued the spiritual exercises that they had always believed held outsize importance in their traditional communities. This would have especially been true at a time when they lacked so much control over their lives, for it was their most sacred practices that helped engage the extraordinary power of higher spiritual forces. Another reason that explains these retentions may have been more pragmatic. In an era of utter dislocation, enslaved people from a variety of diverse ethnic, cultural, and linguistic backgrounds—including Yoruba, Dahomey, Kongolese, Bambara, and others—would have forged new social ties with each other by turning to the few cultural practices that they shared in common. Thus, the first phase of syncretization in African American life occurred between the different cultures of African Americans, and music played an integral role in this process.

In America, when bonded people adapted African rhythms and rituals to new expressive forms, their efforts led to the creation of ring shouts and other diasporic religious practices, or at least that is what some of the extant historical evidence indicates. What is also perhaps attributable to Africa is the spiritual significance that pre-Christianized enslaved people gave to these practices. One theory suggests that the roots of the ring shout actually originated in the African BaKongo ecstatic practice of tracing cosmograms on the ground and dancing over them.[25] Here again, a compelling theory remains constrained by the sheer lack of empirical evidence. Nevertheless, regardless of whether enslaved and disenfranchised Black Americans reconjured African deities on American soil, it seems likely that attributes of their spiritual practice could be traced back to their ancestral lands across the Atlantic. Those who participated in diasporic rituals like the ring shout, therefore, would have succeeded not only in maintaining some semblance of connection to their past but also in forging communal links with others who shared a mutual cultural inheritance.

American Voudou

Of all the colonies and settlements that would eventually be incorporated into the United States, it was Louisiana—and particularly the city of New Orleans—that would remain probably the most permissive for the longest of ecstatic, musical, and religious rituals that were tied to Africa. The reasons for this somewhat accommodating approach are complex and multifaceted. One certainly has to do with demographics and geography. During its first eighty-five years, most of which were as the capital of colonial Louisiana, New Orleans became a prominent port for both European (mostly French) settlement and the transatlantic slave trade, rapidly making it one of the most populous and multiracial cities in North America. With a steady influx of enslaved people arriving regularly under both French control (1718–1763, 1803) and Spanish control (1763–1803), the city acquired a relatively high percentage of African-born people as compared to many other colonial regions—a condition that, especially when considering the confined area within which so many lived, would have provided more opportunities for enslaved people to meet and foster their shared cultural practices and beliefs.

Another reason for New Orleanians' apparently permissive approach to the musically inflected ecstatic activities of African Americans related to their attitude toward religion. In comparison to its British equivalents, the French colonial administration was more tolerant of the cultural and religious customs of enslaved individuals. Formally, the religious practices and beliefs of enslaved people were sharply delimited in the Code Noir, a legal code passed by Louis XIV for the regulation of slavery and the treatment of enslaved people, which in Louisiana was implemented by the French in 1724 and maintained by the Spanish in Louisiana after they took control of the territory in 1763. The code explicitly required enslaved people to be baptized and instructed in Roman Catholicism, and it prohibited them from public displays of any religion other than that faith.[26] In practice, however, the French and Spanish governmental authorities rarely interfered with the religious practices of the local Black population, particularly if they were carried out under the guise of Catholicism.[27] In this context, enslaved people actually had a legally sanctioned right to religious worship: the Code Noir required that enslaved people be guaranteed both "the free exercise of the Catholic religion" and a day free from work on Sundays and holidays.[28] In effect, what this meant was that enslaved people of African descent could maintain aspects of their Old World religious traditions.

What it also meant was that enslaved New Orleanians became increasingly exposed to Christian theology and the pantheon of Catholic saints. For some, such as those who originated from the Kingdom of Kongo, which had nominally converted to Catholicism in the fifteenth century, the tenets of Christianity may already have been familiar. For others, they would have been entirely new. Even for these previously un-Christianized African Americans, though, a few basic features of Christianity may have felt generally familiar, as most traditional religions from West and Central Africa recognized a supreme deity. The Virgin Mary and the saints also had some analogues in the deities and ancestors that populated their traditional spirit worlds.[29] Yet, despite these points of commonality, the adoption of European religious beliefs and practices was always partial.

The peculiar conditions of New Orleans meant that African Americans in that city and its environs were able to foster a truly diasporic religion that incorporated—sometimes nominally and sometimes meaningfully—elements of European Catholicism while also cultivating a rich set of religious practices that were tied to Africa and responsive to their lived experience of bondage in the New World. During much of the eighteenth and nineteenth centuries, the syncretic religion that evolved in this area was usually referred to as Voudou (although other spellings were used).[30] It involved elements of the ring shout as well as various other rituals that incorporated spirit possession, song, and dance as crucial devotional activities. These were intended to engage an almighty God, a few Catholic saints, and some spirits of the dead.[31] Many of these metaphysical entities were blended together in syncretic fashion, such that St. Peter was associated with Papa Laba (also known as Papa Lébat or Papa Limba).[32] The former originated in Christianity while the latter had cognates in the Yoruba religion of West Africa. Both, in their own ways, were known as gatekeepers to the spirit world. Other times, Voudou spirits were not closely twinned with Christian saints, as with Blanc Dani and the Grand Zombi, a deity represented by a serpent but not with Satan. (The word "zombi" had roots in the Kongo Bantu word *nzambi*.)[33] These spiritual intermediaries had a liminal status, connecting the natural sphere of mortal humans to the supernatural realms beyond, and therefore when individuals became possessed by them, their trance may have taken on malleable modal characteristics in ways similar to African tribal trance.

Although few reliable and detailed historical accounts of New Orleans Voudou practices are accessible, particularly from as far back as the eighteenth century, it may be possible to extrapolate some general characteristics of these practices by looking to another Afro-Catholic syncretic religion in the Caribbean—the *Vodou* religion of Saint-Domingue (Haiti), which was another French colony that was closely linked to New Orleans during that era. One of the earliest detailed records of a Saint Dominican Vodou ceremony was recorded in the travelogue of Médéric Louis Élie Moreau de Saint-Méry, a French lawyer who traveled to the colony just prior to the revolutionary war there (1791–1804). His account, published in *Description topographique, physique, civile, politique et historique de la partie française de l'isle Saint-Domingue* (1789), was obviously tainted with racism. Moreau vociferously defended the institution of slavery and represented the white planters in France's National Assembly.[34] His account, however, provided a detailed depiction of a Vodou ceremony in Saint-Domingue that, despite its deficiencies, may help outline some basic practices that were common among practitioners in that colony and others in the region.

Moreau described a number of different dances—"the *Calenda*," "the *Bamboula*," and "the *Chica*"—all of which would have likely been considered Vodou practices by their participants. However, much of his attention focused on one particular dance-based ceremony, which he simply called "le Vaudoux," or the "Voodoo."[35] Although he considered the underlying beliefs of the ceremony nothing more than superstition, Moreau recognized that the participants understood it to facilitate supernatural communication and spirit possession. As he described it, the ceremony revolved around a snake, which was believed to hold access to extraordinary knowledge and who was able to "communicate his power, and to prescribe his will, only by the organ of a high priest whom the followers choose and still more by that of the Negress, that his love elevated to the rank of High Priestess."[36] In Moreau's interpretation, these two figures were given the names of "King and Queen" or "master and mistress" or mother and father. As "chiefs of the *Voodoo*" they had intimate access to the snake and its spirit.[37] Each initiate who participated in the ceremony wore a pair of sandals and a number of red handkerchiefs. The King and Queen stood near an altar of sorts, on which the snake was located in a caged box. The attendees then swore an oath of secrecy as well as an oath of devotion to the snake. Each member of the sect, in order of seniority, then came to implore "the Voodoo" for assistance in their own lives—whether to influence their plantation masters, acquire more money, please a romantic partner, punish a rival, be cured of an ailment, and so forth. The Voodoo King collected these requests—"the spirit works in him."[38] Then, he abruptly moved the snake in its box close to the Queen, so she could stand on it: "As soon as the sacred asylum [the box] is under her feet, new pythoness, she is penetrated by the god, she moves, her whole body is in a convulsive state, and the oracle speaks through her mouth. Sometimes she flatters and promises bliss, sometimes she shocks and bursts into reproaches."[39] After some additional oaths and invocations from the Queen, the "dance of the Voodoo" began. The King drew a circle with a charcoal on the ground and moved an initiate into it, placing in his hands a parcel of herbs, horsehair, and fragments of a horn. Then, he began to sing a refrain in an African language, with the others surrounding the circle responding in chorus:

> Eh! Eh! Bomba, hen! hen!
> Canga, bafio té
> Canga moune dé lé
> Canga do ki la
> Canga, li.[40]

Inside the circle, the initiate began to dance, and after becoming increasingly agitated, "finally [arrived] at convulsions."[41] At last, the initiate was led to the altar to swear his oath and officially join the sect. This marked the beginning of further spirit work of the Queen and King, as both fell into elaborate bodily movements and others joined in.

The queen especially, is in the grip of the most violent agitations; She goes from time to time in search of a new charm with the voodoo serpent; She shakes her box, and the bells of which this one is stuffed . . . the delirium increases. It is further increased by the use of spirits [liquor], that in the intoxication of their imagination the adepts do not spare, and that maintains it in its turn. Failures, swoons succeed in some, & a kind of fury in others; But in all there is a nervous tremor, which they seem unable to control. They revolve endlessly about themselves.

As the trance subsided, the members of the group eventually fell into a state of lassitude.[42]

Moreau's account may have been contorted to align with his racist biases, but it nevertheless probably provided some basic indication of how people of African descent practiced their religions in the New World. Their rituals, it would seem, were highly physical, rhythmic, infused with song, and aimed at facilitating spirit possession with mystic forces and strengthening communal bonds. All of these features were present in the traditional religions of West and Central Africa, and therefore they seem likely to have originated in some fashion from those regions. Elements of the ring shout also appear to have been present in the ceremony: around a circle drawn on the ground, the King sang out a chant with other devotees responding in chorus.

On top of these more traditional elements, participants in the ceremony may have layered on a more political message. Antagonism toward the ruling class, even sentiments of rebellion, were known to be integrated into the religious rituals of Saint Dominican Vodou, especially during the years leading up to the revolutionary war there. In the event described by Moreau, which took place during this fraught period, the devotees may have sung their refrain ("Eh! Eh! Bomba, hen! hen!" and so forth) to articulate their communal aspirations toward liberation and implore their God for assistance in dealing with their white masters. As the religious scholar Ina J. Fandrich has established, that refrain has two potential meanings.[43] One was an invocation to the healing presence of the "Canga" spirit in the Malinke language. The other, interpreted from the KiKongo language, was a more political invocation to "Seize the blacks. Seize the whites. Seize the witches!"[44]

The African aesthetic of the cool similarly appears to have been present in the ceremony described by Moreau. In his account, when an initiate began dancing under the possession of the spirit, participants were always on the lookout for unbridled loss of self-control: "If, unfortunately, the excess of his transport makes him leave the circle, the song ceases immediately, the voodoo king and queen turn their backs to ward off the omen. The dancer returns to him, enters the circle, agitates again, drinks, and finally arrives at convulsions to which the voodoo king orders to stop by striking him lightly on the head of his palette or moves, or even as he thinks fit."[45] This ongoing attention revealed that the group valued regulation and containment of the trance ritual even as they recognized the necessity for self-transcendence. The Queen and King in particular seem to have pursued this control of self and others, even under ecstatic conditions. Indeed, it was they who determined "whether the snake agree[d] to the admission of a candidate into society; [and] who prescribe[d] to him the obligations, the duties which he must fulfill."[46] Despite their obvious proclivity to merge spiritually with the god, they were also required to act as agents in the interest of their community.

The Voudou rituals practiced by African Americans in Louisiana may have resembled the activities in Saint-Domingue set out by Moreau, but they also differed in important ways.[47] For instance, as compared to Saint Dominican Vodou and other syncretic religions that developed in most colonies throughout the Caribbean, New Orleans Voudou had a relatively small pantheon of African spirits, or *lwa*, that were regularly equated with Catholic saints. This discrepancy may have been a result of a higher ratio of white-to-Black populations in New Orleans as well as certain rigid elements of the social system in that city, all of which could have added pressure to strip out the numerous spirits inherited from Africa. However, as Fandrich argues, the absence of the spirits may also have resulted from the different cultural backgrounds of the Black people in that region. During the eighteenth century, it was the Bambara and Kongolese people who made up the majority of Louisiana's enslaved population, and the religious practices associated with these cultures tended to focus on the spirits of the dead.[48] This emphasis contrasted with that of other prominent Caribbean colonies, such as Saint-Domingue and Cuba, where Yoruba and Dahomeyans originally constituted the majority of the enslaved populations and fostered a belief in a multitude of African spirits and deities.[49]

Beyond these differences, however, there were also easy comparisons to be made between Haitian Vodou and Louisianian Voudou. This was particularly true by the 1780s, when Moreau was writing. By this time, the number of West Central Africans, including many Kongolese, had grown to dominate the bonded people residing in Saint-Domingue. Indeed, their presence in the colony may have helped ignite a rebellion there in the 1790s.[50] Their large proportion of the Saint-Domingue/Haitian population meant that during and following the revolution in that country, especially by 1808, Kongolese people and their descendants—some of whom fled as free refugees and others who were forcibly transported while enslaved—constituted a large percentage of the people who moved from Haiti to New Orleans, nearly doubling the population of the city in a short time. The shared ancestry and cultural backgrounds of many Haitian and Louisianian African Americans would have likely made for a relatively smooth merger of their religious practices while simultaneously augmenting the preexisting Kongolese cultural influence in New Orleans.

One early account of a Voudou ceremony in that city took place in the yard of a residence on Dumaine Street in 1825. The home belonged to Sanité Dédé, a mixed-race woman from Haiti who gained a reputation as a Voudou priestess in New Orleans during the first decades of the nineteenth century. The witness who observed the ceremony was a white slaveowner who attended the event because one of his bonded people was an initiate.[51] If his account is to be trusted, some sixty people were in attendance and each of the men and women who participated wore "white kerchiefs tied around the forehead."[52] The yard included a table, on which were placed taxidermied cats and a cypress sapling, along with a black doll wearing a dress emblazoned with signs and animal bones. An older Black man used two sticks to beat a "ra-ra-ta, ra-ra-ta-ta" rhythm on a drum, while another man and woman beat additional rhythms on the side of the drum using animal bones.[53] Nearby, another musician squatted "twirling a long calabash" made of a large gourd filled with pebbles. After a signal from Sanité Dédé, one of them raised a large snake and moved with it, passing it over the heads and around the necks of the initiates. Then, "a long, deep howl of exultation broke from every part of the shed" as the drumming began anew. As a banjo player appeared and started playing, "pandemonium was unloosed."[54] In time, the participants feasted on meat and wine after which a tall Black woman began a dance with an undulating motion. At a certain point, the whole group began dancing as "the beat of the drum, and thrum of the banjo, swelled louder and louder." The women took off their clothing and continued to dance naked as a drummer began to chant.[55]

The New Orleans Voudou ceremony described here bears comparison to the one in Saint-Domingue described by Moreau. Similarities included the wearing of handkerchiefs by devotees, the integral role of a snake, the chanting and drumming, the spirit possession, the imbibition of alcohol, and the presence of a "Queen" figure in Dédé. Other elements were absent; there was no box in which the snake was kept, nor did there appear to be a ring formation for the dancing and rituals. Although one of the drummers seemed to take on a leadership role of sorts, there was also no obvious king, which reinforces Fandrich's and others' historical assertions that Louisiana Voudou was largely female-led.[56] There were also new elements introduced in this ceremony, including a banjo (an instrument of African origin), nudity, and, notably, the diverse and interracial nature of the group. Indeed, attendees included "males and females, old and young, Negroes and Negresses, handsome mulatresses and quadroons" as well as some white men and women.[57]

Much of what is known about Voudou ceremony in New Orleans after this episode in 1825 revolves mainly around Marie Laveau, a prominent Voudou queen of New Orleans. While many aspects of her life are shrouded in legend, it is known that Laveau was born sometime around the turn of the nineteenth century and, as a young woman, she probably worked as a hairdresser and nurse until the 1830s.[58] It was around that time that she was initiated into Voudou and became renowned as a religious oracle and

Figure 3.2. A journalistic depiction of a Voudou ceremony in New Orleans. *Source: The Voudou Meeting in the Old Brick-Yard*, 1882, wood engraving. Library of Congress Prints and Photographs Division.

herbalist. She was a "free person of color" and thus part of a French social category (*gens de couleur libres*) that included individuals of usually mixed African, European, or Indigenous American descent who were not enslaved. People of all races and backgrounds became her clients, paying her for help in predicting their futures and overcoming struggles in their personal lives. While little is known about the precise nature of Laveau's Voudou techniques, the author Carolyn Morrow Long—who has done much to disentangle her myth from her reality—has determined that she "embraced" the syncretic religious practices of New Orleans Voudou, including its "Roman Catholic prayers, chanting, dancing, and spirit possession, followed by a communal feast."[59]

A multitude of other historical descriptions of Marie Laveau's rituals exist, but a great many of them are known to be unreliable or problematic. Nevertheless, while these may be far from accurate portrayals of Laveau's activities, there is a chance they are not completely contrived but instead reflect certain generalizable characteristics of Voudou at that time. One account of Laveau, thought to be apocryphal but nevertheless attributed to an African American man who is said to have seen her when he was a child,[60] describes her as a prolific Voudou dancer and a prominent fixture of Congo Square: "Sometimes them policemens tried to keep Marie Laveau out, but she jest hypnotized 'em and walked in. . . . Well, when she got in the middle of the [Congo] Square she took her snake out of a box and danced wit' it. . . . When she got through dancin' all the other folks would dance—not before."[61] The mysterious provenance of this account makes it impossible to know whether it has any basis in reality. In the event that it did, it may still have been only partially accurate, for instance by reflecting some activities witnessed in Congo Square but not necessarily performed by Laveau, or vice versa. What is notable about the scene are the snake, the box, and the dancing—all features reminiscent of the episodes described in the past ceremonies from New Orleans and Saint-Domingue. What was different was the large public venue. More so than elsewhere, Voudou in New Orleans was considered a racially integrated affair for much of its existence, and those who attended events at Congo Square included a large assembly of enslaved Blacks, free people of color, and whites. Congo Square enabled the gathering of these larger, diverse groups of attendees, observers, and participants.

That Marie Laveau would gain such prominence in New Orleans, not only as a *voodooienne* but also as a mixed-race (and, at times, unmarried) woman, speaks to the unusually fluid racial and social dynamics that characterized New Orleans society from its beginning. In the colonial era, the division between races was starkly codified in the Code Noir and reinforced by legal segregationist policies. However, as one of the most populous and multiracial cities in North America, colonial New Orleans also remained home to a large community of Creoles, a group that originally included American-born descendants of European colonizers in French America, but which expanded to include "Creoles of color," free, mixed-race descendants of enslaved Africans, like Marie Laveau. Creoles of all backgrounds typically knew French, practiced Roman Catholicism, and were from families who had become established in the region before the United States purchased the land.[62] Far from the French metropole, the ruling Creole elite also had the luxury of pursuing policies and attitudes that did not necessarily conform to European standards and expectations. In this context, they encouraged a social hierarchy that was based on legal status more than race and that allowed some potential for social mobility, even among those with low status or African ancestry.[63] Consequently, Creoles of color like Laveau were able to gain some level of respectability in the eyes of social elites. This situation did not mean that slavery was any less brutal or dehumanizing than elsewhere. However, it did mean that, when the United States took over Louisiana in 1803, the city of New Orleans had a legacy of treating race, social hierarchy, and cultural integration in more fluid and complex terms than most other regions in the country with large enslaved populations.

Laveau's popularity among people of all racial backgrounds demonstrates how the dynamic social system of New Orleans could have actually benefited the growth of American Voudou. Perhaps that city was the only one in the United States where a person like Laveau could gain such widespread respect during the antebellum period, and by doing so attract the public at large to elements of an African diasporic religion that would have otherwise felt very foreign to some of them. As the prior quotation suggested, even white policemen may have succumbed to her "hypnotizing" will. It would have helped, of course, that she also seemed to be a dedicated Catholic and attended mass on a regular basis[64]—hallmarks that signaled her status as a Creole and her acceptability among the more elite members of New Orleans society.

Although a concentration of existing historical sources focuses on Voudou in and around New Orleans, comparable practices also took place elsewhere in the United States where African Americans resided. Indeed, the Black abolitionist William Wells Brown recounted a ceremony from St. Louis during the antebellum period (probably around 1840), when devotees met secretly in the middle of the night to partake in the same kinds of rituals practiced farther down the Mississippi River, including the circle dancing, the presence of a ceremonial Queen, the use of a snake (and other animals), and the convulsive movements and "wildest dance," followed by a collapse in exhaustion.[65] Although diverse in gender and age, the racial makeup of the crowd at this ceremony was more exclusively Black than what might have been found in New Orleans during that same period, but it nevertheless suggests that American Voudou existed along the Mississippi River and in areas that had historical connections to New Orleans.

Black Evangelicalism and the Rise of the Spiritual

Black syncretic religion also persisted in the British American colonies and the U.S. states that evolved out of them, but its history was different from that of Louisiana. Here, along the Atlantic seaboard and its interior territories, African religious elements often met with earlier and harsher reactions from the local white elites as compared to what happened in New Orleans. From an early period, British colonial concerns about African religion were bound up closely in fears of slave rebellions. One such rebellion occurred in April 1712, when more than twenty enslaved people living in New York City staged a revolt, ultimately leading to the death and injury of fifteen whites.[66] One of the key organizers of the revolt was known as Peter the Doctor, a free African-born conjurer who was reported to have inspired his fellow rebels toward action by creating a magical powder and rubbing it into their clothes in order to make them impervious to retaliation.[67] The historian Walter Rucker has determined that Peter the Doctor was likely a practitioner of Obeah, a magic tradition derived from the West African Akan culture.[68] As a conjurer, he would have had a "mastery over mystical forces" and possessed "a variety of supernatural powers including the ability to foretell future events through interpreting visions and dreams."[69] No historical evidence is available to confirm whether Peter the Doctor engaged in spirit possession rituals, but his religious pedigree would suggest he had extensive knowledge of such things. There is also no indication that the local white elites acted intentionally to suppress trance rituals in particular. What is known, however, is that they knew Peter to be a conjurer of magic and that they responded aggressively and decisively to prevent any rebellions from occurring again. After arresting seventy rebels and sentencing twenty-one of them to death, the colonial government of New York passed more restrictive slave laws. Now, bonded people were prohibited from carrying firearms, gambling, and gathering in groups of more than three.[70] Many of these actions would have made it exceedingly difficult for African Americans to engage in their musical rites of spirit possession.

In other British colonies, legislators of the slaveocracy resorted to even stricter measures by the mid-eighteenth century. In many colonies with large enslaved populations, they banned bonded people from using drums and other loud instruments that could be used to communicate with each other over relatively long distances using a rhythmic language unknown to whites. "It is absolutely necessary to the safety of this Province," read South Carolina's Negro Act of 1740, "that all due care be taken to restrain the . . . using or keeping of drums, horns, or other loud instruments, which may call together or give sign or notice to one another of their wicked designs and purposes."[71] The law was directly prompted by the Stono Rebellion a year earlier, when African rebels in South Carolina used a drum to signal each other and galvanize themselves toward action.[72] As with the New York laws previously established following the 1712 revolt, the Negro Act did not explicitly proscribe African American rituals of spirit possession, but it did inhibit one of their crucial features. Drumming had been so integral to many forms of African religious practice that its prohibition substantially curtailed Black people's ability to forge communal bonds based on their ancestral cosmologies.

As compared to Louisiana, British American colonies in general also made starker distinctions between races. They had no formal social category equivalent to "Creole" that enabled individuals of mixed-race backgrounds to gain some social status, just as Marie Laveau had done in New Orleans. In the British colonies that were heavily reliant on the institution of slavery—particularly in the Chesapeake colonies, Virginia and Maryland, as well as the other Southern jurisdictions they influenced—social stratification was more strictly delineated in a manner that was uncommon in colonial Louisiana.[73] In these regions, social hierarchies were typically established, following English norms, on a rigid class structure with wealthy white landowners at the top, followed by small farmers, indentured servants, and enslaved individuals. This condition encouraged elites to culturally (and legally) enforce class boundaries and prevent the kind of social mobility afforded to the likes of Marie Laveau.

If African American religion was to survive the censorious purview of white lawmakers, its initiates needed to recast their musical-spiritual rituals into something that their white overseers would find acceptable. Part of this process involved an evolution of form. For instance, ring shouts were changed to exclude overt percussive sounds as a response to the drumming prohibition.[74] This shift helps elucidate why, in certain regions, practitioners of the ring shout replaced drum accompaniment with the use of wooden sticks and planks, handclapping, foot-tapping, and other softer rhythmic expressions.[75]

Adapting to Protestant Christianity, it would seem, provided the best method for African Americans to ensure the survival of some of their traditional religious practices. During colonial times in Louisiana, the Code Noir had officially required bonded people to become Catholic and then protected their religious rights once they were. By contrast, no such legal stipulations existed regarding Protestantism in the Southern colonies of Anglo-America. Early on, English slavemasters had in fact been reluctant to convert their enslaved populations to Christianity. That task would be taken up by the white evangelical preachers who arrived in the South starting in the 1730s. Not only did the preachers encourage the enslaved to convert to Christianity, but they were also somewhat open to methods of exuberant bodily devotion and musical ecstasies that would have seemed considerably more compatible with African rituals than the staid worship of the Old Lights.

Enslaved people who entered into evangelical churches heartily took advantage of preachers' openness to effusive praise. Reverend Samuel Davies, one of the more musical of the white, American-born evangelists of the eighteenth century, preached throughout Virginia from the 1740s to the 1770s and observed that "the Negroes, above all the human species that ever I knew, have an ear for music and a kind of extatic [sic] delight in psalmody."[76] During Sabbath services, Davies took great pleasure listening to the congregants in their segregated gallery "breaking out in a torrent of sacred harmony, enough to bear away the whole congregation to heaven."[77] Instead of being mounted by African gods, they were now being filled with the Holy Spirit. But all the same, they shouted, sang, danced, and fell into trance to achieve their spiritual goals.[78]

Their turn to evangelical Christian cosmology did not mean that enslaved people gave up all their African inheritances;[79] however, in the regions where evangelical proselytism among African Americans was strongest, their syncretic beliefs became more conventionally Christian than, for instance, Voudou in colonial New Orleans. This difference probably had something to do with the strict regulations imposed by white authorities from an early period to curtail African American rituals. However, it was also likely tied to a particular theological stance of Protestant denominations, which discouraged the veneration of saints (particularly those designated by the Catholic Church). As such, Black Protestants had fewer opportunities to integrate African-inherited deities into their ecstatic practices than devotees of Afro-Catholic religions had done when they blended, for instance, St. Peter with Papa Laba. In this way, Black evangelical ecstasy did not take on the malleable modal qualities that were more identifiable within the American Voudou of New Orleans. Instead, they became more conventionally supernatural in their orientation, finding ecstatic release most often in the presence of the Holy Spirit, just as their white counterparts did.

This alignment is what enabled evangelicals of different races to attend the Southern camp meetings of the Second Great Awakening. As Andrew Reed observed in Virginia (see chapter 2), enslaved African Americans were frequently in attendance at such events. Their participation, however, was automatically subordinated to the back of the pulpit or farther reaches of the grounds, and African Americans carried out their own additional services in segregated quarters or in separate camp meetings altogether. John Fanning Watson, an amateur historian from Philadelphia, attended one such session at a Black section of a camp meeting in the 1810s and reported as follows: "In the blacks' quarter, the colored people get together, and sing for hours together, short scraps of disjointed affirmations, pledges, or prayers, lengthened out with long repetition choruses. . . . With every work so sung, they have a sinking of one or other leg of the body alternately; producing an audible sound of the feet at every step. . . . If some in the meantime sit, they strike the sounds alternately on each thigh."[80] While some of these exercises bore many similarities to those of white worshipers in attendance, certain practices, such as the rhythmic, almost dance-like stepping and body-slapping described above, diverged starkly. African Americans' cultural understanding of music and self-transcendence was ostensibly only partly indebted to Euro-American culture and Protestantism. The other inheritance derived from Africa and its tribal religions.

By the Second Great Awakening, the Old World influences on Black evangelical religion were perhaps best represented by African American "spirituals," self-stylized folk hymns developed by enslaved people that synthesized Christian doctrine, in the form of lyrics, with African-derived musical devices familiar to those who were enslaved.[81] The compilers of *Slave Songs of the United States* (1867), the first published collection of African American music, also observed this syncretism in South Carolinian congregants' creative blending of Anglo-style worship with the traditional ring shout format. Following

Figure 3.3. African Americans at a revivalist camp meeting. *Source:* Sol Eytinge Jr., *A Negro Camp Meeting in the South*, 1872, wood engraving. Published in *Harper's Weekly*, August 10, 1872: 620.

regular church services, they reported: "The benches are pushed back to the wall when the form meeting is over, and old and young, men and women, sprucely-dressed young men, grotesquely half-clad field-hands[,] . . . boys with tattered shirts and men's trousers, young girls barefooted, all stand up in the middle of the floor, and when the 'sperichil' is struck up, begin first walking and by-and-by shuffling round, one after the other, in a ring."[82] Most often when they performed a spiritual, "a band, composed of some of the best singers and of tired shouters, [stood] at the side of the room to 'base' the others, singing the body of the song and clapping their hands together or on the knees." Both the song and the dance were "extremely energetic," and sometimes the "monotonous thud, thud of the feet" could be heard lasting well into the night.[83] African-inspired religious practices, it would seem, did persist in the circular worship practices and the songs of evangelical African Americans.

Although documentation of the ring shout is sparse (especially outside of New Orleans) during the first half of the nineteenth century, there is much more evidence of its integration into the Black evangelical liturgy during the second half. One such account comes from the famed landscape architect Frederick Law Olmsted, who was commissioned by the *New York Times* during the 1850s to research the enslaved societies of the American South and published his findings in several volumes. One of these recounted a story of a church member in a "Southern city" who witnessed a revival that had African Americans "leap from their seats, throw their arms wildly in the air, shout vehemently and unintelligibly, cry, groan, rend their clothes, and fall into cataleptic trances."[84] Although it is unknown where exactly this event took place, ecstatic pursuits possibly associated with the ring shout were abundantly on display in this description.

Much evidence of the ring shout in the American South comes from encounters along the southeast coast, including the coastal plains of the Lowcountry and the Sea Islands of South Carolina and Georgia. This region historically included close-knit communities of Black people who became isolated from the rest of the country as they worked on remote rice and indigo plantations. Their seclusion limited their exposure to outside cultural influences and enabled them to come together and foster aspects of their shared African cultural ancestry to a degree that was more difficult to achieve in other places. They ultimately became an ethnic group known as the Gullah (and sometimes Geechee), and they maintained a creole dialect that included some African words. They also carefully nurtured religious practices like the ring shout. Evidence for the shout's prevalence in the region came from, among others, Laura M. Towne, a white abolitionist and prominent educator, who moved to St. Helena Island in South Carolina to teach freed people after the Union Army captured that area during the Civil War. In 1862, she described an event that probably would have been familiar to John Fanning Watson and others who had already witnessed a ring shout: "To-night I have been to a 'shout,' which seems to me certainly the remains of some old idol worship. The negroes sing a kind of chorus,—three standing apart to lead and clap,—and then all the others go shuffling round in a circle following one another with not much regularity, turning round occasionally and bending the knees, and stamping so that the whole floor swings."[85]

Similar observations came from a different account only a few years later, recorded at a nearby location, Port Royal Island, where newly freed people were being supported to farm the land that had been recently abandoned by the local planters. Here, an observer witnessed "a peculiar service in which dozen or twenty jog slowly round a circle behind each other with a peculiar shuffle of the feet and shake of the arms, keeping time to a droning chant and hand-clapping maintained by the by-standers. As the exercise continues, the excitement increases, and occasionally becomes hysterical. Some religious meaning is attributed to it, as 'worldly dancing' is strictly prohibited."[86] There are clearly common features between all of these examples and others that followed[87]—the circle formation, the handclapping and rhythmic foot movements, and the chanting or singing, and the obvious religious meaning for the participants (if not always the observers).

Even freed men who partook in the Civil War efforts during the 1860s continued the spiritual exercises they valued at home. These included men who joined the First South Carolina Volunteers, the earliest officially recognized Black regiment of the Union Army during the war. In his memoirs, Thomas Wentworth Higginson, a white man who served as colonel of that regiment, later recounted how, on many occasions, his soldiers "moved in the rhythmical barbaric dance the negroes call a 'shout,' chanting, often harshly, but always in the most perfect time, some monotonous refrain."[88] The words of those songs were almost always derived in part from biblical references—a clear indication that they were spirituals—and they were sung with only "the clapping of hands and the clatter of many feet."[89] Higginson's mention of the obvious Christian references in these Black spirituals was not reiterated by the other eyewitnesses from the Sea Islands, but it seems likely that explicit Christian elements could be found there and anywhere Black evangelicalism had taken hold.

What neither Higginson nor the other eyewitnesses directly addressed were the actual subjective experiences of those who sang spirituals or joined in ring shouts. It is impossible to know whether these people felt themselves undergoing an ecstatic merger with the Holy Spirit, but there are reasons to suggest they may have, at least on certain occasions. As Bishop Daniel Alexander Payne, a mixed race Methodist and a leading light of the African Methodist Episcopal Church, observed in the 1880s, African Americans continued to advocate for the relevance of the ring shout as integral to the Christian conversion experience: "This young man insisted that 'Sinners won't get converted unless there is a ring.' . . . [At] camp meeting there must be a ring here, a ring there, a ring over yonder, or sinners will not get converted."[90] Protestant Americans, especially evangelicals, had imbued conversion experiences with self-transcendent connotations from the earliest days of Christianity in America. That the shout would be considered integral to this process suggests an ongoing assumption that it could facilitate the profoundest self-transcendent experiences.

Ecstatic connotations also inflected African American worship practices that were not directly linked to the ring shout. The Massachusetts journalist Edward King, who toured the American South during the 1870s, recounted occasions in his published memoirs where former enslaved people would sing the "simplest hymns . . . with almost extravagant intensity."[91] As before, "they arose out of the ecstasy occasioned by the rude and violent dances on the plantation; . . . they bubbled up from the springs of religious excitement."[92] This description spoke to the value of emotional worship practices to African American religion and strongly implied the possibility of self-transcendence, even if it did not fully corroborate the subjective experience of the participants.

With the legacy of spirit possession well intact, it is perhaps no surprise that many African Americans became fervent supporters of the emotionally and musically charged style of worship that characterized the Holiness Movement and Pentecostalism starting in the 1880s. Their attraction was also facilitated by the fact that the new revivalists like Charles Fox Parham and Maria Woodworth-Etter happily appealed to people of all races. Woodworth-Etter felt strongly about this issue. Claiming that her only interest was in the "harvest of souls," she held camp meetings in African American communities and associated with the successful Black Christian leader and songwriter Thoro Harris.[93] Parham had much the same attitude. In 1906, he began a ministry in the city of Houston and preached extensively to African Americans there.[94] Many devotees were deeply affected by Parham's ministry style, including the Black Holiness preacher William J. Seymour, who would go on to become another early leader of the Pentecostal movement.[95]

Both interracial mixing and ecstasy featured prominently in the Azusa Street Revival, which began in Los Angeles in 1906 and helped launch Pentecostalism as a religious movement. The effusive ecstatic experiences, speaking in tongues, and avid musical participation that characterized this revival (see chapter 1) were promoted under the leadership of Seymour, who in turn drew on worship practices encouraged by Parham and often already present in Black evangelicalism. They proved to be key points of attraction for many African Americans who joined the revival, including a woman named Jennie Moore: "I sang under the power of the Spirit in many languages, the interpretation [of] both words and music which I had never before heard, and in the home where the meeting was held, the Spirit led me to the piano, where I played and sang under inspiration, although I had not learned to play."[96] This first-person account confirmed that self-transcendent phenomena was indeed a central feature of Black religious experience under Pentecostalism. Given the strong interracial makeup of the participants at the Azusa Street Revival, it is also possible that other descriptions of that event also represented the experiences of African Americans even if they did not openly confirm as much. These include statements from chapter 1, such as the one describing how "many were slain in the Spirit . . . in a beautiful Holy Spirit cloud" as they sang and praised God, or another that spoke of how people who "claim to be filled with the spirit . . . repeatedly sing the same song."[97]

Following the Azusa Street Revival, many Pentecostalists also seemed to integrate elements of the ring shout formally into their religious practices. The precise history of how and when this integration occurred is still underdeveloped. However, what is known is that sometime early in the twentieth century, Black church services and revivals, especially Pentecostal ones, became increasingly punctuated with what were commonly called "shouts" or "praise breaks." These were high intensity periods, which could last up to half an hour or more, that involved singing (often using call and response), shouts of praise, dancing, handclapping, foot-stomping, up-tempo music, glossolalia, or any combination of these.[98] Features of the ring shout were obviously on display here, although certain traditional elements also seem to have been abandoned, such as the formation of a ring and the circular movement of devotees around it. The enduring influence of the ring shout speaks to the evolving, creative, and syncretic ways in which African Americans maintained their spiritual traditions and integrated them into their religious lives. Moreover, the fact that many Black Christians incorporated elements of the ring shout into the most emotional, ecstatic, and musical moments of their religious ceremonies also suggests that some had never forgotten the self-transcendent potential of what might have been their oldest surviving spiritual practice in America.

The Suppression of African American Ecstasy

Although African American syncretic religion remained profoundly meaningful to its practitioners during the nineteenth and early twentieth centuries, white onlookers regularly found ways to reprimand and denounce its existence. Their reactions varied from outright fear and denigration to bemused concern, and only occasionally happy indifference. Rarer still was true respect. Their negative reactions sometimes led to new laws and policies that curtailed ring shouts and other African-inspired forms of musical spirit possession.

After the 1803 Louisiana Purchase and throughout the antebellum period, traders and planters in Louisiana increasingly interpreted Voudou as challenging their authority over enslaved peoples. These attitudes were probably augmented by the growing migration into southern Louisiana of Americans from other parts of the U.S., where attitudes toward African American rituals, music, and communal gatherings were stricter and racial categories starker. These perspectives countered the local Creole elite's generally more flexible approach to race and religion. Such antagonistic attitudes in New Orleans were also spurred on by the changing demographics of New Orleans and its vicinity during the first years of the nineteenth century. Following the Haitian Revolution, the influx of Black refugees into Louisiana—many of whom had gained military experience fighting during the revolutionary war—heightened concerns of rebellion. These fears were realized when, in January 1811, what would become the largest slave revolt in U.S. history erupted just outside of New Orleans, led by a Black bonded foreman from Saint-Domingue. Hundreds of enslaved people from the St. Charles and St. John the Baptist parishes mobilized and headed toward New Orleans, killing white men and destroying plantations as they went. They were ultimately stopped by a local militia and military troops, and local elites exacted harsh punishments on all those involved. Dozens of rebels were condemned to death and beheaded, their heads planted on poles to warn off other would-be insurgents.[99] The reaction to this rebellion, and the social and legal repercussions that followed, echoed the response to the Stono Rebellion along the East Coast some seventy years prior.

For white Louisianians, concerns about Black religious practices were tightly bound up in their fears of revolt. By the time of the 1811 uprising, it was already believed that Haitian Vodou practitioners had helped instigate the movement to overthrow the French colonial government in Saint-Domingue, and that the rebels performed with courage because they believed their deities made them unbeatable.[100] Many whites also worked hard to mitigate Voudou in New Orleans. First, they attempted to simply limit the frequency with which enslaved African Americans engaged in their own musical rituals, by keeping them working and limiting their free time to one day or several hours a week. Indeed, the advent of Congo Square as a meeting place for African Americans on Sunday afternoons was the result of a city ordinance in 1817 to confine the perceived threat of their religion to a highly localized place and time.[101] As a consequence, enslaved and free Blacks who wanted to practice their rituals and festivities at other times and places were often required to carry out their ceremonies in remote woods, secluded churches, and other places far away from condemning eyes and ears.[102] To quiet what would have normally been relatively raucous musical events in these settings, they may have even placed pots and other barriers in strategic places to absorb the sound and prevent it from traveling too far.[103] On the plantations, the shouts, yells, and moans that African Americans inserted into their music likewise disturbed slavemasters so much that on some occasions owners categorically banned these practices on the plantation grounds, threatening corporal punishment such as burning or whipping to any violators.[104] If enslaved people decided to surreptitiously shirk their masters' injunctions, they needed to do so in even more remote or isolated locations.[105]

As the sentiment of the establishment grew increasingly hostile toward Voudou, New Orleanians in positions of authority became more aggressive in curtailing any activities associated with it. By the 1830s, the city decreed that police surveillance was required for any activities in Congo Square, and by the 1840s the council demanded that bonded attendees acquire written permission from their masters before coming, and further limited the hours in which they could assemble.[106] Then they surrounded the square with posts connected with iron chains and planted the square with sycamore trees before finally surrounding the whole space with a cast iron fence and gates. Within a decade, the local militia began completing drills there on Sunday afternoons, the only time African Americans had originally been permitted to convene there.[107] In 1849, St. John's Parish, located not far from New Orleans, prohibited enslaved people from drumming and from dancing after sunset.[108] In 1850, police arrested dozens of people, mostly women, at a Voudou dance ceremony, and five years later a crowd tried to apprehend a Voudou practitioner who they believed had been casting spells on individuals.[109] All these actions accumulated to effectively quash most festivities at Congo Square, pushing African Americans to carry out their ring shouts and other celebrations in smaller groups and more private settings around the city and in the surrounding countryside.[110] The suppression continued during the Civil War, including under the occupation of the Union Army, which took over the city in 1862.[111] As Reconstruction gave way to the Jim Crow era in the United States, cultural and legal authorities in New Orleans took action to prevent activities in their city that were integral to Voudou practice. These included new ordinances through the 1870s and 1880s that prohibited anything in public spaces that could be construed as loitering, disorderly conduct, bodily displays, as well as meetings and processions of any kind, including religious ones. The practice of medicine without a license was also forbidden.[112]

Beyond the physical and legal actions of New Orleanian elites, their war against Black religion, music, and ecstasy was most often waged through words. For almost as long as they had known about Voudou, ring shouts, and the like, white journalists, diarists, and other published writers had censured them as not only dangerous but also primitive, superstitious, and (at best) frivolous. One way they proceeded was by linking African American ecstasy to egregious physicality, noise, savagery, and excess. For instance, during a visit to New Orleans in 1819, the British architect Benjamin Latrobe happened to hear a "most extraordinary noise, which [he] supposed to proceed from some horse mill, the horses trampling on a wooden floor."[113] The source of the sound, as it turned out, was a great meeting of Black dancers and drummers in Congo Square. Their music Latrobe described as "abominably loud," "uncouth," and "detestable," "brutally savage, and at the same time dull and stupid."[114] For George Washington Cable, the musical exploits of those in Congo Square were appalling less for their noise and more because they represented "a frightful triumph of body over mind, even in those early days when the slave was still a genuine pagan."[115] Accordingly, Cable believed their dance to be not only rife with "madness," but also "gross" and "a forbidden fruit monopolized by those of reprobate will." Only through a "moral education" could an enslaved person begin to understand the depth of his or her depravity.[116] In the ring shout, white observers saw an excessively physical savagery that had no hope of meeting the elite cultural expectations around corporeal control and cultivated comportment.

Of course, not all observers thought Black expressive culture was quite so repulsive. Louis Moreau Gottschalk, one of the best-known American composers and virtuosic pianists of the mid-nineteenth century, found it inspirational. While delirious from a bout of typhoid fever in France from 1844 to 1845, Gottschalk wrote his second opus, *Bamboula: Danse des nègres*, inspired by the ecstatic drumming and dances of bonded and freed Blacks in his native New Orleans.[117] It was a strongly rhythmic piece, with some parts reminiscent of a drum beat that, in comparison to other Romantic music of the day, lent the piece an exotic flair. It seems likely that, in the ring shouts of Congo Square, Gottschalk sensed an emotional force that was compatible with what he believed to be the ecstatic impulse that undergirded all great music. It was an impulse that he also identified in the "phantasmagoria of [Carl Maria von Weber's] *Der Freischütz*," the "mystical inspirations" of Renaissance composer Giovanni Pierluigi da Palestrina, or the Masses of Mozart,[118] which, he believed, like all great art "makes us burst the bonds of material space, through the ideal, and transports us to the celestial spheres."[119] That Gottschalk would find a kindred self-transcendent element in both European and African American music might be at least partly explained by his own blended identity. Born to an Anglo-German-Jewish father and a French-Haitian Creole mother, Gottschalk was able to identify both with European Romanticism and the popular folk traditions of Louisiana and the Caribbean.

Despite his best efforts, Gottschalk's more appreciative views were often overshadowed by patently hostile indictments of Black ecstatic culture. Journalists and authors who wrote sensationalist accounts of Voudou often led this charge, deploring the latter as immoral, un-Christian, and delusional. The author of the previously mentioned account of the 1825 Voudou ceremony led by Sanité Dédé described the events of that night as rife with "satanic discord" and "fetish-worship," and he maintained, "If I ever realized a sense of the real visible presence of . . . the devil, it was that night among his Voudou worshipers."[120] Another account from the *Daily True Delta*, a mid-century New Orleans newspaper, condemned Voudou ceremonies for reviving the "ancient superstitions of Africa" in their creation of a "charmed circle" around which a dance is held, often in the nude, along with cauldrons, snakes (representing "the Spirit of Evil"), and other reptiles.[121] This was all "deviltry" with a "hellish purpose" in which "hags, as ugly as sin, mutter a[n unintelligible] jargon" and try to "impress the participants with a full belief in this superstition, and the effect produced by those incantations upon the credulous." Although the gospel was heard regularly throughout the event, it nevertheless "failed to crush out their heathenish proceedings."[122] Another account from *Appleton's Journal*, a national magazine published during the 1870s, equated Voudou with witchcraft—not that of the European variety, but "a far deeper and deadlier sorcery . . . No mere words can describe the hold which it has on the mind of the Southern negro. Once convince him that he is 'tricked,' and, unless he be able to procure a 'trick-doctor' whom he considers more skilful [*sic*] than the witch under whose spell he has fallen, no human power can save him."[123] Marie Laveau's popularity, it would seem, could not ultimately save Voudou from harsh religious and racial condemnation from the pundits of the establishment.

The war of words against African American ecstasy also continued outside of New Orleans and across the American South. Letitia M. Burwell, a plantation owner's daughter who grew up in Virginia during the antebellum era, described one ring shout pursued on her property at the deathbed of a bonded woman who was beloved by her peers. Burwell described the scene as "a savage dance . . . horrible to hear and see, especially as in this family every effort had been made to instruct their negro depends in the truths of religion . . . But although an intelligent woman, she seemed to cling to the superstitions of her race."[124] Frederick Law Olmsted's account from the 1850s uncovered a comparable, although perhaps less severe attitude from "Mr. X," a plantation owner and slaveholder, who, "endeavored, with but little success, to prevent this shouting and jumping of the negroes at their meetings on his plantation, from a conviction that there was not the slightest element of religious sentiment in it. He considered it to be engaged in more as an exciting amusement than from any really religious impulse."[125] This was perhaps as generous an interpretation as could be found from this context, describing the ring shout practices as nonreligious and frivolous.

One need not have been a member of a slaveholding family to have derogatory views of African American religious practices. In the North, blackface minstrelsy, the most popular form of entertainment during the nineteenth century, was also rife with negative portrayals of African American ecstasy. Claiming to be "authentic delineators of Negroes,"[126] by the 1840s blackface minstrels regularly depicted entranced African Americans as uncontrollable and dangerously corporeal.[127] Richard Pelham, a founding member of the Virginia Minstrels during the 1840s, provided one example. One journalist's review of his musical performance described how he seemed to become "animated by a savage energy; and the [handling of his instrument] . . . nearly wrung him off his seat. His white eyes rolled in a curious frenzy . . . and his hiccupping chuckles were unsurpassable."[128] This description resembled another one from 1857, which mentioned how enslaved people would also "let themselves go" in "dervish-like fury . . . all night long, in ceaseless violent exertions of frenetic dancing."[129] Such portrayals of violent and chaotic ecstasy typified a larger trend within blackface minstrelsy that cast Black culture as essentially and excessively physical. This included portrayals of African Americans with gaping mouths, long dangling lower lips, gigantic feet, and bulging eyeballs—all aberrant physical features that also served to reinforce derogatory assumptions about Black ecstasy.[130] Over time, performances were repeated with such frequency that character tropes quickly emerged, many of which exhibited inclinations toward degenerate corporeality. These included the "dandy darky," an egocentric free Black man with a large sexual appetite who dressed in upper-class fashion.[131] This caricature became only one representation of a growing tendency to depict Black Americans as uglier, dumber, drunker, more violent, and more sexually depraved than anyone else.[132]

These outrageously physical portrayals of African American experience, both ecstatic and otherwise, offered some social benefit to white audiences. Professional blackface entertainers were paid to impersonate African Americans (however inaccurately), so by feigning Black ecstasy, people like Pelham—and the audiences who adored them—were not so much condoning the experience as demonstrating their ability to recognize and even resist it. In short, play-acting ecstasy on the stage may have provided opportunities for white audiences and performers alike to prove their own individual integrity and self-mastery vis-à-vis a dark-skinned other. This kind of veiled public demonstration of white self-control would have probably seemed attractive to whites from all classes who aspired to existing codes of self-propriety that attended claims to respectability during this period.

Northern abolitionists were often not any kinder in their interpretations of African American trance. For instance, Laura M. Towne, the abolitionist from Pennsylvania who came to the Sea Islands of South Carolina in the 1860s to educate formerly enslaved people, described the ring shout in the following way: "I never saw anything so savage. They call it a religious ceremony, but it seems like a regular frolic to me."[133] Towne's condescension was palpable. So too was that of Harriet Ware, another Northerner who volunteered to teach free people of color and help manage a Southern plantation in South Carolina at the end of the Civil War. She had the following to say about the ring shout and the experiences of those who participated in it:

> I let the children sing some of their own songs in a genuine, shouting style, a sight too funny in the little things, but sad and disagreeable to me in the grown people, who make it a religious act. It is impossible to describe it—the children move round in a circle, backwards, or sideways, with their feet and arms keeping energetic time, and their whole bodies undergoing most extraordinary contortions, while they sing at the top of their voices the refrain to some song sung by an outsider. We laughed till we almost cried over the little bits of ones, but when the grown people wanted to "shout," I would not let them. . . . [If] you could have looked in, you would have thought it Bedlam let loose![134]

For Ware, the "energetic" movements were silly and puerile, amusing enough when performed by children but deplorable when committed by adults. And the "extraordinary contortions" of bodies were hardly to be considered "a religious act."[135]

When Elizabeth Kilham, another white school teacher, visited a Black church in the Sea Islands in 1865, she was also repelled by what she believed to be a harsh, discordant mixture of shouts, screams, and stamps that were injected into their hymns and other religious songs. For Kilham, it was a scene that left "an impression like the memory of some horrid nightmare—so wild [was] the torrent of excitement, that, sweeping away reason and sense, [it tossed] men and women upon its waves."[136] The stamping, which gradually intensified during the singing of hymns, eventually proceeded until "the noise was deafening," and the whooping and screaming that sometimes occurred resembled a "savage war-cry."[137] In the minds of so many white elites like Kilham, intense corporeality and thunderous cacophony were entrenched yet disgraceful characteristics of the soundscape of enslavement.

Even after African Americans converted to Protestantism, middle-class authorities, including abolitionists, often refused to accept their expressions of religion and ecstasy as authentically Christian. Instead, they picked out the idiosyncratic or overtly physical elements of African American worship and cast them as foreign, unintelligible (and unintelligent), and excessive. The vast divergence between their moral interpretations and those of most African Americans (who usually saw their syncretic, ecstatic rituals as exceedingly meaningful and positive) represented a larger race-based epistemological divide over Black culture and identity.

From the earliest days of slavery, African Americans pursued and interpreted ecstatic release in multifarious ways. Trance had been foundational to the African religious traditions they brought with them in fragments across the Atlantic, and it remained so as they endured the challenges of adapting to their dislocated surroundings under slavery and after it. That process unfolded differently depending on context. It resulted in the development of several parallel lines in the counterpoint of ecstatic experience, including ones that clustered around both Black evangelicalism and American Voudou. These two clusters evolved separately and under somewhat different circumstances. Notably, Black evangelicalism largely absorbed the supernatural mode of musical ecstasy as it embraced spiritual possession via the Holy Spirit. Voudou, on the other hand, seemed to perpetuate a theological approach that confounded strict modal distinctions between supernatural and naturalized trance. Instead, it permitted spirit possession by a variety of deities and saints that were simultaneously linked to an almighty God and the more profane workings of the earthly realm.

Despite these important differences, Black evangelicalism and American Voudou also shared a great deal in common. Certainly, they were syncretic in a multidimensional way that involved not just the blending of African religions with Christianity, but also the further immixing of different African (e.g., Kongolese, Yoruba) and Afro-Christian religious traditions (e.g., Haitian Vodou and New Orleans Voudou). They were also inherently musical, often involving song and usually including features that could be found in the ring shout and related ritualized practices.

This chapter has revealed that the commonalities did not stop there. American Voudou and Black evangelicalism also shared an inclination toward physicality. While not all African Americans were predisposed to highly physical spiritual practices (or trance for that matter),[138] those many who elevated ecstatic experiences as central to their spiritual lives typically remained open to corporeal expression, as evidenced by their propensity toward effusive dancing and rhythmic music including drumming, hand-clapping, and other forms of percussion. In the eighteenth and nineteenth centuries, such activities stood in stark contrast to the more staid culture of comportment that typified mainstream values and regularly impelled white, patrician Americans to clamp down on overtly physical displays of emotion and self-transcendent experience. This physicality did not mean that African Americans had less self-control than whites, as many contemporaneous white observers presumed. To the contrary, there is evidence that African Americans exerted considerable individual agency over how and under what circumstances they pursued self-transcendent experience. In many (although not all) instances, they treated bodily movement as a preferable method through which to motivate trance. But they also had the means to "cool" down their physicality when necessary.

Another attribute of ecstatic experience shared by American Voudou and Black evangelicalism was resistance. Indeed, the ring shout and other associated musical rituals provided participants with one of their most powerful methods of defying white supremacy. This could take different forms. One was outright rebellion. As this chapter has demonstrated, African Americans were able to incorporate rhythmically charged ecstatic practices into subversive activities, including slave revolts. At the same time, white observers often exaggerated the threat of rebellion when interpreting the physical expressiveness of African American religious rituals.

Another form of Black resistance through ecstasy did not seek to threaten the social hierarchy at all. Instead, for its practitioners, it involved opening up psychic and spiritual channels necessary to transport enslaved people, if even temporarily and incompletely, out of bondage. Certainly, no one could easily escape the physical bonds of forced servitude. In Saidiya Hartman's view, chattel slavery served to make the captive body "an abstract and empty vessel, vulnerable to the projections of others' feelings, ideas, desires, and values."[139] In this sense, Hartman suggests that the logic of slavery leaned toward an enforced dispossession of African selfhood—by making the enslaved person a receptacle for the consciousness of the master. In this view, bondage, by its very definition, insisted on a degree of self-loss. But if enslaved individuals were entirely dispossessed of their bodies, perhaps they believed that their souls could not so easily succumb to the wishes of their white masters. And spirit possession, manifested partly through the ritualized rhythms of African-derived music, would have served to barricade white ownership from the most essential aspects of their identity. According to Katrina Hazzard-Donald, through the ring shout, enslaved people "could and did assert a limited independence from slavery's pain as well as agency in forging their community, personality, and place."[140] In this sense, the ring shout, along with other related Black spiritual practices, ensured that the enforced possession of African American selves by white traders and owners was always incomplete, and could be (partially) contravened via possession by a spirit of one's own choosing.

That entrancement engendered agency for African Americans helps to explain why they continued to eagerly pursue ecstatic experience in the Holiness Movement and Pentecostalism during the late nineteenth and early twentieth centuries. Intense and exuberant religious trance, such as the variety on offer at the Azusa Street Revival, provided more than a profound religious experience. For Black Americans in this era of Jim Crow—during what the historian Rayford Logan called "the nadir" of race relations in America[141]—it also could have provided release from the onslaught of anti-Black violence, lynchings, segregation, and expressions of white supremacy that typified that era. In this context, voluntary spirit possession can also be considered a form of self-possession.

For African Americans, the Holiness/Pentecostal movement was a response to the strictures of racial segregation and subjugation, but as a transracial movement it can also be thought of as a countercultural reaction to other trends within society at large. One was surely the enduring sensibility of tranquil decorum embraced by the genteel classes, which devalued physical expression in all emotional experiences including self-transcendent ones. Another trend that incited a reaction by African American religionists related to an entirely different mode of ecstatic experience. This particular mode did not closely resemble its supernatural or natural counterparts. Its advocates avoided or chafed at the prospect of tying ecstasy to an identifiable deity, spirit, or mystical force. For them, trance comprised a decidedly more immanent experience.

Chapter 4

The Internalization of Enthusiasm

In his 1898 book, *The Psychology of Suggestion*, Boris Sidis recounted the story of a theater actress who underwent a religious conversion some decades before. Walking through town one day, the actress found herself strangely attracted by the songs of a revival meeting. Opening a door, she heard the congregation sing the words "Depth of mercy! can there be, / Mercy still reserved for me?"[1] She could not shake the influence of the hymn, which she felt had surrounded her with its full force. A short time later, the actress walked on stage prepared to perform a song for the opening act of a play. The curtain rose and the orchestra began the accompaniment for her song. Yet, instead of singing, the actress stood "as if lost in thought (she seemed to have fallen into a trance), and as one forgetting all around her and her own situation."[2] So the orchestra started up the music from the beginning, but as her cue to sing came up again, she still did not move her lips. After a third attempt, the actress clasped her hands and, with tearful eyes, she finally started to sing—but not the song from the play. Instead, she began the hymn from the revival meeting: "Depth of mercy! can there be, / Mercy still reserved for me?"

The story, first published by the Baptist pastor Henry Clay Fish of Newark, New Jersey, had originally been interpreted as a powerful example of religious conversion and the piety of Christians who "sang with the Spirit" of their God.[3] However, for Sidis, the actress's musical performance was not an example of divine spirit possession. Rather, it was an excellent illustration of what he called "automatism"—an involuntary mental process that occurred outside or on the margins of conscious awareness and that shaped behavior and experience in ways difficult for the individual to control. Ecstasy, in this view, originated *inside* the individual. Such automatic behavior did not represent an entrancement by external metaphysical entities but instead the power of "suggestion"—the encouragement of often involuntary thought and action through subtle or diffuse cues ("suggestions") exhibited by the people or things in an individual's environment (e.g., speech, gesture, and tone). Thus, for Sidis, the actress's automatic behavior was elicited by the social suggestibility of the hymn-singing members of the congregation who sang so powerfully while she was at the revival meeting.

Sidis's theory was a purely secular and scientific one based on some of the most recent psychological findings emanating from Europe. That Sidis would move away from a religious explanation for the actress's extraordinary experience is unsurprising. He certainly had not been brought up in the evangelical tradition so prevalent among native-born Christian Americans during the nineteenth century. Instead, as a Jewish émigré from Kiev, he had gained a reputation from a young age as a radical thinker who opposed his family's religious tendencies almost as much as he condemned the political authority of the Romanov dynasty. After fleeing the Russian Empire for the United States, Sidis attended Harvard University and studied with the preeminent psychologist William James, under whose guidance he became familiar with the latest scientific theories of the mind.

With his background and education, Sidis was well positioned to conceptualize subjective experience—or "consciousness," as it was increasingly called in academic circles—in thoroughly immanent terms. Instead of referring to an experience that transcended individual selfhood, his idea of ecstasy was simply an experience that transitioned between two different types of self. Indeed, Sidis maintained that the individual contained both a "waking self" and a secondary "subwaking self" that lurked in the shadows of an individual's psyche. The latter could be normally controlled with an effective mental "cleft" that ensured the primacy of the former, but if the subwaking self became too "disaggregated" from the waking form, it could take control of the individual and lead to abnormal experiences and actions. If Sidis believed in self-transcendent experiences, they were, for him, highly mitigated mental forms that involved the transcendence of the normal, rational waking self into one dominated by the irrational subwaking self. Sidis was far from alone in his ideas. Indeed, he was only one contributor to a long line of American and European professionals who confined consciousness within the bounds of the individual. He was also part of an even larger scientific trend in America that emptied meaning and value from conventional objects of self-transcendent experience.

As this chapter demonstrates, Sidis represented a distinct mode of ecstasy that had roots in the seventeenth century but became increasingly robust over the course of the nineteenth century. This mode defined trance as a thoroughly secular phenomenon that was detached from objects of experience that existed outside the self. In contrast, it offered up a thoroughly internal interpretation of experience as enclosed entirely within the mind and body of the individual.[4] This internal mode was not the result of a soft secularizing impulse that naturalized ecstatic experience while still maintaining beliefs in a spiritual other, as was typical of sentimentality and spiritualism. Instead, it involved a more stringent form of secularization that strongly devalued the great bulwarks of religion and spirit and attempted to abrogate any conventional sense of transcendence.[5] This form of secularization was guided and encouraged by a cadre of social scientists, intellectuals, and physicians from both America and Europe who challenged the authority of religious and Romantic cultures by casting trance as an internal experience enclosed within the individual mind or body, or both.[6]

Theories of Enthusiasm

The origins of such an immanent interpretation of ecstasy can be traced back at least to the seventeenth century, when some medical theorists averred that certain experiences resembling self-transcendence were simply illusions created by the individual mind or body. It was at this time that the influential English scholar Robert Burton claimed that phenomena involving the loss of self-control—including what he called "Frenzy," "Ecstasy," "Lycanthropia" (the feeling of being a wolf or some other nonhuman animal), "Chorus sancti Viti" (Saint Vitus' Dance), and "Melancholy"—could all result from the delusional power of "*phantasy*, or *imagination*."[7] Burton further suggested that the intense affections related to these phenomena originated in the human body, via the workings of "animal spirits"—natural impulses produced within the blood that transmitted stimuli between the organs, brain, and heart.[8] Contained as they were within the body, animal spirits were therefore as biological as blood or bile. Stimuli outside the body, including music, could certainly arouse the animal spirits, both for good and ill, but in Burton's view, the body was the wellspring of affection.

For all his emphasis on the body, Burton's view did not entirely exclude the possibility of unitive experiences with a metaphysical other. Indeed, he also attached his theory to a larger Christian cosmology by suggesting that the immanent impulses generated by animal spirits complemented and interacted with the self-transcendent dimension through one's "sensible soul." In this manner, the Devil could manipulate animal spirits to interfere with the workings of the body and mind, for instance, by making a person not only "subject to diabolical temptations" but also to "demoniacal . . . obsession or possession of devils, which *Platerus* & others would have to be preternatural."[9] Thus, the internal impulses of the human body were not fully insulated from the influence of supernatural intervention. In colonial America, this view found purchase among intellectual elites and public figures like Cotton Mather, who wrote similarly about the possibilities of demonic possession via the impaired humors.[10]

By the eighteenth century, the term "enthusiasm" came to represent the kind of phantasmic fabrications that had previously interested the likes of Burton and Mather. During this period, the philosopher David Hume used the term to refer to a process that occurs when the subject's "imagination swells with great but confused conceptions," making him into a "fanatic madman" blindly prone "to the supposed illapses [absorption] of the spirit."[11] This theory was only amplified by the English clergyman and writer Martin Madan, who described raptures and transports as the products of a profound confusion between "the *imaginations of men*" and "the *inspiration of God*" as experienced by the biblical prophets and apostles.[12] The eminent English educator, philosopher, and moralist Samuel Johnson used the phrase "invisible riot of the mind" to denote the same kind of phenomenon, which arose, he suggested, when one willingly "abandons himself to his own fancy."[13] All of these references to "imagination" and "fancy" suggested the presence of a human "mind" (rather than soul) that was separate from any metaphysical entity or space.[14]

In America, Charles Chauncy, along with other Old Light Congregationalists and Baptists, adopted the theory of enthusiasm in their condemnations of the New Lights and their religious experiences. From Chauncy's perspective, the impulses of revivalists resulted from flaws in the body and mind of the subject: "an over-heated imagination," a "bad temperament of the blood," or a melancholic constitution.[15] They also came from "the natural Influence of awful Words and frightful Gestures" or "a mechanical Impression on animal Nature" that worked to enhance the production of animal spirits.[16] Although the assertion of a strong rational will could ideally contain these affections, Chauncy averred that an overabundance of profane impulses was capable of putting "weaker Minds out of Possession of themselves."[17] The self-transcendence that resulted was, in his view, a debased indulgence in the false ecstasy of enthusiasm. At its most benign, Chauncy suggested, this propensity reflected mere flights of fancy propelled by an overactive personal imagination, but at its worst it could be linked more to "the *Suggestions* of *Satan*."[18] Old Lights' derision of ecstasy, therefore, was simultaneously an effort to demote that experience as mere fantasy, uplift the rational will, and stave off the possibility of heretical behavior and demonic engagement.

While New Lights readily endorsed the redemptive potential of self-transcendence, some of them acknowledged the dangers of enthusiasm. For Jonathan Edwards, false ecstasy was possible even when people practiced in the name of religious devotion: "There are many exercises of the affections that are very flashy, and little to be depended on; and oftentimes there is a great deal that appertains to them, or rather that is the effect of them, that has its seat in animal nature, and is very much owing to the constitution and frame of the body."[19] The difficulty for Edwards was in determining which forms of trance were inspired through God's grace and which were fabricated by indulging in unholy affections. On this count, he was reluctant to provide a steadfast heuristic, concluding only that the task must be left to "the skill of the observer."[20]

Medical theorists and conservative religionists were not the only ones who came to attribute ecstasy to the internal workings of the mind and body. Some late eighteenth- and nineteenth-century Romantics likewise considered whether their sublime experiences might be internally generated.[21] They contended that self-transcendent experiences could be fully confined within the individual imagination and were not reliant on external stimuli. As the literary scholar Kiene Brillenberg Wurth notes, this viewpoint was summarized in Immanuel Kant's *Critique of Pure Reason*, which held that sublime transcendence could be achieved by disengaging from sensory experience and turning inward. Such a reorientation, though, was not meant to discount the sublime experiences that were possible when engaging one's senses and exploring the will of Nature. Instead, it was intended to complement them.[22] As the scholar Roger Lundin demonstrates, this turn inward to personal experience gained much traction in transcendentalism and other forms of American Romanticism.[23]

The Rise of Neurology and Psychology

By the late eighteenth century, many scientific thinkers who were already fully committed to Enlightenment principles of rationalization began to adopt mental and physical explanations of experience and tacitly move away from purely religious theories. Benjamin Franklin's previously discussed inquiries into the phenomenon of what Franz Anton Mesmer called animal magnetism helped initiate this shift in the United States. Although Franklin's 1784 French Royal commission on mesmerism revealed that music could help induce magnetic trance, it also concluded that there was no credible evidence to suggest the existence of magnetic fluid, and that any individual's sensation of being magnetized was actually a result of the power of imagination and "mechanical imitation" as opposed to a genuine magnetic connection to a metaphysical other.[24] His ability to explain (away) mesmeric trances without reference to the mystical workings of a numinous force would have far-reaching effects, influencing even Abbé Faria, one of Mesmer's erstwhile disciples, who ultimately helped popularize an early theory of "suggestion."[25]

In the 1840s, the Scottish surgeon James Braid worked from these ideas and advanced a new theory of "rational mesmerism," which labeled mesmeric conditions as "hypnotism." Lacking the "higher phenomena" usually reported by animal magnetists, hypnotism as Braid understood it was instead "a peculiar condition of the nervous system, into which it may be thrown by artificial contrivance."[26] This "nervous sleep" was a "habit of abstraction or mental concentration," in which the "powers of the mind are so much engrossed with a single idea or train of thought, as . . . to render the individual unconscious of, or indifferently conscious to, all other ideas, impressions, or trains of thought."[27] Eventually, Braid would elaborate the different kinds of "suggestion" that could be used to encourage hypnotic conditions in his subjects. These included indirect verbal insinuations, figures of speech, changes in vocal intonation, and similar methods.[28]

Music too, Braid believed, possessed a hypnotically suggestive power. He identified how certain people were known to develop a "taste for dancing . . . on hearing lively music during hypnotism."[29] In demonstrating this point, he recounted an experiment performed on one "Mrs. C," wherein music excited her "to ecstasy . . . [and] graceful dancing."[30] In another case, he described how a different woman "cut a very good figure at waltzing" while melodically induced into a hypnotic sleep.[31] In Braid's estimation, "every variety of passion and emotion can be excited in the mind by music," and hypnosis was a pathway to achieve such an affective response.[32]

Soon, influential professionals on both sides of the Atlantic began recruiting similar theories to target the notion of animal magnetism. In the United States, Nathaniel Hawthorne began to explain mesmeric experiences as grounded in one's physical faculties.[33] Ralph Waldo Emerson also acknowledged animal magnetism as produced by a nervous condition.[34]

These viewpoints did not necessarily diminish the public's (or the authors') fascination with mesmeric phenomena, but they increasingly put advocates of animal magnetism in a defensive position, requiring that they either ignore or address the physiological interpretations of consciousness.

As it turned out, spiritualists—who had adopted many ideas from animal magnetism—proved more open than many traditional mesmerists in accommodating this skepticism. Some of them engaged in empirical studies to distinguish between true spiritual trance and illusions of the imagination, and they admitted that misapprehension, voluntary deception, and imitation could all create false impressions of spiritual contact.[35] Although most spiritualists continued to believe in the possibility of genuine interaction with a mystical realm, some of them also began to take an agnostic view on the topic. Among them was Dr. John Gray, who admitted that "it is impossible for us to know whether [the pronouncements and experiences of mediums] . . . are simply spiritual or simply natural in their authorship, or a mixture from both sources."[36] He, therefore, acknowledged that there was not yet any conclusive way of disqualifying the possibility that a spiritual communication was, in fact, a trick of the imagination.

By the 1860s, scientifically minded professionals of various backgrounds augmented their efforts to internalize all forms of self-transcendent experience, and not just those associated with animal magnetism. Much of the impetus in this direction stemmed from the work of La Roy Sunderland, an American former Methodist minister, mesmerist, and spiritualist who turned into a religious skeptic later in life. He described the mystical experiences of both evangelicals and spiritualists as products of "nervous phenomena" that excited the mind.[37] He also contended that the particular activities and sensations associated with any given religious tradition were encouraged by the "sympathetic imitation" of others and learned mental "habits" of association.[38] The raptures that had previously been imbued with metaphysical qualities now fell under Sunderland's category of "the Trance": "a state of the nervous system, in which the mind is said to pass beyond the use of the external senses; a condition in which the mind is more or less active, without the normal consciousness of the external world."[39] In this form, trance was a diversion of attention away from the outside world, but it did not exactly constitute a fusion with or transcendence of that world. Instead, it was more simply a movement of the mind and nervous system into new and unusual states. Like Braid's theory of hypnotism, Sunderland's formulation of "the Trance" reframed ecstatic experiences as physiologically grounded mental ones.

Sunderland's views often aligned comfortably with those of the American neurologist George Miller Beard, his colleague and sometimes collaborator.

Scarred by a strict Congregationalist childhood, Beard developed as an adult a deep-seated scorn for what he believed were the delusions of religious experience. Addressing what he considered to be the false apparitions of "trance experiences" in particular, he claimed that it was imperative to overcome misguided assumptions that the senses were always "worthy of trust." In the case of trances, he contended that such impressions were best explained by the neurological knowledge of experts, who knew them to represent "a functional disease of the nervous system, in which the cerebral activity is concentrated in some limited region of the brain, with suspension of the activity of the rest of the brain, and consequent loss of volition."[40]

Beard's conclusions echoed and anticipated the ideas of Sunderland, as well as many other American and British scientists and physicians, including the physiologist W. B. Carpenter, the neurologist William A. Hammond, and the alienist (psychiatrist) Henry Maudsley, all of whom wrote in similar terms, if less elaborately, on the topic. Together, their work would help professionalize fields such as neurology and physiology on both sides of the Atlantic.

Although many leaders of the new professional movement originated from the English-speaking world, one of the most influential voices was a French neurologist, Jean-Martin Charcot. During his time at the Salpêtrière Hospital in Paris, Charcot helped popularize the theory that explained subjective experience as primarily resulting from the workings of the physical body. Indeed, he interpreted trance as indicative of an underlying disease of the nervous system involving abnormal activity in certain parts of the brain. An individual, he averred, did not experience spirit possessions or psychic attunements with a magnetic fluid. These were instead examples of "hysteria," a medical condition previously associated with sexual imbalances in the female body (and attributed to a malfunction of the uterus or other female organs), which Charcot now linked directly with hypnosis and lesions on the female brain. While this formulation altered earlier theories, it also perpetuated an enduring cultural tendency that cast women as susceptible to the excesses and automatism of ecstatic madness.

Some of Charcot's research and experimentation involved initiating trances among women he had identified as hysterics. This practice regularly involved sound- and music-based hypnotic techniques, included the use of gongs, tuning forks, and songs, as well as other methods developed originally by mesmerists but now divested of their spiritual framework (see figs. 4.1 and 4.2). After inducing cataleptic fits and loss of self-control, Charcot and his colleagues at the Salpêtrière concluded that hysterical women were

Figure 4.1. A depiction of the automatic response ostensibly provoked in a female patient by the suggestive power of a tam-tam instrument. *Source:* Paul Régnard, "Catalepsy Produced by the Sudden Sound of a Tam-Tam." Published in Paul Régnard, *Les Maladies épidémiques de l'esprit: Sorcellerie, magnétisme, morphinisme, délire des grandeurs* [Epidemic maladies of the spirit: Sorcery, magnetism, morphine addiction, delusions of grandeur] (Paris: E. Plon, Nourrit, et cie., 1887): 262. Public domain.

Figure 4.2. A female "hysteric" at the Salpêtrière Hospital (Paris) exhibiting what is described as an automatic response to the sound of a tuning fork held by a physician. *Source:* Charles Laufeneur, "Des contractures spontanées et provoquées de la langue chez les hystéro-épileptiques," *Nouvelles Iconographie de la Salpêtrière* 2 (1889): 203–7, plate 34 (located between pages 204 and 205). Public domain.

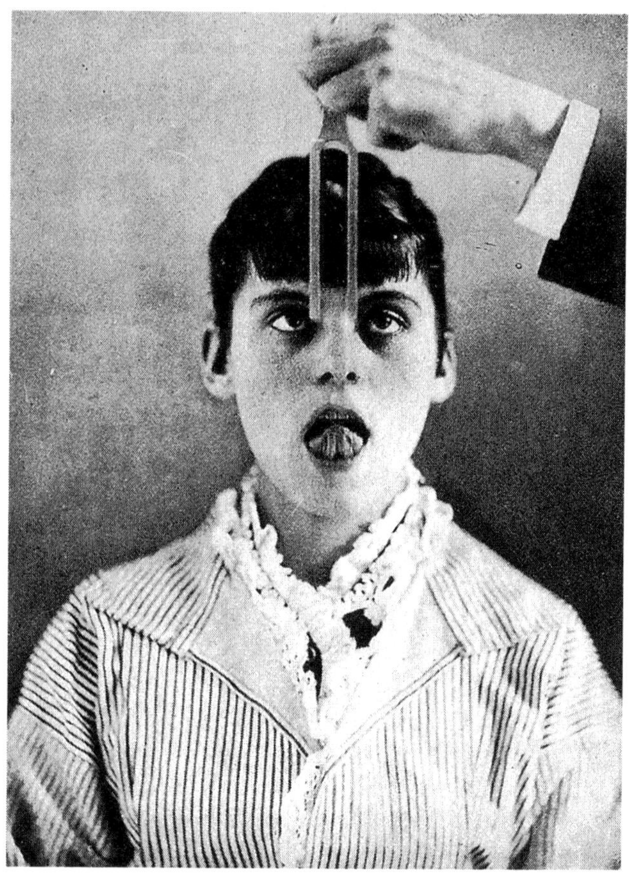

predisposed toward automatism and trance delusions.[41] In doing so, he knotted together insanity, femininity, and sound.[42]

While many researchers supported Charcot's explanation of trance as a physical phenomenon, a growing body of scientists countered that the unusual alterations of consciousness could be explicated in purely psychological terms.[43] For instance, Hippolyte Bernheim, a French professor of medicine, rejected Charcot's claim that trance experiences were solely rooted in the abnormal physiology of certain diseased individuals, such as hysterical women. Instead, Bernheim called unusual forms of consciousness "psychogenic," because he thought they could be triggered by unusual mental activity associated with environmental stimuli rather than a disorder in the physical body. This meant that otherwise healthy and sane people could also become entranced in the same manner as so-called hysterics.[44] Bernheim's ideas grew influential enough that, later in his career, Charcot and his supporters would start to consider the viability of this explanation.[45]

Some professionals, such as Gustave Le Bon, were happy to combine physiological and psychological explanations of trance with the addition of socially suggestive factors. In *The Crowd,* Le Bon's widely read publication from 1896, the author contended that, when acting as a participant in a crowd of emotional peers, individuals could begin to behave automatically based upon ideas and emotions presented to them by other people in their environment. Even people who were normally of sound mind could, in Le Bon's view, more easily succumb to the alluring power of "suggestibility" during these particularly heated moments. In doing so, they lost their rational will and became entranced in much the same way that a hypnotized subject became susceptible to the suggestions of the hypnotizer. What emerged, according to Le Bon, was a crowd "unconsciousness" or "group mind" that possessed its own opinions, values, and beliefs, often in contrast to those of the individual. Under these conditions, the individual's "conscious personality has entirely vanished; will and discernment are lost."[46] In upholding many of the gender biases of his predecessors, he contended that women were particularly sensitive to this crowd psychology because they tended toward emotional "extremes."[47]

Although it would have been possible to consider the "group mind" as existing external to the individual, Le Bon did not frame it as such. Unlike a mystical spirit whose power was conventionally thought to be tied to some metaphysical realm or entity, he assumed the group mind to be entirely a product of the faculties contained within the individual mind. After all, submitting to the crowd unconsciousness rendered one "the slave of all the unconscious activities of his spinal cord."[48] It did not entail fusing one's internal identity with an entirely separate, external one. Instead, it involved acquiescing to the alternate identities and impulses that existed within a subject's own mind in ways that mirrored the subconscious thoughts and actions of others. In short, "group mind" was an emergent by-product of self-hypnotizing individual minds that, upon entering highly "suggestible" states, forewent rational impulses of individual control in favor of the emotional impulses that group members held in common.

Irrespective of whether professionals explained trance as primarily psychological or physiological, or a blend of the two, most researchers and theorists of consciousness during the late nineteenth century joined in the effort to challenge metaphysical explanations of experience, whether religious or Romantic. While most Americans would not consider science to be entirely at odds with religion until the twentieth century,[49] it is clear that over the course of the nineteenth century that many scientific thinkers had begun to retreat from belief systems that relied on the primacy of a spirit world, deity, naturalized numen, or any claims to higher powers or deep universal truths that challenged a materialist or mechanistic view of the world. If these thinkers were not entirely antitheological or antimetaphysical,[50] they nevertheless effectively erased any element of spiritual doctrine from the new science of emotional experience. In its place, they posited that, while the experience of unusual or mysterious phenomena may give the illusion of a metaphysical reality, these were actually the result of psychic or bodily changes.

The Radical Empiricism of William James

Despite the accelerating inclination toward internalization in modern social science, a few scholars nevertheless strove to find compatibility rather than contrast between the different modes of experience. Chief among them was William James, who for a time would become the most influential psychologist in America. The investigation of trance, variously construed, had been a longtime interest of James. In 1882, already fascinated with altered forms of consciousness, he intentionally breathed nitrous oxide, whereupon he experienced an "immense emotional sense of reconciliation" in which "the centre and periphery of things seem to come together. The ego and its objects, the meum and the tuum, are one."[51] The merging of subject and object incited in James an "intense metaphysical illumination," from which he concluded that "Hegelism was true after all"; a dialectic synthesis of opposites was achievable, as was the fusion of self with other. Later he would claim, "Our normal waking consciousness, rational consciousness as we call it, is but one special type of consciousness, whilst all about it, parted from it by the flimsiest of screens, there lie potential forms of consciousness entirely different. We may go through life without suspecting their existence; but apply the requisite stimulus, and at a touch they are there in their completeness, definite types of mentality which probably somewhere have their field of application and adaptation."[52] By the fall of 1884, James had helped institute the American Society for Psychical Research, which established committees to investigate supernatural phenomena, including those associated with trance mediums. By the 1890s, he was writing and lecturing on topics such as automatism, hypnotism, hysteria, multiple personalities, demoniacal possession, and genius. By the early years of the twentieth century, he began expounding his ideas in a variety of formats, including in a lecture series at the University of Edinburgh, a pioneering publication called *The Varieties of Religious Experience*, and his ongoing courses and publications while at Harvard University.[53]

To a certain extent, James accepted materialist explanations of experience. After earning an MD from Harvard Medical School at the age of twenty-seven, where he specialized in anatomy and physiology, he worked for a time as a brain researcher, regularly accumulating empirical data and developing scientific conclusions based on surgical dissection. Some of his best-known theories were grounded in biological materialism. These included his postulation that emotional experience is the result of the mind perceiving physiological responses to an internal or external stimulus. Only the perception of changes in the body created identifiable feelings; for instance, the production of tears actually preceded the feelings of sadness.[54]

Despite his grounding in materialism, though, James accepted that the mind also influenced one's experience, and in this regard, he was convinced that parallel sets, or what he eventually called "streams," of consciousness existed within the mind of an individual. The theory itself had been broadly outlined earlier by Frederic W. H. Myers, a member of the English Society for Psychical Research, who had postulated the existence of additional sets of "subliminal consciousness" in the peripheral regions beyond normal awareness.[55] The notion of a multiplex of consciousnesses would become endorsed by an array of psychologists around the turn of the century, including Boris Sidis whose work, as discussed earlier in this chapter, distinguished between waking and subwaking selves. (Eventually, "subconscious" and "unconscious" would become the primary terms used to identify the different types of multiplex consciousness.) As an ardent supporter and popularizer of the notion of multiple consciousnesses, James was happy to explain subjective consciousness as integrally linked to the individual mind and body.

Yet, notwithstanding his interest in the more internal sources of experience, James was decidedly not a reductionist. Indeed, he was somewhat open to more conventionally metaphysical explanations of experience—those that involved objects that existed outside of the individual. When he was a child, his own father had associated with many mystically minded thinkers of the day, including the Christian theologian Emanuel Swedenborg and Ralph Waldo Emerson, with Emerson becoming the young James's godfather. This background distinguished him from most of his scientific contemporaries and seemed to make him more willing to synthesize physiological and psychological explanations of experience with spiritual ones. His effort to resolve these different considerations came not by rejecting the principles of science, but rather by pushing them to their limit. In this way, James diverged from the French philosopher August Comte's notion of positivism—an increasingly influential approach to scientific inquiry at the time—which required conclusions to be based on objectively verifiable, empirical observations of material entities (including human bodies). Instead of a positivist empiricism, James encouraged a "radical empiricism" that also gave equal attention to those phenomena subjectively experienced by the mind (and therefore not objectively verifiable by others). This theory expanded the definition of empiricism to include sensory perceptions, thoughts, feelings, and experiences of metaphysical phenomena. James considered these as part of what he called science's "unclassified residuum," and he believed they should be given credence despite the impossibility of having an outside party objectively verify them.[56] Contrary to many of his colleagues, he averred that science provided no convincing reasons why empiricism should only be applied to the material world. Pure positivism, he suggested, was philosophically incomplete and unjustifiably narrowed the scope of knowledge.

Wary of relying too heavily on what he believed to be fallible yet institutionalized opinions, James asserted that the truth and value of any explanatory theory of experience should be determined only by the efficacy of its results. (This approach would eventually be enshrined in his philosophy of pragmatism, which he developed toward the end of his career.) Under this logic, if the experience of engaging with a divine or metaphysical force substantially improved the moral and aesthetic quality of one's daily life or the interactions between people, he contended that it was no less valid than a neurological explanation of the same experience. Similarly, if an experience of self-expansion or self-transcendence facilitated some aspect of one's personal or community life, it should also be accepted as valuable and a kind of truth in its own right. This point held even if what James called "medical materialism" deemed these experiences nothing more than the "perverted action of various glands."[57] The "rationalistic" claims of modern science, James believed, were "relatively superficial," but they only benefited from the medical discipline's *"prestige"* and "loquacity."[58]

James's radical empiricism and his pragmatic stance did not just help reconcile religious experience with scientific materialism; his theories also embraced conventional understandings of self-transcendence as potentially valuable.[59] Eventually, he would come up with a morally neutral term, "transpersonal,"[60] that served as an etic label for any kind of intensely emotional experience in which an individual's ordinary understanding of self is felt to be temporarily lost, expanded, or transcended. As with previous labels for ecstasy, the term "transpersonal" also involved a powerful experience that could potentially transform the interior life of those who experienced them by revealing a sense of knowledge unknown to the normal intellect.[61] There is no evidence to suggest James attended any Holiness or Pentecostal revivals around the turn of the century, but if he had done so, he would have almost certainly labeled the participants' experiences of spirit possession as transpersonal.

James's lack of exposure to Pentecostal events and the like perhaps partly explains why he also wrote little about the relationship between music and transpersonal experience. There is also a chance the psychologist was "tone deaf." Although he had entertained the idea of a career in visual arts as a young man, James was known to be unresponsive and indifferent to music at the best of times and rarely felt compelled to write about it, much less attend a concert.[62] What little he did write about music, however, suggested that he believed melody, harmony, rhythm, and lyrics all had an important role to play in the experience of self-transcendence. In *The Varieties of Religious Experience*, for example, James acknowledged that musical sounds, along with "words, effects of light on land and sea, odors . . . , all bring [mystical experience] when the mind is tuned aright."[63] He also wrote of a subject who used a musical metaphor to describe his own ecstasy: "It was like the effect of some great orchestra, when all the separate notes have melted away into the swelling harmony that leaves the listener conscious of nothing save that his soul is being wafted upward, and almost bursting with its own emotions."[64] By publishing these few phrases, James seemed to acknowledge music's power to induce a sense of soulful transport among certain individuals. He would have likely elaborated his observations and insights on the topic if he had more opportunities (and inclination) to attend deeply moving performances where musical expression was strongly tied to mystical feeling.

The Entrenchment of Psychology

Despite William James's prestige within the scholarly community, his theory of radical empiricism never gained wide currency among his peers, colleagues, and students—most of whom chose instead to rely on more internalizing interpretations of consciousness.[65] They included people like James L. Corning, a prominent American neurologist, who developed a keen interest in the therapeutic potential of musical trance. Starting in the 1890s, Corning began to treat people with emotional and behavioral conditions by playing music for them as they entered into hypnotic states or progressed through various phases of sleep and presleep. Hypnosis and slumber were eminently comparable, Corning believed. Both arose as regular waking cognitive processes became dormant, and both involved the loss of one's autonomy and self-control. Likewise, both opened up access to the subconscious, which Corning ascertained to be the psychic location in the mind where morbid thoughts were situated, and from which they could be eliminated.[66] He suggested that, at the level of subconscious awareness, a person was "open to the full suggestive power of impressions . . . [and] the absence of that inhibition which is the penalty, so to speak, of full consciousness."[67] The style of music, in his view, was crucial to the therapeutic efficacy of hypnosis. Corning himself thought the operas of Wagner and other forms of Romantic music served the purpose best, at least for patients of a more sophisticated background.[68] (For an uneducated clientele, he suggested songs with simple melodies.[69]) His ultimate goal was to produce pleasant feelings within the drowsy or somnolent person, possibly even affecting his or her dreams, all of which were thought to improve the subject's disposition during waking hours.

These "musical vibrations," as Corning called them, were administered to patients through an elaborate arrangement of apparatuses and techniques developed by Corning himself. He would cover much of the head of a patient with a leather and canvas hood, while metal cups were placed over the ears, serving as rudimentary headphones. Each cup had a small hole that was attached to a piece of rubber tubing that connected back to an Edison cylinder phonograph—the source of the music (see fig. 4.3).[70] The function of this apparatus was to enhance the desired signal while reducing other environmental sounds that might disrupt the focused listening experience. On some occasions the musical treatment was accompanied by soothing and pleasant visual displays, thereby creating a "dual appeal to the vast affective life" of the individual.[71] Some of Corning's hypnotic

Figure 4.3. "Musical vibrations" being administered to one of James Corning's patients, using the assistance of a phonograph, an acoustic helmet, and slide projections from a stereopticon. *Source:* Published in James Leonard Corning, "The Use of Musical Vibration Before and During Sleep—Supplementary Employment of Chromatoscopic Figures—A Contribution to the Therapeutics of the Emotions," *The Medical Record: A Weekly Journal of Medicine and Surgery* 14 (1899): 84. Public domain.

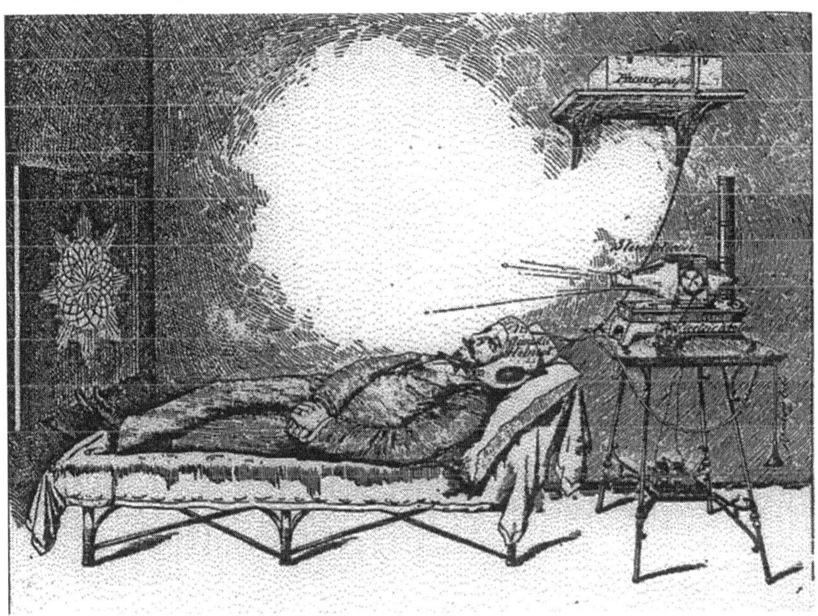

treatments required that the patient be merely drowsy, or presomnolent, while others took place during deep sleep. In an article he wrote in 1899 for the well-known journal *The Medical Record*, Corning reported that his musical therapy sessions had proven successful. Patients, particularly those who had suffered from depression, demonstrated notable improvements in their waking lives, becoming less melancholy and more active and vigorous.[72] Musical self-transcendence, Corning concluded, could be fruitfully leveraged to produce healthier individuals, at least when directed by knowledgeable medical experts such as himself.

The notion of multiple simultaneous consciousnesses—which provided the conceptual scaffolding for Corning's therapeutic experiments—also shaped the thought of the African American intellectual W. E. B. Du Bois, who refashioned it to serve the moral urgency of racial justice and the psychic complexity of Black empowerment. In his seminal 1903 book, *The Souls of Black Folk*, Du Bois developed his theory of a "double consciousness" that resided specifically within African Americans. He described this condition as requiring African Americans to perceive the world in two different ways: one based on their own values, beliefs, and life experiences, and another that involved the "peculiar sensation . . . of always looking at one's self through the eyes of others," namely white Americans.[73] Although Du Bois did not elaborate what this capacity for second sight might feel like subjectively, his description implied that it might have been experienced as a kind of persistent, self-transcendent experience with a negative valence.

However, Du Bois certainly did not consider this capacity for second sight a supernatural, psychic merger with the white perspective. Indeed, although he had been raised as a religious believer, as an adult he soon developed what he described as "strong questions" about the nature of faith, many of which were encouraged following his matriculation at Harvard University.[74] After traveling to Germany for graduate work, he became a free thinker. As a result, *The Souls of Black Folk* articulated no belief in a metaphysical spirit.[75] Instead, Du Bois's notion of double consciousness was probably at least partly inspired by the theories of consciousness emanating from Europe and America.[76] The term "double consciousness" had itself been used since the eighteenth century as a diagnostic category that eventually included "multiple personality disorders and schizophrenia."[77] Mid-nineteenth-century psychologists including La Roy Sunderland and George Miller Beard wrote about double consciousness as a vacillation between what Sunderland described as "two distinct Individualities, so distinct, that when in one state they have no recollection of the other."[78] William James did not employ the exact term, but he used an equivalent form in his popular textbook, *Principles of Psychology*, when he discussed cases of individuals who alternated between "primary and secondary consciousnesses."[79] A French variation, "*double conscience*," also appeared in Josef Breuer and Sigmund Freud's first chapter of *Studies on Hysteria*, published in 1895.[80] In formulating his own notion of "double consciousness," Du Bois seemed to borrow the basic contours of these earlier theories if not always their specific definitions.

Du Bois viewed the clash of double consciousness less as a metaphysical problem and more as a psychological pathology. In his estimation, African Americans' divided awareness alienated them from other aspects of their own identity. Indeed, "seeing" through the eyes of others, even by means of imagination rather than supernatural clairvoyance, meant looking back on oneself from the perspective of those people who made America a racist society. And attempting to live simultaneously as "a Negro and as an American" could give rise to "a painful self-consciousness, an almost morbid sense of personality, and a moral hesitancy which is fatal to self-confidence," as well as "doubt and bewilderment" and a temptation toward "pretence or to revolt, to hypocrisy or to radicalism."[81] In Du Bois's view, the dual consciousness was unrelenting, the conflict unending. "One ever feels his twoness,—an American, a Negro; two souls, two thoughts, two unreconciled strivings; two warring ideals in one dark body."[82] Such characteristics mirrored many of the symptoms described by Charcot when diagnosing hysteria or other hypnoid afflictions.

Ultimately, Du Bois remained hopeful and called for a way to reconcile these two divergent impulses. References to healthy self-transcendence permeated his discussions. "The history of the American Negro is the history of this strife [between consciousnesses]," he contended.[83] However, it also involves a "longing . . . to merge his double self into a better and truer self. In this merging he wishes neither of the older selves to be lost. He would not Africanize America, for America has too much to teach the world and Africa. He would not bleach his Negro soul in a flood of white Americanism, for he knows that Negro blood has a message for the world."[84] How then to achieve this transracial merger of consciousnesses? While Du Bois did not provide specifics, he implied that the process entailed avoiding any force, either external or internal, that favored one consciousness over the other. This meant rejecting the anti-Black sentiment that permeated mainstream American culture without rejecting that same culture in its entirety. It also meant rejoicing in one's African inheritances without shame or remorse. Du Bois, therefore, yearned not for the transcendence of a single consciousness but for the careful reconciliation of both into a healthily integrated whole identity. In broad strokes, his goals for African Americans aligned with the therapeutic objectives of psychotherapy, which also sought to uncover and integrate pathological aspects of an individual's psyche.

For Du Bois, music had a role to play in this process of reconciliation. He dedicated the final chapter of *The Souls of Black Folk* to the old "Sorrow Songs" of enslaved African Americans, which he said made up the bulk of "Negro folk-songs" in America. For him, these "weird old songs" achieved something of an amalgamation of old and new, Black and white, African and European. Written by enslaved people who were "weary of heart," they became "not simply . . . the sole American music, but . . . [also] the most beautiful expression of human experience born this side the seas."[85] Thus, originating in Africa ("where its counterpart can still be heard"), and adapted to an American context, these songs transcended both to become entirely "human."[86] In Du Bois's view, such music provided a crucial element of "hope" that "America shall rend the Veil [that separates Black consciousness from white] and the prisoned shall go free."[87] He found this hope for reconciliation encapsulated in any number of different songs, including the one whose lyrics he placed at the beginning of a chapter. "I Know Moonrise" spoke of the meeting of different souls after some kind of figurative or literal death:

> I walk through the churchyard
> To lay this body down;
> I know moon-rise, I know star-rise;
> I walk in the moonlight, I walk in the starlight;
> I'll lie in the grave and stretch out my arms,
> I'll go to judgment in the evening of the day,
> And my soul and thy soul shall meet that day,
> When I lay this body down.[88]

Simultaneously sorrowful and hopeful, the words suggested the possibility of joining together two alienated "souls," and in doing so it gestured toward a resolution to the paradox of a double consciousness. Considering his distrust of Christianity, Du Bois probably interpreted the song's lyrical allusions to a meeting of the souls as metaphorical rather than spiritual. As such, what the song seemed to represent for Du Bois was the possibility of a deeply integrated African American identity—one that did not suffer from the feelings of disunity evoked by trying to satisfy two contradictory conscious impulses. It was in this way that Du Bois valued the importance of music, as a therapy to relieve the pathological trance of double consciousness.

Evolutionary Theory

The rise of internalized explanations of unusual experiences of consciousness was only reinforced by the growing, demystifying influence of Charles Darwin's theory of evolution, which ultimately served to devalue the cultural authority of both the religious and Romantic modes. As the British naturalist's ideas grew in popularity among American scientists during the 1870s and 1880s, many observers interpreted them to preclude the presence of an omnipotent God in the development of the natural world. Although Darwin never articulated such a position in his writing (preferring to remain agnostic about the issue),[89] he did become one of the champions of positivism, which effectively circumvented metaphysical interpretations of self-transcendent experience. Darwin also dealt a blow to these perspectives when he argued that natural selection, which involved a combination of chance variation and competition, applied as much to the evolution of emotions as it did to biology and physiology. That is to say, emotions of all varieties arose primarily as animals (including humans) adapted to environmental and biological demands in the interest of species survival. In this sense, Darwin suggested that emotional experiences, such as those associated with self-transcendence, revealed a great deal about natural evolution and nothing at all about the presence of some spiritual force.

Music too, Darwin argued, had an evolutionary origin. It gave scientists insight into how early humans experienced and expressed themselves, divulging much about their mental and physical conditions, but nothing about the presence of a spirit world or sublime will. In *The Expression of the Emotions in Man and Animals*, originally published in 1872, Darwin maintained that the sophisticated melodies and harmonies of contemporary music could be traced back to the very simple vocalizations produced by prehumans during their primitive courtship practices. Investigating the sounds produced by apes, young children, and other animals, he inferred that a kind of protomusic actually predated and precipitated the development of systematized language in the human species. "The progenitors of man," he declared, "probably uttered musical tones before they had acquired the power of articulate speech."[90] Darwin's counterpart, Herbert Spencer, disagreed with him regarding the order in which music and language developed in human history,[91] but Spencer's theories of evolution were no less secular. Despite their differences, Darwin, Spencer, and other natural scientists all agreed on one fundamental principle: human practices and emotions were the result of adaptations to environmental and biological demands in the interest of species survival, not the result of some supernatural or otherwise metaphysical force. By establishing this basic premise, the proponents of natural science helped to collapse several preexisting metaphysical and religious doctrines, paving the way for what historian James Turner calls a "model of new truthfulness"—an areligious, positivistic framework that gained traction in American society.[92]

Some of the strongest assaults on traditional interpretations of transcendent phenomena came during the late nineteenth century. At this time, some evolutionary theorists emphasized that the belief in self-transcendent experience was a central feature of so-called "primitive" human cultures, a characteristic that made it easy for them to categorize this perspective as misguided and illusory. Spencer, for instance, described ecstasy as a form of "insensibility" marked mainly by a "high degree of mental excitement," the stiffening of the body, and the suspension of "voluntary motion."[93] These were mental and physical disturbances, not metaphysical ones. For Spencer, only primitive tribal cultures—such as the Zulu of Africa, the Dyak of Borneo, and the Khonds of India—believed that such phenomena also involved going "astray out of the body" or traveling to supernatural realms.[94] These beliefs, according to Spencer, indicated the "lower states" of such cultures within a hierarchy of social development.[95] From the perspective of modern, scientific-minded Westerners, in his view, such ecstatic experiences took on a "pretend" quality; they were associated with "figurative expressions," and no longer held their "original implication." For the British evolutionist, then, a belief in spiritual self-transcendence helped distinguish slow developing humans from highly developed, civilized ones.[96] During the late nineteenth and early twentieth centuries, this hierarchical view of human development became entrenched in the mainstream of American culture. It often framed primitive beliefs as akin to the immature illusions of children, and it required that white Anglo-Americans emphasize their distance from such forms of consciousness.

The conflation of primitive cultural beliefs, including trance, with the consciousness of children was encapsulated in the recapitulation theory, originally developed by the German naturalist Ernst Haeckel. It stated that the development of an individual human being (ontogenesis) mimicked the species-level evolution of humans (phylogenesis). In the United States, G. Stanley Hall, a Harvard graduate and the first American to earn a PhD in psychology, became the most vocal supporter of Haeckel's theory. Among other things, he found strong parallels between the unusual hypnotic experiences of adolescents and those of "savages," including shared propensities toward "manias, trance, lycanthropy, demonology, and especially in revivals and other great religious movements," as well as "enthusiasm, and fanaticism, . . . frenzies, and calentures." All of these activities, according to Hall, were simply exaggerated "tendencies and characteristics normal to this [adolescent] age" and stage. In this sense, they could be compared to play, which Hall also considered a normal part of the development of both the human individual and the human species.[97]

Many evolutionists believed that musical rhythm represented a crucial feature not only of the early phases of human evolution but also of the trance experiences associated with them. In 1889, the psychologist J. Donovan suggested that rhythm played a strong role in eliciting powerful emotions and "feelings of self-expansion" in both the earlier phylogenetic and ontogenetic stages of humans.[98] For the psychologist Carrie Ransom Squire, rhythm similarly played a central role in the trance experiences of childhood. In her dissertation, published just after the turn of the century, she stated that

> the greater pleasure which children find in rhythm is due to the efficacy of rhythm to set up vibrations in other organs of the body, and the consequent harmonious activity of the several bodily organs. The affective tone increases in proportion as the summation of excitation increases, till a state bordering on ecstasy may be reached. Ecstasy, when it follows upon rhythmical stimulation, is due to a spreading of the excitations to a greater and greater number of centers, till the body and the whole consciousness are set in co-vibration. At such times the rhythm has become automatic, and the attention is directed solely upon the sensations accompanying the diffused bodily movements.[99]

Squire fell short of fully authenticating children's sense of trance, being careful to qualify that the sensations were grounded in bodily changes and only "bordered" on ecstasy. However, the psychologist nevertheless affirmed that rhythms induced physiological and psychological changes that amounted to trance, and that such an experience was an integral feature of childhood. The German philosopher Karl Groos similarly wrote of the power of rhythm and repetition to elicit "trance-like or ecstatic state[s]" during the play activities of early humans.[100] James H. Tufts, a philosopher at the University of Chicago, did not address self-transcendent experiences in particular. However, he came close when he argued that when early tribal peoples engaged in play behavior they often used "common rhythmic action" to both stimulate and reinforce "sympathy and social accord."[101] These feelings of sympathy and accordance suggested, even if they did not directly describe, the same kind of self-transcendence discussed by Donovan, Squire, and Groos. Altogether, these academicians stitched together evolutionary theories with trance experiences to reframe them as the illusory views held by those occupying the early stages of human development.

The Freudian Influence

After William James died in 1910, he would continue to be praised as a leading figure in modern psychology, but his transpersonal theories would gain far less currency than his other more mainstream theories. Indeed, it is telling that James's *Principles of Psychology*, which provided a capacious and insightful overview of psychologists' primary problems, theories, and questions, remained central to the field, while *Varieties of Religious Experience* did not. In James's absence, those who became members of the American Psychological Association and published in the discipline's most prestigious organs rarely wavered from theories that assumed emotion and consciousness—including those involving experiences of self-transcendence—were states unequivocally internal to the individual.[102]

The pivot away from James was accompanied by a growing embrace among psychologists of another theorist, Sigmund Freud. The Viennese neurologist would travel to the United States only once in his life, in 1909, when he went to Worcester, Massachusetts to provide a series of lectures at Clark University, at the invitation of its president, G. Stanley Hall, who headed the American Psychological Association at the time. By then, Freud's writings were already well known to many academics and intellectuals, and following his visit they would quickly grow popular within the larger society, especially following the translation into English of several of his better-known publications.

Whereas James had not been particularly enamored of music, Freud's feelings were both stronger and bleaker. He had reportedly despised music as a young man, and later he came to regard a love of music as reflective of an obsessive disorder in need of treatment.[103] He also feared that its deeply emotional connection to human consciousness might tempt others to treat it as a rival to his own therapeutic methods. His immense influence on his discipline meant that music would remain of virtually no interest to most psychologists for much of the twentieth century.

Freud was also more critical than James of what might be called the external modes of ecstasy, that is to say, those modes that supposed an individual's consciousness could merge with entities in the outside world. He deplored religious ideas and experiences, including ecstasies, as delusions of the mind, and he speculated how they came to occupy such a prominent space in human culture.[104] He also reinforced his field's increasingly commonplace conceit that human consciousness was entirely discrete from its external environment, making statements such as "towards the outside, the ego seems to maintain clear and sharp lines of demarcation."[105] In that sense, for Freud, all experiences of merger with the outside world were actually false projections generated by the internal workings of one's own mind.

From this position, Freud readily accepted the internal interpretations of self-transcendent experience that had been circulating among his colleagues and disciplinary forebearers. As a young professional, he had studied with the leading French theorists, including Jean-Martin Charcot and Hippolyte Bernheim, and his early work correspondingly framed hypnosis as a beneficial tool for accessing the hard to reach corners of a patient's psyche. One of his first books, *Studies on Hysteria* (1895), which was cowritten with his colleague and mentor Josef Breuer, discussed this therapeutic potential at length.[106]

Yet Freud's attitude toward hypnosis would soon bend toward the negative. In fact, before long, Freud lost interest in hypnosis altogether, finding that his theories of it never garnered widespread acclaim and that his corresponding therapeutic practice achieved inconsistent results. Ultimately, he would begin to disparage therapeutic hypnosis as "a fanciful, and so to speak, mystical, aid."[107] (At the time, the word "mystical" was often employed as a term of opprobrium leveled by critics at anyone who was deemed to be out of touch with the modern scientific theories of experience.) Instead of hypnosis, Freud now turned to "psychoanalysis," or "the talking cure" as it would be colloquially called, as his preferred therapeutic method. In this practice, a trained professional typically analyzed the words and gestures of a waking subject in order to infer obliquely the hidden workings of the unconscious mind. It was here in the unconscious, Freud theorized, that an individual's repressed emotions and memories resided, and it was from here that they impacted the waking consciousness and behavior of the subject. A cohort of advocates and authors helped glamorize psychoanalysis to such an extent that by the 1920s it became fashionable in some circles to be in need of Freudian therapy.[108]

Freud's loss of faith in the therapeutic benefit of hypnosis did not mean that he was against altered experiences altogether. Rather, he felt that, when pursued not by patients but by trained psychoanalysts who themselves were educated in the complex workings of the unconscious, these experiences remained perfectly acceptable because such professionals were more capable of manipulating their experiences for therapeutic benefit. It was for this reason that in 1912 he called for psychoanalysts to engage a new therapeutic approach, which involved an " 'evenly suspended attention' in the face of all that one hears."[109] The goal of this particular technique was for the therapist to "give himself over completely" to his unconscious activity and become "like a receptive organ toward the transmitting unconscious of the patient," just as a telephone receiver is adjusted to the signal from the transmitting microphone.[110] This kind of deep attunement between the "evenly suspended attention" of the therapist and the unconscious of the patient exhibited a meditative, almost hypnotic quality itself. And the reassignment of hypnotic experience from patient to psychoanalyst fit with Freud's long-standing proclivity to elevate the cultural authority and agency of the therapist-as-expert. Despite its draw, though, the concept of evenly suspended attention never accrued much traction among early twentieth-century psychoanalysts.[111] They either dismissed the method as unprofessional because it required "hardly any work at all" on the part of the analyst,[112] or they watered it down into a set of vague guidelines that made analysts aware of their own subtle biases or preconceptions when interacting with a patient.[113] Most professional psychologists, it would seem, simply lost interest in exploring the positive potential of hypnotic experience.

Upon failing to embrace evenly suspended attention, Freudian psychologists and psychoanalysts had few options other than to cast trance experiences as pathological, primitive, or both. Freud himself provided a rich foundation for such a perspective, having elaborated such interpretations throughout his career. *Studies on Hysteria*, for instance, framed spontaneous trance experiences (that were not induced by therapeutic hypnotic methods) as hallucinatory by-products of a tumultuous unconscious overflowing with repressed desires and traumas, often leading to "hysterical psychosis."[114] To support this portrayal, Freud and Breuer's publication described the experiences of several women. Perhaps the best known subject was given the pseudonym "Anna O." She was reported as having regular, vivid daydream-like hallucinations in which she would leave the present reality and enter into an alternate reality of time and space. Anna O. described these experiences as her "private theatre,"[115] while Breuer and Freud would label them as a form of "double consciousness." The latter, they asserted, exhibited a "tendency to dissociation and thereby to the emergence of abnormal states of consciousness" and existed "in a rudimentary form in every hysteria."[116]

Later in his career, Freud would discuss another particular kind of ecstatic experience using language that was less overtly pathological. He called the experience in question the "oceanic feeling"—borrowing the term from his friend Romain Rolland, who had used it in a letter he wrote to Freud in 1927. In the letter, Rolland encouraged Freud to explore "la sensation de l'éternel (qui peut très bien n'être pas éternel, mais simplement sans borne perceptibles)" (the feeling of the eternal [which can very well not be eternal, but simply without perceptible limits]). Freud would embrace the term as as a reference to subjective sensations of "'eternity,' a feeling of something limitless, unbounded," or the experience of "an indissoluble bond, of being one with the external world as a whole."[117] While Freud refrained from discussing such an experience as a form of hysteria, he was nevertheless quick to describe it as a vestige of illusory, infantile experiences that occurred in the early development of a human being before a strong sense of rational individuality could develop. He remained fascinated with such experiences, not least because he saw them as generating the "religious energy" that motivated the world's religions, as well as the sensation of losing oneself while in love. At bottom, however, Freud viewed the oceanic feeling as resting on the same unsound logic as conventional mysticism: it falsely projected an engagement with the internal depths of one's own unconscious onto an external reality. Such confusion, for Freud, was understandable enough in the undeveloped minds of the young, but it was undesirable when this primitive proclivity persisted into what were supposed to be the more rational years of adulthood. Freud himself admitted to never knowingly having such an experience as an adult, and therefore he found it difficult to fully appreciate its importance in the lives of others. For him the oceanic feeling was different from pathological states associated with hysteria, in the sense that it was not known to be generated by repressed trauma or conflicting impulses. However, at a general level, he found both conditions comparable to the degree that they involved experiences in which, using Freud's words, "the boundary lines between the ego and the external world become uncertain or in which they are actually drawn incorrectly."[118]

Freud's rise to prominence only served to further embed what was already by his time a well-established mode of internal trance in American culture. It was a process that had been set in motion centuries prior. In the seventeenth century, this mode was represented by the supporters and theorists of enthusiasm. Over time, it modulated into a more thoroughly secular, usually areligious, and increasingly antireligious interpretation. Although the perspective on trance was associated early on with physiological disturbances within the human body, over the course of the nineteenth century, it progressively became linked to the inner workings of the mind. The external world still had a role to play, for instance through the power of suggestion, but no longer was it considered the actual source or object of self-transcendent experience. Instead, with the rise of modern psychology, unitive experiences with an entity or metaphysical space external to the self were now squarely framed as, at best, a benign illusion and, at worst, a pathological delusion that required attentive treatment. This consolidation of opinion ensured that the internal interpretation of ecstasy would mature into a fully formed mode and a formidable counterpoint to the supernatural and natural modes already entrenched in American culture.

In addition to reframing trance as an immanent mental phenomenon, the internal mode also departed from other perspectives in its relationship to music. Whereas religious and Romantic devotees were thoroughly invested in the power of music to motivate ecstasies, during the nineteenth and early twentieth centuries the scientific-minded elites who popularized the internal mode only occasionally employed musical expression to elicit hypnotic states and the like. Charcot experimented with sound and musical instruments, and Braid and Du Bois accepted the power of song, but during this era it was only Corning who systematically applied music as a way to induce trance. Music, then, remained an occasionally important tool for psychologists, but, especially after Freud's influence on American culture, it did not maintain the same status it had within the other modes.

Despite these notable differences, the internal interpretation of ecstatic phenomena still shared important commonalities with the external (supernatural and natural) modes. Importantly, it maintained a semblance of self-transcendence. Although it largely disabled the possibility of ecstatic mergers with an external deity or spiritual presence beyond the individual, it nevertheless permitted the experience of transcendence between at least two kinds of consciousnesses that coexisted within the same individual. Depending on the specific theory, such an experience could entail a transition or union between an ordinary (waking) consciousness and an altered (sub- or un-) consciousness, or between multiple coequal consciousnesses. In all these cases, there occurred some transcendence of a central locus of awareness, though not exactly a transcendence of the individual as a whole.

The internal mode resembled the supernatural and natural varieties in other ways too. In specific contexts, the likes of Corning, Le Bon, Bernheim, Beard, or Sunderland could easily have characterized the experiences they studied using the same descriptors that William James used to describe common varieties of religious experience: ineffable, noetic (revealing knowledge that is inaccessible through the "discursive intellect"), transient (usually temporary and difficult to sustain), and passive (involving the sense of being acted upon). These, then, were attributes that typified ecstatic states, irrespective of how they were ultimately explained.

The expanding influence of social sciences within American culture starting in the late nineteenth century enabled the internal mode to present a serious challenge to its counterpoints. From about the 1880s onwards, all competing modes of musical ecstasy would be increasingly expected to address the scientific effort to derealize the authenticity of externalized ecstasy in favor of psychological and physiological explanations. Yet those who refused to bend entirely to such empirical arguments or elite theories still had a few options. This is why some doubled down on religious trance, as the Pentecostalists did. Others took a still different approach by uplifting an alternative mode of ecstatic musical entrancement.

Chapter 5

The Carnivalization of Consciousness

On July 22, 1865, an advertisement appeared in the *New York Clipper*, the city's "sporting and theatrical journal," announcing that a young impresario named Tony Pastor was opening a new variety theater in New York City's Bowery district.[1] The Tony Pastor Combination, a wildly popular ensemble of diverse entertainers managed by Pastor, would perform on opening day. While the act featured different dances and comic skits,[2] music remained a central part of the show. Indeed, the advertisement pledged that Pastor himself would grace the stage with "all his NEWEST AND BEST COM-POSITIONS," including "New Comic Songs, Humorous Ballads and Admirable Adaptations."[3] Indeed, music had always run deep for Pastor. Earlier in his career, he had found success as a songwriter and singer and published numerous songbooks for use in stage performances.[4]

A single prominent line in the 1865 advertisement dripped with connotations of self-transcendence. It promised that the performance would produce "ladies in extasies [*sic*] and . . . gentlemen highly delighted."[5] This statement obviously reiterated a gendered distinction, common during the mid-nineteenth century, that framed women as more inclined toward emotion and less able to control themselves than their male counterparts. However, another of Pastor's descriptions made no such distinction, proclaiming that "Tony's company . . . has a galaxy of talent which enraptures the Bowery girls and boys."[6] Beyond the gendered language, what is striking about both of these statements is their utter lack of contextualizing detail. No further information was provided to explain what "extasies" and "enraptures" might actually entail.

How was the reader of the advertisements meant to interpret these experiences? Since such terms were originally borrowed from religion, they may have suggested the possibility of a mystical experience with the Holy Spirit. Or perhaps they instead referenced the sublime experiences of Romantic art music, which also borrowed those terms. For that matter, they may have been alluding to a psychological interpretation of trance—an illusion of the mind, ungrounded in external reality. These were all possibilities, and yet the content and context of the performances did not seem to favor any one reading. Upon admission to the event, patrons were neither required nor expected to find themselves merging with a supernatural god, a naturalized numen, or the hidden reaches of their own psyches. The song lyrics did not betray some hidden preference. Indeed, Pastor's description lacked an attachment to any of the modes described in earlier chapters.

Perhaps, then, Pastor was referring to a different form of self-transcendent experience altogether, one that required no sacred texts or formal philosophy. Or maybe the words were not really referring to *any* kind of self-transcendent experience whatsoever. Long before the 1860s, Americans began to incorporate the term "ecstasy" into their vernacular usage to signify feelings like "excessive joy" or "extreme delight"—a definition that was only loosely aligned with the more radical subjective experiences originally associated with the term.[7] In this sense, the concept of ecstasy became something closer to hyperbole than genuine representation, a rhetorical device used to render a statement more emphatic and vivid. Perceived this way, Pastor's words could have been chosen primarily as a commercial ploy to attract attention, build expectations, and ultimately sell tickets. (Certainly, his shows were wildly popular, attracting what another advertisement described as fifty consecutive nights of "HOUSES CROWDED TO EXCESS."[8]) If one can say anything definitive about Pastor's descriptions of musical ecstasy, it is that they lacked a singular meaning, and this absence of clarity left open the possibility of a multiplicity of readings.

This chapter argues that Pastor's "extasies" spoke to a larger equivocal mode of musical entrancement in America that paralleled, overlapped with, and in many ways counterbalanced the others discussed in previous chapters. This mode always treated ecstasy as something like a double entendre, an experience that remained open to multiple interpretations simultaneously. In one way, it permitted a certain amount of credence to the metaphysical sensibilities entrenched within both the supernatural and naturalized modes, which endorsed the feeling of genuine psychic or spiritual merger with the external world. In another way, it also permitted immanent explanations that portrayed ecstasy as by-products of the individual mind and body. In a third way, it suggested that ecstasy was not quite the experience of self-transcendence at all, whether externalized or internalized, but more a metaphor for intensity or delight. Characterized primarily by ambiguity, ecstasy now simultaneously encompassed different interpretations. It also drew attention to the contradictions between them without necessarily trying to reconcile such differences.

This chapter investigates the roots of the equivocal mode in the premodern Christianity of Europe and its modulation over time under the influences of modernity. In America, it would evolve quickly under the pressures of immigration, urbanization, and industrialization—ultimately finding expression in "rough music," Mardi Gras, and blackface minstrelsy, as well as other commercialized music traditions. Cultural elites who had previously distanced themselves from the people and practices historically associated with this mode eventually came to embrace ambiguous inter-pretations of ecstasy as well, especially when faced with the particular circumstances in which they found themselves during the late nineteenth century and early twentieth centuries. The equivocal mode seemed to thrive whenever meaning-making became fraught, and for Americans of all kinds such conditions were becoming increasingly common in the modern era.

The Deritualization of Ecstasy

The origins of the equivocal mode can be traced back centuries to long-standing religious tensions in Western Christianity. These revolved around the premodern Carnival, a popular event throughout Europe that was originally attached, at least nominally, to Christian doctrine and officially labeled as a religious "ritual."[9] Throughout the Middle Ages and into the early modern era, European Carnival centered mainly around the Christian calendar—particularly the festive season that preceded Lent. Many Europe-ans treated this time, as well as related saints' days throughout the year, as periods of bodily excess involving not only music-making and dancing but also eating, drinking, sexual activity, and hedonistic abandon.[10] Practiced mainly, although certainly not exclusively, by the "lower sorts," these displays often included intentional mockery of authority through ribald humor or role reversals—for instance, by temporarily elevating a man of low status to the role of "lord of misrule" or "king of the fools," or dressing men as women.[11] Many of these customs were on display in *The Fight Between*

Carnival and Lent, the famous 1559 painting by the Flemish artist Pieter Bruegel the Elder (see fig. 5.1). All of these practices shared a common goal of upending normative notions of order, hierarchy, and stability. According to the Russian literary critic Mikhail Bakhtin, a "carnivalesque" sensibility not only characterized certain holidays but it also informed much of the expressive culture of the medieval and early modern eras in general.

It seems likely that the dissolution of social boundaries that characterized Carnival could have easily been paralleled by a similar breakdown of the psychic boundaries that normally confined notions of selfhood. This much is suggested by the account of a traveler to Wales in the twelfth century, who described a scene of emotional and physical abandon that he

Figure 5.1. Detail of the musician from Bruegel's *The Fight Between Carnival and Lent*, which includes an elaborate depiction of revelers celebrating Carnival activities. *Source:* Pieter Bruegel the Elder, *The Fight Between Carnival and Lent*, 1559, oil on wood panel. Original located at Kunsthistorisches Museum, Vienna. Public domain.

encountered: "You can see young men and maidens, some in the church itself, some in the churchyard and others in the dance which wends its way round the graves. They sing traditional songs, all of a sudden they collapse on the ground, and then those who, until now, have followed their leader peacefully as if in a trance, leap up in the air as if seized by a frenzy."[12] The "trance" and "frenzy" of the Welsh participants aligned with Carnival rites described elsewhere across Europe. They also corresponded with what Bakhtin describes as the " 'carnivalization' of human consciousness"—a process that, in creating "the possibility of a complete exit from the present order of this life," ultimately erased "limits between man and the world."[13] According to the literary critic, this process of dismantling the boundaries of the self through music, dance, and reveling was also "closely combined" with excessive eating and drinking.[14] Such "grotesque" acts of carnal consumption, Bakhtin argued, effectively enabled one's personal body to transgress "its own limits," by swallowing, devouring, and rending apart the external, material world.[15] By assimilating the "cosmic elements: earth, water, air, and fire; he [Man] covered them and became vividly conscious of them in his own body. He became aware of the cosmos within himself."[16] Carnival, then, not only provided the ecstatic opportunity to blur self and other, it also, in Bakhtin's view, empowered participants to initiate this process, configuring the carnival "trance" as a liberatory opportunity for self-expansion rather than a circumscribed act of self-surrender to some greater force.[17]

Yet, if Carnival offered, as Bakhtin suggested, some alternate opportunity for metaphysical *ekstasis*, it also involved a strong element of theatrical make-believe. Playacting informed the role reversals, masking, and other forms of social abandon that typified Carnival practice. Violence, when it was enacted by participants, was often of a mitigated or simulated variety, for instance in the form of food fights. The holiday always held a degree of play, fun, and performance, and its ethos embraced mockery in both senses of the word—both as derision and imitation. It was this artificial quality that helped medieval powerbrokers accept Carnival practices as (mostly) lighthearted transgressions to the status quo rather than radical rejections of it. As ersatz upheaval, then, Carnival could moreover be regulated to ensure that it remained only a temporary, symbolic challenge to social and ecclesiastical hierarchies.

Yet these qualities of play and performance also made it difficult to discern a single interpretation of Carnival performance. The twelfth-century description mentioned above seemed to acknowledge this ambivalence, qualifying the descriptions of trance and frenzy by preceding them with the words "as if." Did the young men and maidens actually experience a sense of entrancement? Were they really seized by a frenzied power outside of their control? Did they experience any kind of profound expansion of their subjectivities, as Bakhtin described it? Perhaps so. Or perhaps the witness was using exaggerated language for rhetorical purposes in order to accentuate the intensity of their behavior. A lack of detailed description meant that no possibilities were closed off entirely. This ambiguity would remain a hallmark of the carnivalesque consciousness into the modern era.

Ultimately, the uncertain, topsy-turvy ethic that imbued Carnival's psychic, social, and cultural activities would place it at odds with the church hierarchy and its more formal religious stance. Without clear-cut boundaries, playful transgression always risked erupting into radical revolution. While medieval elites sought to regulate and limit Carnival's liberatory impulses (including its challenge to social and ecclesiastical hierarchies),[18] by the early modern era elite fears of disorder had grown and Carnival was now viewed as a serious existential threat to the social status quo and the very principles that undergirded Christianity. In short, Carnival was deemed a profane counterculture masquerading as a holy rite. The fears of church leaders were somewhat founded. According to Bakhtin, there was an aspect of the carnivalesque consciousness that laughed in the face of religious doctrines and practices, abiding only by "the laws of its own freedom."[19] And those laws made it easy to reject "God, authority and social law."[20] They also made carnivalesque activities more inclined toward conflict or rebellion. Wary of such antiauthoritarian tendencies, church leaders decided to demote Carnival from a religious "ritual" to a profane "festivity."[21] This official deritualization process was, in effect, a way for ecclesiastical elites to disassociate Carnival from religion altogether, leaving it to float alone as a secular phenomenon with few ties to Christian doctrine or, for that matter, to any other sacred entity or ideal.

Despite the demotion, popular support continued for Carnival, and its (now unholy) festivities proliferated among common people within the secular sphere even amid official efforts to condemn, prohibit, and regulate them out of existence. What resulted was a diverse array of vernacular traditions of song, dance, and sensory overload, social inversion, role reversals, humor, sport, and sacrifice, as well as masking and costuming.[22] While these practices were no longer always tied together through association with a single set of holidays or rituals, the varied traditions that developed nevertheless shared common "carnivalesque" attributes. In this way, Carnival—along with its self-transcendent possibilities—progressed away from a specific calendrical event toward what Peter Stallybrass and Allon White call "a mobile set of symbolic practices, images and discourses which were employed throughout social revolts and conflicts," not to mention celebrations.[23] Across early modern Europe, including the British Isles, the carnivalesque sensibility proliferated in a myriad of folk customs, including those called "charivari" and "skimmington."[24]

Dancing manias also broke out across Europe at this time, which religious commentators condemned as a kind of madness that was probably sent as a curse from St. John or St. Vitus. During these events, peasants, mechanics, and housewives were known to leave their normal duties to join in wild scenes of what must have seemed to onlookers like senseless abandon. They formed circles hand in hand and danced for hours together, often accompanied by elaborate visions of spirits and holy figures.[25]

Many carnivalesque folk customs maintained a strong reliance on sound, including most notably those associated with "rough music." Sometimes treated interchangeably with terms such as skimmington, charivari, callithumpian, or ran-tan, rough music involved the performance of raucous sounds that created psychic upheaval with the goal of maintaining community cohesion or affecting social transformation. Often it was performed by a procession of concerned neighbors in order to authorize or condemn certain kinds of behavior among community members. This included sanctioning unusual marriage pairings (e.g., second or third marriages) or confronting more deplorable activities, such as adultery and spousal abuse. If mellifluous music was meant to represent a social and moral status quo, then rough music symbolized its opposite. It was characterized by cacophonous playing (noisy enough to be hardly considered music at all) using not only conventional instruments such as drums and horns but also pots, pans, basins, spades, bells, and tongs, as well as much whooping and hollering by the participants. The resulting din, which could often be heard for up to a mile away, was intended to cause a psychic disturbance; the term "charivari" is thought to derive from the Latin word *caribaria*, which meant "headache."[26] Ultimately, it acted as a form of local, community-enforced justice.[27] As such, it became a secular exercise that tacitly acknowledged a vague moral order without holding a strict allegiance to a metaphysical entity.[28]

From time to time, certain folk customs' metaphorical assaults on authority were also known to unravel into serious physical aggression. Indeed, descriptions of revels transforming into rebellions go back at least to the sixteenth century.[29] It was during these kinds of tensions that the term "emotion" came into colloquial usage among English speakers.[30] Initially associated with

Figure 5.2. An eighteenth-century depiction of "rough music" by English satirist William Hogarth. The image portrays an unruly procession gathering outside the home of a domineering wife and subservient husband, who are mocked by their neighbors. Rough music is played by members of the procession as they bang on pots and pans, blow a horn, and squeeze a bagpipe. *Source:* William Hogarth, *Hudibras Encounters the Skimmington*, 1726, etching and engraving. Metropolitan Museum of Art. Drawings and Prints Collection. Public domain.

any disruption or movement, either physical or social, the term soon came to denote public agitations and civil unrest, precisely the kinds of popular revolt and political action that, as Stallybrass and White claim, were nearly inextricable from connotations of Carnival for centuries to come.[31]

Carnival Comes to America

When Europeans migrated to America they brought carnivalesque customs with them. Thomas Morton, for example, modified such practices to orchestrate an uprising. After settling in Massachusetts in the 1620s as a senior partner of a trading venture led by Captain Wollaston, Morton took advantage of the captain's absence one day by arranging a feast for the local indentured servants. There, he explained to them that they would be sold into slavery in Virginia unless they rose up against their master.[32] Promising them freedom from servitude and equal partnership in a new colony, Morton convinced many and managed to usurp Captain Wollaston's leadership and start a new colony based on his own utopic vision. William Bradford, the governor of Plymouth Colony at the time, wrote disparagingly in his diary of these antics, decrying how Morton and his consociates "fell to great licentiousness and led a dissolute life, pouring out themselves into all profaneness." They set up a maypole, "drinking and dancing about it many days together" and composed "sundry rhymes and verses, some tending to lasciviousness, and others to detraction and scandal." For Bradford, a strict moralist, "pouring out" oneself through dance, verse, and other illicit practices was a deplorable act of exuberance and would have constituted nothing less than an insult to God. It is on these grounds that Bradford claimed Morton "became lord of misrule and maintained (as it were) a school of atheism."[33]

The activities Bradford described and the language he used were all derived from the carnivalesque traditions of European folk celebrations. They were full of music and dance; they were "profane" and "dissolute," and, by using phrases like "pouring out themselves," they strongly hinted at experiences of self-transcendence. The sincerity and intentions of the participants were also up for debate. Morton, for his part, defended his activities as "harmless mirth" and undeserving of such strong condemnations.[34] In all these ways, the episode remained firmly aligned with the ambiguous, carnivalesque sensibility inherited from Europe.

Morton was not an anomaly. It is fair to say that, even amid condemnation from local religious elites, carnivalesque elements were regularly transplanted to Britain's American colonies and evolved there over the centuries. Dozens of examples come up in the historical record, including a rough music incident on January 21, 1757, when a group of yeomen farmers rioted in front of the house of another yeoman, Joseph Smith, at Cortlandt Manor, New York. The rioters approached Smith's house at about two o'clock in the morning armed with "Clubs, and Staves Fiddles French Hornes & making hideous and umber [dark or earthy] noises," whereupon they proceeded to terrify Smith for several hours.[35] During times of civil unrest and political discontent, including the revolutionary years, dissenting groups often recruited rough music for political goals. On July

4, 1778, for instance, in the midst of the Revolutionary War, a ran-tan crowd marched through the streets of Philadelphia and eventually stopped at a tavern where genteel men and women presumed to be Loyalist leaning were attending a private ball.[36] Instead of the usual array of pots and pans and other makeshift noisemakers, a soldier beat out a rowdy march on his drum, perhaps the "Rogue's March" or the "Whore's March" (both tunes that were customarily played as delinquent soldiers or "idle" women were being expelled from military encampments during the eighteenth century).[37] One of the participants in this group was a woman. She marched at the center of the rowdy crowd, with her hair coiffed high above her head in mockery of the elite female hairstyles of the day. Practices of social and sonic inversion were obviously on full display, and perhaps so too were experiences of psychic transport.

During the first half of the nineteenth century, a wide range of carnivalesque folk customs continued to flourish along the East Coast of the United States, invigorated by the arrival of millions of laboring immigrants from Ireland and Germany.[38] Philadelphia in particular became known as a hotbed for carnivalesque festivities. These included the German "Belsnickle," a Christmas Eve celebration that involved a noisy party centered around a Saint Nicholas figure who dressed in furs and perambulated around town shaking bells (often cowbells), holding a club or whip to frighten children, and sometimes delivering small gifts. Belsnickle was followed by the Mummers Parade on New Year's Day, which involved masked and costumed revelers ringing bells and banging pots and pans as they marched throughout the city. In Philadelphia, as well as in New York and Boston, rough music processions became widespread in the form of callithumpians. Appearing around the same time of year as mummers parades and sharing their proclivity for noisy celebration, callithumpian bands also dressed in outrageous costumes and mocked, intimidated, and jousted with both the higher and lower social strata—wailing on drums, whistles, horns, pots, pans, and kettles as they went.[39] As the Philadelphia *Public Ledger* reported, "Some [callithumpian troupes], . . . extravagant in the expression of their pleasure, were tricked out in burlesque garb and whimsical costume, and excited much amusement in the crowd, while musical instruments, from the trumpet to the penny whistle, enlivened the air with sound."[40] Since all of these customs were rooted in Carnival and shared a common emphasis on music and noisemaking, the term "rough music" might fairly be said to stand in as an appropriate synecdoche for the entire category of activities.

The North was not the only area with rich carnivalesque customs. These were also present in Southern communities along the Gulf Coast, particularly in New Orleans and Mobile. Originally colonized by the French and oriented more to the Caribbean, these places originally celebrated Carnival in a manner that was markedly different from that in the North. One defining feature of the Southern tradition was the importance it placed on masked balls. Such events had been popular among members of the European aristocracy since the Renaissance and were transplanted to Louisiana by colonial elites and plantation owners during the eighteenth century.[41] By the mid-eighteenth century, society balls, banquets, and masquerades—all of which combined poetic verse, music, and dancing—were held regularly during the days and weeks leading up to Mardi Gras, the day before Lent.[42] Many of these were also relatively cosmopolitan affairs, open to different classes, including the local-born Creole elite and occasionally free or enslaved people of color.[43]

New Orleans' status as a mature colonial enclave within the French sphere of influence made its Mardi Gras customs relatively distinct from those practiced elsewhere in North America.[44] However, there was also some notable overlap with folk customs popular in areas of the continent that were more influenced by the British Isles and Northern Europe. For instance, the informal and street-oriented practices associated with the rough music of New York or Philadelphia were not unknown in New Orleans. In that city in 1804, an immense charivari confronted Madame Louise de la Ronde de Almonaster in order to protest her marriage to her unpopular new husband. Her house was "mobbed by thousands of the people of the town, vociferating and shouting with loud acclaim . . . many in disguises and masks; and all with some kind of discordant and loud music, such as old kettles, shovels and tongs and clanging metals. . . . All civil authority and rule seems laid aside."[45] Similar kinds of raucous events regularly took place in the communities of the North around this time.

The United States' purchase of Louisiana in 1803 provided new opportunities for blending the Northern and Southern carnivalesque cultures. For instance, on Christmas Eve of 1831, Michael Krafft, a cotton broker from Pennsylvania living in Mobile at the time, strung together several cowbells and attached them to a rake. Described by a contemporary as "a fellow of infinite jest and . . . fond of fun," Krafft clattered around town with his noisy contraption and eventually gathered a crowd. His boisterous antics that night were not simply the brainchild of a waggish and intoxicated mind.

Instead, it is likely they also drew on the German rough music tradition associated with "Belsnickle." This much seems likely when considering that Krafft was originally from the Philadelphia area, where Belsnickle was already popular, and that his name also suggests a German ancestry. Regardless of its source, however, Krafft's activities that night had a resounding influence on the carnivalesque culture of America's Gulf Coast. A local group in Mobile created the "Cowbellion de Rakin" Society, a carnival club inspired by Krafft's raucous displays. When business growth occurred in New Orleans starting in the 1830s, many members of the society moved to that city and brought with them the Cowbellion customs, thereby initiating a new blossoming of Mardi Gras street culture.[46] In 1835, an observer in New Orleans recorded boisterous scenes of commingling races, genders, and classes that were infused with a carnivalesque sensibility: "Men and boys, women and girls, bond and free, white and black, yellow and brown, exert themselves to invent and appear in grotesque, quizzical, diabolical, horrible, humorous, strange masks and disguises. . . . [They] march on foot, on horseback, in wagons, carts, coaches, cars, & c. in rich confusion up and down the street wildly shouting, singing, laughing, drumming, fiddling, fifing, and all throwing flour broadcast as they went their reckless way."[47] Mardi Gras' noisy musical confusion seemed to evoke the breakdown of boundaries between conventional social identities, if even for a short time. Perhaps, too, it perpetuated the ecstatic breakdown of psychic boundaries.

Although certain carnivalesque folk customs persisted relatively intact in the United States throughout the nineteenth century, many also underwent profound transformations in response to the demands of industrialization and immigration. This was particularly apparent in America's largest urban centers, such as New York, Boston, and Philadelphia, where traditional carnivalesque customs were regularly adapted for commercial purposes. America's and Western Europe's growing capitalist economies during this period encouraged the creation of strict barriers between laborers' work and leisure. This division profoundly affected notions of time and space. Certain hours of the day and certain days of the week became reserved exclusively for labor, as did certain spaces like the factory. Sometimes these delineations proved incompatible with the more spontaneous revels associated with preindustrial rough music. So, America's laboring classes increasingly endeavored to extract the carnivalesque sensibility out of its traditional customs and adapt it to more strictly defined times and spaces.[48] Now, secular working-class "leisure activities" became centered in saloons, popular theater, and social or vocational clubs, all of which catered to the after-work period.

Figure 5.3. A historical illustration of Mardi Gras celebrations in New Orleans. *Source:* B. West Clinedinst, *Promiscuous Maskers on Canal Street—New Orleans Mardi Gras*, 1893. Published in *Frank Leslie's Illustrated Weekly*, March 2, 1893, 137. Public domain.

Blackface Minstrelsy

According to the musicologist Dale Cockrell and the social historian Eric Lott, the folk theatricals associated with traditional rough music created a cultural setting in which a new commercial festivity could flourish in America: blackface minstrelsy.[49] Adapted into a new form of leisure by the emerging working class in the industrializing cities of the North, many features of minstrelsy were actually rooted in the carnivalesque tradition. These included a strong reliance on music. Although the stage performances of minstrelsy involved a series of comic skits and variety acts, some of its biggest attractions comprised dances and songs, including the massively popular tunes "Jump Jim Crow," "Zip Coon," "Oh, Susannah," and "Dixie." Moreover, most of the famous minstrel personalities became renowned for their musical performances—including prominent stage personalities like Thomas D. Rice, Dan Emmett, and E. P. Christy, and a slew of songwriters. According to one estimation, minstrelsy was approximately two-thirds musical.[50] Its other carnivalesque inheritances included an emphasis on spontaneous civil participation (often taking place at night), a strong support base among the laboring classes, and connotations of rebellion, role reversal, artificiality, playacting, and, of course, an association with upending normative psychic activities and notions of self.

These shared qualities meant that the songs and activities of the minstrel theater were easily recruited for the more rowdy antics associated with rough music protest. The series of antiabolitionist riots that swept through New York in 1834 exemplified this musical convergence between the stage and street. On July 9 of this year, a mob descended on the New York house of the abolitionist Lewis Tappan—shattering doors, windows, and furniture as they went. Elsewhere that night, several thousand whites collected at the Chatham Street Chapel, the headquarters of the revivalist and abolitionist Charles Grandison Finney, where an antislavery meeting was planned for that evening. Finding the meeting place empty (the abolitionists had already fled), the crowd might have normally resorted to the noisy drumming, blowing of horns, and the banging of pans that were the mainstay of rough music. This time, though, they drew on the minstrel stage tradition to convene their own mock "emancipation meeting." The performance included satirical renditions of the kind of abolitionist rhetoric that might have occurred there that night, an ersatz sermon from the pulpit presented in a "mock Negro style" typical of the minstrel stage, and finally the performance of "Jump Jim Crow," minstrelsy's signature song of that era.[51] Not far away, several thousand rioters also broke into the Bowery Theatre after discovering the owner, an English-born abolitionist by the name of George Farren, had earlier made an anti-American remark, complaining "damn the Yankees; they are a damn set of jackasses and fit to be gulled."[52] Disrupting a play that was in progress, the throng erupted into rowdy demands for Farren's apology.[53] The tension grew until the manager unfurled an American flag and the well-known blackface performer George Washington Dixon quelled the crowd with the popular minstrel songs "Yankee Doodle" and "Zip Coon."[54]

Did the New York rioters experience a self-transcendent frenzy during those summer nights in 1834? Concerned observers seemed to leave open that possibility even if they never fully substantiated it. *Niles' National Register*, one of the most influential newspapers in the United States at the time, described New York's rioters who destroyed abolitionist churches as hundreds of "infuriated devils" who tore out the windows and doors of nearby houses with "fiend-like" rage.[55] Another observer declared that New York was drowning in "an ocean of madness."[56] Such phrases echoed similar accounts of uproarious rough music in Philadelphia from Christmas Eve the year prior, which described how "gangs of boys and young men howled and shouted as if possessed by the demon of disorder."[57] Those events fell on Christmas Eve and were intended as celebratory folk customs. However, an article in the city's *Daily Chronicle* complained that they too brimmed with a "riot, noise, and uproar [that] prevailed, uncontrolled and uninterrupted in many of our central and most orderly streets."[58]

In some ways, an artificial quality pervaded the ecstatic connotations of these descriptions. The words "as if" reappeared in the latter description, just as they had in accounts of carnivalesque possession from previous centuries. Likewise, while the word "infuriated" was once associated with spirit possession by Greek Furies,[59] such connotations were already considered archaic by the nineteenth century. Thus, the experiences of rough music and minstrel revelers could easily have gestured obliquely to the process of soul possession without actually engendering it.

Nevertheless, suggestions of authentic entrancement might have also been detectable by contemporaneous readers. A phrase such as "possessed by the demon of disorder" was explicit enough, and it would have evoked the same kind of language used by devout evangelicals and other believers in genuine soul possession. Moreover, while the ecstatic connotations of the term "infuriate" were largely outdated, the same could not be said for a related term, "furious." Indeed, the 1828 edition of *Webster's Dictionary* defined the word as "raging; violent; transported with passion."[60] Connotations of self-transport also imbued definitions of "madness," another descriptor used in the *Niles' National Register* article. *Webster's* described the term as "a state of disordered reason . . . in which the patient raves or is furious."[61] Indeed, the dictionary provided the "madness of a mob" as a potent example of this definition. The word "riot," too, had similar connotations of passionate abandon, linked as it was to "act[ing] or mov[ing] without control or restraint."[62] Therefore, the language used by journalists to describe the activities in New York in 1834 played with the possibility that a musical mob's unruly behavior was directly tied to the ecstatic experience of its participants.

Market Economy Equivocation

Ambivalent interpretations of musical self-transcendence did not only appear in rough music, minstrelsy, and other direct outgrowths of the Carnival tradition. They could arise anywhere a single, coherent explanation of experience was difficult to discern. Hence, under uncertain circumstances, equivocal framings of self-transcendence could even be ascribed to music that was formally tied to metaphysical modes of transcendence—especially the traditions associated with Romanticism.[63] Chapter 2 has established that Romantic music could foster mystical interpretations that were understood to be completely genuine, such as when John S. Dwight's journal described the Germania Musical Society's 1853 American debut of Beethoven's Ninth Symphony as a "sublime whole."[64] The naturalized mode of musical ecstasy, however, did not represent the experiences of all who attended that storied concert. Dwight himself admitted as much, confessing that although the performance was eminently successful, it was impossible to deny that there were "all shades of opinions and feelings about it, from utter indifference to unqualified enthusiasm."[65] Another review of the same performance, this time by a local businessman and avid patron of art music named Henry Higginson, was more cynical: "Dwight, I believe says . . . [the performance] was very fine, beautiful, etc., but no doubt most of the audience thought it terribly dull."[66] Ecstatic encounters with the "sublime whole" were not obviously apparent to everyone who patronized the show that night.

The famous American virtuoso, Louis Moreau Gottschalk, who performed and composed music in the Romantic style, demonstrated his own equivocal attitude toward the ecstatic experience of art music. Writing down his thoughts in 1862, the pianist described his frenzied experiences while playing show after show during a relentless touring schedule across America:

> I have become stupid with it. I have the appearance of an automaton under the influence of a voltaic pile. My fingers move on the keyboard with feverish heat. . . . The sight of a piano sets my hair on end. . . . Whilst my fingers are thus moving, my thought is elsewhere. Happier than my poor machine, it traverses the field, and sees again those dear Antilles, where I gave tranquilly a little concert every two or three months comfortably, without fatiguing myself, where I slept for weeks the sleep of the spirit, so delicious, so poetical, in the midst of the voluptuous and enervating atmosphere of those happy lands.[67]

The description avoided any mention of a transcendent spirit, but did it reject the possibility of self-transcendent experience altogether? On one hand, Gottschalk felt his bodily movements take on an automatic quality, and he also felt transported through time and space—back to the Antilles during a peaceful period earlier in his life. On the other hand, Gottschalk's movements only had the "appearance" of being automatic, and his transports might have occurred within his "thought" rather than as a result of some literal escape from his body. In this regard, he may have considered his transport an imaginary engagement with the outer reaches of his personal consciousness rather than with a metaphysical entity. Although Gottschalk's experience was undeniably powerful, his vague description made it impossible to categorize as a true self-transcendent experience. It could have just as easily been what Samuel Johnson earlier called an "invisible riot of the mind."[68]

How could Gottschalk's equivocal understanding coexist alongside Dwight's metaphysical interpretation of musical ecstasy within the setting of the concert hall? The reasons for this transition were sundry and related to large economic and cultural changes that were occurring throughout American society. One major factor stemmed from the rise of a capitalist, market-driven economy. With the pursuit of profit as its primary goal, capitalist enterprise often encouraged an indifference toward conventional worldviews and belief systems that elevated spiritual values over economic ones. In the *Communist Manifesto*, Karl Marx described this disenchanting view. "All that is solid melts into air, all that is holy is profaned," he declared in reference to the consequences of capitalism. Indeed, the accumulation of capital thrived on the principle of commodification—a process that involved extracting activities and goods from their original frameworks of meaning and making them amenable to new contexts where they could be sold and bought in a market, preferably by the greatest number of highest-paying customers. The underlying goal of profitability was best served if commodities required little other than payment from their potential consumers. Therefore, whether someone understood a commodity as part of a rich tradition of sacred meaning was ultimately less important than one's willingness to pay for it.

Market culture had a strong historical congruence with the carnivalesque sensibility. From its beginnings, carnivalesque culture had been staged in marketplace settings and linked with market activities that also fostered the dislocation of cultural practices and products from dominant spiritual and social traditions.[69] This certainly helps explain why the outgrowths of Carnival, including minstrel theater, became easily commercialized throughout North America and especially in the industrialized areas of the Northeast. The sheer strength of the market economy in America, however, also meant that it indirectly applied something of the carnivalesque ethos to any tradition it touched. Importantly, this included Western classical music and religious music traditions. During and before the eighteenth century in Europe, the music of these traditions was not heavily commercialized. At that time, small groups of aristocrats and religious elites constituted the principal patrons of the music, and they often commissioned musical works in order to support their own spiritual, aesthetic, and social interests.[70] But by the nineteenth century, especially in the United States, the "public" came to replace the old patrons.[71] Moreover, those who constituted the public grew in number, as the rise of economies of scale encouraged the mass production of sheet music and its distribution to diverse regions of the country. Consequently, if it was to be sustainable, music's composition and performance—regardless of its provenance—had to accommodate the demands of an increasingly expansive community of paying individuals. To complicate matters more, new patrons of commercial music—many of them recent immigrants—often hailed from a variety of cultural, linguistic, and educational backgrounds, and, as such, they were not necessarily trained in the subtleties of religious or Romantic musical appreciation.[72]

Accordingly, music in general became increasingly framed as a cultural commodity that could be simultaneously open to a diverse array of different meanings. Opening musical meaning to the possibility of double entendre could be achieved in a number of ways. One involved simply advertising and selling songs from different genres or traditions. For instance, in sheet music catalogs and in shops, entrepreneurs took songs associated with sacred traditions and sold them, quite literally, alongside decidedly profane minstrel tunes, thereby creating a sense of equivalency.[73] Another way involved the pervasive use of "musical borrowing," a technique that typically involved taking an existing melody and setting it to new lyrics (although it could also include applying an original melody or music style to recognizable lyrics). Yet another way to evoke multiple musical meanings, and the method most relevant to this chapter, was through the use of ambiguous language that invited varied interpretations.

Trance at the Turn of the Century

Although Americans of all kinds skirted the boundary between belief and unbelief in musical ecstasy during earlier parts of the nineteenth century, it was not until the period spanning from about the 1880s to the 1920s that this carnivalesque dynamic became fully accepted by cultural elites in the United States. It was at this time, according to the historians T. J. Jackson

Lears and John Higham, that bourgeois Americans began to yearn increasingly for authentic experiences amid nagging concerns that the spread of industrialization, secular science, and technology was creating a setting of unnaturally soft decadence—or what was often called overcivilization.[74] Certainly, many agreed that the comfort and stability afforded by such programs were worthy of veneration. Yet many of the elites who benefited most from such luxuries also believed they exacerbated a sense of artificiality in modern life, thereby sapping one's will and perverting one's decisiveness—much like the medical anesthetics that became prevalent during this era.[75] During the Gilded Age, fears of this modern languor were often associated with the illness "neurasthenia"—a condition marked by physical and mental exhaustion, fatigue, anxiety, and depressed mood, often without an identifiable physical cause. For an antidote to this condition, many concerned elites were motivated to look beyond comfort and stability toward more intense sensations that seemed altogether more real.[76] In this context, activities associated with premodernity, such as historic arts and crafts techniques, seemed satisfying precisely because they were strenuous enough to counterbalance the synthetic softness of modern life. The yearning for authenticity could rarely be fully satisfied, but elites pursued it nonetheless, thus perpetuating and entrenching the dynamic of in/authenticity.

For many bourgeois Americans, notions of self-transcendence became a focal point for this tension between authentic and artificial experience. This was certainly the case for William James, who has been described in more detail in chapter 4. In many ways, James embodied much of the overcivilized dissatisfaction typical of his class and generation. Born into a wealthy family in 1842, he had a privileged childhood and access to all the comforts of modern living, yet he developed neurasthenia as a young man and began longing for an invigoration of his will. Initially, he found curatives to his depression by seeking out travel and adventure, such as when he took a year out of his studies at Harvard to explore the Amazon River with the naturalist Louis Agassiz.[77] As he matured, though, James also came to recognize that mental transports could be just as uplifting as geographical travel. This realization prompted his experiments with nitrous oxide and his investigations as a member of the American Society for Psychical Research. Yet, even as he became fascinated with the possibility of genuine transcendence, he remained dedicated to reconciling these interests with the theories that proliferated among the professionals in his own field—theories that treated experiences of transcendence outside the individual as entirely artificial. In this context, his theory of radical empiricism and his notion of transpersonality might be understood as part of an attempt to synthesize modern science with his personal yearning for authentic, mystical self-transport. James was, of course, only one of the best-known American elites who became fascinated with authentic experience amid a perceived pandemic of artificiality. Literary Romantics, philosophical vitalists, avant-garde artists, all participated in this fin-de-siècle movement.[78] So too did music performers and enthusiasts.

This ambivalent perspective certainly appeared to inform the ecstasies of Lucy Emerson Lowell, a young woman from Massachusetts who attended a Richard Wagner opera festival at Boston's Mechanics Hall on April 15, 1884. On that evening, *Götterdämmerung*, the last installment of Wagner's four-part Ring cycle, was being performed. As the daughter of a district court judge from an illustrious Massachusetts family,[79] twenty-four-year-old Lucy had enjoyed both the means and opportunities to hear Wagner's music before. This was, in fact, her second night in a row attending the festival. Yet Lowell's familiarity with the music did not mean that her experience that night would be ordinary. Transcribing her impressions in a personal diary, Lowell would later recount the exquisite sensation that overcame her upon hearing one tenor, Walter Winkelmann, perform his prized song. "Never in my life was I so perfectly carried away, excited, overcome," she enthused. And part of this musical captivation seemed to have been shared by the performer himself. Lowell wrote: "[It] was perfectly superb. . . . Winkelmann sits all the time perfectly unmoved & as tho' in a dream (almost)."[80] A great number of others in attendance at Mechanics Hall must have shared something of Lowell's feelings, as she noted that one of the final performances became "a scene of wild enthusiasm [such as] I've never seen." After the performance, the audience called the singers back on stage repeatedly and met them each time with a standing ovation bursting with exuberance. The audience, in Lowell's words, "shouted & cheered, stamped, waved handkerchiefs & were actually beside themselves. Cousin Lewis & I rushed forward so that we were close to them as they went up & down fr. the stage & they [the singers] were tremendously excited & pleased."[81] Lucy Lowell's description was replete with ecstatic terminology. Her feeling of being "carried away" or "overcome" in extraordinary ways suggested a vast reframing of her boundaries of selfhood. Likewise, her account of the audience being "beside themselves" brimmed with connotations of personal transcendence: the term implied a simultaneous splitting of self into two adjacent parts.

How could these ecstasies be categorized? Wagner and his admirers had long equated experiences of his music with the Romantic sublime.

And Lowell could certainly have been familiar with the philosophies of nature associated with Romanticism. Her family was recognized by others to be "renowned in all its branches for learning and integrity." She was also the granddaughter of the famous educator George Barrell Emerson and a distant cousin of Ralph Waldo Emerson.[82] If this family connection was not enough to guarantee her familiarity with Romantic philosophies of the sublime, then her bourgeois upbringing may have been. Indeed, by the 1880s, the patrician elites on both sides of the Atlantic had become current with Wagner's theories.

Yet, despite her possible knowledge of Romantic metaphysics, Lowell's descriptions never referred to Emerson's attunement with "the currents of the Universal Being"[83] or Wagner's ecstatic encounters with the "universal currents of Divine Thought."[84] Lowell's account also avoided conventionally religious language. Nowhere did she speak of the concert experience as some unitive experience with the will of Nature, God, or some other metaphysical essence. Instead, she employed unconventional descriptions, such as being "carried away" or "beside" herself, which were vague enough to be attached to any mode of musical ecstasy, or none at all.

Lowell's descriptions also wavered on the authenticity of such experiences. On one hand, she was "perfectly" carried away and the audience members were "actually" beside themselves, both adjectives that suggested a degree of genuineness. Her exceedingly detailed descriptions, evocative vocabulary, and admission that the events were unlike anything she had ever seen or felt also suggested that she approached them earnestly. On the other hand, certain elements of her writing subtly questioned the authenticity of some of the self-transcendent phenomena that night. This was most obvious in her description of Winkelmann's performance, who she described as sitting on the stage "as tho' in a dream (almost)."[85] The words "as tho'" and "almost" suggested that the great tenor's dream state was not necessarily literal in the strictest sense. Lowell's account, therefore, remained expressly open to the possibility of real self-transcendence even as some of her language invalidated such sensations.

Lilli Lehmann, the famous German soprano who performed regularly at the New York Metropolitan Opera during the late nineteenth century, also found a similar double quality in the character of musical transports. For her, operatic music, especially that of Wagner, elicited deeply moving experiences: "In the whole world there was nothing that could free greater emotions in me than [my *Tristan und Isolde*] performances in New York, where the audiences sat still for minutes, silent and motionless in their places, as though drunk or in a transport, without being conscious that the opera was over."[86] Like Lowell, Lehmann referred to the profound power of musical transport but also qualified it with the words "as though" and compared it to drunkenness, opening the possibility that audience ecstasies may not have been truly psychic or soulful journeys beyond personal subjectivity, but merely intoxicated delusions that resembled such experiences.

Lucy Lowell and Lilli Lehmann were not alone in their ambivalent yearning for authentic ecstasy through music. Their basic impulses were paralleled by the German philosopher Friedrich Nietzsche. Instead of looking to the overcivilization of his own era, however, Nietzsche maintained that Western culture had been sapped of its vital force for more or less its entire existence. In his first book, *The Birth of Tragedy* (published in German in 1872), Nietzsche traced the origin of an enervating force back to the rationalism of Socrates, which he maintained had provided the central ethos of the entire Judeo-Christian intellectual tradition up until modern times. As an antidote to what he saw as the West's compulsion toward reason-making, Nietzsche looked to the precepts and practices of the pre-Socratic era—particularly those associated with preclassical Greek tragedy—which he believed better balanced the natural human instincts and drives. It was during this ancient period, Nietzsche contended, that a proper equilibrium existed between what he called the Apollonian principle, which impelled order, restraint, discipline, and form, and the Dionysian principle, which prompted disorder, abandon, dissolution, and formlessness. The former reinforced distinct boundaries and therefore a sense of duality and individuality, whereas the latter smashed individuality and united it with "primordial existence."[87] In this sense, human access to the Dionysian impulse was an ecstatic act, and represented nothing less than a merger with the heart of creation.[88] In much of his writing, Nietzsche highlighted music—especially wordless music—as the purest expression of the Dionysian principle.[89] Just as the ancient practitioners of Dionysian rites employed melody, rhythm, and harmony to instigate the "annihilation of the ordinary bounds and limits of existence,"[90] so too, Nietzsche believed, did the best concert music of his own day.

Yet Nietzsche's views on ecstasy also remained slippery. For one thing, he was always limited in his ability to describe it, because he had to use language, an Apollonian tool, to convey what was ultimately an ineffable Dionysian quality. By his own logic, the most he could do in his philosophical writings was to gesture toward an amorphous experience. This condition made it impossible to identify a definitive object of ecstatic experience, whether supernatural, natural, or internal. Ambiguity was all that remained. To make matters more nebulous, Nietzsche also firmly believed in the possibility of counterfeit ecstasy. His changing views on Richard Wagner's music evinced this perspective. The two Germans had been one-time friends, and Nietzsche's early writing lauded Wagner's music as a "dance-song of metaphysics" that exposed listeners to the "vast void of cosmic night" and "the heart-chamber of the world-will" in ways that had them "collaps[ing] all at once" and "flying irresistibly towards [their] primitive home."[91] In short, he upheld Wagner's music as embodying the boundary-dissolving Dionysian principle. Yet the friendship between the two men eventually soured, and, by the 1880s, several of Nietzsche's publications performed a drastic about-face, and he chastised the composer for adhering to beliefs that actually stymied a properly balanced Dionysian ethos. In two treatises, *The Case of Wagner* and *Nietzsche Contra Wagner*, Nietzsche railed against Wagner for his German nationalism, anti-Semitism, and affinity for Christianity. As for his operas, Nietzsche now condemned them for being far too theatrical: "Wagner makes one ill—What do I care about the theatre? What do I care about the spasms of its moral ecstasies in which the mob . . . rejoices? What do I care about the whole pantomimic hocus-pocus of the actor? . . . [Wagner] was essentially a man of the stage, an actor, the most enthusiastic mimomaniac that has perhaps existed on earth, even as a musician."[92] What repulsed Nietzsche about Wagnerian operas was, among other things, their infusion of an artificial "pantomimic" quality into the "moral ecstasies" of the audiences—amplifying their emotion without directing their focus. In Nietzsche's view, Wagner's obsession with undirected theatricality and emotionalism is what made him a "mimomaniac"; moreover, he was a "master of hypnotic trickery" and his music was incapable of eliciting true Dionysian trance.[93] Regardless of Wagner's aspirations toward the sublime, then, Nietzsche ultimately found his music to fall short. Authentic ecstasy, it would seem, resided uncomfortably close to its false counterpart.

Whether Lucy Lowell or her peers were acquainted with Nietzsche and his writings in the 1880s is unknown, and perhaps unlikely. During the early decades of his career, the philosopher's intellectual influence was not yet directly felt in North America. Few English speakers west of the Atlantic were particularly amenable to the German's writings during the 1870s and 1880s; and his *Birth of Tragedy* would not be translated into English until 1909.[94] Both Nietzsche and Lowell, however, nevertheless seemed to share a longing for ecstatic release through music while simultaneously accepting the impulse that sought to diminish ecstasy to nothing more than an "as if" experience.

☙

When compared to its counterpoints in earlier chapters, the equivocal mode discussed here stands somewhat on its own. Although the supernatural, natural, and internal interpretations of musical ecstasy diverged from each other in numerous ways, what they all shared was a relatively clearly defined object of experience. To be sure, the members of different traditions conceptualized their chosen object differently, using words such as God, Nature, animal magnetism, the unconscious, and so forth. They also varied in the ways they related to these objects. Nevertheless, they all articulated the basic character of their experience in relatively certain terms. Advocates of the equivocal mode described in this chapter, by contrast, provided no such certainty. They permitted not only the possibility of multiple objects of ecstatic experience but also none at all. In this sense, the equivocal mode stands out as a true alternative to the others.

The reasons for this difference are historical. Rooted in medieval European Carnival and its outgrowths in America, including different traditions of rough music, blackface minstrelsy, and Mardi Gras, this mode can be linked back to what Bakhtin called the " 'carnivalization' of human consciousness," a process that enabled the breakdown of psychic (as well as spiritual and social) norms and challenged conventional notions of stable selfhood at the same time that it embodied an attitude of playful performance, mockery, and imitation. In the absence of clear frameworks of meaning, it transformed the ecstatic loss of subjectivity into a relatively dubious experience. What emerged was the possibility of an objectless ecstasy that involved the subjective experience of moving or expanding through metaphysical space or time, or both, but with no identifiable union with other identifiable entities exterior to the individual. This self-transcendence was unmoored from its foundations and available to be employed simply for its own sake.

The rise of such an alternative form of entrancement in America was related to a number of factors. One can be attributed to the growing number of immigrants who openly pursued vague ecstasies during the nineteenth century. Laborers from Europe, whose affiliation to carnivalesque musical practices went back centuries, enlarged the population of the United States. A second factor involved the dissociative logic of the market economy, which also grew in size and strength during that period. The market process of commodification, which impacted all musical traditions, disconnected songs and performances from conventional frameworks of meaning and opened them up to different contexts, audiences, and interpretations. A third factor was the growing participation of cultural and economic elites, such as Lucy Lowell, in the carnivalesque perspective. The impetus for this elite involvement was certainly related to the other two factors, but it also had its own distinct origin in upper-class and middle-class ennui. If these three factors entrenched the equivocal mode of musical ecstasy as a mainstay in American culture during the nineteenth century, a fourth factor would establish it as arguably the most prominent interpretation of ecstatic experience during the next century.

Chapter 6

The Industrialization of Ecstasy

In 1903, the German writer Gustav Kuhl underwent a profound experience upon attending a musical masquerade ball on Jekyll Island, one of the Sea Islands off the coast of Georgia. The event, he recalled, took place amid a group of "hilarious" dancers who moved noisily to the "peculiarly jerky and clappering sounds" of two African American men playing a piano and a double bass in a "rag-time" style. The music was played in a distinctively American style known for its syncopated rhythms, which began to appear in published forms in the mid-1890s and inundated the music publishing industry by the early 1900s.[1] While ragtime was played mainly in the Southern and Midwestern United States, it was also present on the country's East and West Coasts and became a trend in Europe as well. This is how it came to be known by Kuhl, a scholar and lover of music, who traveled to the U.S. specifically to investigate the country's ragtime phenomenon for an upcoming publication.[2]

He recounted that, when he entered the ballroom on this particular occasion, his senses were "captivated against [his] will by the music, which seemed to be produced by a little army of devils to [his] left."[3] Astounded that anyone could move in time to such a cacophonous rhythm, he also admired the dexterity of the musicians. Before long, Kuhl found that the music once again became irresistible:

> Suddenly I discovered that my legs were in a condition of great excitement. They twitched as though charged with electricity and betrayed a considerable and rather dangerous desire to jerk me from my seat. The rhythm of the music, which had seemed

> so unnatural at first, was beginning to exert its influence over me. It wasn't that feeling of ease in the joints of the feet and toes, which might be caused by a Strauss waltz, no, much more energetic, material, independent as though one encountered a balking horse, which it is absolutely impossible to master.[4]

Only with the assistance of two other people was he able to wrest control of his own feet. The victory would be short-lived, however. Every time the music started up, Kuhl's body began jittering with "rhythmic compulsion" even before his ears registered what was happening.

In many ways, Kuhl's experience was exemplary of the equivocal mode of ecstasy. Read one way, it could be interpreted as a metaphysical form of ecstatic experience involving some kind of merger between himself and a spiritual other, whether supernatural or natural. Much of his description suggested that his ecstasy originated in the music itself, particularly the rhythm, which Kuhl described as overriding his own sense of self-control. At other times, the German indicated that the special ability to possess his bodily functions may have stemmed from the power of the musicians rather than the music. As he described it, the music was produced by "a little army of devils"—a term that could have referred to some supernatural beings, but, given the levity of the writer's tone, was more likely a figurative representation of the people playing the music. In this sense, Kuhl's ecstasy involved some kind of psychic attunement between himself and the musicians.

Racial dynamics, of course, may have inflected this rapture. After all, Kuhl was white and of European descent, while the musicians (not to mention the other dancers) were African American. The music's heavily rhythmic, syncopated style—what was, at the time, sometimes called a "ragged" rhythm—was a common feature of music produced by Black Americans from St. Louis, New Orleans, and elsewhere. The origins of this style were undoubtedly diverse;[5] but they were at least partly rooted in the ring shouts, Congo Square dances, and other music traditions of the African diaspora in the Americas.[6] (Certainly, ragtime's syncopated style, which one practitioner described as "playing two different times at once," perhaps approximated the effect of African polyrhythm even if it did not fully achieve it.[7]) As such, Kuhl's emotional merger with the sounds and psyches of the musicians might have also constituted some kind of racial ecstasy, whereby his white identity perhaps absorbed aspects of the African American performers' consciousness. Despite their differences, all of these variations fit within the metaphysical traditions of supernatural and natural self-transcendence.

Other aspects of Kuhl's description, however, reveal that his experiences may not have been quite so metaphysical after all. Although it recruited the language of transcendence, his description also accommodated a psychological view that grounded all human experience within the mind of the individual. This much was indicated when Kuhl wrote that "there is no magic connected with" ragtime. This disenchanted view was also instantiated by his further efforts to explain the human nervous system's role in heightening the experience of music. Specifically, he described how one's body "involuntarily . . . strive[d] to oppose and balance the weakly accented principal beats of the bar" in syncopated music. Musical experience, from this perspective, arose as a result of one's own involuntary (perhaps subconscious) effort to compensate for the production of irregular rhythms in one's aural environment. It was a response to the suggestive sway of the external sounds. In Kuhl's particular case, the efforts of his mind and body to interpret or attune to the ragtime rhythms compelled him to dance. Understood in this way, did Kuhl's experience actually constitute a metaphysical form of self-transcendence? Kuhl seemed to provide two contrasting answers to this question. One cast his actions as something like a spiritual enthrallment to the power of music or musicians; the other explained them by looking at the internal workings of his mind and body.

It was no coincidence that ragtime music prompted an ambivalent experience of entrancement in Kuhl. Not only was it one of the most well-liked music styles of its era, but it was also one of the most heavily commercialized ones, and Kuhl's early exposure to it had occurred via a rapidly expanding music industry that emerged in the United States during the last decades of the nineteenth century. This chapter argues that America's commercial music and entertainment industry became a powerful vehicle for advancing the equivocal mode. Between the 1880s and the 1920s, the producers and consumers of commercial "popular music" helped institutionalize it within American mainstream culture.

As amply demonstrated by historians such as David Suisman, Timothy Taylor, Karl Hagstrom Miller, and Russell Sanjek, entrepreneurs and corporations in search of popular appeal developed techniques, technologies, and strategies that augmented the cultural influence of mass entertainment from about the 1880s to the 1920s.[8] This process involved numerous music industry professionals, but came to center mainly around those affiliated with Tin Pan Alley, an erstwhile neighborhood and then coterie of music publishers and songwriters based in New York City that greatly influenced popular music of the United States during this fifty-year period. The process also involved, among other things, the industrialization of sheet music production, the refinement of song advertisement techniques, the commercialization of automated music players, and the expansion of copyright laws.[9] Songwriting techniques changed too during this period, as writers put greater focus on making songs hummable, memorable, and "catchy" enough to invite repeated listening or performance.

This chapter contributes to the literature by demonstrating how, by promoting music and seeking popular appeal, participants in America's burgeoning music industry highlighted the self-transcendent qualities of the music while remaining open to multiple interpretations of altered experience. Many kinds of people eagerly contributed to this effort, including performers, producers, advertisers, audience members, and journalists.

These figures explored the multiple possibilities of ecstatic interpretation, hedging their claims, diffusing certainty, and leaving space for both belief and denial. Their repertoire of strategic ambiguities was partly inherited from earlier forms of commercial entertainment in America, including minstrelsy, where a carnivalesque sensibility had long held sway. It was also related to new innovations that accompanied the rapidly industrializing era around the turn of the twentieth century. The approach could take many forms. Some, for example, engaged a metaphysical perspective by referring to conventional supernatural and natural numens, such as deities and spiritual forces, while others advanced a more social interpretation that—while still metaphysical—saw transcendent opportunities between the individual consciousnesses of different people. Some aligned with a psychological perspective, which approached trance as an internal experience generated by the unusual workings of the mind and body. All the while, many also referenced ecstasy more as a metaphor for emotional intensity than as an experience of self-transcendence. In advancing these multiple meanings, participants in the music industry made use of new media technologies, while others relied primarily on older formats of live stage performance. As with Kuhl, some discussions also took on specifically racial overtones, particularly when they involved white Americans pursuing ecstatic experience vis-à-vis the music most closely associated with (if not always performed by) African Americans—including ragtime and its stylistic successor, jazz.[10] In all of these settings, Americans of varying backgrounds participated in the discourse of ambiguity surrounding self-transcendent experiences.

Spiritual Rapture

At times, industry professionals advanced the equivocal mode by drawing on the metaphysical language of religion and spirituality. While popular songs occasionally referenced Christianity, they more often leaned toward Romanticism's spirit of Art, which held music as a quasi-sacred source of transcendence. Yet even as they invoked the metaphysical, these expressions remained tethered to the playful artifice of mass entertainment—offering visions of the numinous cloaked in the language of make-believe.

This paradox was in full force among aficionados of opera. Because of its nineteenth-century association with the Romantic sublime, opera had long demonstrated an enduring attachment to naturalized interpretations of self-transcendence. However, the authenticity of that mode, which had already been thrown into question by the likes of Lucy Lowell in the late nineteenth century, became consistently challenged by members of the commercial music industry starting in the early twentieth century. This became apparent in appraisals of performances by Enrico Caruso—not only the best-known tenor of his day, but probably the most famous musical performer of his era. Born in Naples, Caruso began touring and recording throughout America and Europe in 1902, and much of his international renown was achieved after he took a multiyear contract to sing for the Metropolitan Opera in New York City in 1903. According to one newspaper article in the *New York World* from this period, "a motley but spellbound audience" would gather in the lobby outside the door of Caruso's rehearsal parlor as he prepared for opening night of the opera *Rigoletto*.[11] At times, the admirers could be seen "gushing rapturously" and humming along to the muffled melodies that emanated from his room. What was the source of their spellbound rapture? A clearer answer came two years later, following a London performance of *Madama Butterfly*, when Thomas Burke wrote rhapsodically about the "captivating" power of Caruso's voice. The singer's dulcet tones, remarked Burke, educed Caruso's "first fine careless rapture" and sprung forth with a "lyric of ecstasy," an "incomparable magnificence . . . [and an] intangible quality that smites you with its own mood."[12] Although Burke's encomium never went so far as to affirm a mystical encounter with Nature, his words described something close to a sublime spirit of music.

A *New York Telegraph* article from 1910 went a step further, invoking conventional religious terminology to describe the ecstatic power of Caruso's operatic voice. The author described his performance as "not only good, great, overwhelming," but also "divine."[13] Even before the concert began, experiences of overwhelming divinity were ostensibly at work, as the spectator felt an "irresistible impulse" driving him from the street into the concert hall. That impulse seemed to originate not from him, but from the music. After witnessing the great tenor perform, the author's "soul was transfixed" by the "magnificent, enthralling" performance. According to the article, these sensations of soul possession appeared to be shared by the performer himself. While onstage, Caruso could be seen "singing, and pouring forth the music with such abandon, with such devotion" that he appeared to become a "vessel" for the music and for "God's voice." As powerful as it was, this overt affirmation of sincere metaphysical (and indeed religious) ecstasy was not actually typical of most descriptions of musical performances during the early twentieth century.

In many instances, journalistic descriptions of musical experience—even those affiliated with Caruso or opera in general—were written in ways that remained open to both sides of the debate regarding the "possessive" power of music. This included the 1914 *New York Herald* headline that proclaimed "Caruso Carried Away by His Song."[14] Did the music's capacity to "carry away" Caruso actually involve some unitive experience with an external musical force? The headline insinuated as much, yet the content of the article also pointed to the mental effects that arise from hypnotic suggestion. It described Caruso as "carried away" not only by music but also by "his own emotion" and "on the waves of . . . emotional intensity." These latter descriptions seemed to remain open to the possibility that his experience was not rooted in the external world or the spirit of music but in the workings of his own mind and body. Such conflicting assumptions remained unresolved in the article. Indeed, the fact that both points were left unelaborated suggests that the author seemed happy enough to leave the debate open.

Neither Caruso nor his preferred genre of music held a monopoly on the rhetoric of spiritual entrancement in American popular music. Some observers followed Gustav Kuhl in locating such a power in ragtime and other popular styles of the 1910s. These included the writers of "coon songs," which were written by white and Black songwriters alike and combined elements of ragtime rhythm with crude, parodic caricatures of stereotypical African American culture. One example, Harry A. Fischler's 1910 piece "Chili Sauce," included lines such as "You coons is in a trance, Dis is no place to dance . . . But I am willin', Chilun' to take a chance, On dat entrancin' melody," and "Don't try to stop yo' twitchin', keep on, dat tune's bewitchin'."[15] Another song, "That Coon Town Rag," written by Herm

Siewert and Gilbert Perry in 1913, also told of the rapture experienced by a group of African Americans listening to a ragtime tune:

> Down across the border lives a rag-time coon,
> Who plays upon a banjo such a rag-time tune
> We slides and sways when he sings and plays
> Such a syncopated trance,
> And I'm gone, that's all, when that man does call
> "Come on hon' an' do dat dance."[16]

As with the other songs, the full complex of metaphysical, psychological, and metaphorical interpretations could be appropriate to the "bewitchin'" effect and "syncopated trance" they described. Both songs also framed the music itself, in this case an "entrancin' melody" and "a rag-time tune," as motivating the trance experience. Lastly, the songs' lyrics and obvious use of the so-called minstrel show dialect cast African Americans as the susceptible to ecstatic release, a trend in much popular music of the day.

Even the most famous Tin Pan Alley songwriters participated in a discourse of ambiguity surrounding self-transcendent experiences. These included Irving Berlin, who avowed that his success as a songwriter was partly due to his ability to write a tune that "grips each member of the audience."[17] Similarly, the accomplished British pianist and composer Francesco Berger, in writing about his introduction to American jazz music in 1919, described how "the music . . . thrilled and overpowered" the listener.[18] While both Berlin's and Berger's comments suggested the possibility of metaphysical entrancement, they stopped short of fully affirming a genuine achievement of it. The best jazz ensembles, Berger declared, were

> a blend of uncongenial elements, bewildering, exasperating, and yet appealing. . . . Your familiar codes and laws are defied and upset. Your *terra ferma* [*sic*] is withdrawn. You are adrift on an unexplored ocean. The anchor of your traditions, by which you held so reliantly, has failed you. Whether you will ever reach sunlit meadows and shady groves, whether you will ever again safely tread the highroads which your forefathers trod before you, is a question which only Time, the inscrutable, can solve.[19]

Did Berger's use of metaphor—including references to losing touch with solid ground and being set adrift upon an ocean—imply a theory of transcendent experience that was in line with the oceanic feeling popularized by Freud? Did it point toward a sublime encounter that would always exceed the capacity of normal language to describe it? Was it a convenient tool for imagining a mystical experience of spiritual self-transport? Even if one possibility seemed more plausible to the reader, all remained open, and highlighting the paradox may have been precisely what Berger had intended.

Such ambivalence contrasted with the more straightforward psychological analysis of some social scientists. For instance, the German psychologist Ludwig Gruener, and many of his American counterparts, discussed the phenomenological effect of popular music as a purely mental occurrence and diagnosed it as representing an underlying mental illness. In a newspaper article, Gruener wrote that ragtime was akin to a "germ" that makes anyone "dippy" if they become too fond of syncopated melodies. His theory was supposedly derived from studies of the criminally insane, which Gruener took to indicate that ragtime created "mental disease" and "acute mania" associated with hysteria and "idiocy."[20] These conclusions seem to have been based on a logical fallacy: Gruener assumed that if "90 per cent" of inmates at American asylums were "abnormally fond of ragtime," then the musical form itself must be a cause of the disease. Despite the obvious error, the opinion was published and served to corroborate a more general attitude among many American psychologists that considered self-transcendent experiences to be pathological delusions.

For some musicians during the 1920s, the sensations they felt while listening to jazz were completely at odds with Greuner's theories. Instead, they suggested the possibility of a truly mystical merger with some metaphysical entity. Such an interpretation is certainly what the banjoist and guitarist Eddie Condon described as a young man in 1924 when he heard King Oliver and his Creole Jazz Band perform live in his hometown of Chicago. As soon as Oliver lifted his horn to play, Condon reported, "the first blast of *Canal Street Blues* hit me."[21] In this moment Condon, along with his friends Bud Freeman and Jimmy McPartland, felt themselves each losing control of their own individual wills: "[Musical] notes I had never heard were peeling off the edges and dropping through the middle; there was a tone from the trumpets like warm rain on a cold day. Freeman and McPartland and I were immobilized; the music poured into us like daylight running down a dark hole."[22] Transfixed by the improvised melodies of Oliver and his soon-to-be famous bandmate, Louis Armstrong, Condon and his friends experienced the music penetrating them much like the sublime experiences that overwhelmed the most spiritual of American Romantics. To a lesser extent the description was also comparable to evangelical accounts of baptisms by the

Holy Spirit. Condon seemed to recognize such a parallel when he admitted that he and his cohort of fellow aficionados—most of whom would later become well-known jazz musicians in their own right—would often talk about jazz "as if it were a new religion just come from Jerusalem."[23] Such feelings of entrancement did not occur only in the presence of their idols. Indeed, Condon described one of his friends, a musician named Dave Tough, as "possessed" nearly anytime he played the drums.[24]

Yet, for all of his endorsement of metaphysical trance, Condon also provided subtle cues to suggest that these feelings did not always or entirely need to be approached with sincerity. Indeed, when he described his first live experience of the King Oliver band that night in Chicago as "hypnosis at first hearing," Condon may have acknowledged the psychological premise that his experience of musical absorption was a consequence of an excited subconscious mind more than some possession by an outside force. Even if Condon remained a true believer in the spiritual power of jazz, he nevertheless sometimes refrained from treating jazz trance as a sincere and profound experience. For him, music was one of the "two things in the world which obviously were fun" (the other being "girls").[25] This playful attitude even informed his choice of songs. As a young musician, some of the tunes he loved to play included titles such as "Ain't We Got Fun" and "Make Believe."[26] The songs may have symbolized a mindset in Condon that complicated his beliefs in the metaphysical potential of music and trance.

Social Trance

While exploring the fluidity of beliefs in spiritual experiences, many Americans gestured toward the possibility of what might be called *social* trance—the absorption of one's psyche or will into those of other individuals or communities such that the consciousness of the individual is subsumed into that of the collectivity. In many ways, this impulse was a variation of the eighteenth- and nineteenth-century philosophy of sentimentality, which had encouraged tender feelings such as empathy and benevolence to bond together societies of people. Now, in the context of turn-of-the-century commercial entertainment, feelings of social entrancement were also infused with a skepticism that Gustave Le Bon echoed in his writings on crowd psychology.

By the 1890s, Americans even expressed ambivalence about social trance when discussing musical traditions that strongly promoted self-control, such as John Philip Sousa's marching band music, which became popular throughout that decade and beyond (see fig. 6.1). As scholars like Neil Harris, Patrick Warfield, and others have demonstrated, Sousa's background in the military, his cultivation of personal rigor and authority, and his aversion to bodily excess strengthened his reputation as a paragon of masculine discipline.[27] This was, unquestionably, a characteristic that helped popularize his music and earn him his moniker—"The March King." What is less studied, however, is how the bandleader's advocacy for self-control concealed, even relied upon, certain kinds of self-surrender. Indeed, he quietly insisted that his band members give up aspects of their own individuality in the name of higher goals, such as the production of strong, bold, coordinated music. Believing himself the best authority on how to achieve this standard, Sousa was known to be a demanding bandleader, requiring his orchestra to become highly attuned to his every direction. One Michigan newspaper reported that such training enabled Sousa to hold his men "as under a spell," as they responded to his "quiet and unassuming" conducting.[28] In this quotation, as in other instances, the word "as" inflected the statement with a figurative quality that challenged belief in conventional magic; however, it simultaneously suggested that each band member's individuality should nevertheless be mitigated while performing Sousa's songs.

As it turned out, Sousa was fully aware and supportive of something like communal trance during his performances. In his memoirs, the March King admitted as much:

> This is what I am constantly trying to do all the time—to make my musicians and myself a one-man band! Only, instead of having actual metallic wires to work the instruments I strike after magnetic forces. I have to work so that I feel every one of my eighty-four musicians is linked up with me by a cable of magnetism. Every man must be as intent upon and as sensitive to every movement of my baton as I am myself.[29]

Sousa's reference to animal magnetism could have been used hyperbolically for effect, for by the turn of the century, the theory had been discredited in mainstream society. But such language also suggested that the March King believed his own consciousness should coordinate with his band members to the point of fusion.[30] In a press package for the band from 1895, the distinguished actor Otis Skinner expanded this capacity for psychic possession, claiming that it extended from the music through Sousa and not just to his band but also to his audiences: "Watch him . . . in his abandon to the character of the music . . . , and his magnetic capture of his audience."[31] Some observers were, in fact, immensely pleased by his display of authoritarian control over others in pursuit of musical perfection. One review from 1899 purported that "to be able to command men is a gift possessed by comparatively few, and the great general is no more difficult to discover than the great conductor. . . . Not the least enjoyable thing about a Sousa band concert is the masterly control of the leader over the human instrumentality before him."[32] It would seem, therefore, that Sousa's aural and visual projection of individual strength, discipline, and refinement was accompanied by loud echoes of psychic merger with orchestras and audiences alike.

Such an effect would not have been lost on Irving Berlin, who, despite his reputation as a Tin Pan Alley tunesmith, adored brass band music written in the Sousa style. An article Berlin published in 1913 in the entertainment magazine *The Billboard* marveled at how audiences, and not just the musicians themselves, could have profound, even trance-like, experiences

Figure 6.1. An illustration of John Philip Sousa and his concert band. *Source:* H.A. Thomas & Wylie Company, Sousa's Grand Concert Band: Sousa's Band at Manhattan Beach, 1895/1896, lithograph. Huntington Digital Library. Jay T. Last Collection of Graphic Arts and Social History. Public domain.

when listening to such performances.[33] These included the huge crowds of people who flocked to amusement parks like Coney Island during hot summer nights and made "a bee-line" for resident brass bands that usually performed in a corner theater. It was in witnessing these performances, Berlin commented, that audiences "go into fits of ecstasy." Such responses were not exactly the submission of will to the authority of a commanding conductor, as Sousa himself had described it. Instead, for Berlin, the ecstatic feeling had a more equalizing effect. A well-prepared band, he claimed, possessed a "sympathetic soul . . . that feels as we feel and speaks in our own heart-to-heart language." Its loud and bold voice became a "mammoth aggregation of soul-felt thought reflectors, shouting forth the fundamental sentiment of its listeners, with all the fervor an individual soul feels, and in actual, sincere, naturally-harmonized tones!" This fundamental element of all souls amounted to, in Berlin's words, "the spirit of the music," and, as such, it was only expressible through music. It had the capacity to bind together people over space and time, for instance, by capturing "the voices of the living and the dead ringing together in a vital, clear sound." This power, according to Berlin, is what caused people to weep or sing joyfully during a patriotic air. For some older men and women, he recognized, it was almost as if they were "receiving a blessing from the creator." In this manner, he compared brass band performances to a revival meeting or the work of an "oracle of old," since they captured something of the "universal soul" that passed through the music, the performers, and the audiences alike.[34] Berlin's description was comparable in several ways to Victor Turner's concept of *communitas*.[35]

Yet, despite the earnestness of Berlin's tone, his assessment of the metaphysical power of music may also have been couched in hyperbole and metaphor. This possibility becomes apparent when considering his stunted introduction to religious training and spiritual philosophy. Born into a Jewish community in Russia in 1888, Berlin—whose original name was Israel Isidore Baline—gained a deep exposure to religion only during the first few years of his life. In his Russian hometown, religious observance was seamlessly integrated into social life.[36] At this time, his father worked as a *shochet* (a ritual slaughterer of animals according to kosher religious laws) and a cantor in the local synagogue. However, when the Balines immigrated to Manhattan's Lower East Side in the 1890s, they underwent a rapid process of secularization.[37] When young Israel's father suddenly died, the family's assimilation accelerated, as the children were forced to leave school in order to seek out any kind of employment that would help support the family. Similar kinds of pressures had, in fact, led many Jews to start abandoning their religious rituals during this period, even if they never completely stopped thinking of themselves as ethnically or culturally distinct from the rest of American society. After growing up and becoming a famous songwriter, Irving Berlin exhibited very little, if any, affinity for the religious teachings of his ancestors. His daughter, Mary Ellin, would later confirm that her father was "not a religious person."[38] Berlin's own reading of the power of music to speak the language of a "universal soul," therefore, should be read in the context of his own incidental experience of secularization.

Other successful Tin Pan Alley songwriters also wrote ambivalently about social trance. They included those who penned popular lyrics on the topic of hypnosis, which usually involved a hypnotized person giving up self-control and agency to their hypnotizer. One example was "It Must Have Been Svengali," written by Vincent Bryan and Harry Von Tilzer in 1902. The song maintained that the power of "Hypnotism" had instigated a variety of tragic outcomes, from Adam and Eve's migration out of Eden to a doctor's fall down a well.[39] In the chorus, each of these occurrences was explained to be "Svengali in disguise," a reference to a fictional "hypnotist" character in the popular novel *Trilby*, by George du Maurier. In referencing hypnotism, the song seemed to accept scientific theories of consciousness that framed trance as a result of a highly suggestible mental state more than a genuine soulful fusion or psychic possession. Other songs took a similar approach. These included "That Hypnotizing Man," written by Lew Brown and Albert Von Tilzer (Harry's brother),[40] as well as "Hip Hip Hypnotize Me" by Will Dillon and Harry von Tilzer.[41]

Tin Pan Alley's recurring Svengali character, however, was also loaded with metaphysical connotations. Published in 1895, du Maurier's original story played upon a persistent cultural interest in what was at the time regularly called the "occult"—an umbrella term meant to encompass mystical and magical phenomena from a variety of backgrounds largely outside of the Christian fold, such as spiritualism, divination, clairvoyance, alchemy, and astrology. Popularized by the likes of Helena Blavatsky, Rudolf Steiner, and Alice Bailey, occult topics garnered considerable interest and often appeared in popular literature of the day. The song lyrics for "It Must Have Been Svengali" hinted at this occult quality when they described Svengali not only as a manipulative hypnotist, but in more abstract terms as "the force by which the world is ruled." This cast the character as an agent of magic or mystical influence that slipped beyond the grasp of rational explanation and unsettled the boundaries between self and other.[42]

Yet the formal features of songs about hypnosis also encouraged metaphorical interpretations of self-transcendence by employing the art of exaggeration.

"Hip Hip Hypnotize Me," for instance, was written in a flagrantly joyful, even silly, style, and its title seemed to be a play on the common celebratory cheer of the day, "hip hip hooray." Meanwhile, "That Hypnotizing Man" was composed in a minor key and characterized by an overembellished eerie style. Despite the contrasting moods, the effect of both songs was much the same: their exaggerated character lent a satirical quality to the lyrics and seemed to act as invitations to listeners and performers alike to refrain from taking the songs too seriously and to treat their references to hypnosis as trivial.

The hand-drawn cover art of the songs' sheet music illustrated the unanswered question of what the hypnotic experience actually entailed. These images provided colorful caricatures of men's hands projecting what might be described as magnetic waves, which—in one picture—appear to have cast a spell on an entranced woman (see figs. 6.2 and 6.3). Were these cover images simply lighthearted advertisements intended to spark the imagination, tantalize

Figure 6.2. Sheet music cover for "Hip Hip Hypnotize Me" by Will Dillon and Harry Von Tilzer. *Source:* Will Dillon and Harry Von Tilzer, "Hip Hip Hypnotize Me" (Harry Von Tilzer Music Publishing, 1910). Public domain.

Figure 6.3. Sheet music cover for "That Hypnotizing Man" by Lew Brown and Albert Von Tilzer. *Source:* Lew Brown and Albert Von Tilzer, "That Hypnotizing Man" (York Music Co., 1911). Public domain.

audiences, and ultimately sell sheet music? Were they representations of pure animal magnetism or some other mystical force psychically connecting one individual to another? Did they depict a highly suggestible person under the influence of a charismatic Sousa-like figure? All of these understandings of hypnosis in action may have been available to the viewer.

Equivocal commentary on social trance within popular music also had much to say about gender relations. The lyrics for "That Hypnotizing Man," for instance, were written from the perspective of a woman and ran as follows:

> Oh! that hypnotizing man:
> When he makes those motions at you
> Ev'rything he bids you must do.
> . . .

> Oh those wonderful eyes,
> How they seem to tantalize.
> When that feeling o'er you does creep,
> Your eyes are open but you're fast asleep.

Here again, the lyrics proposed that social entrancement, however explained, could effectively submit one's psychic and bodily control to the will of another. The female focus of the song was not coincidental; it perpetuated the long-standing tradition of associating women with a weakened will and susceptibility to self-transcendence. "Hip Hip Hypnotize Me" continued the gender stereotype and even indicated that fully conscious women lacked a sufficient degree of self-control, for they could be willing participants in their own entrancement. The song told the story of how "A Hypnotist once in a Vaudeville Show was admired by a maid in the very front row . . . she said, 'if you hypnotize me, then I won't know . . . I don't care what you do; I'll take my chances with you, if I'm hip, hip hypnotized, hypnotized.'"[43] The woman in this song seemed to be not just willing but happy to succumb to the trance induced by the performer. Taken together, then, both Tin Pan Alley songs framed women as highly susceptible to the beguiling methods of men. In this formulation, it did not matter whether hypnosis was an immanent mind-based phenomenon or generated by a numinous spirit external to the individual. Whatever it was, its power was relentless and consuming of the psychic agency of women.

Despite this enduring legacy, America's popular music industry did not entirely downplay the ecstatic agency of females. This much becomes apparent when investigating the career of Nora Bayes, who made a name for herself in vaudeville and shot to fame on the Broadway stage during the early 1900s. Having gained a reputation for "awaken[ing] the enthusiasm of . . . large audience[s],"[44] Bayes became even more famous during her time at the popular theatrical revue *The Ziegfeld Follies*. One review from 1912 described her as having a "bewitching," "ethereal," and "entrancing" stage presence.[45] By 1917, as she was gaining international attention with the song "Over There," her smash First World War anthem, Bayes continued to receive an array of accolades. Many reviews from this period described how she "captivated her hearers," "capture[d] the hearts of a Brooklyn audience," or exhibited "the power to conjure audiences."[46] For Bayes's supporters (or at least her reviewers), therefore, ecstasy might have amounted to an attunement between the performer and her audience, perhaps through some kind of genuine psychic merger or maybe via a scientifically grounded process of synchronized mental states.

Nora Bayes herself seemed to be fully aware and supportive of the self-transcendent possibilities of her effect on audiences. She acknowledged as much in a 1917 article she published in *Theatre Magazine,* titled "Holding My Audience."[47] In it, she provided a ringing endorsement of the power of creative expression to bind together performers and audiences (of any gender) into a unified whole marked by "unbridled self-abandon" and an "exchange of feeling with other human beings who understand you." Achieving this ever-so desirable effect, Bayes argued, required "absolute sincerity" from the performer and became something akin to an act of "magic."[48] Bayes presented a similar perspective in another article she wrote for *American Magazine* in 1918, where she contended: "If you can make anybody cry, you make them forget themselves. The minute you make them forget themselves they are being entertained. If you can set them to thinking about your blues instead of their own, they are taken completely out of themselves."[49] In short, Bayes reasoned that true entertainment involved a "complete" transcendence of self. And yet, despite this apparent embrace of metaphysical transcendence, some of Bayes's words also infused an illusory element into the experiences of musical ecstasy. For instance, in the previous quotation Bayes interpreted audiences "thinking about" someone's troubles as tantamount to being "taken completely out of themselves," a conflation that either elevated the former or diminished the latter—and opened up the possibility for reducing self-transcendence to the inner workings of the imagination. Bayes, then, perpetuated the music industry's ambivalence toward trance experiences and by doing so demonstrated that women were just as capable as men at advancing the equivocal mode in the early twentieth century.

Race relations also informed the framing of social trance. This was especially true by the late 1910s and 1920s, when jazz emerged as a popular musical idiom, and Americans of all races began to encounter it at nightclubs, ballrooms, and theaters, as well as through audio recordings.[50] In many cases for the first time, these venues provided white Americans with opportunities to encounter Black musicians and their music directly. (Until that point, most were only familiar with the minstrel theater's contrived and distorted misrepresentations of African American culture.) In the jazz context, a fascination with what might be called cross-racial unitive experiences likely motivated white Americans' attraction to jazz. According to James Weldon Johnson—the famous African American author, civil rights leader, and sometime songwriter—white patrons of Black dance music in the 1920s, including jazz, were "striving to yield to the feel and experience of abandon; seeking to recapture a state of primitive joy in life and living; trying to work their way back into that jungle which was the original Garden of Eden; in a word, doing their best to pass for colored."[51] In this statement, Johnson effectively suggested that white Americans participated in African American music culture partly as a way to blend white and Black subjectivities, civilized and "primitive" consciousnesses, and individual and collective experiences. Whether that merger was metaphysical, metaphorical, or otherwise was not clear.

Many popular jazz and dance tunes of the 1920s directly fed this ambiguous white longing to blend with Black consciousness. For instance, Perry Bradford's lyrics to the song "Black Bottom" ran as follows:

> Now learn this dance somehow
> Started in Georgia and it went to France
> It's got everybody in a trance,
> It's a wing, that Old Black Bottom Dance.[52]

Like almost all references to ecstasy in the popular music environment of the era, the reference to "trance" here could easily have been interpreted in a variety of ways, including as a true psychic merger, a hypnotic mental state, or a vicarious experience of the feelings and actions of others through the power of an individual's imagination. Whatever was entailed in the experiential process, it may have involved somehow bridging the racial divide. Written by a composer of color, "Black Bottom" was usually performed with a dance that originated among the African American communities of Florida and was subsequently shaped and popularized by the Black choreographer Billy Pierce. (The name "Black Bottom" itself referred to a historically African American neighborhood in Detroit.) Despite such strong African American roots, the song and its accompanying dance grew into a national craze and became famous among white jazz-lovers. For these Americans, the Black Bottom "trance" might have been considered an opportunity not only for self-transcendence but also for blending white identity with features of Black consciousness.

A similar longing for cross-racial transcendence may have informed the allusions to ecstasy in the 1929 song "You Do Something to Me," by the white songwriter Cole Porter.

> You do something to me,
> something that simply mystifies me.
> Tell me, why should it be
> you have the power to hypnotize me?
> Let me live 'neath your spell,
> Do do that voodoo
> that you do so well.[53]

Even as the word "hypnotize" pointed toward immanent explanations of ecstasy, the phrase " 'neath your spell" suggested a more magical form of mystification. And while the object of the singer's desire might be assumed to be a woman, it could have also been interpreted as the entire African American community. In fact, the reference to "voodoo" made this alternative seem entirely possible. In this scenario, the word "you" would be treated as second-person plural, and the effect would consist of embodying Black experience through the power of song and dance. Such a process may have constituted a more metaphysical impulse of what the author Norman Mailer would later call the "white Negro"—a name he gave to those white hipsters who shrugged off the tendency toward totalitarian conformity and "absorbed the existentialist synapses of the Negro."[54] Social transport, it would seem, could take on racialized formations as well.

Technological Transport

Although ambivalence over the character of ecstasy never disappeared, the advent of new media technologies and commercial techniques during the closing decades of the nineteenth century would serve to reinforce cultural interest in metaphorical interpretations of entrancement. Thomas Edison's invention of the phonograph in 1877 became a crucial early component in the process of "artificializing" aural experience more generally.[55] Edison's promotion of the device as a "talking machine" provided an effective way of describing its hybrid features. On one hand, it possessed something close to human characteristics. It could reproduce the sounds made by humans with uncanny accuracy. On the other hand, it was obviously mechanical. Indeed, it captured aural experiences in superhuman ways, retaining and accurately re-creating them across long distances of time and space; and its method of reproduction actually signified the very mechanical nature of the process itself. The hissing and popping and scratching that typified the earliest recordings, including those on wax cylinders and later on celluloid or vinyl discs, could never be made by the human body.[56] Moreover, the phonograph's design was entirely inorganic, replete with metal, wax, and wires. In this manner, if the device was "talking" like a person, it also had all the characteristics of a "machine." As such, it became easy enough (although not inevitable)[57] to treat phonographic experience as somehow less authentic than face-to-face human interaction.

Americans recognized the relative fakeness of mechanical recording experiences early on. An 1877 article from the popular magazine *Scientific American* exclaimed that it was impossible for a man to listen to the recording "without his experiencing the idea that his senses are deceiving him."[58] The article reinforced these connotations of deception by describing recordings as a "little contrivance" (on par with stereoscopic photographs) and by marveling at their power to create "the illusion of real presence." Notably, the term "real presence" had theological connotations, serving as a synonym for a transcendent entity.[59] But, in these terms, as impressive as the phonographic experience was, it only ever mimicked a spiritual one.

The counterfeit quality that typified the phonograph was less obvious but still on display in the player piano, the more profitable and arguably more important music reproduction technology of the early twentieth century.[60] The contrivance of this instrument lay in the rolls of perforated paper—originally recorded by a human player—that, when processed through a mechanism inside the piano, caused its hammers to strike different strings at different times, thereby creating melodies, harmonies, and rhythms almost like a human player would. While many features of the reproduced music were quite similar to the original, the technology also revealed its mechanical nature to the listener relatively quickly. As the piano roll was processed, keys played in time, but the musical dynamics (the relative loudness or softness) as well as the tempo of the original performance could not be retained. With these limitations, it was not uncommon for music critics and journalists to describe the instrument as "ingenious artifice" or "a curious artificial device."[61]

More than even the phonograph and player piano, the greatest opportunity for technological trickery came with the introduction of moving picture devices. These included Edison's Kinetoscope, which was intended for viewing by one person, and the Vitascope, which could support multiple simultaneous viewers. Although the primary function of such devices was to project images on a lens or screen, even from an early era their visual phenomena were rarely presented without an added auditory component.

Indeed, nearly from the beginning of the commercial cinema industry, "watching" moving pictures almost always relied on multiple forms of media and therefore a range of sensory experiences. In this regard, the tendency to label the early decades of the twentieth century as the "silent era" of film is a gross misrepresentation.[62]

Producers of early cinema suffused movies with reminders of their artificiality. Some of these were unintentional, produced by the mechanical limitations of film recording, which tended to create grainy reproductions that could be easily distinguished from phenomena mediated only through the human eye. Other times, the effect was entirely deliberate, for instance when characters broke with onscreen action to smirk and wink knowingly at the audience or bowed to the spectators after performing some remarkable feat.[63] In this regard, screen actors mimicked performers on the vaudeville stage, which was still the most popular commercial entertainment at the time. (Vaudeville actors themselves drew on a long-practiced convention of "breaking the fourth wall" that was rooted in early modern theatrical "asides.") Similarly, the artificiality of films was sometimes put on display in order to demonstrate the novel capabilities of the recording technology itself, as with close-up shots or reproductions of otherwise inaccessible locations, like the front of a fast-moving train. According to film historians such as Tom Gunning and Charles Musser, an emphasis on novelty and an ability to draw attention to its own contrivance characterized the early style of filmmaking, which has been labeled the "cinema of attractions."[64]

Nevertheless, the focus on artifice did not make new communication technologies entirely ill-suited to imbuing altered experiences of consciousness with feelings of metaphysical authenticity. According to the media theorist Marshall McLuhan, all technologies act as an extension of the human body.[65] Put another way, the primary role of technologies is to augment what the human mind, body, and senses can already do—seeing, hearing, moving, remembering, and so forth—by strengthening their actions or extending them across time or space. Long before McLuhan popularized it, many Americans implicitly accepted this theory when they expressed an earnest belief in the power of the phonograph, the player piano, and especially the multimedia technologies of the cinema to extend themselves out into the cosmos.

Film creators' attempts to alter the consciousness and self-awareness of audience members were amply demonstrated by films within the cinema of attractions tradition that included sequences taken from unusual or other- wise inaccessible perspectives—including from atop trains, rollercoasters, or other moving vehicles. For the movies about locomotives, the intent could be ascertained even before the movie started. Some theaters were decorated and arranged as a train car, including a conductor who took tickets and a recording of clacking wheels and hissing brakes.[66] Such details probably encouraged what the film scholar Miriam Hansen refers to as the "derealization" of the theater space.[67] In some instances, the effect was augmented when the film began. This notably occurred during screenings of *The Black Diamond Express*, which projected an image taken not from the front of the train, but from the tracks as a locomotive approached. As the train barreled toward the audience "with a roar and rumble, the noise being simultaneously produced by the phonograph,"[68] more than one audience member "involuntarily . . . scramble[d] to get out of the way" as it seemed to reach the front of the stage.[69] With such stimulation of their auditory and visual senses, audience members may have experienced what Mary Ann Doane calls the "progressive despatialization and disembodiment of the spectatorial position."[70] This involved shifting spectators' awareness away from their known environment or normal sense of self toward other versions far removed in time or place. Contemporary film scholars, including Kathryn Kalinak, have written about this effect, describing the cinematic experience as having "an ability to make us forget where we are or who we are when we are engrossed in watching it."[71]

Yet, considering that cultural assumptions had long tied mechanical reproduction technologies to illusion, how strong or convincing were these apparent transports? By most accounts, the cinema of attractions did not excel at authenticating the metaphysical interpretations of ecstasy. The film scholar Lauren Rabinovitz, for example, acknowledges that cinematic experiences always involved some blending between the phantasmagoric space of the screen and the theater itself. But she counters Doane's arguments by contending that early film-viewing experiences typically maintained spectators' normative sense of self-embodiment.[72] Similarly, according to the film historian Leon Gurevitch, reports about transported audiences in *The Black Diamond Express* were "most likely exaggerated precisely because they served a promotional function that benefited all involved."[73] Other scholars have made similar observations about the so-called transports of early cinema audiences.[74] It would seem, then, that—even with the accompaniment of realistic sound effects—the majority of audiences were never wholly convinced that a physical locomotive emerged from the screen. In a similar manner, most audiences probably did not frame their own feelings of cinematic self-transcendence in purely metaphysical terms.

Contemporaneous psychologists' theories of film experience only reinforced audience members' disbelief in sensations of self-transport. These included the writings of the German-American psychologist Hugo Münsterberg, who compared movie watching to hypnosis. In his publications from the 1900s and 1910s, Münsterberg claimed that the mind states of hypnotized subjects and film spectators were comparable to each other in that both groups suffered from an "over-attention" that "narrow[ed] the contents of consciousness," resulting in "a heightened state of suggestibility."[75] As a result, this form of consciousness stood in "complete isolation from the practical world."[76] In short, Münsterberg's theories of cinematic experience framed cinematic self-transcendence as fictional, powered by "suggestion," and generated through constraints on an individual consciousness.[77]

Nonetheless, filmmaking techniques popularized during the late 1900s and 1910s also helped focus attention away from the artificial element. Much of the impetus in this direction came as a result of filmmakers' rapid transition away from the cinema of attractions and toward more narrative-based movies, wherein characters developed and action unfolded through plot. The primary focus of this format was not to showcase the novel and spectacular capabilities of the technology itself (which often drew attention to its manufactured quality). Instead, the emergent cinema focused on the creation of what theorists call diegesis—the imagined, narrative world of the film.[78] This consisted of the projected sights and sounds that were intended to give a spectator/listener what the film scholar Annabel J. Cohen describes as the "emotional information he or she needs to make a coherent story."[79] A mark of success for this narrative style of filmmaking included the creation of a convincing or compelling diegetic world. (As such, technology needed to serve the story instead of reminding spectators of its contrivance.) Toward these ends, narrative filmmaking always elevated techniques that were more likely to make audiences feel immersed or absorbed in the story.

The multimedia nature of the cinematic environment became especially effective at achieving this sense of immersion. Indeed, the combination of visual and aural technologies often worked better to downplay the illusoriness of audience experience than either technology on its own. The early practice of including human musicians in the cinematic theater space, performing in close proximity to audience members, may have contributed a sense of authenticity to the sonic environment of the theater even after musicians were replaced by machines. Moreover, even when recorded music became normative, it also served to distract audience attention away from the more obvious artificial aspects of the visual component. For instance, a beautiful melody was able to drown out rattling projectors or give the appearance of continuity in an otherwise choppy sequence of shots and scenes.[80] According to the cultural critic Theodor Adorno and the film composer Hanns Eisler, one of the vital functions of music in the cinematic experience was its ability to act as "a cement, which holds together elements that otherwise would oppose each other unrelated—the mechanical product and the spectators."[81] By distracting spectators from the film's mechanical foundation, therefore, music was able to mitigate considerations of artifice, and, in the words of Kalinak, "suspend our disbelief in the two-dimensional, larger-than-life images posing as reality."[82] The desired result was, as Cohen points out, a heightened level of "absorption" in the film context.[83]

Filmmakers recognized this audiovisual synergy early on. The earliest nickelodeons—small indoor cinema spaces that originally cost five cents for admission and featured a series of short movies—were not always accompanied by sound, but by the 1910s most movie theaters did incorporate music in some form or another. At first, most film music was created by live musicians, who would play "incidental music" within the theater space itself. Producing the desired emotional response among audiences became of crucial importance, and, toward this goal, studios, trade publications, and theater managers began to develop "cue sheets"—documents that specified musical pieces (or at least styles) that should be played at precise moments throughout the film.[84] The songs chosen for the cue sheets took any number of different forms. They included popular tunes from vaudeville, classical music, folk melodies, and other compositions written by musicians specifically to accompany particular emotions or actions portrayed onscreen. These pieces were often published in encyclopedic catalogs of songs that producers, managers, and musicians could consult when customizing a cue list.[85]

Some catalogs, such as Malvin M. Franklin's *Favorite Moving Picture Music Folio* from 1914, explicitly described film music as having an authenticating influence on the sensations of cinematic transport. An advertisement for the songbook in a monthly magazine made abundant references to self-transport as it endeavored to encourage musically adept amateur players to purchase the publication for use at home:

> Begin at the very beginning. A few bars of the opening "Grand March" and the fun is on. You are literally carried away as your mind's eye pictures you part of some splendid court scene. The theme changes. "Hurry Up" music stirs you to imaginative

participation in some stern and exciting struggle or pursuit. That done, the first few notes of "Mysterious Burglar Music" halt your galloping brain. You feel it backing instinctively into a conveniently dark corner, where it watches some stealthy night prowler—on evil bent—flicker across the screen of the imagination. Then the warm strains of seductive "Oriental Music" chase the goose-flesh from your back. You loll languidly in unaccustomed splendor 'neath Asiatic skies. A bugle call! Gone is the breath of the lotus. Your mind marks time to the beat of "War Music"—or whoops madly with hard-riding cowboys to the tune of a wild "Gallop." And so on through 20 pages of the Favorite Moving Picture Music Folio takes you through the entire gamut of human sensations. Not a dull bar in it. Never be without it. It's a whole evening's pleasure at home.[86]

By playing the film music at home, the advertisement suggested, one could "literally" float out of a mundane life and magically visit any number of exotic destinations, from a royal court to the Orient or the Wild West. This act of being "carried away," as the advertisement described it, certainly suggested a form of metaphysical ecstasy; indeed, the physical presence of one's body seemed to have no bearing on the flexible potential of one's consciousness.

Yet, beyond these references to self-transcendence, there was also a simulated, psychological quality to the experiences the advertisement described. The ecstasy it marketed, after all, was a transport of the "imagination" that could be achieved "at home." It was not based on the testimonies of people who had performed music from the book. Instead, the experiences it described had the appearance of a daydream. Like the films from which they were derived, these experiences always had some element of artifice. They were projections or facsimiles of reality conjured up within the "mind's eye," not the external reality outside it. In this regard, even the advertisement's use of the word "literally," which it employed to describe the act of being "carried away," took on an ambiguous meaning. Its obvious connotations of being factual or unexaggerated may have been twinned with a more colloquial usage, which even at the time was used to add hyperbolic emphasis more than to delineate authentic reality.[87]

Not only advertisers, but also film creators and spectators believed that musical motion pictures facilitated self-altering experiences of the diegetic world in ways that simultaneously validated and challenged the metaphysical paradigms. One article published in a leading film trade publication,

Moving Picture World, made explicit this duality when describing the musical accompaniment for the film *The Old Fiddler*, which was produced in the 1910s. The movie told the story of an elderly fiddle-playing man, shunned from his house following complaints from his daughter-in-law. His son went out in search for him, eventually finding him and bringing him home to a remorseful daughter-in-law. "It will be a hard-hearted person indeed who can look upon this picture without shedding a tear, and if it is presented with the strains of a violin following the movements of the old fiddler, and, at the end of the search, if a gradual crescendo is effected to denote the approach to the fiddler, the illusion will be complete and will captivate any audience."[88] This passage revealed a great deal about the relationship between music and cinematic self-transcendence. The violin music—appropriately chosen to symbolize the fiddle-playing father at a crucial moment in the story—"completed" the "illusion." But it also worked to "captivate any audience," implying a degree of spectator absorption that could be likened to, if not exactly equated with, true metaphysical transport.[89]

According to an article in the magazine *The Strad*, music was a vital factor for the cinematic transport of audiences who attended any high-caliber movie:

> Anyone who has sat through the performance of a complete film to which there has not been a single bar of musical accompaniment, will readily admit how absolutely dead the whole play seems. Even the most "furioso" parts seem unable to make one oblivious of one's surroundings. Add music of any description, and there is a distinct improvement, though often one is conscious of an emotional pull in one direction by the music and a distinctly opposing pull by the action on the screen. Cause the music to fit the emotion and something of rhythm, and one can become quite absorbed in the play, but add to the perfect fitting *suitable* music and one becomes steeped in the whole atmosphere of the play, seems almost to live in the scenes portrayed, and take away a vivid impression of the whole play that is never quite forgotten. And add even more feature[s], and that is a theme (or two) which accompanies a principal character or the meeting of the two principals, and the audience can take away something tangible.[90]

In this account, music's "distinct" role in making one "oblivious" to one's surroundings amounted to psychically extracting one from the nondiegetic realm and, if well executed, permitting audiences to become "absorbed"—or even "steeped"—in the diegetic world. At their most immersive, these musical experiences became something "tangible," a term that seemed to imply that the audiovisual experience of the cinema could somehow evolve into a tactile one as well.

According to *The Strad* article, such an effect was successfully achieved by a number of movies produced in 1924. One of these was *Monsieur Beaucaire*, a film about court life and society before the French Revolution, which achieved an appropriate air of grace and ceremony through the use of minuets, gavottes, and "stately rhythms."[91] Another movie, *The Thief of Bagdad*, required a "most extravagant" music to accompany its portrayals of mythical winged horses, flying carpets, deep-sea monsters, and magic crystals. These images were accompanied by some commissioned works of "modern music" and "oriental music" composed by Mortimer Wilson. Meanwhile, the film *Peter Pan* achieved its success through the orchestra's ability to make audience members feel as though they could fly. Through the proper use of music, all of these films were able to create "vivid" enough impressions that audiences felt "absorbed" into a cinematic world.

Although the language of absorption retained aspects of metaphysical authenticity, *The Strad* article also imbued such experiences with figurative qualities. Indeed, even as the movies made spectators feel "steeped in the whole atmosphere of the play," the author implied some element of diegetic illusion when using the phrase "seems almost" to describe the sensation of living in the scenes. In doing so, the author also perhaps unwittingly betrayed an acknowledgment that, as realistic as the sensation of transport may "seem," it was always "almost" real. An article in the music magazine *Metronome* made a similar point when it contended that the combination of appropriate music, sound effects, and the visual content of the screen worked together to "carry the illusion" and mystify the audiences.[92] Thus, film music presented a clear departure from everyday reality, but when well executed it served to authenticate the diegetic world to some degree.

It was not only journalists in the film industry who made such claims about the ambiguous self-transcendent effect of film music. Social scientists corroborated these points too. This much was determined after the University of Chicago sociologist Herbert Blumer was commissioned by the Payne Fund, a private foundation, to carry out a survey of filmgoers' subjective experiences of movies. Focusing specifically on children, but with the implication that adults also shared many of the younger generation's impulses, Blumer concluded that filmgoers were prone to what he called "emotional possession"—a loss of self-awareness and control whereby "the individual identifies himself so thoroughly with the plot or loses himself so much in the picture that he is carried away from the usual trend of conduct . . . [and] impulses usually latent or kept under restraint gain expression."[93] Blumer's professional grounding in mainstream scientific theories of his day meant that he almost certainly did not intend these references to self-transport to be interpreted literally in supernatural or natural terms. And yet, by referring to individuals "losing" themselves and being "carried away," Blumer indulged heavily in the language of cinematic entrancement. In this sense, his remarks could be easily compared to the ambiguous description provided by Lucy Lowell after her experience at the 1884 Wagner concert in Boston.

The introduction of synchronized recorded sound into films during the last half of the 1920s sparked new debates regarding music's efficacy in promoting transport. After the release of the 1926 film *Don Juan*, which included a fully recorded musical soundtrack by the New York Philharmonic Orchestra, followed the next year by *The Jazz Singer*, which included synchronized recorded talking as well as music, some Americans resolved that the filmgoing experience had moved one step closer to verisimilitude. For one studio publicist, though, the construction of realistic movie experiences was always simply a process of perfecting what was fundamentally an "illusion."[94] For others, the increased mechanization was more than enough to deauthenticate mystical music experience. Not surprisingly, the American Federation of Musicians—the national labor union representing professional musicians—became one of the most outspoken opponents of recording technology of all kinds. For professional "live" musicians, of course, the increasing ubiquity of recorded music posed an existential threat, and therefore the union had more than one reason to denigrate sound recording in the cinema. A large advertisement published by the organization in the *Pittsburgh Press* and elsewhere in 1929 decried the vapidity of what it called "canned music." Recorded sound was guilty of "corruption of musical appreciation and discouragement of musical education," the advertisement accused.[95] Even more seriously, mechanical performance required that "the soul of the Art is lost" and the "emotional rapture is lost." With this last statement, the American Federation of Musicians effectively proposed that one of the central goals of any musical experience—its capacity to promote emotional entrancement—was no longer available. For some musical Americans, it would seem, recorded sound actually disrupted the delicate balance between illusion and authenticity or metaphor and metaphysics that was required for a truly pleasurable experience of art and entertainment.

❧

By the 1920s, a rapidly expanding mass entertainment industry had promulgated an ambivalent mode of musical ecstasy in America. Much of its work consisted in framing self-transcendence as not only secular but also illusory. This perspective was compatible with the psychological view of experience proffered by modern science, which rooted trance internally in the psychology and physiology of each individual. However, this mode also went a step further, by insinuating that references to ecstasy could be treated as metaphors for intensity more than gestures to transcendence. The lighthearted character of so much writing in and around the commercial music industry certainly helped both these interpretations. Yet commercial entertainment was never entirely sustained on connotations of make-believe. Even the most enthusiastic celebrants of entertainment continued to remain open to some measure of metaphysical merger in their and others' experiences. If individual consciousness was capable of producing trivial illusions of self-transcendence, should such phenomena be considered fake or inconsequential in all cases? Could some semblance of legitimacy be salvaged from what many believed were archaic interpretations of ecstasy? Americans increasingly began to pose these kinds of questions starting in the last decades of the nineteenth century, at precisely the same time that artificiality became so pervasive. Consequently, psychological interpretations and notions of make-believe never fully eclipsed a metaphysical sensibility when it came to questions of musical trance.

In describing audiences' reception of popular music in America during the first decades of the twentieth century, words like "ecstasy," "entrancement," being "carried away," "beside oneself," "overwhelmed," and the like, continued to be referenced—perhaps more frequently than ever. Yet now they played multiple roles. In one way, they were affirmations of mystical entrancement. In other ways, they also opened up a rhetorical space for diminishing the truth of these same declarations and transforming them into hyperbolic statements created for effect. Through lack of elaboration these descriptions remained perpetually available to all of these readings. Sometimes context tilted an interpretation in one particular direction, but a notable degree of equivocation always remained.

In some cases, especially for individuals who were less commercially minded and cared little about appealing to popular lines of thought, the ambiguation of self-transcendence could even come down more heavily on the side of spirit than psychology. Take for instance the 1927 writings of D. H. Lawrence, the British author who—following a lengthy journey through North America and many years studying American culture[96]—wrote earnestly about the ecstatic possibilities of popular entertainment. It is in entertainment settings, he claimed, that "we want to be taken out of ourselves."[97]

> We lean down from the plush seats [of the theatre] like little gods in a democratic heaven, and see ourselves away below there, on the world of the stage, in a brilliant artificial sunlight. . . . The secret of it all, is that we detach ourselves from the painful and always sordid trammels of actual existence, and become creatures of memory and of spirit-like consciousness. We are the gods and there's the machine, down below us. Down below, on the stage, our mechanical or earth-bound self stutters or raves, Pa Potter or King Lear. . . . The audience in the theatre is a little democracy of the ideal consciousness. . . . Which is very soothing and satisfying so long as you . . . instinctively feel that there is some supreme, universal Ideal Consciousness swaying all destiny. . . . A few people, the so-called advanced, have grown uneasy in their bones about the Universal Mind. But the mass are absolutely convinced. And every member of the mass is absolutely convinced that he is part and parcel of this Universal Mind. Hence his joy at the theatre. His even greater joy at the cinematograph. In the moving pictures he has detached himself even further from the solid stuff of earth. . . . That is our idea of entertainment.[98]

In this lengthy quotation, Lawrence captured much of what it meant to lose oneself in the age of mass amusement. His first equivocal statement about desiring self-transcendence in the theater was quickly revealed to be a modern appeal to turn spirit-like. Not only did Lawrence interpret this process as the transfiguration of human spectators into gods, he also perceived it to be a fusion of consciousness with others in order to populate the "Ideal Consciousness" or "Universal Mind." Entrancement, in this frame, was perceived as both spiritual and social, and if divorced from "actual experience" then still somehow authentic in its own right. Such ecstasy was also mediated through technology—not only through the human "machines" on the theatrical stage, but also through the mechanisms of the cinematograph and other moving picture devices, which—despite a degree of contrivance—still augmented one's feelings of self-transcendence.

Although Lawrence did not discuss music's integral role in this process, his statement succinctly summarized the views of many producers and participants in the commercial music industry. It demonstrated how Americans were able to extract ecstasy from its metaphysical settings, brush it off and repurpose aspects of it for an ostensibly metaphorical context without entirely rejecting conventional beliefs in the possibility of authentic mergers with entities beyond the self. Therefore, even as trance was interpreted as a benign illusion or a trick of the mind, whereby the sensation of escaping from one's ordinary subjectivity was pursued simply for fun, it was also—usually more quietly—inferred to be not disconnected from its enchanted past. The modern, secular world of industrialized music and entertainment, therefore, seemed to validate self-transcendent experiences even as it acknowledged them to be false and trivial.

Conclusion

From the early colonial era to the Jazz Age, music both mirrored and molded the American quest for self-transcendence. *Counterpoints of Ecstasy* has illuminated its integral role in this respect. This book, therefore, is a music history, but less a study of notes and melodies and more a phenomenological investigation of how musical expression became woven into the fabric of American consciousness. In many circumstances, music accompanied moments of mystical experiences; at other times it catalyzed and shaped them. From the spirituals sung by enslaved African Americans to the rhapsodic symphonies that filled concert halls, music became a vital part of the individual's journey beyond the self. As such, American music became instrumental in both the generation and endurance of distinct modes of unitive experience. Each of these modes—supernatural, natural, internal, and equivocal—approached the objects of ecstatic experience differently, whether as an ethereal entity, an earthly spirit or force, a mental phenomenon, or a set of simultaneous possibilities. These modes were not uniform; they were contrapuntal formations that each consisted of several lines of interpretation unfolding in parallel. Nor were these modes static; they evolved over time, influenced by the shifting conditions of the cultural environment and societal change, as well as each other. Indeed, the evangelicals who fervently sang hymns as pathways to divine connection during the Great Awakenings were not exactly the same as the Pentecostals of the Azusa Street Revival; and neither of these groups had a great deal in common with Tin Pan Alley songwriters and their audiences, who often muddled their proclivity for trance through a multitude of contradictory explanations. The musical history of American ecstasy, therefore, included both dissonant and consonant harmonies.

The Cultural Dynamics of Musical Ecstasy

If musical concepts like counterpoint, dissonance, and consonance are abundantly useful for the purpose of this analysis, others have factored less prominently into this study but nevertheless deserve some attention. Prime among them is the musical notion of *dynamics*, which is a technical term that corresponds to the relative loudness or softness of a musical line. In the counterpoint of American entrancement, all modes persisted and evolved over time, but in any given era certain modes and interpretative lines rang out with more resonance and volume than others. While this book has not extensively investigated these effects during the period in question, it would probably not be controversial to claim that the orthodox enchantment of supernatural trance resounded loudly in American culture throughout the seventeenth and eighteenth centuries, but gradually gave way to the disenchanted and re-enchanted interpretations associated with the other modes over the course of the nineteenth century. By the first half of that century, the cultures of sentimentality, sublimity, and animal magnetism began to present alternatives to evangelical Christianity. Then, during the last decades of the nineteenth century, the rising cultural authority of scientific experts and commercial entrepreneurs augmented the volume of internal and equivocal voices. While there was a certain amount of complementarity between these latter two modes, it could be said that, by the end of the 1920s, the dominant lines within the counterpoint of ecstasy were mainly equivocal in character. Powered by the commercial bulwark that was the modern, industrialized music industry, these voices sounded more resonantly than any of the supernatural, natural, and internal voices they endeavored to accommodate.

As a mark of its pervasiveness, hints of the equivocal perspective even began appearing in the social sciences around this period. While Freud's influence originally did much to barricade such influences, some scientific-minded scholars who worked outside of mainstream psychology endeavored to accommodate immanent, mind-based theories of consciousness while continuing to countenance the possibility of genuine transcendent experience beyond the individual. Chief among these scholars was the French sociologist Émile Durkheim, who was already well-known among American social scientists by the 1910s. His groundbreaking book from 1912, *The Elementary Forms of Religious Life*, claimed that "Homo duplex" was an appropriate label for humans because people were capable of at least two basic levels of consciousness. One level focused on an individual's self-serving desires, instincts, and goals. The other level subsumed individual concerns in favor of common values, beliefs, and practices that served the interests of a group. This was a form of shared awareness or common understanding that constituted a larger "collective consciousness"—the will of the social group. (It was no coincidence that the word "consciousness" translates into the French word "*conscience*," a term that was also associated with socially determined morals.)

According to Durkheim, certain activities were more conducive than others in facilitating experiences of the collective consciousness. Among the most effective were "cries, songs, music, . . . [and] dance." They created what he called a state of "collective effervescence,"[1] which enabled participants to be "carried outside [themselves] . . . and diverted from [their] ordinary occupation and preoccupations."[2] At bottom, these activities constituted rituals that made participants forget their self-serving identities and become more emotionally attached to the social will. In Durkheim's view, this transfer of awareness is what created sensations of ecstasy.

What is remarkable about the French sociologist's work is that, in an era when most scientific theories strictly confined all forms of consciousness within the mind of the individual, Durkheim never definitively advanced this perspective. Certainly, he recognized that collective consciousness was an amalgamation of several individual "states of consciousness." When these states were "identical," they began reinforcing and "intermingling with one another" to create "a new idea that absorbs the former ones."[3] However, was the collective consciousness, with its "new idea," an external entity that transcended individuals and had a mind of its own, so to speak? Or was it simply shorthand for what was essentially the work of many atomized individual minds, abstracted to the level of the social? Durkheim never provided a clear argument for either viewpoint. By remaining reticent about the issue, though, he left open the possibility of both explanations. For the psychologist R. Keith Sawyer, Durkheim was neither a strict "utilitarian atomist" nor a "metaphysical organicist" but instead suggested that the individual and the social levels of consciousness were simultaneously distinct from as well as contingent upon each other.[4] In this manner, the collective consciousness emerged from the actions and ideas of individuals, but it also, in turn, exerted its own agency back on individuals.[5]

Durkheim demonstrates how pervasive the equivocal mode had become by the early decades of the twentieth century, but the question remains as to why this mode become so prevalent in American culture. Although this book has not endeavored to answer this question in detail, it seems clear that the reasons were manifold. One certainly has to do with the industrial power of commercial entertainment, which was structured to appeal to as broad a consumer base as possible, including people with vastly different interpretations of experience and subjectivity. In pursuit of these diverse audiences, the producers of commercialized music of the 1910s and 1920s may have found it conducive to offer something for everyone.

Another part of the explanation may lie in a deeply ingrained longing among Americans to reconcile contradictory impulses even if they were not always successful at it. The anthropologist Claude Lévi-Strauss fortified this point when he argued that the human mind is naturally drawn to reconcile opposites presented to it through contradictory cultural symbols, such as nature and culture, male and female, raw and cooked, and so forth. This process, he argued, occurs through the myths of traditional societies or the more technologically mediated stories of modern, Western society.[6] However, he also recognized that the mere juxtaposition of contradictions is not sufficient for their reconciliation, and indeed the tension is often left unresolved. When this happens, new narratives are generated that reframe the opposition, allowing the process of symbolic negotiation to continue in new forms. Put another way, juxtaposition without reconciliation only instigates a new attempt at resolution under different circumstances.[7] In this light, the equivocal mode might be understood as presenting Americans with something equivalent to a mythic act: it may have highlighted the cultural contradictions that existed between the supernatural, natural, and internal interpretations of self-transcendence without fully resolving them. This tension would have, in turn, reiterated the longing for resolution and motivated consumers to search out new opportunities to fulfill it. However, the rise of a cultural industry mobilized to reproduce equivocal juxtapositions and unresolved half-myths would have only perpetuated the cycle of yearning.[8]

Whatever the reasons, it would seem that the commercial entertainment industry had much to gain from preserving the paradoxes at the core of the equivocal mode. Indeed, by using musical entertainment to promise a certain kind of ecstatic escape and simultaneously indicating that such a transport was possibly never truly attainable, American musical entrepreneurs effectively established an irreconcilable contradiction that may have been tempting enough to pay for but never fully satiating for the consumer. This combination of attraction and dissatisfaction could have easily reinforced itself, causing Americans to consume music in order to seek the resolution of an irresolvable paradox. Put another way, such a condition could have placed twentieth-century Americans in a contradictory situation whereby they were encouraged to yearn for a certain kind of self-transcendence, while at the same time they were reminded of the impossibility of attaining it. Here, the chronic consumption of popular musical culture would have been a desirable—if not wholly effective—means of managing the dissonant contrapuntal relationships that existed between ecstatic modes. Such a dynamic certainly would have served the purposes of a commercial cultural industry by maintaining engagement.

The fledgling theory of consumer culture presented above engages less with the work of Theodor Adorno, perhaps the best-known theorist of popular music, and more with that of other scholars like Colin Campbell, T. J. Jackson Lears, and Jean-Marc Philibert, to name a few. They have indicated the ways in which related tensions between authenticity and inauthenticity or belief and disbelief were integral to the generation of a robust consumer culture in America and beyond.[9] This theory also contributes to the growing body of historical literature that seeks to understand how the contradictions of belief and authenticity played out in the arena of American popular culture and entertainment during the period in question.[10] Commercial music's incorporation of multiple interpretations of ecstasy could have generated a similar tension between authenticity and artificiality that also encouraged Americans to consume more musical entertainment, whether in the form of vaudeville, opera, ragtime and jazz, film scores, and any number of other recorded and live performances.

The Persistence of Modes

Of course, the sheer volume of voices within the equivocal mode by the 1920s did not signal the obsolescence of the other modal traditions. Although the temporal scope of chapters 1–4 ends around the turn of the twentieth century, the interpretations addressed in those chapters never disappeared. The supernatural mode maintained a strong following under Christian evangelicalism and the growth of Pentecostalism. Although the natural mode may have become less popular over time, it persisted in a variety of settings, including with American avant-garde composers such as Charles Ives, Dane Rudhyar, Henry Cowell, Carl Ruggles, and Ruth Crawford Seeger. Their music, which embraced radical sonic dissonance, was—in different ways and to different extents—grounded in mystical precepts and spiritualist beliefs and linked to occult traditions within Western esotericism, such as Theosophy.[11] As for the internal mode, a few early twentieth-century psychologists and psychiatrists—including Clark Hull, Milton Erickson, and Ernest Hilgard—remained interested in the academic study and therapeutic practice of hypnosis, and they continued to explore altered consciousness at the peripheries of their disciplines.[12] By the 1960s, many of these modes underwent revival and growth. Among other factors, they were compelled by the advent of the charismatic movement in American Christianity, the rise of a counterculture fascinated with esoteric thought and Eastern mysticism, the development of the subdiscipline of transpersonal psychology, and new research on psychedelics, out-of-body experiences, altered states, and psychosis. All of these influences came to bear on the popular music industry, thereby reiterating the ambiguity that resided at the core of the equivocal mode.

The history of ecstatic experience in America, then, is a history of multiplying traditions. This process exemplifies one of the fundamental characteristics of secular modernity: an expanding set of ontological and epistemological options. Even as some gained prevalence, none disappeared completely.

Beyond Modes

Counterpoints of Ecstasy has demonstrated the utility of modes when thinking about self-transcendent experience, and it has established that all the relevant modes were fully entrenched in American culture by at least the 1920s. However, it is also important to acknowledge some limitations of these modal categories. First, not all modes were comparable in the same way. On one hand, the supernatural, natural, and internal modes might be considered integrated in the sense that each one was created by communities of supporters and contributors who agreed with each other about what constituted the object(s) of their ecstatic experience. For instance, supporters of the internal mode concurred that trance engaged obscure aspects of the mind. The equivocal mode, on the other hand, might be described as unintegrated because its followers did not cohere around a single object of experience but instead remained open to the possibility of different, contradictory experiences simultaneously. In this sense, the equivocal mode actually engaged in modal interplay.

Second, not all interpretations of trance fit comfortably within the modal categories described here. American Voudou, for instance, seemed to possess characteristics that could be classified as both supernatural and natural but not equivocal. While Voudou was a syncretic religion in several respects, its formation did not result from practitioners blending discrete supernatural and natural viewpoints. Similar to the African tribal religionists from whom many of them descended, African American practitioners of Voudou saw (and heard) their belief system as unified. They did not consider it a hybrid phenomenological framework. Moreover, when it came to describing the objects of their ecstatic experiences, they rarely recognized the boundaries between supernatural and natural interpretations as particularly meaningful. In this sense, their perspective might be considered modally malleable.

Lastly, there are subtle ways that this book as a whole challenges the modal categories by seeking to embrace and transcend them in a transmodal perspective. In analyzing the different modes side by side, comparing them, and drawing out their shared features—namely a fascination with transcendence and a longing to encounter something beyond the self—*Counterpoints of Ecstasy* suggests that ecstatic experience writ large can be understood in ways that exceed specific modal categories or cultural frameworks. In this way, and in keeping with William James's reflections in *The Varieties of Religious Experience*, it might be worth considering ecstasy as a fundamental feature of human life. As people across time and place have shaped self-transcendent experiences within their own cultural worlds, the expressions have varied, yet the fascination and longing have endured. Along this journey, musical expression has been considered an excellent means for facilitating and articulating these transcendent impulses. All this points to a strong resonance between the patterns and structures of music, mind, culture, and history.

Notes

Introduction

1. The focus on the United States and its colonial predecessors is not intended to imply that interpretations of musical ecstasy were dissimilar elsewhere. Much of what occurred in the American context also occurred in other parts of the modern world. At the same time, the United States' unique combination of diverse cultural influences in combination with its political, legal, economic, and geographic circumstances provided an atypically rich environment for subjects to explore the intricacies and varieties of trance and to elaborate these understandings in ways that were not found elsewhere. This book, therefore, frequently employs the word "America" to acknowledge both the distinct and shared cultural histories of the United States. The term is chosen intentionally because of its ambiguity. On one hand, it is meant to refer in the conventional ("Usonian") sense to the United States. On the other hand, it simultaneously gestures toward the transnational context of the American continent(s) and beyond.

2. In this book, "selfhood" or subjectivity can be defined broadly as an intimate locus of awareness, or consciousness, that is regularly juxtaposed against exterior others. The general concept is assumed to be transhistorical to the degree that it is an integral element of all human consciousness irrespective of temporal or cultural context.

3. Although other scholars (e.g., Judith Becker and Gilbert Rouget) maintain that there are important differences that distinguish ecstasy, trance, and mystical experiences from each other, this study emphasizes at least one attribute that the varying definitions hold in common, namely the experience of drastically altered subjectivity. Judith Becker, *Deep Listeners: Music, Emotion, and Trancing* (Indiana University Press, 2004), 1, 8; Gilbert Rouget, *Music and Trance: A Theory of the Relations Between Music and Possession* (University of Chicago Press, 1985), 7.

4. Although some modern definitions of "music" focus specifically on instrumental varieties, this book also expands the definition to include songs with lyrics.

5. Ferdia J. Stone-Davis, ed., *Music and Transcendence* (Routledge, 2015).

6. Jamie James, *The Music of the Spheres: Music, Science, and the Natural Order of the Universe* (Copernicus, 1993); Joscelyn Godwin, *Harmonies of Heaven and Earth* (Inner Traditions, 1978); Joscelyn Godwin, *Music, Mysticism, and Magic: A Sourcebook* (Routledge and Kegan Paul, 1986).

7. La Roy Sunderland, *Book of Psychology* (Stearns & Co., 1853), 28–29; Editors of the American Heritage Dictionaries, *Word Histories and Mysteries: From Abracadabra to Zeus* (Houghton Mifflin, 2004), 45–46.

8. Editors of the American Heritage Dictionaries, *Word Histories and Mysteries*, 45–46.

9. 1 Samuel 10:5; 2 Samuel 6:14–21; 2 Kings 3:15–16; Ex. 15:1–21; Deut. 31:19–32:44; Judges 5:1–12; Psalms 1–150; Hab. 3; 1 Chronicles 25.

10. Some of the great medieval mystics, including Hildegard of Bingen and Richard Rolle, entered musically inflected trances. And during the Italian Renaissance, Marsilio Ficino revived the Music of the Spheres philosophy and encouraged its connection to ecstasy.

11. Roger Scruton, "Music and the Transcendental," in *Music and Transcendence*, edited by Ferdia J. Stone-Davis (Routledge, 2015), 77.

12. Charles Taylor, *A Secular Age* (Belknap Press of Harvard University Press, 2007), 27. In the 1980s, the anthropologist Clifford Geertz famously defined individual selfhood in a compatible way, describing it as "a bounded, unique, more or less integrated motivational and cognitive universe, a dynamic center of awareness, emotion, judgement, and action organized into a distinctive whole and set contrastively both against other such wholes and against its social and natural background." See Clifford Geertz, *Local Knowledge: Further Essays in Interpretive Anthropology*, 3rd ed. (Basic Books, 2000), 57.

13. Raymond Williams, *Keywords: A Vocabulary of Culture and Society*, rev. ed. (Oxford University Press, [1976] 1983), 161–65.

14. The nineteenth-century Swiss historian Jacob Burckhardt was among the first to locate the roots of this modern conception of selfhood in the Italian Renaissance. It was in this context, he argued, that the common medieval assumption that all identity was essentially shared with others "melted into air" revealing personal subjects to be separate and unique entities. See Jacob Burckhardt, *The Civilization of the Renaissance in Italy* (Dover, 2012), 81. On the longer history of individuality, see, for example, Charles Taylor, *Sources of the Self: The Making of the Modern Identity* (Harvard University Press, 1989); Larry Siedentop, *Inventing the Individual: The Origins of Western Liberalism* (Belknap Press of Harvard University Press, 2014).

15. Taylor, *Sources of the Self*.

16. Accompanying the rise of the individual was also a growing sense of individual self-awareness. See Peter Abbs, "The Development of Autobiography in Western Culture: From Augustine to Rousseau," PhD diss., University of Sussex,

1986, 131–32; Roy F. Baumeister, *Identity: Cultural Change and the Struggle for Self* (Oxford University Press, 1986), 39.

17. Norbert Elias, *The Civilizing Process, Volume 1: The History of Manners*, trans. Edmund Jephcott (Pantheon Books, 1982); Barbara Ehrenreich, *Dancing in the Streets: A History of Collective Joy* (Metropolitan Books, 2007), 137, and chap. 5.

18. R. H. Tawney, *Religion and the Rise of Capitalism* (Harcourt, Brace and Co., 1926).

19. Émile Durkheim, *The Division of Labor in Society*, trans. W. D. Halls (Free Press, 2014).

20. Joyce Appleby, *Inheriting the Revolution: The First Generation of Americans* (Harvard University Press, 2000).

21. Taylor, *Secular Age*, 42.

22. The term "disenchantment," as it is attributed to Weber, was first published in 1946, in the English translation of Weber's 1917 lecture "Science as Vocation," contained in Hans H. Gerth and C. Wright Mills' compendium of Weber's translated work titled *From Max Weber: Essays in Sociology*. Weber wrote in German and died in 1920, decades before Gerth and Mills's publication. The original German word he used, *Entzauberung*, has no direct equivalent in English and no common etymological link to "enchantment." Therefore, the translation would have required some creative interpretation. Interestingly, the first time *Entzauberung* was translated into English, "disenchantment" was not chosen. This occurred when American sociologist Talcott Parsons first translated Weber's *Die protestantische Ethik und der Geist des Kapitalismus* into *The Protestant Ethic and the Spirit of Capitalism* in 1930. It would be another sixteen years before Gerth and Mills used "disenchantment" as the English equivalent to Weber's *Entzauberung*. See Max Weber, *The Protestant Ethic and the Spirit of Capitalism*, trans. Talcott Parsons (Routledge, [1930] 2005); Max Weber, *From Max Weber*, ed. H. H. Gerth and C. Wright Mills (Oxford University Press, 1946). Although Weber wrote quite extensively on music history and theory, it is unlikely that Weber's translators were thinking of the musical connotations of the word "enchantment" when they used this term; the musical connotations were not commonly recognized by the early twentieth century. For Weber's interest in music, see Max Weber, *The Rational and Social Foundations of Music*, trans. D. Martindale, J. Riedel, and G. Neuwirth (Southern Illinois University Press, 1958). For the early twentieth-century connotations of "enchantment," see, for instance, Noah Webster, Robert Arrowsmith, and Harry Thurston Peck, *Webster's New Modern English Dictionary* (Consolidated Book Publishers, 1922), https://archive.org/stream/webstersnewmoder00web.

23. Max Weber, *Protestant Ethic and the Spirit of Capitalism*, trans. Talcott Parsons (Routledge, [1930] 2005), xxxviii.

24. Charles Taylor, *A Secular Age* (Belknap Press of Harvard University Press, 2007), 542. The historian Glenn W. Olsen has similarly described a "loss of

transcendence" within the West. Glenn W. Olsen, *The Turn to Transcendence: The Role of Religion in the Twenty-First Century* (Catholic University of America Press, 2010), x. Both Taylor and Olsen follow Weber's observation that "the modern man is in general, even with the best will, unable to give religious conscience a significance for the conduct of life, culture and national character which it had [in the past]." Weber, *Protestant Ethic and the Spirit of Capitalism*, 125.

25. Taylor, *Secular Age*, 280.

26. For a comprehensive overview of scholarly explorations of the "dividual," see Antje Linkenbach and Martin Mulsow, "Introduction: The Dividual Self," in *Religious Individualisation: Historical Dimensions and Comparative Perspectives*, ed. Martin Fuchs, Antje Linkenbach, Martin Mulsow, Bernd-Christian Otto, Rahul Bjørn Parson, and Jörg Rüpke (De Gruyter, 2020), 323–44, accessed November 18, 2023, https://doi.org/10.1515/9783110580853-015.

27. Guy L. Beck, *Musicology of Religion: Theories, Methods, and Directions* (State University of New York Press, 2023), 2–3.

28. Matt Karush, "Music in History: Overcoming Historians' Reluctance to Tackle Music as a Source," *OUPblog* (January 15, 2019), accessed November 18, 2023, https://blog.oup.com/2019/01/musicology-analyzing-music-in-history/. Karush is not the only one to have questioned this disconnect between history and music. See Jeffrey H. Jackson and Stanley C. Pelkey, *Music and History: Bridging the Disciplines* (University Press of Mississippi, 2005), vii.

29. Ralph Waldo Emerson, "The Oversoul," in *The Complete Works of Ralph Waldo Emerson: Essays, First Series*, vol. 2 (Houghton, Mifflin and Company, 1903), 2:282; William James, *The Varieties of Religious Experience: A Study in Human Nature* (Longmans, Green, and Co., 1902), 380–81.

30. Siglind Bruhn, ed., *Voicing the Ineffable: Musical Representations of Religious Experience* (Pendragon Press, 2002); Vladimir Jankélévitch, *Music and the Ineffable*, trans. Carolyn Abbate (Princeton University Press, 2003); David Allen Erickson, "Language, Ineffability and Paradox in Music Philosophy," master's thesis, Simon Fraser University, 2005.

31. George Steiner, *Real Presences* (University of Chicago Press, 1989), 20. Decades later, the English composer Frederick Delius similarly proclaimed that music "only begins to be significant where words and actions reach their uttermost limit of expression." Quoted in Carol Kimball, *Song: A Guide to Art Song Style and Literature* (Hal Leonard, 2006), 361.

32. James, *Varieties of Religious Experience*, 380. The philosopher Ludwig Wittgenstein studied the ideas of James and understood his attitude toward music and meaning. He once posed a thought experiment in which James listened to a glorious piece of music but could not explain why it moved him, saying only that "our vocabulary is inadequate." Ludwig Wittgenstein, *Philosophical Investigations*, trans. G. E. M. Anscombe (Macmillan, 1953), 610.

33. Rudolf Otto, *The Idea of the Holy: An Inquiry into the Non-rational Factor in the Idea of the Divine and Its Relation to the Rational*, 2nd ed. (Oxford University Press, 1936), 50. Also see 191–98.

34. For a few examples, see "A New Art—'Silent Music,' " *Musical Leader* 43 (1922): 515. On Libby Holman, see Francis Fergusson, "What Is the Revue?" *The Bookman: A Literary Journal* 72 (1930), 411; Becker, *Deep Listeners*, 43; Christopher Ballantine, *Music and Its Social Meanings* (Gordon and Breach, 1984), xvi; Jeffrey H. Jackson and Stanley C. Pelkey, *Music and History: Bridging the Disciplines* (University Press of Mississippi, 2005), vii.

35. See Christopher Partridge, *The Lyre of Orpheus: Popular Music, the Sacred and the Profane* (Oxford University Press, 2014); Robin Sylvan, *Traces of the Spirit: The Religious Dimensions of Popular Music* (New York University Press, 2002); David Chidester, *Authentic Fakes: Religion and American Popular Culture* (University of California Press, 2005); Rupert Till, *Pop Cult: Religion and Popular Music* (Continuum, 2010); Vaughan S. Roberts and Clive Marsh, *Personal Jesus: How Popular Music Shapes Our Souls* (Baker Academic, 2012). See also Peter Bebergal, *Season of the Witch: How the Occult Saved Rock 'n' Roll* (Penguin, 2014); Graham St. John, *Global Tribe: Technology, Spirituality and Psytrance* (Equinox Publishing, 2012); Robin Sylvan, *Trance Formation: The Spiritual and Religious Dimensions of Global Rave Culture* (Routledge, 2005); Graham St. John, ed., *Rave Culture and Religion* (Routledge, 2004); Barbara Ehrenreich, Elizabeth Hess, and Gloria Jacobs, "Beatlemania: Girls Just Want To Have Fun," in *The Adoring Audience*, ed. Lisa A. Lewis (Routledge, 1992), 84–105; Susan J. Douglas, *Where the Girls Are: Growing Up Female with the Mass Media* (Times Books, 1994); Greil Marcus, *Mystery Train: Images of America in Rock 'n' Roll Music*, 6th ed. (Plume, 2015).

36. John Lennon, for instance, admitted that it was an "acid trip" that inspired him to write the opening lines to the Beatles' 1967 tune, "I am the Walrus," which began, "I am he as you are he as you are me / And we are all together." By the time that song was released, Lennon and his bandmates were avidly practicing transcendental meditation and would soon make their famous trip to India to study it with the Maharishi Mahesh Yogi. David Sheff, *All We Are Saying: The Last Major Interview with John Lennon and Yoko Ono* (St. Martin's, 2000), 184.

37. Albert L. Blackwell's *The Sacred in Music* is an exception to this approach in that it offers a sustained focus on the role of music in religious life, while also engaging with the nature of ecstatic experience in a range of historical and theological settings. Albert L. Blackwell, *The Sacred in Music* (Westminster John Knox Press, 1999).

38. William G. McLoughlin, *Modern Revivalism: Charles Grandison Finney to Billy Graham* (Ronald Press, 1959); William G. McLoughlin, *Revivals, Awakenings, and Reform: An Essay on Religion and Social Change in America, 1607–1977* (University of Chicago Press, 1980); Elaine A. Heath, "Ecstasy: Mysticism and Mission in the

Wesleyan Tradition," presentation of a paper to the Oxford Institute of Methodist Theological Studies, July 2007; Timothy E. Fulop and Albert J. Raboteau, *African-American Religion: Interpretive Essays in History and Culture* (Taylor and Francis, 2013); Albert J. Raboteau, *Slave Religion: The "Invisible Institution" in the Antebellum South* (Oxford University Press, 2004); Albert J. Raboteau, *Canaan Land: A Religious History of African Americans* (Oxford University Press, 1999); Stephen D. Glazier, *Encyclopedia of African and African-American Religions* (Routledge, 2001); Kenneth Thomas, *The Religious Dancing of American Slaves, 1820–1865: Spiritual Ecstasy at Baptisms, Funerals, and Sunday Meetings* (Edwin Mellen, 2008); C. Eric Lincoln and Lawrence H. Mamiya, *The Black Church in the African American Experience* (Duke University Press, 1990); Noel Leo Erskine, *Plantation Church: How African American Religion Was Born in Caribbean Slavery* (Oxford University Press, 2014); Mechal Sobel, *Trabelin' On: The Slave Journey to an Afro-Baptist Faith* (Princeton University Press, 1988); Blackwell, *The Sacred in Music.*

39. Stephen A. Marini, *Sacred Song in America: Religion, Music, and Public Culture* (University of Illinois Press, 2010); David W. Music, *Hymnology: A Collection of Source Readings* (Scarecrow Press, 1996); David W. Music and Paul Westermeyer, *Church Music in the United States, 1760–1901* (MorningStar Music, 2014); John Ogasapian, *Music of the Colonial and Revolutionary Era* (Greenwood, 2004); John Ogasapian, *Church Music in America, 1620–2000* (Mercer University Press, 2021).

40. Joshua Landy and Michael Saler, eds., *The Re-Enchantment of the World: Secular Magic in a Rational Age* (Stanford University Press, 2009), 7.

41. Ann Braude, *Radical Spirits: Spiritualism and Women's Rights in Nineteenth-Century America* (Free Press, 1989); Marianna Torgovnick *Primitive Passions: Men, Women, and the Quest for Ecstasy* (University of Chicago Press, 1997); Barbara Goldsmith, *Other Powers: The Age of Suffrage, Spiritualism, and the Scandalous Victoria Woodhull* (Harper, 1999).

42. Taylor gestured toward the concept of re-enchantment in *A Secular Age*, when he wrote of how the immanent frame could be interpreted as open toward transcendent possibilities. However, he only began employing the term "re-enchantment" after the publication of that book. See Charles Taylor, *Dilemmas and Connections: Selected Essays* (Belknap Press of Harvard University Press, 2014), chap. 12.

43. See also Joseph Bottum, *An Anxious Age: The Post-Protestant Ethic and the Spirit of America* (Image Books, 2014); Michael Saler, *As If: Modern Enchantment and the Literary Prehistory of Virtual Reality* (Oxford University Press, 2012); Jane Bennett, *The Enchantment of Modern Life: Attachments, Crossings, and Ethics* (Princeton University Press, 2011); Michael Warner, Jonathan Van Antwerpen, and Craig Calhoun, eds., *Varieties of Secularism in a Secular Age* (Harvard University Press, 2010); Gordon Graham, *The Re-Enchantment of the World: Art Versus Religion* (Oxford University Press, 2010); Joshua Landy and Michael Saler, eds., *The Re-Enchantment of the World: Secular Magic in a Rational Age* (Stanford University Press, 2009); Jackson Lears, *Rebirth of a Nation: The Making of Modern America, 1877–1920* (HarperCollins,

2009); George Levine, *Darwin Loves You: Natural Selection and the Re-enchantment of the World* (Princeton University Press, 2008); Kristina Karin Shull, "Is the Magic Gone? Weber's 'Disenchantment of the World' and Its Implications for Art in Today's World," *Anamesa* (Fall 2005): 61–73; Richard Jenkins, "Disenchantment, Enchantment and Re-Enchantment: Max Weber at the Millennium," *Max Weber Studies* 1, no. 1 (November 2000): 11–32; Jackson Lears, *Fables of Abundance: A Cultural History of Advertising in America* (Basic Books, 1994); T. J. Jackson Lears, "From Salvation to Self-Realization: Advertising and the Therapeutic Roots of the Consumer Culture, 1880–1930," in *The Culture of Consumption: Critical Essays in American History, 1880–1980*, ed. Richard Wightman Fox and T. J. Jackson Lears (Pantheon Books, 1983); T. J. Jackson Lears, *No Place of Grace: Antimodernism and the Transformation of American Culture, 1880–1920* (University of Chicago Press, 1981); Morris Berman, *The Reenchantment of the World* (Cornell University Press, 1981); George Steiner, *Nostalgia for the Absolute* (CBC Publications, 1974); Robert Bellah, "Civil Religion in America," *Journal of the American Academy of Arts and Sciences* 96, no. 1 (Winter 1967): 1–21; Philip Rieff, *The Triumph of the Therapeutic: Uses of Faith After Freud* (Harper & Row, 1966).

44. Ann Taves, *Fits, Trances, and Visions: Experiencing Religion and Explaining Experience from Wesley to James* (Princeton University Press, 1999).

45. June McDaniel, *Lost Ecstasy: Its Decline and Transformation in Religion* (Palgrave Macmillan, 2018).

46. Scruton, "Music and the Transcendental," 77.

47. By investigating these different modes, this study partly assumes what the scholar Jon Michael Spencer calls a "theomusicological" perspective. Spencer defines the latter as a method for exploring musical meaning that involves "theologizing about the sacred, the secular, and the profane" and treating the "symbols, myths, and cannon of the culture being studied . . . [as] authoritative/normative sources." Jon Michael Spencer, *Theological Music: An Introduction to Theomusicology* (Greenwood, 1991), 3–4; Jon Michael Spencer, "Musicology as a Theologically Informed Discipline," in *Theomusicology*, ed. Jon Michael Spencer (Duke University Press, 1994), 36–63. *Counterpoints of Ecstasy* also moves beyond, or perhaps expands, that perspective by incorporating cultural dispositions that denied any theological presuppositions and focused entirely on the secular and the profane.

48. Philosophers of music have long recognized how music and musical improvisation serve as a representation and facilitator of social interaction; and they have also investigated the ethical implications of these relationships. While these scholars have explicitly invoked the concept of "counterpoint" only occasionally, their discussions of interactivity and improvisation are nevertheless related to that topic. See, for example, Marcel Cobussen, *The Field of Musical Improvisation* (Leiden University Press, 2017); Marcel Cobussen and Nanette Nielsen, *Music and Ethics* (Routledge, 2011); Kathleen Marie Higgins, *The Music of Our Lives* (Temple University Press, 1991); Jeff R. Warren, *Music and Ethical Responsibility* (Cambridge University Press, 2014).

49. In his writings, Weber occasionally framed the spread of rationalization as flexible enough to incorporate certain salvageable features of orthodox enchantment, including those associated with Christianity and other organized religions or supernatural belief systems that gained prominence in premodern eras. On the topic of trance Weber suggested that "mystic contemplation and a rational attitude are not in themselves mutually contradictory." Rather, both rational thought and mystic experience, he asserted, could be traced back to the same religious root, namely the early Protestant tradition, which upheld both impulses simultaneously. Modern life, Weber suggested, did not so much deny as obscure this interconnectivity. As such, some form of mystical experience continued to remain possible even in the modern disenchanted context. Weber, *Protestant Ethic*, 189; Jason A. Josephson-Storm, *The Myth of Disenchantment: Magic, Modernity, and Birth of the Human Sciences* (University of Chicago Press, 2017), chap. 10; Taylor, *Secular Age*. Furthermore, Weber argued, the most rational forms of disenchantment could actually generate enchanted forms if pursued dogmatically enough. In this manner, Weber maintained, rationalization challenged orthodox monotheistic European religion but ultimately ended up replacing it with a new polytheistic panoply of "warring gods," each of which acted as a divine figurehead of a distinct value system (e.g., capitalism). Secular belief in these fragmented value systems still required an irrational leap of faith similar to that needed for conventional religion. See William T. Cavanaugh, "Strange Gods: Idolatry in the Twenty-First Century," *Commonweal*, January 21, 2020, accessed November 18, 2023, https://www.commonwealmagazine.org/strange-gods; Sung Ho Kim, "Max Weber," in *The Stanford Encyclopedia of Philosophy* (Fall 2012), ed. Edward N. Zalta, http://plato.stanford.edu/archives/fall2012/entries/weber/.

50. Landy and Saler, *Re-Enchantment of the World*, 2.

51. Saskia Sassen, "Organized Religions in Our Global Modernity," *Publications of the Modern Language Association of America* 126, no. 2 (2011): 455–59; Tom Rosentiel, "Religion and Secularism: The American Experience," Pew Research Center, December 3, 2007, accessed November 18, 2023, https://www.pewresearch.org/2007/12/03/religion-and-secularism-the-american-experience/.

Chapter 1

1. Camp meetings and their associated devotional activities had not been a part of Reed's early education as a Congregationalist in Britain. See Andrew Reed, George Collision, and Robert Winter, *The Ordination Service of the Reverend Andrew Reed* (T. Rutt, 1812).

2. Andrew Reed and James Matheson, *A Narrative of the Visit to the American Churches, Vol. 1* (Jackson and Walford, 1835), 272.

3. Reed and Matheson, *A Narrative of the Visit to the American Churches*, 1:271, 275.

4. Reed and Matheson, *A Narrative of the Visit to the American Churches*, 1:77.

5. Reed and Matheson, *A Narrative of the Visit to the American Churches*, 1:272.

6. Reed and Matheson, *A Narrative of the Visit to the American Churches*, 1:274.

7. Reed and Matheson, *A Narrative of the Visit to the American Churches*, 1:283.

8. Reed and Matheson, *A Narrative of the Visit to the American Churches*, 1:283.

9. Reed and Matheson, *A Narrative of the Visit to the American Churches*, 1:283.

10. Reed and Matheson, *A Narrative of the Visit to the American Churches*, 1:284–85.

11. *Ephesians* 5:18–19.

12. Catholic mystics during the medieval era sometimes experienced musical ecstasies, even as they engaged in the ostensibly silent practice of contemplative devotion. These included Hildegard of Bingen, Richard Rolle, and Henry Suso. See Godwin, *Harmonies of Heaven and Earth*, 63, 71. For an extensive overview of medieval trances associated with musical expression, see Laurence Wuidar, *Fuga Divina: La musique dans l'écrit mystique du Moyen Âge à la première modernité* (Droz, 2021).

13. Rene Descartes, *Passions of the Soul*, trans. Stephen H. Voss (Hackett, 1989), 46 (Article 48); Taylor, *Sources of the Self*, 115–16.

14. Taylor, *Sources of the Self*.

15. In taking this stance, radical Protestants also drew on a long-held impulse within Christianity illustrated by Paul's biblical aphorism, "Let all things be done decently and in order." 1 Corinthians 14:40.

16. The nominalists, led originally by people like William of Ockham, purported that universalism logically worked to challenge God's ascendancy, because it could not deny the presence of other universals (e.g., "truth," "beauty," "goodness," or even "being-ness") in all things. God, the nominalists claimed, could only remain completely sovereign over the world if separate from it and its universals. *Stanford Encyclopedia of Philosophy*, s.v., "William of Ockham," by Paul Vincent Spade and Claude Panaccio, accessed November 28, 2023, http://plato.stanford.edu/entries/ockham/.

17. Emery John Batis, *Saints and Sectaries: Anne Hutchinson and the Antinomian Controversy in the Massachusetts Bay Colony* (University of North Carolina Press, 1962), 27.

18. Richard Rath, *How Early American Sounded* (Cornell University Press, 2003), 129.

19. Rath, *How Early American Sounded*, 129.

20. Increase Mather, *Remarkable Providences: Illustrative of the Earlier Days of American Colonisation* (Reeves and Turner, 1890), 241–42.

21. Rath, *How Early American Sounded*, 133–34.

22. Quoted in Rath, *How Early American Sounded*, 136.

23. Christopher Marsh, *Music and Society in Early Modern England* (Cambridge University Press, 2010), 48.

24. John Wallis, "XIII. A Letter of Dr. John Wallis, to Mr. Andrew Fletcher; Concerning the Strange Effects Reported of Musick in Former Times, Beyond What

is to be Found in Later Ages," in *Philosophical Transactions: Giving some Account of the Present Undertakings, Studies and Labours of the Ingenious, in Considerable Parts of the World*, vol. 20 (Royal Society, 1698), 298; also cited in Marsh, *Music and Society in Early Modern England*, 34.

25. Wallis, "XIII. A Letter of Dr. John Wallis," 298; also cited in Marsh, *Music and Society in Early Modern England*, 34.

26. Gretchen L. Finney, "Ecstasy and Music in Seventeenth Century England," *Journal of the History of Ideas* 8, no. 2 (April 1947): 185.

27. John Hollander, *The Untuning of the Sky* (Princeton University Press, 1961).

28. April Lee Hatfield, *Atlantic Virginia: Intercolonial Relations in the Seventeenth Century* (University of Pennsylvania Press, 2004), 115, 119; Carla Gardina Pestana, *The English Atlantic in the Age of Revolution, 1640–1661* (Harvard University Press, 2004), 21.

29. Lauren F. Winner, *A Cheerful and Comfortable Faith: Anglican Religious Practice in the Elite Households of Eighteenth-Century Virginia* (Yale University Press, 2010), 190n7.

30. Edward L. Bond, *Damned Souls in a Tobacco Colony: Religion in Seventeenth-Century Virginia* (Mercer University Press, 2000), 245.

31. John Page, *A Deed of Gift: To My Dear Son, Captain Matt* (Henry B. Ashmead, [1687] 1856), 94.

32. John K. Nelson, *A Cheerful and Comfortable Faith: Parishes, Parsons, and Parishioners in Anglican Virginia, 1690–1776* (University of North Carolina Press, 2001), 207.

33. Ogasapian, *Music of the Colonial and Revolutionary Era*, 60.

34. Cotton Mather, *Memorable Providences, Relating to Witchcrafts and Possessions*, Evans Early American Imprint Collection, accessed June 24, 2024, https://name.umdl.umich.edu/n00392.0001.001.

35. Cotton Mather, *The Wonders of the Invisible World, Being an Account of the Tryals of Several Witches Lately Executed in New-England* (John Russell Smith, [1693] 1862), 80, accessed June 24, 2024, http://doi.org/10.5479/sil.15551.39088001220250.

36. Colin Campbell, *The Romantic Ethic and the Spirit of Modern Consumerism* (Blackwell, 1987),123; Ursula Brumm, "Passions and Depressions in Early American Puritanism," *La passion dans le monde anglo-américain aux XVIIe et XVIIIe siècles* 7, no. 1 (1978): 85–96.

37. Richard Baxter, "The Cure of Melancholy and Overmuch Sorrow, by Faith," in *The Practical Works of Richard Baxter*, vol. 4 (George Virtue, 1838), 923.

38. Quoted in Brumm, "Passions and Depressions in Early American Puritanism," 85–96.

39. Cotton Mather, *Diary of Cotton Mather, 1681–1724* (Massachusetts Historical Society, 1911), 98.

40. Thomas Mace, *Musick's Monument; or, a Remembrancer of the Best Practical Musick*, quoted in Finney, " 'Organical Musick' and Ecstasy," 283.

41. Quoted in Marsh, *Music and Society*, 66.

42. Robert Burton, *The Anatomy of Melancholy*, ed. Arthur Richard Shilleto and Arthur Henry Bullen, vol. 2 (George Bell and Sons, 1896), 2:134.

43. Quoted in Marsh, *Music and Society*, 66.

44. McLoughlin, *Modern Revivalism*, 95–98.

45. Perry Miller, "From Edwards to Emerson," in Miller's *Errand into the Wilderness* (Belknap Press of Harvard University Press, 1956), 198.

46. Mather, *Diary of Cotton Mather*, 187.

47. Cotton Mather, *The Accomplished Singer* (B. Green for S. Gerrish, 1721), 13. Also quoted in Karen L. Shadle, "Singing with Spirit and Understanding: Psalmody as Holistic Practice in Late Eighteenth-Century New England," PhD diss., University of North Carolina at Chapel Hill, 2010.

48. George Wither, *A Preparation to The Psalter* (1619), quoted in Finney, "Organical Musick," 280.

49. Kenneth L. Carroll, "Singing in the Spirit in Early Quakerism," *Quaker History* 73, no. 1 (Spring 1984): 1–13.

50. Carroll, "Singing in the Spirit in Early Quakerism," 5.

51. Marsh, *Music and Society*, 64.

52. Thomas S. Kidd, *The Great Awakening: The Roots of Evangelical Christianity in Colonial America* (Yale University Press, 2009). Arminianism was a theological perspective originating in the teachings of the Dutch theologian Jacobus Arminius in the early seventeenth century. It emphasized free will, the possibility of resisting grace, and the belief that Christ's atonement is available to all individuals. It contrasted with Calvinist doctrines of predestination and limited atonement.

53. Jonathan Edwards, *Sinners in the Hands of an Angry God* (S. Kneeland and T. Green, 1741).

54. Thomas Foxcroft, *Some Seasonable Thoughts on Evangelic Preaching, Its Nature, Usefulness, and Obligation* (G. Rogers and D. Fowke, 1740), 43.

55. William Law, *Serious Call to a Devout and Holy Life*, 2nd ed. (William Innys, 1732), 286–87.

56. Jonathan Edwards, *The Works of Jonathan Edwards*, ed. Edward Hickman, vol. 1 (William Ball, 1819), 1:lv.

57. Jonathan Edwards, *Works of Jonathan Edwards*, 1:xii.

58. George Whitefield, *A Continuation of the Reverend Mr. Whitefield's Journal* (James Hutton, 1740), 5:71–72.

59. Isaac Watts, "Thoughts on Poetry and Musick," in *The Grounds and Rules of Musick Explained: or, An Introduction to the Art of Singing by Note*, ed. Thomas Walter (Benjamin Mecom, 1760).

60. Joseph Strong, "The Duty of Singing, Considered as a Necessary and Useful Part of Christian Worship" (Thomas and Samuel Green, 1773), 20, quoted in Shadle, "Singing with Spirit and Understanding," 89.

61. Shadle, "Singing with Spirit and Understanding," 94–95.

62. M[artin] M[adan], *A Full and Compleat Answer to the Capital Errors, Contained in the Writings of the Late Rev. William Law* (1763), quoted in Susie I. Tucker, *Enthusiasm: A Study in Semantic Change* (Cambridge University Press, 1972), 27. English philosophers and jurists had made use of the term in similar ways for at least a century. Jon Mee, *Romanticism, Enthusiasm, and Regulation: Poetics and the Policing of Culture in the Romantic Period* (Oxford University Press, 2003), 3.

63. Charles Chauncy, *Seasonable Thoughts on the State of Religion in New-England* (Rogers and Fowle, 1743), 182.

64. Chauncy, *Seasonable Thoughts*, 239.

65. Jonathan Edwards, *The Works of President Edwards, in Four Volumes*, vol. 1 (Leavitt, Trow and Company, 1844), 1:531.

66. Jonathan Edwards, *Thoughts on Revival of Religion in New England, 1742* (Dunning and Spalding, 1832), 122.

67. Harold P. Simonson, *Jonathan Edwards: Theologian of the Heart* (Mercer University Press, 1982), 50, 58–59. See also Jonathan Edwards, *A Treatise Concerning Religious Affections, in Three Parts* (Boston: S. Kneeland and T. Green, 1746; Ann Arbor: Text Creation Partnership, 2011), part 2:37–38, accessed November 28, 2023, https://quod.lib.umich.edu/e/evans/N04635.0001.001.

68. Edwards, *A Treatise Concerning Religious Affections*, part 2:332–33.

69. Quoted in Ann Taves, *Fits, Trances, and Visions: Experiencing Religion and Explaining Experience from Wesley to James* (Princeton University Press, 1999), 37.

70. Richard P. Heitzenrater, *Wesley and the People Called Methodists*, 2nd ed. (Abington, 2013).

71. Henry Moore, *The Life of the Rev. John Wesley, A. M.*, vol. I (Printed for John Kershaw, 1824), 1:95.

72. Moore, *Life of the Rev. John Wesley*, 1:95.

73. Steve McCormick, "Theosis in Chrysostom and Wesley: An Eastern Paradigm on Faith and Love," *Wesleyan Theological Journal* 26 (1991): 50.

74. Wesley, too, would strive to make distinctions between what he called "proper enthusiasm" and "reasonable [or improper] enthusiasm." W. Stephen Gunter, *The Limits of "Love Divine": John Wesley's Response to Antinomianism and Enthusiasm* (Kingswood Books, 1989), 127, 134–37.

75. John Wesley, *The Works of Reverend John Wesley* (John Jones, 1809), 186–87 (February 1736).

76. J. Steven O'Malley, "Pietistic Influence on John Wesley: Wesley and Gerhard Tersteegen," *Wesleyan Theological Journal* 31, no. 2 (Fall 1996): 66.

77. John Wesley, *The Journal of John Wesley* (Oxford University Press, 1980), 66.

78. Wesley, *Journal of John Wesley*, 67.

79. Charles Wesley, *The Early Journal of Charles Wesley* (Charles H. Kelly, 1909), 147.

80. Roger J. Green, "1738 John & Charles Wesley Experience Conversions," *Christian History Home* 28 (1990), accessed November 28, 2023, http://www.christianitytoday.com/ch/1990/issue28/2844.html.

81. John Wesley, *The Works of John Wesley*, vol. 7: *Letters* (Zondervan Publishing House, 1872), p. 71. (Quoted in Taves, *Fits, Trances, and Visions*, 51.)

82. Leslie Griffiths, "Traditions and Spiritual Guidance: Spirituality and the Hymns of Charles Wesley," *The Way* 31 (1991): 333.

83. Jack Stephen Kroll-Smith, "In Search of Status Power: The Baptist Revival in Colonial Virginia, 1760–1776," PhD diss., University of Pennsylvania, 1982, 163.

84. James Downey, "The Music of American Revivalism," PhD diss., Tulane University, 1968, 93.

85. Downey, "Music of American Revivalism," 93–95.

86. Quoted in Alan Heimer and Perry Miller, eds., *The Great Awakening: Documents Illustrating the Crisis and Its Consequences* (Bobbs-Merrill, 1967), 202–3.

87. Daniel Fristoe's journal 1771, in Lewis Peyton Little, *Imprisoned Preachers and Religious Liberty in Virginia: A Narrative Drawn Largely from the Official Records of Virginia Counties, Unpublished Manuscripts, Letters, and Other Original Sources* (J.P. Bell Co., 1938), 243.

88. Clifton Ellis, "Dissenting Faith and Domestic Landscape in Eighteenth-Century Virginia," in *Everyday Landscapes: Perspectives in Vernacular Architecture, VII*, ed. Annmarie Adams and Sally McMurry (University of Tennessee Press, 1997), 32.

89. Quoted in Little, *Imprisoned Preachers*, 230.

90. "Waller, Rev. John," in *The Baptist Encyclopaedia*, ed. William Cathcart, D.D. (Everts, 1881), 1205–6.

91. Quoted in Little, *Imprisoned Preachers*, 231.

92. Quoted in Little, *Imprisoned Preachers*, 231.

93. Stephen J. Stein, *The Shaker Experience in America: A History of the United Society of Believers* (Yale University Press, 1992), 3–9; Edward Deming Andrews, *The People Called Shakers: A Search for the Perfect Society* (Dover, 1963), 3–7.

94. Benjamin Seth Youngs, et al, *The Testimony of Christ's Second Appearing*, 2nd ed. (E. and E. Hosford, State Street, 1810), xxv, accessed December 15, 2024, https://archive.org/details/testimonyofchris1810youn/.

95. Stein, *Shaker Experience in America*, 3–9; Andrews, *People Called Shakers*, 3–7.

96. Stein, *Shaker Experience in America*, 3–9; Andrews, *People Called Shakers*, chap. 1.

97. Stein, *Shaker Experience in America*, 10–24; Andrews, *People Called Shakers*, chap. 1.

98. S. Y. Wells, ed., *Testimonies Concerning the Character and Ministry of Mother Ann Lee and the First Witnesses of the Gospel* (Packard & Van Benthuysen, 1827), 101, accessed December 12, 2024, https://babel.hathitrust.org/cgi/ssd?id=umn.319510014985649. Also quoted in D. W. Patterson, *Gift Drawing and Gift Song: A Study of Two Forms of Shaker Inspiration* (United Society of Shakers, 1983), 18.

99. Quoted in Flo Morse, *The Shakers and the World's People* (University Press of New England, 1980), 23.

100. Stein, *Shaker Experience in America*, 25–37.

101. Valentine Rathbun, *Some Brief Hints of a Religious Scheme, Taught and Propagated by a Number of Europeans, Living in a Place Called Nisqueunia, in the State of New-York* (Benjamin Edes and Sons, 1782), 6–7, accessed December 15, 2024, https://name.umdl.umich.edu/N13973.0001.001.

102. Stein, *Shaker Experience in America*, 47.

103. Daniel W. Patterson, *The Shaker Spiritual* (Dover, 2000), 107–15; Kimerer L. Lamothe, "Enlivening Spirits: Shaker Dance Ritual as Theopraxis," *Théologiques* 25, no. 1 (2017): 114–15.

104. Patterson, *Shaker Spiritual*, 116–21; Lamothe, "Enlivening Spirits," 114–15.

105. Patterson, *Shaker Spiritual*, 122–30; Lamothe, "Enlivening Spirits," 114–15.

106. Janet Sarbanes, "The Shaker 'Gift' Economy: Charisma, Aesthetic Practice and Utopian Communalism," *Utopian Studies* 20, no. 1 (2009): 130–34; Patterson, *Shaker Spiritual*, 316–76.

107. Quoted in Patterson, *Shaker Spiritual*, 323–24.

108. Sarbanes, "Shaker 'Gift' Economy," 130.

109. For the most comprehensive overview of the meaning and content of Shaker songs, see Patterson, *Shaker Spiritual*.

110. Stein, *Shaker Experience in America*, 184–214.

111. Stein, *Shaker Experience in America*, 200–354.

112. Works that support this viewpoint include John Bodo, *The Protestant Clergy and Public Issues, 1812–1848* (Princeton University Press, 1954); Charles C. Cole Jr., *The Social Ideas of the Northern Evangelists, 1820–1860* (Columbia University Press, 1954); Charles Foster, *An Errand of Mercy: The Evangelical United Front, 1790–1837* (University of North Carolina Press, 1960); Perry Miller, *Nature's Nation* (Belknap Press of Harvard University Press, 1967), 115; Donald Mathews, "The Second Great Awakening as an Organizing Process, 1780–1830: An Hypothesis," *American Quarterly* 21, no. 1 (Spring 1969): 23–43.

113. Nathan Hatch, *The Democratization of American Christianity* (Yale University Press, 1989); John H. Wigger, *Taking Heaven by Storm: Methodism and the Rise of Popular Christianity in America* (Oxford University Press, 1998).

114. By 1811 the Methodist bishop Francis Asbury reported in his journal that over four hundred camp meetings were held annually along the frontier from Georgia to Michigan. *Encyclopædia Britannica Online*, s. v., "Camp Meeting," accessed November 28, 2023, http://www.britannica.com/topic/camp-meeting.

115. Kenneth O. Brown, *Holy Ground: A Study of the American Camp Meeting* (Garland, 1992), 18.

116. The concerned Presbyterian ministers in attendance were named John Rankin, William Hodge, and James McGready. See John McGee to Thomas L. Douglas, June 23, 1820, *Methodist Magazine* 4 (1821): 191, quoted in John B.

Boles, *The Great Revival: Beginnings of the Bible Belt* (University of Kentucky Press, 1972), 54.

117. Robert Davidson, *History of the Presbyterian Church in the State of Kentucky* (R Carter, 1847), 138, accessed November 28, 2013, https://archive.org/details/historyofpresbyt00davi/page/138/.

118. Davidson, *History of the Presbyterian Church in the State of Kentucky*, 138.

119. Robert Stuart Sanders, *Presbyterianism in Paris and Bourbon County, Kentucky, 1786–1961* (Dunne Press, 1961), 210.

120. Sanders, *Presbyterianism in Paris and Bourbon County, Kentucky, 1786–1961*, 211.

121. Sanders, *Presbyterianism in Paris and Bourbon County, Kentucky, 1786–1961*, 211.

122. Sanders, *Presbyterianism in Paris and Bourbon County, Kentucky, 1786–1961*, 214.

123. Sanders, *Presbyterianism in Paris and Bourbon County, Kentucky, 1786–1961*, 210.

124. Sanders, *Presbyterianism in Paris and Bourbon County, Kentucky, 1786–1961*, 211, 214.

125. Dickson D. Bruce, *And They All Sang Hallelujah: Plain-Folk Camp-Meeting Religion, 1800–1845* (University of Tennessee Press, 1973), 80–82.

126. Catherine A. Brekus, *Strangers and Pilgrims: Female Preaching in America, 1740–1845* (University of North Carolina Press, 1998), 148.

127. Chauncy, *Seasonable Thoughts*, 105.

128. Reed and Matheson, *Narrative of the Visit to the American Churches*, 1:277.

129. Although they do not focus specifically on ecstatic experiences, John F. Kasson, Lawrence Levine, and other historians have identified the growth of an ethos of controlled conduct in American concerts during the nineteenth century. Admittedly, critics have called out these authors for overstating both the periodization and the effectiveness of this regulatory movement. Acknowledging these limitations, the general thrust of their observations nevertheless remains relevant to the topic of this chapter. See Kasson, *Rudeness and Civility*, 239–45. See also David Scobey, "Anatomy of the Promenade: The Politics of Bourgeois Sociability in Nineteenth-Century New York," *Social History* 17, no. 2 (May, 1992): 203–27; Levine, *Highbrow/Lowbrow*; James H. Johnson, *Listening in Paris: A Cultural History* (University of California Press, 1996); William Weber, "Did People Listen in the 18th Century," *Early Music* 25, no. 4 (November 1997): 678–91.

130. Historians and social theorists including Max Weber, E. P. Thompson, Christopher Hill, Paul E. Johnson, Steven Mintz, and Karen Halttunen have argued that the rise of capitalism impelled its would-be beneficiaries to endorse the creation of (1) a disciplined, consistent labor force that was conducive to the smooth functioning of industry; and (2) moral entrepreneurs, protected from the temptations of unfettered capitalism. See Weber, *Protestant Ethic and the Spirit of*

Capitalism, 2005; Weber, *Sociology of Religion*; E. P. Thompson, *Customs in Common: Studies in Traditional Popular Culture* (New Press, 1993); Christopher Hill, *Society and Puritanism in Pre-Revolutionary England* (St Martin's, 1997); Paul E. Johnson, *A Shopkeeper's Millennium: Society and Revivals in Rochester, New York, 1815–1837* (Hill and Wang, 2004); Steven Mintz, *Moralists and Modernizers: America's Pre–Civil War Reformers* (Johns Hopkins University Press, 1995); Karen Halttunen, *Confidence Men and Painted Women: A Study of Middle-Class Culture in America, 1830–1870* (Yale University Press, 1982).

131. Johnson, *Shopkeeper's Millennium*; Stowe, *How Sweet the Sound*.

132. Sven Beckert and Julia Rosenbaum, eds., *The American Bourgeoisie: Distinction and Identity in the Nineteenth Century* (Palgrave Macmillan, 2010). In this volume, see in particular Michael Broyles, "Bourgeois Appropriation of Music," 235.

133. In many regards, this goal perpetuated and elaborated the Wesley brothers' efforts to reconcile "cold rationalism" with "overheated enthusiasm" during the eighteenth century. For reference to "cold rationalism," see Gunter, *Limits of "Love Divine,"* 127, 134–37.

134. See [James Fanning Watson], *Methodist Error* ([n.p.], 1814); Watson, *Methodist Error*, 27. Both sources are cited in Taves, *Fits, Trances, and Visions*, 76n3.

135. Charles Grandison Finney, *Memoirs of Rev. Charles G. Finney* (Applewood Press, [c. 1876] 2009), 19.

136. Finney, *Memoirs of Rev. Charles G. Finney*, 19–20.

137. Finney, *Memoirs of Rev. Charles G. Finney*, 20.

138. Finney, *Memoirs of Rev. Charles G. Finney*, 20.

139. In his *Lectures on Revival of Religion,* Finney claimed that "God has found it necessary to take advantage of the excitability there is in mankind to produce powerful excitements among them before he can lead them to obey." In another tract, *How to Experience Revival,* Finney similarly stated that "pray[ing] with a lack of feeling" prevented the effectiveness of worship. Finney and Leavitt, *Lectures on Revival of Religion*, 9, 194–97; Charles Finney, *How to Experience Revival* (Whitaker House, 2010), 29.

140. Charles Finney, "Letters on Revivals: No. 8," *Oberlin Evangelist* 7 (1845): 75.

141. Finney, "Letters on Revivals: No. 8," 75.

142. Sean McCloud, *Divine Hierarchies: Class in American Religion and Religious Studies* (University of North Carolina, 2009), 165, 132–33; Hatch, *Democratization of American Christianity*, 199.

143. Finney and Leavitt, *Lectures on Revival of Religion*, 66, 250.

144. Thomas Hastings, *Dissertation on Musical Taste* (Mason Brothers, 1853), 249, 250.

145. Hastings, *Dissertation on Musical Taste*, 267, 250.

146. Hastings, *Dissertation on Musical Taste*, 271.

147. Hastings, *Dissertation on Musical Taste*, 171.

148. Hastings, *Dissertation on Musical Taste*, 278.

149. Over the course of his career, Mason composed or arranged approximately sixteen hundred tunes and compiled more than eighty songbooks. His most influential role, however, was as a music educator. After founding the Boston Academy of Music with William Channing Woodbridge in 1833, Mason ran free juvenile classes at Boston's Bowdoin Street Church and also taught at two private schools in the area. He also headed up an initiative that introduced music classes to all public schools in Boston and eventually other cities across America. James A. Keene, *A History of Music Education in the United States* (Glenbridge Publishing, 2010), 102–35.

150. Lowell Mason, *Juvenile Lyre, or Hymns and Songs, Religious, Moral, and Cheerful, Set to Appropriate Music* (Richardson, Lord & Holbrook, 1831), iii–iv.

151. John Ogasapian and N. Lee Orr, *Music of the Gilded Age* (Greenwood, 2007), 88.

152. Kathryn Teresa Long, *The Revival of 1857–1858: Interpreting an American Religious Awakening* (Oxford University Press, 1998); Heath, "Ecstasy."

153. See, for example, McLoughlin, *Revivals, Awakenings, and Reform*.

154. Vinita Hampton and C. J. Wheeler, "The Gallery," *Christian History Magazine* 9, no. 25 (1990): 13.

155. William R. Moody, *The Life of Dwight L. Moody* (Book for the Ages, 1997), 127.

156. Edgar Johnson Goodspeed, *A Full History of the Wonderful Career of Moody and Sankey in Great Britain and America* (John O. Robinson, 1876), 566.

157. Ira Sankey, *Sankey's Story of the Gospel Hymns and of Sacred Songs and Solos* (Sunday School Times Company, 1906), 224–25.

158. Sankey, *Sankey's Story of the Gospel Hymns*, 224–25.

159. Tamara J. Van Dyken, "Singing the Gospel: Evangelical Hymnody, Popular Religion, and American Culture; 1870–1940," PhD diss., University of Notre Dame, December 2008, 39–40, 93; Stowe, *How Sweet the Sound*, 105.

160. Lyle W. Dorsett, *A Passion for Souls: The Life of D. L. Moody* (Moody Publishers, 2003).

161. A. M. Kiergan, *Historical Sketches of the Revival of True Holiness and Church Polity from 1865–1916*, quoted in Donald W. Dayton, *Theological Roots of Pentecostalism* (Francis Asbury, 1987), 177–78.

162. Maria Woodworth-Etter, *Signs and Wonders* (Whitaker House, 1997), 85.

163. Woodworth-Etter, *Signs and Wonders*, 248–50.

164. On the roots and early history of Pentecostalism, see Vinson Synan, *The Holiness-Pentecostal Tradition: Charismatic Movements in the Twentieth Century* (W.B. Eerdmans, 1997); Grant Wacker, *Heaven Below: Early Pentecostals and American Culture* (Harvard University Press, 2001); Dayton, *Theological Roots of Pentecostalism*.

165. Charles Parham, *A Voice Crying in the Wilderness* (CreateSpace Independent Publishing), 11.

166. Parham, *Voice Crying in the Wilderness*, 11.

167. Adolfo C. Valdez, "Fire on the Street," quoted in Gastón Espinosa, "Tongues and Healing at the Azusa Street Revival," in *Religions of the United States in Practice*, ed. Colleen McDannell, vol. 2 (Princeton University Press, 2001), 2:222. Although its most intense period of participation took place during its first three years, the Azusa Street Revival would last for nearly a decade, until 1915.

168. "Weird Fanaticism Fools Young Girl," *Los Angeles Daily Times*, July 12, 1906, quoted in Larry Martin, *The Life and Ministry of William J. Seymour: And a History of the Azusa Street Revival* (Christian Life Books, 1999), 249.

169. Jon Butler, *Awash in a Sea of Faith: Christianizing the American People* (Harvard University Press, 1992).

170. "II. Religion in Eighteenth-Century America," *Religion and the Founding of the American Republic*. Library of Congress, accessed November 28, 2023, https://www.loc.gov/exhibits/religion/rel02.html.

171. Richard J. Carwardine, *Evangelicals and Politics in Antebellum America* (Yale University Press, 1993), 44.

172. Daniel Cavicchi, *Listening and Longing: Music Lovers in the Age of Barnum* (Wesleyan University Press, 2011), 59.

173. Finney and Leavitt, *Lectures on Revival of Religion*, 381.

Chapter 2

1. *Dwight's Journal of Music*, February 5, 1853, 141.

2. "Concerts of the Past Week," *Dwight's Journal of Music*, February 12, 1853, 150.

3. *Dwight's Journal of Music*, April 9, 1853, 6.

4. "Concerts of the Past Week," *Dwight's Journal of Music*, February 12, 1853, 151.

5. *Dwight's Journal of Music*, April 9, 1853, 5.

6. *Dwight's Journal of Music*, April 9, 1853, 5.

7. *Dwight's Journal of Music*, April 9, 1853, 5.

8. *Dwight's Journal of Music*, April 9, 1853, 6.

9. *Dwight's Journal of Music*, April 9, 1853, 5.

10. For an overview of the transcendentalist idea of art, see Ralph Waldo Emerson, "Art," in *The Complete Works of Ralph Waldo Emerson: Society and Solitude*, vol. 7 (Houghton, Mifflin and Company, 1903–1904), 7:37–57.

11. Jamie James, *The Music of the Spheres: Music, Science, and the Natural Order of the Universe* (Copernicus, 1993).

12. Mee, *Romanticism, Enthusiasm, and Regulation*. Although the term "enthusiasm" was more consistently used as a pejorative in Protestantism, John Wesley too distinguished between what he called "proper enthusiasm" and "reasonable [or improper] enthusiasm." Gunter, *Limits of "Love Divine*," 127, 134–37.

13. For an elaboration on the supernatural qualities of Romanticism, see M. H. Abrams, *Natural Supernaturalism: Tradition and Revolution in Romantic Literature* (W.W. Norton, 1971).

14. Otto, *The Idea of the Holy.*

15. Admittedly, using "Romanticism" as an umbrella term to encompass all the traditions discussed in this chapter might be seen as controversial by some, because the term was often associated exclusively with those traditions that venerated notions of the sublime. Historically, however, the term was also used more loosely to identify the amalgam of traditions that encouraged a sincere emotional engagement with earthly entities. This chapter employs that broader, more versatile usage of the word.

16. See Shirley Samuels, ed., *Culture of Sentiment* (Oxford University Press, 1992).

17. Olsen, *Turn to Transcendence*, 210.

18. Olsen, *Turn to Transcendence*, 211.

19. Matthew Stewart, *Nature's God: The Heretical Origins of the American Republic* (W.W. Norton, 2014).

20. The liberal view accepted, even celebrated, religious beliefs but only as long as they did not enable the ascendency of one religious belief system over another in the public sphere. In this sense, it installed toleration and moderation as core principles of society. These were supra-religious in the sense that they were intended to override immoderate tendencies within any individual faith, denomination, or sect and they prevented the devotees of one religious tradition from claiming the final authority over public life. Ultimately, the supremacy of a secular, civic institution ensured that Puritans, Quakers, Baptists, and other religious groups could coexist without resorting to a permanent state of internecine conflict. This scenario also helped create a united national identity, and it encouraged economic growth by allowing people from diverse regions and backgrounds to immigrate and join a rapidly growing labor force. This view is cogently summarized by Stanley Fish, "Liberalism and Secularism: One and the Same," *New York Times*, September 2, 2007. Admittedly, historians have debated the importance of secularity (i.e., nonreligious values) in early philosophies of liberalism in America. See, for instance, Mark D. McGarvie, *One Nation Under Law: America's Early National Struggles to Separate Church and State* (Northern Illinois University Press, 2004); Philip Hamburger, *Separation of Church and State* (Harvard University Press, 2002).

21. According to Campbell, this moral belief stemmed from an enduring orientation he calls the "Other Protestant Ethic," going back to the earliest days of the Reformation. Campbell, *Romantic Ethic*, 99–137.

22. Campbell, *Romantic Ethic*, 120, 141. Some of Cambridge University's Platonists happened to take an interest in music. Thomas Mace, a well-known musician, composer, and theorist, taught singing to one Cambridge Platonist (John Worthington), for instance, and was well known to another (Henry More). See Penelope Gouk, *Music, Science and Natural Magic* (Yale University Press, 1999), 44.

Mace also appears to have shared his Cambridge associates' penchant for emotional experience. In his well-known publication, *Musick's Monument*, Mace described the rapture he experienced when singing psalms together with organ accompaniment: "When *that Vast-Conchording-Unity* of the whole *Congregational-Chorus*, came (as I may say) *Thundering in*, even so, as it made the very *Ground shake* under us; *(Oh the unutterable ravishing Soul's delight!)* In the which I was so *transported*, and *wrapt* up into *High Contemplations*, that there was no room left in my *whole Man*, viz. *Body, Soul* and *Spirit*, for any thing below *Divine* and *Heavenly Raptures*; Nor could there possibly be any *Thing* in *Earth*, to which *That* very *Singing* might be truly compar'd, except the Right apprehensions or conceivings of *That glorious and miraculous Quire* [choir], recorded in the *Scriptures*, at the *Dedication* of the *Temple*." Thomas Mace, *Musick's Monument* (L. T. Ratcliffe and N. Thompson, for the Author, 1676), 19.

23. According to Campbell, this turn toward tender sentiments would have been reinforced not only by the positive emotionalism that accompanied benevolence. It also would have resulted indirectly from the residue of "negative emotionalism" inherited from Calvinism—specifically, the melancholy, self-doubt, and morbidity that Puritans accepted (if not admired) as appropriate dispositions for pious individuals aware of their inherent depravity but ignorant of their election. While not exactly tender, these sentiments nevertheless represented a tacit tradition of emotionalism that had long been rooted in Calvinism and that lingered on even as the orthodox strains of that tradition began to wane. Campbell, *Romantic Ethic*, 131.

24. Campbell, *Romantic Ethic*, 131.

25. It was during this period that "sentimentality" lost its general affiliation with all types of affect and gained its more specific, modern connotation with benevolent feelings, empathy, and high emotional responsiveness. Campbell, *Romantic Ethic*, 139.

26. Michael Ferber, *Romanticism: A Very Short Introduction* (Oxford University Press, 2010), 15.

27. Occasionally, and early on in the movement, sentimentalists connected the feelings of sensibility to a Christian God. For instance, the Anglo-Irish novelist and clergyman Laurence Sterne declared that a degree of pity, sympathy, and benevolence constituted "God's contact with mankind." It was, according to Sterne, an act of grace that worked through the human nervous system, such that a display of tears incited a Man (or Woman) of Feeling to make proclamations like "I am positive I have a soul." Likewise, the English novelist Samuel Richardson contended that his own sentimental writing conveyed "the great doctrines of Christianity." Sterne quoted in Campbell, *Romantic Ethic*, 141. Richardson quoted in Lori Branch, *Rituals of Spontaneity: Sentiment and Secularism from Free Prayer to Wordsworth* (Baylor University Press, 2006), 136.

28. As Allison Coudert observes, moral sense philosophers like Adam Smith made "no mention whatsoever of religion or revelation" in their discussion of sentimentality and sensibility. Allison Coudert, *Religion, Magic, and Science in Early Modern Europe and America* (Praeger, 2011), 117.

29. One example of the spiritual quality of sentimentality comes from the English writer Hannah More's poem *Sensibility*, from 1782, which described a "sweet" and "secret" power that ineffably "eludes the chains of definition" and is imparted only to a select few at birth. Such a description was comparable to the Calvinist notion of grace as described in its doctrine of predestination. Hannah More, *The Works of Hannah More*, vol. 1 (S. G. Goodrich, 1827), 35.

30. J. M. S. Tompkins, *The Popular Novel in England 1770–1800*, quoted in Campbell, *Romantic Ethic*, 139.

31. R. F. Brissenden, *Virtue in Distress: Studies in the Novel of Sentiment from Richardson to Sade* (Macmillan, 1974), 20.

32. Branch, *Rituals of Spontaneity*, 136.

33. Walter Francis Wright, *Sensibility in English Prose Fiction, 1760–1814: A Reinterpretation* (Folcroft Press, [1937] 1970), 24.

34. Knott also demonstrates how, beyond fostering social cohesion within a new nation, American displays of sensibility enabled sentimentalists to showcase a level of identification with the genteel, sentimental classes of Europe, which many American elites counted as equals. Sarah Knott, *Sensibility and the American Revolution* (University of North Carolina Press, 2009).

35. Torre argues that the growing market economy in America encouraged a reassessment of the concept of "value." In the early republic, many Americans found themselves deeply in debt and interested in increasing their capital quickly. Therefore, they began to reject older notions of value as something intrinsic and objective in favor of a new conception, promoted by David Hume and other moral sense philosophers, which approached value as something constructed, malleable, and based on subjective feeling. This shift was meant to promote paper credit and the lending capacity of banks while simultaneously sparking a new era of sociability and interdependence in the commercial sphere. Jose Torre, *The Political Economy of Sentiment: Paper Credit and the Scottish Enlightenment in Early Republic Boston, 1780–1820* (Pickering & Chatto, 2007).

36. Denis Diderot described the overwhelming sensations he experienced, as a Man of Feeling, when he contemplated anyone else who led a virtuous life: "Then it seems as if my heart were distended even beyond my body, as if it were swimming; a delicious and sudden sensation of I know not what passes over my whole body; I can hardly breathe; it quickens over the whole surface of my body like a shudder." Here, the author's empathy transformed into outright identification with the objects of his feelings. But Diderot's was not a religious experience in the conventional sense. It was neither instigated by nor directed at a supernatural source, but instead seemed to stem from the self-transcendent power of emotion itself. Quoted in Campbell, *Romantic Ethic*, 140. Adam Smith also discussed a similar phenomenon when he wrote of a profound sympathetic tendency (paramount to modern notions of "empathy") among individuals who recruited the power of one's imagination to almost "carry us beyond our own person." In this capacity, he

contended that "we place ourselves in [another's] situation . . . we enter as it were into his body, and become in some measure the same person with him." The power of the imagination, Smith clarified, was not capable of completely re-creating one's experience within another individual, making the sensations of the latter "weaker in degree." However, the similarity of the sentiments was close enough in his estimation to elicit a kind of social, secular ecstasy. Adam Smith, *The Theory of Moral Sentiments*, ed. Knud Haakonssen (Cambridge University Press, 2002), pt. 1, sec. 1, paragraph 2, pp. 11–12.

37. Victor Turner, *The Ritual Process: Structure and Anti-Structure* (Routledge & Kegan Paul, 1969); Victor Turner, *Dramas, Fields, and Metaphors: Symbolic Action in Human Society* (Cornell University Press, 1974); Edith Turner, *Communitas: The Anthropology of Collective Joy* (Palgrave Macmillan, 2012); Victor Turner, "Liminal to Liminoid in Play, Flow, and Ritual: An Essay in Comparative Symbology," *Rice University Studies* 60, no. 3 (1974): 53–92.

38. Quoted in David Warren Steel, "Sacred Music in Early Winchester," *Connecticut Historical Society Bulletin* 45 (1980): 36.

39. G. J. Barker-Benfield, *Abigail and John Adams: The Americanization of Sensibility* (University of Chicago Press, 2010).

40. According to the historian Joyce Appleby, the first generation of the early republic fashioned an image of the ideal citizen as an autonomous individual who voluntarily participated in civil society (e.g., temperance societies, foreign missions, antislavery movement), free enterprise, the political process, and other trappings of a liberal society. Joyce Appleby, *Inheriting the Revolution: The First Generation of Americans* (Harvard University Press, 2000).

41. William Hill Brown and Hannah Webster Foster, *The Power of Sympathy and the Coquette* (Penguin, 1996), 87.

42. Brown and Foster, *Power of Sympathy and the Coquette*, 48–49.

43. Richard Walser, "Boston's Reception of the First American Novel," *Early American Literature* 17, no. 1 (1982): 72.

44. James Hook, "I Leave My Heart With Thee" (I & M Paff, 1804), located in Johns Hopkins University, Levy Sheet Music Collection, Box 110, Item 010.

45. Thomas Moore and John Stevenson, *A Selection of Popular National Airs* (V. Thurston, 1818), 51–53.

46. *Godey's* magazine regularly referenced music in articles and published songs every week. Julia Eklund Koza, "Music and the Feminine Sphere: Images of Women as Musicians in 'Godey's Lady's Book' 1830–1877," *Musical Quarterly* 75, no. 2 (Summer 1991): 103.

47. Miss Mary E. Macmichael, "The School-Fellows," *Godey's Lady's Book* 13, no. 2 (August 1836), 68–69.

48. Macmichael, "School-Fellows," 68–69.

49. Thomas R. Lounsbury, ed., *Yale Book of American Verse* (Yale University Press, 1912), 11.

50. Charles Hamm, *Music in the New World* (W.W. Norton, 1983), 176.

51. Quoted in Tawa, *Sweet Songs for Gentle Americans*, 139.

52. Some professional music families included the Cheney Family, the Rogers Family, the Baker Family, and the Wright Family.

53. Hutchinson Family, "The Old Granite State" (Oliver Ditson, 1843).

54. Nicholas E. Tawa, *Sweet Songs for Gentle Americans: The Parlor Song in America, 1790–1860* (Bowling Green University Popular Press, 1980), 82.

55. Jesse Hutchinson Jr. and E. W. Hazard, "The Case of Judson Hutchinson" (letters to the editor), *Spiritual Philosopher* 1, no. 15 (November 9, 1850): 113–14.

56. Scott Gac, *Singing for Freedom: The Hutchinson Family Singers and the Nineteenth Century* (Yale University Press, 2007), 102.

57. Jesse Hutchinson, "Get off the Track!" (Jesse Hutchinson, 1844). In advocating for moral causes sometimes in defiance of orthodox Christian doctrine, the Hutchinsons might be said to have been part of a larger liberal religious order during the antebellum era that rejected conventional Christianity's sanctification of pain and suffering as an undue justification for slavery. See Elizabeth B. Clark, " 'The Sacred Rights of the Weak': Pain, Sympathy, and the Culture of Individual Rights in Antebellum America," *Journal of American History* 82, no. 2 (September 1995): 463–93.

58. Henry Dickinson Stone, *Personal Recollections of the Drama or Theatrical Reminiscences* (Charles van Benthuysen & Sons, 1873), 10.

59. Emma Stebbins, ed., *Charlotte Cushman: Her Letters and Memories of Her Life* (Houghton, 1879), 87.

60. Wilhelm Heinrich Wackenroder, *Confessions and Fantasies*, trans. Mary Hurst Schubert (Pennsylvania State University Press, 1971), 179. In another essay, Wackenroder wrote a fictional story about a composer during the mid-eighteenth century who struggled to distance himself from the mundane duties of a utilitarian life by listening to music and embracing the passionate trance it induced in him. Wackenroder, *Confessions and Fantasies*, 155.

61. Ludwig Theobald Kosegarten, *Die Harmonie der Sphaeren* (1797), reproduced in Godwin, *Music, Mysticism, and Magic*, 190.

62. Kosegarten, *Die Harmonie der Sphaeren* (1797), reproduced in Godwin, *Music, Mysticism, and Magic*, 189.

63. The German philosopher Friedrich Schelling affirmed the spiritual assessment of nature when he proclaimed that "nature shall be visible spirit, and spirit invisible nature." Friedrich Schelling, "Ideas for a Philosophy of Nature as Introduction to the Study of This Science" (1797), trans. Albert Hofstadter, in *Philosophy of German Idealism: Fichte, Jacobi, and Schelling*, ed. Ernst Behler (Continuum, 2003), 202.

64. Edmund Burke, *A Philosophical Enquiry into the Origin of Our Ideas of the Sublime and the Beautiful* (Oxford University Press, [1757] 1990); Immanuel Kant, *Observations on the Feeling of the Beautiful and the Sublime*, trans. John T.

Goldthwait (University of California Press, [1764] 1960); Immanuel Kant, *Critique of Judgement*, trans. James Creed Meredith (Clarendon Press, [1790] 1964).

65. Christopher Partridge, *The Lyre of Orpheus: Popular Music, the Sacred, and the Profane* (Oxford University Press, 2014), 122.

66. Jeanette Bicknell, *Why Music Moves Us* (Palgrave Macmillan, 2009), 34.

67. Bicknell, *Why Music Moves Us*, 36.

68. David Hume's philosophies, which argued that selfhood was essentially malleable, seemed to validate this inclination toward secular entrancement. Hume theorized that the true self could not narrowly be attributed to any natural state, for instance as the agent of rational will. Although he acknowledged the concept of a singular, unified "self" was a useful category for dealing with matters of personal accountability and jurisprudence, he claimed that the true self was always divisible and mutable. As such, the illusion of normal selfhood arose only from the habitual associations one's mind makes between similar experiences. See Becker, *Deep Listeners*, 91; Mary Douglas, "The Person in an Enterprise Culture," in *Understanding the Enterprise Culture: Themes in the Work of Mary Douglas*, ed. Shaun Hargreaves Heap and Angus Ross (Edinburgh University Press, 1992), 44.

69. E. T. A. Hoffmann, "Beethoven's Instrumental Music (1813)," in *Strunk's Source Readings in Music History (Revised Edition)*, ed. Oliver Strunk (W.W. Norton, 1998), 1194–96.

70. Arthur Schopenhauer, "Music as the Cosmic Will Revealed," in *The World as Will and Idea*, trans. R. B. Haldane and J. Kemp (Kegan Paul, Trench, Trübner & Co., 1907), 1:143.

71. Schopenhauer, "Music as the Cosmic Will Revealed," 1:340.

72. Many of the founding members of transcendentalism pursued extensive religious education at Harvard Divinity School or trained as Unitarian ministers. Ian Frederick Finseth, "'Liquid Fire Within Me': Language, Self and Society in Transcendentalism and Early Evangelicalism, 1820–1860," master's thesis, University of Virginia, 1995.

73. In venerating emotional experiences, Emerson and his colleagues tended to reject a prevailing impulse among many Unitarians to favor calm, cool reason. Andrea Greenwood and Mark W. Harris, *An Introduction to the Unitarian and Universalist Traditions* (Cambridge University Press, 2011).

74. Ralph Waldo Emerson, "The Transcendentalist: A Lecture Read at the Mason Temple, Boston, January 1842," in *The Complete Works of Ralph Waldo Emerson, Nature: Addresses and Lectures*, vol. 1 (Houghton, Mifflin and Company, 1903–1904), 1:329–59.

75. Emerson, *Complete Works of Ralph Waldo Emerson*, 1:9.

76. Emerson, *Complete Works of Ralph Waldo Emerson*, 1:10.

77. Emerson, *Complete Works of Ralph Waldo Emerson*, 2:270.

78. Emerson himself had traveled to Britain and talked in person with these poets as well as to Thomas Carlyle. Emerson, *Complete Works of Ralph Waldo Emerson*, 1:xxiii.

79. The two poets' co-publication in 1798 of the seminal compendium of Romantic literature, *Lyrical Ballads, with a Few Other Poems*, suggested they, like the ancient Greeks, conflated ballads and poems.

80. William Wordsworth, *The Miscellaneous Poems of William Wordsworth*, vol. 2 (Longman, Hurst, Rees, Orme, and Brown, 1820), 2:157.

81. Samuel Taylor Coleridge, "Kubla Khan" in *The Oxford Book of English Verse: 1250–1900*, ed. Arthur Quiller-Couch (Clarendon, 1904), 650–51.

82. Emerson's conflation of song and poetry is exemplified by his 1836 poem commemorating a battle fought in Massachusetts at the outbreak of the Revolutionary War, which he musically titled "Concord Hymn." Ralph Waldo Emerson, *Complete Works of Ralph Waldo Emerson*, 9:158–59.

83. Quoted in Irving Lowens, "Writings About Music in the Periodicals of American Transcendentalism (1835–50)," *Journal of American Musicological Society* 10, no. 2 (Summer 1957): 79.

84. Amos Bronson Alcott, *The Journals of Bronson Alcott*, ed. Odell Shepard (Little, Brown, 1938), 240–41, entry for February 9, 1951.

85. Quoted in Lowens, "Writings About Music in the Periodicals of American Transcendentalism," 71.

86. "The First Night of 'Fidelio' in America," *The Corsair*, September 14, 1839: 423. (Originally printed in *The American*, September 10, 1839.)

87. George Templeton Strong's diary entry from April 16, 1843, quoted in Vera Brodsky Lawrence, *Strong on Music*, vol. 1: *Resonances, 1836–1849* (University of Chicago Press, 1988), 1:182.

88. George Templeton Strong's diary entry from November 2, 1841, quoted in Lawrence, *Strong on Music*, 1:115.

89. Nicholas E. Tawa, *From Psalm to Symphony: A History of Music in New England* (Northeastern University Press, 2001), 107.

90. "On Music," an unpublished essay in the Boston Public Library, as cited in Lowens, "Writings About Music in the Periodicals of American Transcendentalism," 75. Many of the ideas set out in this essay were reiterated and elucidated in Dwight's later article for Elizabeth P. Peabody's publication *Aesthetic Papers*.

91. John Sullivan Dwight, "Music," in *Aesthetic Papers*, ed. Elizabeth P. Peabody (AMS Press, [1849] 1967), 30.

92. Tawa, *From Psalm to Symphony*, 126.

93. Louis Moreau Gottschalk, *Notes of a Pianist* (Princeton University Press, 2006), 127.

94. H. Earle Johnson, "The Germania Musical Society," *Musical Quarterly* 39, no. 1 (January 1953): 75–93.

95. "Concerts of the Past Week," *Dwight's Journal of Music*, February 12, 1853, 151.

96. "Concerts of the Past Week," *Dwight's Journal of Music*, February 12, 1853, 151.

97. "Concerts of the Past Week," *Dwight's Journal of Music*, February 12, 1853, 149–51, 150.

98. Walt Whitman, *The Complete Writings of Walt Whitman*, ed. Richard M. Bucke, Thomas B. Harned, and Horace L. Traubel, vol. 7 (G.P. Putnam's Sons, 1902), 7:106.

99. John Townsend Trowbridge, "Reminiscences of Walt Whitman," *Atlantic Monthly* 89, no. 2 (February 1902), 166.

100. Donald Barlow Stauffer, "Opera and Opera Singers," in *The Routledge Encyclopedia of Walt Whitman*, ed. J. R. LeMaster and Donald D. Kummings (Routledge, 1998), 484–86.

101. Walt Whitman, "Letters from Paumanok," *New York Evening Post*, August 14, 1851, [1].

102. Stauffer, "Opera and Opera Singers," in *Routledge Encyclopedia of Walt Whitman*, 484–86.

103. See, for example: "Out of the Cradle Endlessly Rocking," "When Lilacs Last in the Dooryard Bloom'd," "Proud Music of the Storm," "Chants Democratic," "Italian Music in Dakota," "I Hear America Singing," "Vocalism." Stauffer, "Opera and Opera Singers," in *Routledge Encyclopedia of Walt Whitman*, 484–86.

104. Whitman, *Complete Writings of Walt Whitman*, 1:67.

105. Whitman, *Complete Writings of Walt Whitman*, 2:150.

106. Whitman, *Complete Writings of Walt Whitman*, 4:288.

107. Richard Wagner, *Wagner on Music and Drama: A Compendium of Richard Wagner's Prose Works*, ed. Albert Goldman and Evert Sprinchorn, trans. H. Ashton Ellis (Da Capo, 1964), 186.

108. Wagner, *Wagner on Music and Drama*, 186, 184.

109. As reported by Engelbert Humperdinck in Arthur M. Abell, *Talks with Great Composers* (Citadel, 1998), 137–38.

110. Richard Wagner, *Tristan und Isolde (Tristan and Isolda): Opera in Three Acts* (Fred Rullman, 1865), 55. This English translation of the libretto was provided to patrons during the early decades of the opera's performance at New York's Metropolitan Opera House.

111. Burton D. Fisher, ed., *Wagner's Tristan and Isolde*, Opera Journeys Mini Guides Series (Opera Journeys Publishing, 2002), 18–19.

112. Fisher, *Wagner's Tristan and Isolde*, 18–30.

113. M. Carey Thomas Papers, *M. Carey Thomas to Mary Garrett, March 3, 1891* (letter), Bryn Mawr College Library, Special Collections, Reel 148, accessed December 1, 2024, https://digitalcollections.tricolib.brynmawr.edu/object/bmc25087.

114. M. Carey Thomas Papers, *M. Carey Thomas to Mary Garrett, August 23, 1891*, Reel 148, accessed December 1, 2024, https://digitalcollections.tricolib.brynmawr.edu/object/bmc22818.

115. Ella Wheeler Wilcox, "The Prelude to 'Tristan und Isolde,'" *Munsey's*, December 1894, 288.

116. Taves, *Fits, Trances, and Visions*, 127.

117. John Anthony Andola, "Nathaniel Hawthorne's Use of Mesmerism in Four Major Works," PhD diss., Bell State University, 1977; Samuel Coale, "The Romance of Mesmerism: Hawthorne's Medium of Romance," in *Nathaniel Hawthorne, Updated Edition*, ed. Harold Bloom (Chelsea House, 2009); Maria M. Tatar, *Spellbound: Studies on Mesmerism and Literature* (Princeton University Press, 1978); Samuel Chase Coale, *Mesmerism and Hawthorne: Mediums of American Romance* (University of Alabama Press, 1998); David S. Reynolds, " 'Its Wood Could Only Be American!' Moby-Dick and Antebellum Popular Culture," in *Herman Melville's Moby-Dick*, ed. Harold Bloom (Infobase, 2007).

118. Tatar, *Spellbound*.

119. H. W. Brands, *The First American: The Life and Times of Benjamin Franklin* (Doubleday, 2000), 325; David A. Gallo and Stanley Finger, "The Power of a Musical Instrument: Franklin, the Mozarts, Mesmer, and the Glass Armonica," *History of Psychology* 3, no. 4 (November 2000): 326–43; Peregrine Horden, "Commentary on Part V, with Notes on Nineteenth-Century America and on Mesmerism and Theosophy," in *Music as Medicine: The History of Music Therapy Since Antiquity*, ed. Peregrine Horden (Ashgate, 2000), 326; James Kennaway, "Musical Hypnosis: Sound and Selfhood from Mesmerism to Brainwashing," *Social History of Medicine* 25, no. 2 (May 2012): 273.

120. From *Report of Dr. Benjamin Franklin, and other Commissioners, charged by the King of France, with the Examination of the Animal Magnetism, as Now Practiced at Paris* (Johnson, 1785), 25–27.

121. In a report on animal magnetism in 1836, Poyen stated: "Now . . . magnetizers . . . help themselves neither with the influence of music nor the power of imitation." Henri Marie Husson and Charles Poyen St Sauveur, *Report on the Magnetical Experiments: Made by the Commission of the Royal Academy of Medicine, of Paris, Read in the Meetings of June 21 and 28, 1831* (D. K. Kitchcock, 1836), xii.

122. Herman Melville, *Pierre; or, The Ambiguities* (Harper & Brothers, 1852), 172–73.

123. Emanuel Swedenborg, *Heaven and Its Wonders and Hell: From Things Heard and Seen* (Swedenborg Foundation, 2009).

124. Taves, *Fits, Trances, and Visions*, 178.

125. Because spiritualists envisioned the spirit realm as somewhat separate from the natural world, their tradition might be said to incorporate supernatural beliefs that fit uncomfortably within the naturalized mode. In this respect, spiritualism did not fit exclusively within any single modal framework and therefore might be considered modally malleable—a concept that is further discussed in chapter 3. However, spiritualism might still be described as an example of the naturalized mode to the extent that its supporters believed the activities of otherworld spirits could be made manifest to the natural senses of living humans and therefore also had some

form of material existence. The historian Ann Taves has described spiritualism as representing perhaps the first modern instance of "religious naturalism," a philosophy that endeavored to reconcile anything supernatural with verifiable scientific knowledge derived from the study of nature. Taves, *Fits, Trances, and Visions*, 175.

126. J. B. Packard, *The Spirit Minstrel; A Collection of Hymns and Music, for the Use of Spiritualists, in Their Circles and Public Meetings* (Bela Marsh, 1853); James Martin Peebles, *The Spiritual Harp; a Collection of Vocal Music for the Choir, Congregation, and Social Circle* (W. White, 1868). Also see Esther C. Henck, *Spirit Voices: Odes, Dictated by Spirits of the Second Sphere, for the Use of Harmonial Circles* (G. D. Henck, 1854); Emma Hardinge Britten [and Henry Wadsworth Longfellow], *The Footsteps of Angels; Recitative & Air* (H. Waters, 1856); John Stowell Adams, *The Psalms of Life; a Compilation of Psalms, Hymns, Chants, Anthems, &c., Embodying the Spiritual, Progressive and Reformatory Sentiment of the Present Age* (O. Ditson, 1857).

127. W. G. Haskell, "The Hymnology of Spiritualism," *Religio-Philosophical Journal*, July 28, 1888: 2.

128. Emma Hardinge Britten, *Autobiography of Emma Hardinge Britten*, ed. Margaret Wilkinson (John Heywood, 1900), 50.

129. Haskell, "Hymnology of Spiritualism," 2.

130. Ann Leah (Fox Fish) Underhill, *The Missing Link in Modern Spiritualism* (Thomas R. Knox & Co., 1885), 415–20.

131. Bret E. Carroll, *Spiritualism in Antebellum America* (Indiana University Press, 1997), 138.

132. Samuel Byron Brittan, in the *Spiritual Telegraph*, as quoted by Emma Hardinge, *Modern American Spiritualism: A Twenty Years' Record of the Communion Between Earth and the World of the Spirits* (Emma Hardinge, 1870), 202–3.

133. Hardinge, *Modern American Spiritualism*, 104, 155, 201, 202, 288, 314, 317, 463, 464; Daniel Dunglas Home, *Incidents in My Life* (Carlton, 1863), 85; Aura Satz, "Music of Its Own Accord," *Leonardo Music Journal* 20 (2010): 73–78.

134. Jesse Hutchinson Jr., "The Hutchinson Family," letter to the editor, *Spiritual Philosopher* 1, nos. 11–12 (October 19, 1850), 81–82.

135. Hutchinson and Hazard, "Case of Judson Hutchinson," 113–14.

136. William Lloyd Garrison, "Modern Phenomena," *The Liberator* 24, no. 9 (March 3, 1854), 34.

137. Quoted in Leigh Eric Schmidt, *Hearing Things: Religion, Illusion, and the American Enlightenment* (Harvard University Press, 2000), 237.

138. Peebles, *Spiritual Harp*, 3.

139. Nicole Eustace, *Passion Is the Gale: Emotion, Power, and the Coming of the American Revolution* (University of North Carolina Press, 2011).

140. Lisa Spiro, "Reading with a Tender Rapture: Reveries of a Bachelor and the Rhetoric of Detached Intimacy," *Book History* 6 (2003): 61.

141. Ute Frevert, *Emotions in History: Lost and Found* (Central European University Press, 2011), 109–10.

142. Thomas Moore, "Oh! Why Should the Girl of My Soul Be in Tears" (Carr & Schetky, 1809).

143. Frevert, *Emotions in History*.

144. Macmichael, "School-Fellows," 68–69.

145. George Templeton Strong, *The Diary of George Templeton Strong: Post-War Years, 1865–1875*, ed. Allan Nevins and Milton Halsey Thomas (Macmillan, 1952), 4:116 (December 15, 1866).

146. Strong, *Diary of George Templeton Strong*, 2:467 (September 1, 1851).

147. Daniel Cavicchi has also made this point in *Listening and Longing*, 173.

148. "Concerts of the Past Week," *Dwight's Journal of Music*, February 12, 1853, 151.

149. *Dwight's Journal of Music*, April 9, 1853, 6.

150. George Templeton Strong, *The Diary of George Templeton Strong: The Turbulent Fifties, 1850–1859*, ed. Allan Nevins and Milton Halsey Thomas (Macmillan, 1952), 2:467.

151. Strong, *Diary of George Templeton Strong*, 2:467.

152. Strong, *Diary of George Templeton Strong*, 2:445 (April 8, 1859); 373 (November 30, 1857).

153. Strong, *Diary of George Templeton Strong*, 2:63 (September 1, 1851).

154. Strong, *Diary of George Templeton Strong*, 2:371 (November 21, 1857).

155. John Erskine, *The Philharmonic-Symphony Society of Its First Hundred Years* (Macmillan, 1943).

156. Kasson, *Rudeness and Civility*, 234–38.

157. Quoted in Lawrence W. Levine, *Highbrow/Lowbrow: The Emergence of Cultural Hierarchy in America* (Harvard University Press, 1988), 134.

158. George Gladden, "Is Applause Necessary?," *Music: A Monthly Magazine* 8 (May 1895 to October 1895): 435.

159. Gladden, "Is Applause Necessary?" 433, 431.

160. According to Finseth, for both Romanticism and evangelicalism, "the central event of human existence" was the spiritual transformation that accompanied ecstatic conversion experiences. Finseth, " 'Liquid Fire Within Me.' "

Chapter 3

1. George Washington Cable, "The Dance in Place Congo," *Century Magazine* 31 (February 1886): 517–32.

2. Cable, "Dance in Place Congo," 523.

3. Earliest direct references to the ring shout as an African retention go back to at least the 1840s. See Dena J. Epstein, *Sinful Tunes and Spirituals: Black Folk Music to the Civil War* (University of Illinois Press, 1977), 232. For one of the earliest scholarly works in the twentieth century that claims the ring shout as

an African cultural retention, see Harold Courlander, *Negro Folk Music, U.S.A.* (Columbia University Press, 1963).

4. Katrina Hazzard-Donald, *Mojo Workin': The Old African American Hoodoo System* (University of Illinois Press, 2013), 46–48; Mark Knowles, *Tap Roots: The Early History of Tap Dancing* (Mcfarland & Co, 2002), 59–60; Samuel A. Floyd, "Ring Shout! Literary Studies, Historical Studies, and Black Music Inquiry," *Black Music Research Journal* 22 (2002): 50; Robert Winslow Gordon, "Negro 'Shouts' from Georgia," in *Mother Wit from the Laughing Barrel: Readings in the Interpretation of Afro-American Folklore*, ed. Alan Dundes (Garland, 1981); John Storm Roberts, *Black Music of Two Worlds*, 2nd ed. (Schirmer, 1998), 19–68. According to Samuel A. Floyd Jr., Cable's observation that "some are responsive; others are competitive" suggested the presence of call-and-response figures and polyphony that was likely inherited from Africa. Samuel A. Floyd Jr., *The Power of Black Music: Interpreting Its History from Africa to the United States* (Oxford University Press, 1995), 37.

5. Knowles, *Tap Roots*, 59.

6. Knowles, *Tap Roots*, 60.

7. Exceptionally, during this era a few African Americans did pursue ecstatic experiences that fell quite squarely within the European-American traditions of entrancement addressed in earlier chapters. One of these people was Paschal Beverly Randolph, a free Black man of mixed race origin (who descended from several prominent Southern planters). He was a spiritualist trance medium and occultist who was an avid practitioner of Rosicrucianism, a mystical and esoteric movement that emerged in Europe during the early seventeenth century. Randolph toured Europe extensively, although he also traveled across the American South in the 1860s and gained some interest in African American "hoodoo" practices. John Patrick Deveney, *Paschal Beverly Randolph: A Nineteenth-Century Black American Spiritualist, Rosicrucian, and Sex Magician* (State University of New York Press, 1996).

8. Joseph E. Holloway, "The Origins of African-American Culture," in *Africanisms in American Culture*, 2nd ed., ed. Joseph E. Holloway (Indiana University Press, 2005), 1–18.

9. Catherine L. Albanese, *America Religions and Religion*, 5th ed. (Wadsworth, 2012), 138–40.

10. John M. Chernoff, "The Rhythmic Medium in African Music," *New Literary History* 22, no. 4, Papers from the Commonwealth Center for Literary and Cultural Change (Autumn 1991): 1093; Raboteau, *Slave Religion*, 65.

11. Floyd, *Power of Black Music*, 20, 26. Also see Sheila S. Walker, *Ceremonial Spirit Possession in African and Afro-America: Forms, Meanings, and Functional Significance for Individual and Social Groups* (Brill, 1972).

12. Peoples Gabriel, "A Circular Lineage: The BaKongo Cosmogram and the Ring Shout of the Enslaved Africans and Their Descendants on the Georgian and South Carolinian Sea Islands," master's thesis, Cornell University, 2008.

13. Raboteau, *Slave Religion*, 10; Robert Farris Thompson, *Flash of the Spirit: African and Afro-American Art and Philosophy* (Vintage, 1984), 9.

14. John Miller Chernoff, *African Rhythm and African Sensibility* (University of Chicago Press, 1981). Chernoff's study is based on Ghana and not necessarily representative of all African music, or even West African music for that matter, as Chernoff himself acknowledges.

15. Chernoff, *African Rhythm and African Sensibility*.

16. Sam Mickey, "The Rhythm of Spirit Possession: An Entrancing Legacy," *Nomos Journal* (May 14, 2014), accessed November 18, 2023, http://nomosjournal.org/columns/sounding-sacred/the-rhythm-of-spirit-possession/.

17. Linkenbach and Mulsow, "Introduction: The Dividual Self"; Berman, *Reenchantment of the World*, 2.

18. Chernoff, *African Rhythm and African Sensibility*, 169.

19. Robert Farris Thompson, "An Aesthetic of the Cool," *African Arts* 7, no. 1 (Autumn 1973): 40–43, 64–67, 89–91.

20. Thompson, "Aesthetic of the Cool," 41.

21. Thompson, "Aesthetic of the Cool"; Timothy Brennan, *Secular Devotion: Afro-Latin Music and Imperial Jazz* (Verso, 2008).

22. Katrina Hazzard-Gordon, "Dancing Under the Lash: Sociocultural Disruption, Continuity, and Synthesis," in *African Dance: An Artistic, Historical, and Philosophical Inquiry*, ed. Kariamu Welsh Asante (Africa World Press, 1996), 105.

23. For some of the better known publications on the topic of African retentions in African American music, see Floyd, *Power of Black Music*; Roberts, *Black Music of Two Worlds*; Eileen Southern, *The Music of Black Americans: A History* (Norton, 1983); Portia K. Maultsby, "Africanisms in African-American Music," in *Africanisms in American Culture*, ed. Joseph E. Holloway (Indiana University Press, 1990), 185–210; Samuel Charters, *The Roots of the Blues: An African Search* (Da Capo, 1981); LeRoi Jones (Amiri Baraka), *Blues People* (William Morrow, 1963).

24. Floyd, *Power of Black Music*; Otto Karolyi, *Traditional African and Oriental Music* (Penguin, 1998), 12–13.

25. Gabriel, "Circular Lineage."

26. Kevin Arlyck, "The 'Code Noir': North American Slavery in Comparative Perspective," *OAH Magazine of History* 17 no. 3 (2003): 39.

27. Carolyn Morrow Long, "Perceptions of New Orleans Voodoo: Sin, Fraud, Entertainment, and Religion." *Nova Religio: The Journal of Alternative and Emergent Religions* 6, no. 1 (2002): 87.

28. Arlyck, " 'Code Noir,' " 39.

29. Carolyn Morrow Long, *A New Orleans Voudou Priestess: The Legend and Reality of Marie Laveau* (University of Florida Press, 2007), 11.

30. This chapter mostly uses the archaic spelling, "Voudou," because it was more common during much of the eighteenth and nineteenth centuries.

31. Ina J. Fandrich, "Yorùbá Influences on Haitian Vodou and New Orleans Voodoo," *Journal of Black Studies* 37, no. 5 (May 2007): 786.

32. Fandrich, "Yorùbá Influences on Haitian Vodou and New Orleans Voodoo," 787.

33. Fandrich, "Yorùbá Influences on Haitian Vodou and New Orleans Voodoo," 786.

34. Laurent Dubois, *Avengers of the New World: The Story of the Haitian Revolution* (Belknap Press of Harvard University Press, 2004), 241.

35. The spelling "Voodoo" is used in discussing Moreau's description because it has been used in the translated version of this account: Médéric Louis Élie Moreau de Saint-Méry, *Description of the French Part of Saint Domingue, Volume 1*, trans. Jonathon B. Schwartz (Bradford Colonial Press, 2018), part 1.

36. Moreau, *Description of the French Part of Saint Domingue*, 158.

37. Moreau, *Description of the French Part of Saint Domingue*, 159.

38. Moreau, *Description of the French Part of Saint Domingue*, 160, 162.

39. Moreau, *Description of the French Part of Saint Domingue*, 163.

40. Moreau, *Description of the French Part of Saint Domingue*, 303.

41. Moreau, *Description of the French Part of Saint Domingue*, 166.

42. Moreau, *Description of the French Part of Saint Domingue*, 168.

43. Ina Johanna Fandrich, *The Mysterious Voodoo Queen, Marie Laveaux: A Study of Powerful Female Leadership in Nineteenth-Century New Orleans* (Routledge, 2005).

44. Fandrich, *The Mysterious Voodoo Queen, Marie Laveaux*, 133–34.

45. Moreau, *Description of the French Part of Saint Domingue*, 166.

46. Moreau, *Description of the French Part of Saint Domingue*, 159–60.

47. Hélène d'Aquin Allain (1832–1925), a white Creole woman from New Orleans, in fact stole Moreau's description and, in her memoirs, passed it off as her own eyewitness account of a Voudou ceremony in New Orleans when she was a girl. There is in fact nothing to suggest Allain ever observed such a ceremony, and so it would be inappropriate to take her memoirs as reliable.

48. Fandrich, "Yorùbá Influences on Haitian Vodou and New Orleans Voodoo"; Fandrich, *Mysterious Voodoo Queen, Marie Laveaux*, 42.

49. Fandrich, "Yorùbá Influences on Haitian Vodou and New Orleans Voodoo"; Fandrich, *Mysterious Voodoo Queen, Marie Laveaux*, 42.

50. Chris Davis, "Before They Were Haitians: Examining Evidence for Kongolese Influence on the Haitian Revolution," *Journal of Haitian Studies* 22, no. 2 (2016): 4–36.

51. James William Buel, *Mysteries and Miseries of America's Great Cities: Embracing New York, Washington City, San Francisco, Salt Lake City, and New Orleans* (A.L. Bancroft & Co., 1883), accessed November 18, 2023, https://books.google.ca/books?id=rklAAAAAYAAJ.

52. Buel, *Mysteries and Miseries of America's Great Cities*, 524.

53. Buel, *Mysteries and Miseries of America's Great Cities*, 525.

54. Buel, *Mysteries and Miseries of America's Great Cities*, 526.

55. Buel, *Mysteries and Miseries of America's Great Cities*, 528.

56. See Fandrich, *Mysterious Voodoo Queen, Marie Laveaux.*

57. Buel, *Mysteries and Miseries of America's Great Cities*, 524.

58. Long, *A New Orleans Voudou Priestess.*

59. Long, *A New Orleans Voudou Priestess*, 118.

60. Janet L. Allured, "Evaluating a New Orleans Icon: Evidence and Reinterpretation," review of *The Mysterious Voodoo Queen, Marie Laveaux: A Study of Powerful Female Leadership in Nineteenth-Century New Orleans* by Ina Johanna Fandrich, and *Voodoo Queen: The Spirited Lives of Marie Laveau*, by Martha Ward. H-Net Reviews (March 2006), accessed November 18, 2023, http://www.h-net.org/reviews/showrev.php?id=11484.

61. Quoted in Robert Tallant, *Voodoo in New Orleans* (Macmillan, 1962), 56–57.

62. Long, *New Orleans Voudou Priestess*, xxi.

63. Shannon Lee Dawdy, *Building the Devil's Empire: French Colonial New Orleans* (University of Chicago Press, 2008).

64. Long, *New Orleans Voudou Priestess.*

65. William Wells Brown, *My Southern Home, or, The South and Its People* (A.G. Brown, 1880), 68–72, accessed November 18, 2023, https://archive.org/details/06248562.4740.emory.edu/page/n81/mode/2up?q=Voudooism.

66. John Sharpe, "The Negro Plot of 1712," *New York Genealogical and Biographical Record* 21 (1890): 162–63; Walter Rucker, "Conjure, Magic, and Power: The Influence of Afro-Atlantic Religious Practices on Slave Resistance and Rebellion," *Journal of Black Studies* 32, no. 1 (2001): 84–103.

67. Sharpe, "Negro Plot of 1712," 162–63; Rucker, "Conjure, Magic, and Power."

68. Rucker, "Conjure, Magic, and Power," 88–89.

69. Rucker, "Conjure, Magic, and Power," 100.

70. "New York Slave Rebellion of 1712," *Encyclopedia Britannica*, March 30, 2023, accessed November 28, 2023, https://www.britannica.com/event/New-York-slave-rebellion-of-1712.

71. 1740 South Carolina Slave Code, Acts of the South Carolina General Assembly, 1740 # 670, South Carolina Department of Archives and History, Columbia, South Carolina. Reproduced in U.S. Department of Education, *Teaching American History in South Carolina Program*, accessed November 18, 2023, http://www.teachingushistory.org/ttrove/1740slavecode.htm.

72. John Jeremiah Sullivan, "Talking Drums," *Oxford American* 107 (Winter 2019), accessed November 18, 2023, https://oxfordamerican.org/magazine/issue-107/talking-drums.

73. Ira Berlin, *Many Thousands Gone: The First Two Centuries of Slavery in North America* (Harvard University Press, 1998).

74. Raboteau, *Slave Religion*, 64–65; Hazzard-Donald, "Hoodoo Religion."

75. Raboteau, *Slave Religion*, 64–65; Hazzard-Donald, "Hoodoo Religion."

76. Quoted in Lawrence W. Levine, *Black Culture and Black Consciousness: Afro-American Folk Thought from Slavery to Freedom* (Oxford University Press, 1977), 21.

77. Quoted in Levine, *Black Culture and Black Consciousness*, 21.

78. Raboteau, *Slave Religion*, 64.

79. The African American intellectual W. E. B. DuBois maintained that "the [Black] church [in America] was not at first by any means Christian but instead was a co-mingling of plantation rites roughly designated as Voodooism." W. E. B. Du Bois, *The Souls of Black Folk: Essays and Sketches* (A. C. McClurg & Co., 1903), 196.

80. Watson, *Methodist Error*, 16.

81. Floyd, "Ring Shout!" 50; Knowles, *Tap Roots*, 59.

82. William Francis Allen, Charles Pickard Ware, and Lucy McKim Garrison, *Slave Songs of the United States* (Peter Smith, [c. 1867] 1951), xiii–xiv.

83. Allen, Ware, and Garrison, *Slave Songs of the United States*, xiv.

84. Frederick Law Olmsted, *A Journey in the Seaboard Slave States; With Remarks on Their Economy* (Dix and Edwards, 1856), 450. Electronic ed., accessed November 18, 2023, https://docsouth.unc.edu/nc/olmsted/olmsted.html.

85. Laura M. Towne, *The Letters and Diary of Laura M. Towne, Written from the Sea Islands of South Carolina, 1862–1884*, ed. Rupert Sargent Holland (Riverside Press, 1912), 20, accessed November 18, 2023, https://babel.hathitrust.org/cgi/pt?id=coo1.ark:/13960/t82j7197m&seq=52&q1=%22shout%22.

86. "The Freedmen at Port Royal," *North American Review* 101, no. 208 (1865): 1–28.

87. Lydia Parrish, who collected spirituals and other African American songs over the course of twenty-five years on the Georgia Sea Islands, similarly observed Black participants in church "using the same rhythmic shout step." She further speculated it was a "survival of an African tribal dance, and that the accompanying chants in their form and melody are quite as typical of Africa as the dance itself." Lydia Parrish, *Slave Songs of the Georgia Sea Islands* (University of Georgia Press, 1992), 54.

88. Thomas Wentworth Higginson, *Army Life in a Black Regiment* (Fields, Osgood and Co. 1870), 198, accessed November 18, 2023, https://repository.wellesley.edu/object/wellesley30338.

89. Higginson, *Army Life in a Black Regiment*, 198.

90. Daniel Alexander Payne, *Recollections of Seventy Years*, 2nd ed. (Arno Press and the New York Times, [c. 1888] 1968), 254.

91. Edward King, *The Great South; A Record of Journeys in Louisiana, Texas, the Indian Territory, Missouri, Arkansas, Mississippi, Alabama, Georgia, Florida, South Carolina, North Carolina, Kentucky, Tennessee, Virginia, West Virginia, and Maryland* (American Publish Co., 1875), 609.

92. King, *The Great South*, 609.

93. Wayne Warner, *Maria Woodworth-Etter: For Such a Time as This* (Bridge-Logos, 2004), 281.

94. Randall Herbert Balmer, "Charles Fox Parham," in *Encyclopedia of Evangelicalism, Revised and Expanded Edition* (Baylor University Press, 2004), 523–24.

95. Edith L. Blumhofer, *Restoring the Faith: The Assemblies of God, Pentecostalism, and American Culture* (University of Illinois Press, 1993), 55–56.

96. Jennie Moore, "Music from Heaven."

97. Valdez, "Fire on the Street," 2: 222; "Weird Fanaticism Fools Young Girl," 249. See chapter 1 for longer quotations.

98. Dan Cusic, *Saved by Song: A History of Gospel and Christian Music* (University Press of Mississippi, 2012), 163; Andrew Legg and Carolyn Philpott, "An Analysis of Performance Practices in African American Gospel Music: Rhythm, Lyric Treatment and Structures in Improvisation and Accompaniment," *Popular Music* 34, no. 2 (2015): 197–225.

99. Daniel Rasmussen, *American Uprising: The Untold Story of America's Largest Slave Revolt* (Harper, 2011).

100. Long, "Perceptions of New Orleans Voodoo," 88.

101. Long, "Perceptions of New Orleans Voodoo"; Henry A. Kmen, *Music in New Orleans: The Formative Years, 1791–1841* (Louisiana State University Press, 1966), 227.

102. Raboteau, *Slave Religion*, 215–20.

103. Hazzard-Donald, "Hoodoo Religion and American Dance Traditions," 204; Paul Harvey, *Through the Storm, Through the Night: A History of African American Christianity* (Rowman & Littlefield, 2011), 57.

104. See Shane White and Graham White, *The Sounds of Slavery: Discovering African American History Through Songs, Sermons, and Speech* (Beacon Press, 2005), 109.

105. See White and White, *Sounds of Slavery,* 108–9.

106. Jerah Johnson, *Congo Square in New Orleans* (Louisiana Landmarks Society, 1995).

107. Johnson, *Congo Square in New Orleans*, 44–46.

108. Epstein, *Sinful Tunes and Spirituals*, 60.

109. Tallant, *Voodoo in New Orleans*, 24–25.

110. Johnson, *Congo Square in New Orleans*, 48.

111. Blake Touchstone, "Voodoo in New Orleans," *Louisiana History: The Journal of the Louisiana Historical Association* 13, no. 4 (1972): 371–86.

112. Long, *A New Orleans Voudou Priestess*, 128.

113. Edward Carter II, John C. Van Horne, and Lee W. Formwalt, eds., *Journals of Benjamin Henry Latrobe, 1799–1820: From Philadelphia to New Orleans,* vol. 3 (Yale University Press, 1980), 3:203–4.

114. Carter, Horne, and Formwalt, *Journals of Benjamin Henry Latrobe, 1799–1820*, 3:203–4.

115. Cable, writing during the 1880s, was referring to the activities of enslaved people during the first half of the nineteenth century. George Washington Cable, "Dance in Place Congo," 525.

116. George Washington Cable, "Dance in Place Congo," 525.

117. Louis Moreau Gottschalk, *Notes of a Pianist: The Chronicle of a New Orleans Music Legend*, ed. Jeanne Behrend (Princeton University Press, 2006).

118. Gottschalk, *Notes of a Pianist*, 108.

119. Gottschalk, *Notes of a Pianist*, 200.

120. The author also described the music of the event as the sound that might have been created if "the chorus of Dante's hell had entered into the mad shouts of Africa." Buel, *Mysteries and Miseries of America's Great Cities*, 525, 528, 530.

121. "The Voudou or Hoodoo Orgies," *Daily True Delta*, no. 124 (October 21, 1860): 1, accessed November 18, 2023, https://news.google.com/newspapers?id=2PozAAAAIBAJ&sjid=RyMIAAAAIBAJ&pg=6622%2C1380130.

122. "The Voudou or Hoodoo Orgies," 1.

123. Mrs. M. P. Handy, "Witchcraft Among the Negroes," *Appletons' Journal: A Magazine of General Literature* 8, no. 194 (December 14, 1872): 666–67, accessed November 18, 2023, http://quod.lib.umich.edu/m/moajrnl/acw8433.1-08.194/670.

124. Letitia M. Burwell, *A Girl's Life in Virginia Before the War* (Federick A. Stokes Company, 1895), 163, electronic ed., accessed November 18, 2023, https://docsouth.unc.edu/fpn/burwell/burwell.html.

125. Olmsted, *Journey in the Seaboard Slave States*, 450.

126. Robert C. Toll, *Blacking Up: The Minstrel Show in Nineteenth-Century America* (Oxford University Press, 1974), 42.

127. During the earlier era of blackface minstrelsy in America, specifically around the 1820s and 1830s, blackface minstrelsy was often used by working-class participants to critique bourgeois elites. By the 1840s, though, their critique turned more racial in orientation—directed not toward white authority figures, but toward dark-skinned others. The reason for this shift can be attributed to a number of factors, including the influx of working-class European immigrants during the 1840s who competed for jobs with Black Americans, and the corresponding threat of white supremacy in the North. See Toll, *Blacking Up*; David R. Roediger, *The Wages of Whiteness: Race and the Making of the American Working Class* (Verso, 1991).

128. The quotation is taken from an 1846 review of the Ethiopian Serenaders, printed in a pamphlet in England. Quoted in Hans Nathan, *Dan Emmet and the Rise of Early Negro Minstrelsy* (University of Oklahoma Press, 1962), 125.

129. Quoted in Nathan, *Dan Emmet and the Rise of Early Negro Minstrelsy*, vii–viii.

130. Blackface minstrelsy's depictions of African Americans also included other attributes that would have been considered vulgar, such as an uneducated dialect and a taste for "possum and coon." Toll, *Blacking Up*, 67.

131. Other character tropes include the "Old Darky," an elderly, practically asexual, enslaved Southern male who upheld a vision of a sentimental plantation life free from concerns; and the "Mammy," a beloved motherly plantation woman and counterpart to "Old Darky." Toll, *Blacking Up*, chap. 3.

132. LeRoy Ashby, *With Amusement for All: A History of American Popular Culture Since 1830* (University Press of Kentucky, 2006), 53.

133. Towne, *Letters and Diary*, 20, accessed November 18, 2023, https://babel.hathitrust.org/cgi/pt?id=cool.ark:/13960/t82j7197m&seq=52&q1=%22shout%22.

134. Elizabeth Ware Pearson, ed., *Letters from Port Royal: Sung at the Time of the Civil War* (W.B. Clarke Co., 1906), 292–93.

135. Similar views were reflected in an observer's account from Port Royal Island around the same period, which described the shout as "hysterical," "decidedly material," possessing a "few slight traces of superstition," and carried out by people who "bear themselves like fearless children before the Unseen Presence,—with . . . an unthinking recognition." "Freedmen at Port Royal," 10.

136. Elizabeth Kilham, "Sketches in Color: Fourth," *Putnam's Magazine of Literature, Science, Art, and National Interests* 5, no. 27 (March 1870), 305.

137. Kilham, "Sketches in Color," 306.

138. In the postbellum era, some African Americans endeavored to embody the principles of autonomous self-restraint by attending mainline Christian churches that were not especially oriented toward ecstatic experiences or effusive outbursts. One such individual was Bishop Daniel A. Payne of the African Methodist Episcopal Church. He deplored the extemporaneous enthusiasm that often accompanied the singing of spirituals, and he condemned rural congregants as "fist and heel worshipers" who engaged in a "voudoo dance" that would "render them as easy prey to Satan" and "drive out all the intelligence, refinement, and practical Christians" from the church. Although they did not always take as harsh a stance as Payne, certain African Americans, particularly those living in the urban centres of the North, also set out to purge their expressive culture of what they considered vulgar displays of corporeal passion. See Payne and Smith, *Recollections of Seventy Years*, 254–56.

139. Saidiya Hartman, *Scenes of Subjection: Terror, Slavery, and Self-Making in Nineteenth-Century America* (Oxford University Press, 1997), 21.

140. Hazzard-Donald, *Mojo Workin'*, 48.

141. Rayford Logan, *The Negro in American Life and Thought: The Nadir, 1877–1901* (Dial Press, 1954).

Chapter 4

1. Boris Sidis, *The Psychology of Suggestion: A Research into the Subconscious Nature of Man and Society* (D. Appleton and Co., 1898), 306.

2. Sidis, *Psychology of Suggestion*, 307.

3. Henry Clay Fish, *The Handbook of Revivals: For the Use of Winners of Souls* (James H. Earle, 1874), 313.

4. The primary constitution of the individual, whether physical or mental (or otherwise), was a topic of debate during this period, and it had been for centuries. However, in public discourse and common usage, many implicitly agreed that, even if one element constituted the epicenter of selfhood, all of them blended into each other in the making of a bounded and inviolable self. Even Descartes's dualism, which starkly distinguished the mind from the body, recognized that the two were so closely intertwined as to form something like a union—the body being ideally contained within the mind-dominated self even as it was formally an extension of it. As this chapter demonstrates, the debate between mind-based and body-based theories of individuality continued into the nineteenth and twentieth centuries, but so too did implicit assumptions that both aspects were tightly entangled and could be somehow nested together within the individual. See John Barresi and Raymond Martin, "History as Prologue: Western Theories of the Self," in *The Oxford Handbook of the Self*, ed. Shaun Gallagher (Oxford University Press, 2011), and Quassim Cassam, "The Embodied Self," in *The Oxford Handbook of the Self*, ed. Shaun Gallagher (Oxford University Press, 2011).

5. Many proponents of this mode did not altogether deny the existence of God or any other numinous spirit. Instead, they agreed (following a Deistic line of reasoning) that any metaphysical spiritual force had little or no discernible effect on human life and experience. According to Edward S. Reed, "psychology succeeded in becoming a science in large part because of its defense of a theological conception of human nature typically associated with liberal Protestant theology." If the defense was nominal, it was not atheistic—an important distinction that lent more credibility to the social scientists. Edward S. Reed, *From Soul to Mind: The Emergence of Psychology from Erasmus Darwin to William James* (Yale University Press, 1997), 7.

6. Although Georges Bataille's notion of "inner experience" is a somewhat comparable concept to the internalized experience described in this chapter, the comparison is not perfect. First, Bataille remained vague about whether "inner" experience could still involve ecstatic mergers with metaphysical entities, as natural or supernatural ecstasy did. Proponents of the internal ecstasy discussed in this chapter, by contrast, were much more explicit and precise about these issues. Second, Bataille considered inner experience to be largely positive and meaningful. However, the historical figures addressed in this chapter had a tendency to denigrate and pathologize trance phenomena. Georges Bataille, *Inner Experience*, trans. Leslie Anne Boldt (State University of New York Press, 1988).

7. Robert Burton, *The Anatomy of Melancholy*, ed. Arthur Richard Shilleto, Arthur Henry Bullen, vol. 1 (George Bell and Sons, 1896), 1:229, 159.

8. For Robert Burton, music affected the ears instantly and the other primary faculties of the body as well: "the very arteries, the vital & animal spirits; it erects

the mind, and makes it nimble." In this manner, it became a superlative method of remedying both the body and mind of those who suffered from melancholy. Burton, *Anatomy of Melancholy*, 2:133.

9. Burton, *Anatomy of Melancholy*, 1:229, 164.

10. See chap. 1.

11. David Hume, "Essay X: Of Superstition and Enthusiasm," in *Essays, Moral, Political, and Literary, Part 1*, ed. Eugene F. Miller (Liberty Classics, 1987), 74.

12. M[artin] M[adan], *A Full and Compleat Answer to the Capital Errors, Contained in the Writings of the Late Rev. William Law* (1763), quoted in Susie I. Tucker, *Enthusiasm: A Study in Semantic Change* (Cambridge University Press, 1972), 27. About a century earlier, Thomas Hobbes and John Locke had defined the word in similar terms. Jon Mee, *Romanticism, Enthusiasm, and Regulation: Poetics and the Policing of Culture in the Romantic Period* (Oxford University Press, 2003), 3.

13. Samuel Johnson, "No. 89 Tuesday, January 22, 1751," in *The Works of Samuel Johnson, LL.D., in Nine Volumes, Volume the Second The Rambler, Volume I* (Talboys and Wheeler, 1825), 418. Writing in 1853, the Finneyite music director Thomas Hastings similarly proclaimed that the "trivial character" of parlor music—the sheet music marketed to middle-class amateur musicians and bourgeois tastes—had an effect on listeners that was tantamount to an "invisible riot of the mind." Hasting, *Dissertation on Musical Taste*, 169.

14. Reed, *From Soul to Mind*.

15. Charles Chauncy, *Enthusiasm Described and Caution'd Against* (J. Draper, for S. Eliot and J. Blanchard, 1742), 3–5; Taves, *Fits, Trances, and Visions*, chap. 1.

16. Chauncy, *Seasonable Thoughts*, 109, 80.

17. Chauncy, *Seasonable Thoughts*, 94.

18. Chauncy, *Seasonable Thoughts*, 182.

19. Edwards, *Thoughts on Revival of Religion*, 122.

20. Quoted in Taves, *Fits, Trances, and Visions*, 37.

21. The historian Jon Mee makes this case for British Romantics. Mee, *Romanticism, Enthusiasm, and Regulation*, 3.

22. See Kiene Brillenburg Wurth, *Musically Sublime: Indeterminacy, Infinity, Irresolvability* (Fordham University Press, 2009), 3–4.

23. Roger Lundin, *From Nature to Experience: The American Search for Cultural Authority* (Rowman & Littlefield, 2005).

24. *Report of Dr. Benjamin Franklin*, 25–27; Taves, *Fits, Trances, and Visions*, 125–26.

25. During the 1810s, Faria conducted mesmeric experiments in Paris in order to disprove the existence of magnetic fluid and to demonstrate how the alterations in consciousness that followed mesmeric crises were entirely generated within the individual subject. In his view, trance was basically an unusual form of sleep. After Faria's early death in 1819, his theories were taken up and expanded by a French physician and former mesmerist, Alexandre Jacques François Bertrand. See Abbé

Faria, *Of the Cause of Lucid Sleep or Study of the Nature of Man* [De la cause du sommeil lucide ou Étude de la Nature de l'Homme], trans. Manoharrai Sardessai (CinnamonTeal, 2014).

26. James Braid, *Observations on Trance or Human Hibernation* (John Churchill, 1850), vi.

27. James Braid, *Magic, Witchcraft, Animal Magnetism, Hypnotism, and Electro-Biology* (John Churchill, 1852), 53–54.

28. Braid's theory of suggestion was taken up and expanded by the French physician Hippolyte Bernheim. See Hippolyte Bernheim, *Hypnosis and Suggestion in Hypnotherapy* (Aronson, 1884), 179.

29. James Braid, *Neuropnology; or, The Rationale of Nervous Sleep, Considered in Relation with Animal Magnetism* (John Churchill, 1843), 56.

30. Braid, *Neuropnology*, 132.

31. Braid, *Neuropnology*, 138.

32. Braid, *Neuropnology*, 95.

33. Coale, "Romance of Mesmerism," 85–103; Coale, *Mesmerism and Hawthorne*.

34. Ralph Waldo Emerson, *The Journals and Miscellaneous Notebooks of Ralph Waldo Emerson*, vol. 5, ed. Linda Allardt (Belknap Press of Harvard University Press, 1965), 5:388.

35. Taves, *Fits, Trances, and Visions*, 200.

36. Quoted in Taves, *Fits, Trances, and Visions*, 201.

37. La Roy Sunderland, letter to the editor, *Banner of Light*, November 13, 1858.

38. La Roy Sunderland, *The Trance and Correlative Phenomena* (James Walker, 1868), 49, 71, 75–76, 100–104.

39. Sunderland, *Trance and Correlative Phenomena*, 109–10.

40. See George M. Beard, "Psychology of Spiritism," *North American Review* 129 (1879): 67; George M. Beard, *The Scientific Basis of Delusions: A New Theory of Trance and Its Bearings on Human Testimony* (G.P. Putnam's Sons, 1877), 5; Rhodri Hayward, *Resisting History: Religious Transcendence and the Invention of the Unconscious* (Manchester University Press, 2007), 41–43; S. E. D. Shortt, "Physicians and Psychics: The Anglo-American Medical Response to Spiritualism, 1870–1890," *Journal of the History of Medicine and Allied Sciences* 39 (1984): 344.

41. Jean-Martin Charcot, *Oeuvres complètes* (Paris: Bureau de Progres Medical, 1886–93), referenced in Kennaway, "Musical Hypnosis," 5.

42. Kennaway, "Musical Hypnosis," 5.

43. See Kennaway, "Musical Hypnosis," 5.

44. Taves, *Fits, Trances, and Visions*, 247.

45. According to Pierre Janet, a former mentee of Charcot, the existence of abnormal experiences suggested not so much an abnormal neurology as a *désagrega-tion* of consciousness. By this, Janet referred to a section in the mind that was split

off or dissociated from normal waking experience. This disaggregated consciousness was thought to comprise its own "chain of memory" that was inaccessible except through hypnosis or other mind-altering techniques.

46. Gustave Le Bon, *The Crowd: A Study of the Popular Mind* (Macmillan, 1896), 11.

47. Le Bon, *The Crowd*, 35.

48. Le Bon, *The Crowd*, 11.

49. According to Drew Gilpin Faust, "most Americans continued to regard science and religion as in alliance rather than in conflict well into the late nineteenth century." Drew Gilpin Faust, *This Republic of Suffering* (Vintage, 2009), 173.

50. According to the historian Edward Reed, most psychologists into the twentieth century continued to accommodate the possibility of a human soul and a superior deity even as they pursued more secular-oriented models of self and experience. Reed, *From Soul to Mind*.

51. William James, "Subjective Effects of Nitrous Oxide," *Mind* 7 (1882): n.p. Retrieved from http://www.erowid.org/chemicals/nitrous/nitrous_article1.shtml.

52. James, *Varieties of Religious Experience*, 388.

53. Eugene Taylor, "William James and Transpersonal Psychiatry," in *Textbook of Transpersonal Psychiatry and Psychology*, ed. Bruce W. Scotton, Allan B. Chinen, and John R. Battista (Basic Books, 1996), 21–27.

54. James was also among the earliest scholars in America to adopt Darwin's naturalist theories. Taylor, "William James and Transpersonal Psychiatry," in *Textbook of Transpersonal Psychiatry and Psychology*, 22.

55. E. Gurney, F. W. H. Myers, and F. Podmore, *Phantasms of the Living*, 2 vols. (Society for Psychical Research and Trubner and Co., 1886), xlvi. Myers contended that the existence of "subliminal" regions beyond normal awareness was evinced in those people with double or multiple personalities, who were a growing topic of interest for the scientific community during the late nineteenth century. In support of his multiplex theory of consciousness, Myers stated: "I hold that . . . it is perfectly possible that other thoughts, feelings, and memories, either isolated or in continuous connection, may now be actively conscious, as we say, 'within me,'—in some kind of co-ordination with my organism, and forming some part of my total individuality." Frederick W. Myers, "The Subliminal Consciousness," *Proceedings of the Society for Psychical Research* 7 (1891–1892): 305.

56. William James, *The Works of William James: Essays in Radical Empiricism*, ed. Frederick Burkhardt and Fredson Bowers (Harvard University Press, 1976).

57. James, *Varieties*, 13.

58. James, *Varieties*, 73.

59. Frederic W. H. Myers also remained open to the possibility of self-transcendence on par with those proffered by religionists and Romantics. He asserted that what he called the "subliminal self" was often superior to everyday consciousness because it extended well beyond the limits of the body and could conceivably

persist after death. See Frederic W. H. Myers, *Human Personality and Its Survival of Bodily Death*, 2 vols. (Longmans, Green, and Co., 1903).

60. The term "transpersonal" is said to have first appeared on the syllabus of one of James's Harvard courses in 1905. See Taylor, "William James and Transpersonal Psychiatry," 21–27.

61. James, *Varieties of Religious Experience*, 380–81.

62. Oliver Sacks, *Musicophilia: Tales of Music and the Brain, Revised and Expanded Edition* (Vintage Books, 2008), xiii.

63. James also acknowledged that "not conceptual speech, but music rather, is the element through which we are best spoken to by mystical truth. Many mystical scriptures are indeed little more than musical composition." James, *Varieties of Religious Experience*, 383, 420–21.

64. James, *Varieties of Religious Experience*, 66.

65. As the scholars Joel Pfister, Nancy Schnog, and others demonstrate, such views also resonated strongly with a cultural interest in psychic (and physical) interiority that had begun in the nineteenth century, as exemplified by the literature of Louisa May Alcott, the art of Thomas Eakins, the rise of popular psychology, and the proliferation of psychology textbooks in college. See Joel Pfister and Nancy Schnog, eds., *Inventing the Psychological: Toward a Cultural History of Emotional Life in America* (Yale University Press, 1997).

66. During this period, Freud also theorized that the stages of sleep provided clues as to the workings of the unconscious, and therefore he would discuss patients' dreams with them at length. Sigmund Freud, *The Interpretation of Dreams* (Macmillan, 1913).

67. James Leonard Corning, "The Use of Musical Vibration Before and During Sleep—Supplementary Employment of Chromatoscopic Figures—A Contribution to the Therapeutics of the Emotions," *Medical Record: A Weekly Journal of Medicine and Surgery* 14 (1899): 80.

68. Corning, "Use of Musical Vibration Before and During Sleep," 84.

69. "Music for Insanity," *New York Daily Tribune*, April 8, 1900, 4; Corning, "Use of Musical Vibration Before and During Sleep," 84.

70. Corning, "Use of Musical Vibration Before and During Sleep," 84.

71. Corning, "Use of Musical Vibration Before and During Sleep," 83.

72. Corning, "Use of Musical Vibration Before and During Sleep," 82–84.

73. Du Bois, *Souls of Black Folk*, 3.

74. W.E.B. Du Bois, *The Autobiography of W.E.B. Du Bois: A Soliloquy on Viewing* (International Publishers, 1968), 227–88.

75. Edward J. Blum, *W.E.B. Du Bois: American Prophet* (University of Pennsylvania Press, 2011).

76. Dickson D. Bruce Jr., "W.E.B. Du Bois and the Idea of Double Consciousness," *American Literature: A Journal of Literary History, Criticism, and Bibliography* 64, no. 2 (1992): 299–309.

77. Becker, *Deep Listeners*, 39.

78. Sunderland, *Book of Psychology*, 13.

79. William James, *The Principles of Psychology* (Henry Holt and Co., 1890). See especially 1:379–93.

80. Josef Breuer and Sigmund Freud, *Studies on Hysteria*, trans. Nicola Luckhurst (Penguin, 2004), viii, xviii, 14.

81. Du Bois, *Souls of Black Folk*, 202.

82. Du Bois, *Souls of Black Folk*, 3.

83. Du Bois, *Souls of Black Folk*, 4.

84. Du Bois, *Souls of Black Folk*, 4.

85. Du Bois, *Souls of Black Folk*, 251.

86. Du Bois, *Souls of Black Folk*, 191.

87. Du Bois, *Souls of Black Folk*, 263.

88. Du Bois, *Souls of Black Folk*, 250.

89. Darwin contended that an individual "can be an ardent Theist and an evolutionist" and wrote about his own beliefs in the following way: "I have never been an atheist in the sense of denying the existence of a God.—I think that generally . . . but not always, that an agnostic would be the most correct description of my state of mind." Charles Darwin to John Fordyce, May 7, 1879, Letter no. 12041, in Darwin Correspondence Project, accessed November 18, 2023, http://www.darwinproject.ac.uk/DCP-LETT-12041.

90. Charles Darwin, *The Expression of the Emotions in Man and Animals* (John Murray, 1873), 87. See also Darwin's discussion of birdsong in Charles Darwin, *The Descent of Man, and Selection in Relation to Sex* (John Murray, 1871).

91. In an 1857 article, Herbert Spencer argued that animal vocalizations were not enough to constitute the origins of music, and what moderns called music would have more likely evolved after the development of vocal language. Herbert Spencer, "The Origin and Function of Music," *Fraser's Magazine* 56 (October 1857): 396–408.

92. Turner, *Without God, Without Creed*, 213.

93. Herbert Spencer, *The Principles of Sociology*, vol. 1 (D. Appleton and Co., 1883), 1:160, 161.

94. Spencer, *Principles of Sociology*, 1:163–64.

95. Spencer, *Principles of Sociology*, 1:164.

96. This hierarchical view of human development came to dominate popular theories of evolution, though Darwin himself did not share it. Instead, he took a "branch" approach to evolution, contending that the differences between cultures could be explained based on the unique environments and circumstances they encountered over time. His was a three-dimensional theory that prevented perfect comparisons between cultures and therefore made it difficult for naturalists to judge the degree to which any culture or group was more or less "civilized." Spencer, by contrast, took a scalar view of evolution, portraying human development as existing

along a two-dimensional "ladder" of evolution. At the lower rungs resided primitive peoples, such as the Zulu or Dyak, and at the highest rungs existed the more civilized races, including the white, English-speaking world, particularly Anglo-Saxons. Twentieth-century detractors would later call this approach "Social Darwinism" but a more accurate label might have been "Social Spencerism." David Hoogland Noon, "The Evolution of Beasts and Babies: Recapitulation, Instinct, and the Early Discourse on Child Development," *Journal of the History of the Behavioral Sciences* 41, no. 4 (Fall 2005): 384.

97. G. Stanley Hall also compared the adolescent tendency toward trance with play, which he also considered a normal part of the development of both the human individual and the human species. G. Stanley Hall, *Adolescence: Its Psychology and Its Relations to Physiology, Anthropology, Sociology, Sex, Crime, Religion and Education*, vol. 1 (D. Appleton, 1904), 265–66.

98. J. Donovan, *Music and Action, or, The Elective Affinity Between Rhythm and Pitch* (Kegan Paul, Trench, & Co, 1889), 132, 137.

99. Carrie Ransom Squire, *A Genetic Study of Rhythm* (O.B. Wood, 1901), 98.

100. Karl Groos, *The Play of Man*, trans. Elizabeth L. Baldwin (Appleton, 1901), 405. Also see 367–69.

101. James H. Tufts, "On the Genesis of the Aesthetic Categories," *Philosophical Review* 7, no. 1 (January 1903): 12.

102. D. B. Baker, *The Oxford Handbook of the History of Psychology: Global Perspectives* (Oxford University Press, 2011); Michael Wertheimer, *A Brief History of Psychology* (Psychology Press, 2011); Margaret P. Munger, ed., *The History of Psychology: Fundamental Questions* (Oxford University Press, 2003); G. Mandler, *A History of Modern Experimental Psychology: From James and Wundt to Cognitive Science* (MIT Press, 2007).

103. Beck, *Musicology of Religion*, 113–14.

104. See, for example, Sigmund Freud, *The Future of an Illusion* (W.W. Norton, 1927).

105. Sigmund Freud, *Civilization and Its Discontents*, in *The Standard Edition of the Complete Psychological Works of Sigmund Freud*, trans. and ed. J. Strachey, vol. 21 (Hogarth Press, 1964), 21:66.

106. Breuer and Freud, *Studies on Hysteria*.

107. Sigmund Freud, "The Origin and Development of Psychoanalysis," *American Journal of Psychology* 21, no. 2 (April 1910): 191.

108. Joel Pfister, "Glamorizing the Psychological: The Politics of the Performances of Modern Psychological Identities," in *Inventing the Psychological: Toward a Cultural History of Emotional Life in America*, ed. Joel Pfister and Nancy Schnog (Yale University Press, 1997), 167–216.

109. Sigmund Freud, "Recommendations to Physicians Practicing Psychoanalysis," in *The Standard Edition of the Complete Psychological Works of Sigmund Freud*, trans. and ed. James Strachey, vol. 12 (Hogarth Press, [c. 1912] 1955), 12:111–12;

Mark D. Epstein, "On the Neglect of Evenly Suspended Attention," *Journal of Transpersonal Psychology* 16, no. 2 (1984): 193–205.

110. In Freud's words: "Just as the receiver converts back into sound waves the electrical oscillations in the telephone line which were set up by sound waves, so the doctor's unconscious is able, from the derivatives of the unconscious which are communicated to him, to reconstruct that unconscious, which has determined the patient's free associations." Sigmund Freud, "Recommendations to Physicians Practicing Psychoanalysis," in *The Standard Edition* (Hogarth Press, [c. 1912] 1955), 12:111–12, 115. Also see Sigmund Freud, *Two Encyclopedia Articles*, in *The Standard Edition of the Complete Psychological Works of Sigmund Freud*, trans. and ed. James Strachey, vol. 18 (Hogarth Press, [c. 1923] 1955), 18:239.

111. According to the psychiatrist and author Mark D. Epstein, "no specific training in the cultivation or maintenance of . . . [Freud's] attentional attitude ever developed." Epstein, "On the Neglect of Evenly Suspended Attention," 198.

112. Otto Fenichel, quoted in Mark D. Epstein, "Freud's Influence on Transpersonal Psychology," in *Textbook of Transpersonal Psychiatry and Psychology*, ed. Bruce W. Scotton, Allan B. Chinen, and John R. Battista (Basic Books, 1996).

113. Accordingly, the technique of "evenly suspended attention" remained "one of the least discussed, [and] certainly one of the least well conceptualized aspects of psychoanalysis." Paul Gray, *The Ego and Analysis of Defense* (Jason Aronson, 2005), 5.

114. Breuer and Freud, *Studies on Hysteria*, 13.

115. Breuer and Freud, *Studies on Hysteria*, 26.

116. Breuer and Freud, *Studies on Hysteria*, 14.

117. Freud, *Civilization and Its Discontents*, 21:64, 65.

118. Freud, *Civilization and Its Discontents*, 21:66.

Chapter 5

1. "Tony Pastor's Opera House," *New York Clipper*, July 22, 1865, 120.

2. Parker Zellers, *Tony Pastor: Dean of the Vaudeville Stage* (Eastern Michigan University Press, 1971), 27–28.

3. Zellers, *Tony Pastor*, 27–28.

4. These songbooks included *Tony Pastor's Comic and Eccentric Songster* (1862), *Tony Pastor's Great Sensation Songster* (1864), and *Tony Pastor's 201 Bowery Songster* (1867). See Norman Cazden, Herbert Haufrecht, Norman Studer, eds., *Notes and Sources for Folk Songs of the Catskills, Supplement*, vol. 2 (State University of New York Press, 1982), 182–83.

5. "Tony Pastor's Opera House," *New York Clipper*, July 22, 1865, 120.

6. "Tony's Opera House," *New York Herald*, October 6, 1865: 4.

7. "Ecstasy," in *Webster's Unabridged Dictionary*, ed. Noah Webster (George and Charles Merriam, 1862), 379, accessed November 18, 2023, https://ia600307.

us.archive.org/27/items/americandiction00webs/americandiction00webs.pdf; "Ecstasy," in *American Dictionary of the English Language / Webster's Dictionary 1828* [electronic edition] (MasonSoft Technology, 2022), accessed November 28, 2023, https://webstersdictionary1828.com/Dictionary/ecstasy.

8. "Tony Pastor's Opera House," *New York Clipper*, July 22, 1865, 120.

9. Carnival is apocryphally assumed to be a Christianized adaptation of ancient festivals associated with *enthousiasmos*. Even if this connection is overstated, however, both rituals appear to have shared an inclination toward self-transcendence.

10. Peter Stallybrass and Allon White, *The Politics and Poetics of Transgression* (Cornell University Press, 1986).

11. Ehrenreich, *Dancing in the Streets*, 88; Peter Burke, *Popular Culture in Early Modern Europe*, 3rd ed. (Routledge, 2009); Michael D. Bristol, *Carnival and Theatre: Plebeian Culture and the Structure of Authority in Renaissance Britain* (Routledge, 1985).

12. Giraldis Cambrensis, *The Journey Through Wales and the Description of Wales* (Penguin Classics, 1978), 92.

13. Mikhail Bakhtin, *Rabelais and His World*, trans. Helen Iswolsky (Indiana University Press, 1984), 273, 275, 281.

14. Bakhtin, *Rabelais and His World*, 223–24.

15. Bakhtin, *Rabelais and His World*, 281.

16. Bakhtin, *Rabelais and His World*, 336.

17. Bakhtin's original assessment of Carnival's self-transcendent potential has been reiterated by many of his scholarly successors. Peter Stallybrass and Allon White, for instance, affirm that the inversion of "everyday hierarchies, structures, rules and customs" resulted in "the immixing of the subject, to the heterodox, messy, excessive and unfinished informalities of the body and social life." In this way, they agree that Carnival embodied what Bakhtin called the "unfinished nature of being" and the "flux of becoming." Applying these "messy," "unfinished," and perpetually unstable attributes to notions of selfhood could indeed have made for explosive self-experiences. Stallybrass and White, *Politics and Poetics of Transgression*, 183; Bakhtin, *Rabelais and His World*, 52, 53.

18. Scholars such as Julia Kristeva and Michel Foucault have tended to emphasize Carnival's liberatory impulses. Others, such as Terry Eagleton, have focused on the ways that it was licensed by religious, social, and political authorities. The most expansive assessments of Carnival, however, come from Stallybrass and White, who suggest that the history of Carnival resulted from the continuously evolving interplay of liberatory and licensed impulses. See Julia Kristeva, "Word, Dialogue and Novel," in *The Kristeva Reader*, ed. Toril Moi (Columbia University Press, 1986); Julia Kristeva, *La révolution du langage poétique: L'avant-garde à la fin du Xixe siècle, Lautréamont et Mallarmé* (Éditions du Seuil, 1974); Terry Eagleton, *Walter Benjamin: or, Towards a Revolutionary Criticism* (New Left Books, 1981), 148; Stallybrass and White, *Politics and Poetics of Transgression*.

19. Bakhtin, *Rabelais and His World*, 7, chap. 1.

20. Kristeva, "Word, Dialogue and Novel," 49.

21. Ehrenreich, *Dancing in the Streets*, 94.

22. Ehrenreich, *Dancing in the Streets*, 88.

23. Stallybrass and White, *Politics and Poetics of Transgression*, 15.

24. According to the historian Natalie Zemon Davis, this festivity sometimes challenged traditional gender hierarchies by placing "women on top" and ritually humiliating men. "Skimmington" became associated with rites of economic protest, involving male youths in female dress and painted faces defending their forests against the encroachment of capitalist enterprise. Natalie Zemon Davis, "Women on Top: Symbolic Sexual Inversion and Political Disorder in Early Modern Europe," in *Society and Culture in Early Modern France* (Stanford University Press, 1975).

25. Ehrenreich, *Dancing in the Streets*, 85; J. F. C. Hecker, *The Dancing Mania of the Middle* Ages, trans. B. G. Babington (Franklin, 1970), 8; John Waller, *The Dancing Plague: The Strange, True Story of an Extraordinary Illness* (Sourcebooks, 2009).

26. Michael Jarrett, *Drifting on a Read: Jazz as a Model for Writing* (State University of New York Press, 1999), 159.

27. Marsh, *Music and Society in Early Modern England*, 45–47. Also see David Underdown, *Revel, Riot and Rebellion* (Oxford University Press, 1985), 106–11; D. A. Johnson, "'Johnson Is Beaten!' A Case of 'Rough Music' at West Bromwich in 1611," *Transactions, Lichfield and South Staffordshire Archaeological and Historical Society* 25 (1983/1984): 31–34; Martin Ingram, "Ridings, Rough Music and Mocking Rhymes in Early Modern England," in *Popular Culture in Seventeenth-Century England*, ed. Barry Reay (Routledge, 1988), 166–97; E. P. Thompson, *Customs in Common: Studies in Traditional Popular Culture* (New Press, 1993), chap. 8.

28. Rough music's ostensible secularity meant that it continued to bear the scorn of cautionary critics fearful of its apparent disregard for religion. For some, rough music was only the most egregious form of a larger category of sonic expression that could spellbind subjects in a completely un-Christian manner. For example, one sixteenth-century Protestant reformer from England warned that most music was dangerous, not least "bycause it carieth awaye the eare, with the sweetnesse of the melodie, and bewitcheth the minde with a *Syrenes* sounde, pulling it from that delite, wherin of duetie it ought to dwell, unto harmonicall fantasies." According to the author of this quotation, the bewitching quality of the melody could be likened to the trance-inducing and thoroughly pagan songs sung by mythical Greek sirens. Quoted in Marsh, *Music and Society in Early Modern England*, 50–51.

29. Emmanuel Le Roy Ladurie, *Carnival in Romans*, trans. Mary Feeney (Braziller, 1979).

30. *Oxford English Dictionary*, under "emotion," accessed November 18, 2023, http://www.oed.com.proxy.libraries.rutgers.edu/view/Entry/61249.

31. Stallybrass and White, *Politics and Poetics of Transgression*, 96.

32. William Bradford, *Of Plymouth Plantation, 1620–1647* (McGraw-Hill, 1981), 226–27.

33. Bradford, *Of Plymouth Plantation*, 227.

34. Thomas Morton, *New English Canaan*, ed. Jack Dempsey (Digital Scanning, 2000), 139.

35. Deposition of Joseph Smith and Philip Scheffer, n.d., Kempe Papers, quoted in Steven J. Stewart, "Skimmington in the Middle and New England Colonies," in *Riot and Revelry in Early America*, ed. William Pencak, Matthew Dennis, and Simon P. Newman (Pennsylvania State University Press, 2002), 50.

36. Susan E. Klepp, "Rough Music on Independence Day: Philadelphia, 1778," in *Riot and Revelry in Early America*, ed. William Pencak, Matthew Dennis, and Simon P. Newman (Pennsylvania State University Press, 2002), 158.

37. Klepp, "Rough Music on Independence Day: Philadelphia, 1778," 161.

38. Elliot Robert Barkan, ed., *Immigrants in American History: Arrival, Adaptation, and Integration*, vol. 1 (ABC-CLIO, 2013).

39. Dale Cockrell, *Demons of Disorder: Early Blackface Minstrels and Their World* (Cambridge University Press, 1997), 32.

40. "Christmas Eve," *Public Ledger* (Philadelphia), December 25, 1844: 2.

41. R. Randall Couch, "The Public Masked Balls of Antebellum New Orleans: A Custom of Masque Outside the Mardi Gras Tradition," *Louisiana History: The Journal of the Louisiana Historical Association* 35, no. 4 (Autumn 1994): 405.

42. Kmen, *Music in New Orleans*; Robert Tallant, *Mardi Gras . . . as It Was* (Pelican Publishing, 1994).

43. Couch, "Public Masked Balls of Antebellum New Orleans," 403–31.

44. Jerah Johnson, "Colonial New Orleans: A Fragment of the Eighteenth-Century French Ethos," in *Creole New Orleans: Race and Americanization*, ed. Arnold R. Hirsh and Joseph Logsdon (Louisiana State University Press, 1992), 44–45.

45. John F. Watson, "Notitia of Incidents at New Orleans in 1804, 1805," *American Pioneer* 2 (May 1843), 229.

46. See Jessica Atkins, "Setting the Stage: Dance and Gender in Old-Line New Orleans Carnival Balls, 1870–1920," PhD diss., Florida State University, 2008, 51.

47. James R. Creecy, *Scenes in the South and Other Miscellaneous Pieces* (Thomas McGill, 1860), 43.

48. Peter Bailey, *Music Hall: The Business of Pleasure* (Open University Press, 1986); Hugh Cunningham, *Leisure in the Industrial Revolution, c1780–c1880* (Croom Helm, 1980); Hugh Cunningham, "Leisure," in *The Working Class England, 1875–1914*, ed. J. Benson (Croom Helm, 1985); John Storey, ed., *Culture Theory and Popular Culture: A Reader*, 4th ed. (Routledge, 2008); Lowerson and Myerscough, *Time to Spare*; Keith Robbinson, *Nineteenth-Century Britain* (Oxford University Press, 1988); John K. Walton, *The English Seaside Resort* (St. Martin's, 1983).

49. Cockrell, *Demons of Disorder*; Eric Lott, *Love and Theft: Blackface Minstrelsy and the American Working Class* (Oxford University Press, 1993).

50. Ashby, *With Amusement for All*, 52.

51. John Jentz, "Artisans, Evangelicals, and the City: A Social History of Abolition and Labor Reform in Jacksonian New York," PhD diss., City University of New York, 1977, 249.

52. Quoted in Don B. Wilmeth and Christopher Bigsby, eds., *The Cambridge History of American Theatre, vol. 1: Beginnings to 1870* (Cambridge University Press, 1998), 1:361.

53. Philip Hone, *Diary of Philip Hone*, July 10, 1834.

54. From the *Enquirer*, quoted in Sean Wilentz, *Chants Democratic: New York City and the Rise of the American Working Class, 1788–1850* (Oxford University Press, 1984), 265.

55. "Mobs in New York," *Niles' Register*, July 19, 1834, 359.

56. Quoted in Joanne Reitano, *The Restless City: A Short History of New York from Colonial Times to the Present*, 2nd ed. (Routledge, 2010), 45.

57. *Daily Chronicle* (Philadelphia), December 26, 1833, quoted in Alfred Lewis Shoemaker, *Christmas in Pennsylvania: A Folk-Cultural Study* (Stackpole Books, 1999), 91.

58. *Daily Chronicle* (Philadelphia), December 26, 1833. Quoted in Shoemaker, *Christmas in Pennsylvania*, 91–92.

59. In colonial New England, William Bradford had described Thomas Morton and his cronies as acting like "furies" when they danced and frisked together during Carnival festivities. See Bradford, *Of Plymouth Plantation*, 227.

60. "Furious," in *American Dictionary of the English Language / Webster's Dictionary 1828*, accessed November 18, 2023, http://webstersdictionary1828.com/Dictionary/furious.

61. "Madness," in *American Dictionary of the English Language / Webster's Dictionary 1828*, accessed November 18, 2023, http://webstersdictionary1828.com/Dictionary/madness. To "rave," one of the characteristics of madness, was "to wander in mind or intellect; to be delirious; to talk irrationally; to be wild. When men thus rave we may conclude their brains are turned." "Rave," in *American Dictionary of the English Language / Webster's Dictionary 1828*, accessed November 18, 2023, http://webstersdictionary1828.com/Dictionary/rave.

62. "Riot," in *American Dictionary of the English Language / Webster's Dictionary 1828 Webster's Dictionary 1828*, accessed November 18, 2023, http://webstersdictionary1828.com/Dictionary/riot.

63. Indeed, several of the quotations used in chapters 1–4 exhibited a degree of ambiguity that, in the absence of proper contextualization, may have allowed for a multiplicity of readings. This was especially true of those quotations that employed phrases like "as if," "as it were," or "kind of" when describing self-transcendent experiences. Such descriptions are included in the previous chapters because they were more clearly connected to supernatural, natural, and internal perspectives. However, they also indicate that an element of equivocation was always present in the other modes as well.

64. "Concerts of the Past Week," *Dwight's Journal of Music*, February 12, 1853, 150.

65. "Concerts of the Past Week," *Dwight's Journal of Music*, February 12, 1853, 150.

66. Bliss Perry, *Life and Letters of Henry Lee Higginson* (Atlantic Monthly Press, 1921), 78.

67. Gottschalk, *Notes of a Pianist*, 102–3.

68. Devoted defenders of the transcendent sublime perhaps also concluded this much, for some of them were quick to condemn Gottschalk. The influential music critic John S. Dwight, for instance, connected Gottschalk's flamboyant musical style with thoroughly secular, commercial ambitions. The virtuoso's music, he judged, was aimed to "dazzle or to appeal to [a base] sentimentality" more than to elicit a lofty reverence for a numinous entity. Quoted in Tawa, *From Psalm to Symphony*, 112.

69. Lears, *Fables of Abundance*, 24.

70. The German composer J. S. Bach, for instance, was employed for much of his life by a variety of Protestant churches (although he also composed secular music for royal courts). Peter Williams, *J.S. Bach: A Life in Music* (Cambridge University Press, 2007).

71. James, *Music of the Spheres*, 14.

72. H. Wiley Hitchcock, *Music in the United States: A Historical Introduction* (Prentice Hall, 1988), 17, 61–62.

73. For instance, in music catalogs it was possible to find songbooks titled *Church Music* or *Hart's Christmas Carols* next to other titles like *We Will Dance Like Elves and Fairies*, the latter containing "Stomp Ovations, Burlesque Lectures, Negro Songs . . . , Comic Conversation, Darkey Witticisms, . . . and Patent Sermons." All books, regardless of their cultural valence, could be sold for approximately the same price, a condition that only augmented a sense of exchangeability between sacred and secular interpretations of musical experience. See *The Musical Times*, November 1, 1880, 581.

74. This state had been brought on by modernity's "ethic of self-control and autonomous achievement, its cult of science and technical rationality, [and] its worship of material progress." Lears, *No Place of Grace*, 4. See also John Higham, "Reorientation of American Culture in the 1890s," in *Origins of Modern Consciousness*, ed. John Weiss (Wayne State University Press, 1966).

75. On the rise of anesthetics, see Joseph M. Gabriel, "'Anesthetics and the Chemical Sublime," *Raritan: A Quarterly Review* 30, no. 1 (2010): 69–74.

76. Lears, *No Place of Grace*; Lears, "From Salvation to Self-Realization," in *The Culture of Consumption*; Higham, "Reorientation of American Culture in the 1890s."

77. Maria Helena P. T. Machado, *Brazil Through the Eyes of William James: Letters, Diaries, and Drawings, 1865–1866* (Harvard University Press, 2006).

78. Lears, *No Place of Grace*, 4–5.

79. Richard Herndon and Edwin Bacon, *Men of Progress: One Thousand Biographical Sketches and Portraits of Leaders in Business and Professional Life in the Commonwealth of Massachusetts* (New England Magazine, 1896), 69–70.

80. Lucy Lowell Diary, April 14, 1884, quoted in Cavicchi, *Listening and Longing*, 107–8.

81. Lucy Lowell Diary, April 17, 1884, quoted in Cavicchi, *Listening and Longing*, 109.

82. Harvard College, *Records of the Class, 1883–1908* (Harvard College, 1908), 89; Ralph Waldo Emerson, *The Letters of Ralph Waldo Emerson*, ed. Eleanor M. Tilton, vol. 10, *1870–1881* (Columbia University Press, 1995), 10:108.

83. Emerson, *Complete Works of Ralph Waldo Emerson*, 1:10.

84. As reported by Engelbert Humperdinck in Abell, *Talks with Great Composers*, 137–38.

85. Lucy Lowell Diary, April 14, 1884, quoted in Cavicchi, *Listening and Longing*, 107–8.

86. Lilli Lehmann, *My Path Through Life* (G.P. Putnam's Sons, 1914), 366.

87. Friedrich Nietzsche, *The Birth of Tragedy*, trans. Clifton P. Fadiman (Dover, 1995), 27.

88. Nietzsche, *Birth of Tragedy*, 19.

89. Nietzsche, *Birth of Tragedy*, 19.

90. Nietzsche, *Birth of Tragedy*, 23.

91. Nietzsche, *Birth of Tragedy*, 78.

92. Friedrich Nietzsche, *The Case of Wagner, Nietzsche Contra Wagner, and Selected Aphorisms*, 3rd ed., trans. Anthony M. Ludovici (T.N. Foulois, 1911), 59–60.

93. Nietzsche, *The Case of Wagner, Nietzsche Contra Wagner*, 14.

94. Around this same time, two well-known American writers—James Huneker and H. L. Mencken—both published detailed studies of Nietzsche and his philosophies, and in 1913, Oscar Levy published an eighteen-volume English translation of the German philosopher's works. Michael Oriard, *Sporting with the Gods: The Rhetoric of Play and Game in American Culture* (Cambridge University Press, 1991), 407; Ratner-Rosenhagen, *American Nietzsche*.

Chapter 6

1. Edward Berlin, *Ragtime: A Musical and Cultural History* (Open Road Distribution, 2016).

2. Christoph Knüppel, "Kühl, Gustav: geb. 9.9.1869 Lübeck, gest. 20.10.1906 Berlin; ev.; Lehrer, Schriftsteller, Bibliotheksangestellter," in *Neue Lübecker Lebensläufe* (Wachholtz Verlag, 2009), 357–60.

3. Gustav Kuhl, "The Musical Possibilities of Ragtime," trans. Gustav Saenger, *Metronome* 19 (March 1903): 11.

4. Kuhl, "Musical Possibilities of Ragtime," 11.

5. One of the influences on ragtime came from American marching band music, which had remained a fixture of American culture since at least the Civil War and was also heavily rhythmic and beat-oriented. Marching band music, however, had never been as overtly syncopated as ragtime.

6. Brennan, *Secular Devotion*; Ned Sublette, *The World That Made New Orleans: From Spanish Silver to Congo Square* (Chicago Review Press, 2009); Ned Sublette, *Cuba and Its Music: From the First Drums to the Mambo* (Chicago Review Press, 2007); John Storm Roberts, *The Latin Tinge: The Impact of Latin American Music on the United States* (Oxford University Press, 1999); John Storm Roberts, *Black Music of Two Worlds*.

7. Rudi Blesh and Harriet Janis, *They All Played Ragtime: The True Story of an American Music* (Alfred A. Knopf, 1950), 227. The ragtime style had the melody anticipate or follow the main beat of a song, a technique that simultaneously avoided and accentuated that beat. Rudi Blesh, introduction to *Scott Joplin Complete Piano Works*, by Scott Joplin, ed. Vera Brodsky Lawrence (New York Public Library, 1981), xv.

8. Timothy D. Taylor, *The Sounds of Capitalism: Advertising, Music, and the Conquest of Culture* (University of Chicago Press, 2012); Karl Hagstrom Miller, *Segregating Sound: Inventing Folk and Pop Music in the Age of Jim Crow* (Duke University Press, 2010); David Suisman, *Selling Sounds: The Commercial Revolution in American Music* (Harvard University Press, 2009); Russell Sanjek, *American Popular Music and Its Business: The First Four Hundred Years Volume III: From 1909 to 1989* (Oxford University Press, 1988). See also David Sanjek, "They Work Hard for Their Money: The Business of Popular Music," in *American Popular Music: New Approaches to the Twentieth Century*, ed. Rachel Rubin and Jeffrey Paul Melnick (University of Massachusetts Press, 2001).

9. Suisman, *Selling Sounds*.

10. Jazz was a predominantly African American stylistic tradition that emerged following the First World War. As a musical form, it drew deeply from the ragtime styles that typified the prewar era, and for several years the terms were interchangeable in some settings. However, by the 1920s, the term jazz began to represent a variety of distinct musical features. Stylistically, it became associated with a greater emphasis on ensemble performances and improvisation than conventional ragtime tunes. Thomas Brothers, *Louis Armstrong's New Orleans* (W. W. Norton, 2006), 133; Nat Hentoff and Albert J. McCarthy, eds., *Jazz: New Perspectives on the History of Jazz by Twelve of the World's Foremost Jazz Critics and Scholars* (Da Capo Press, 1975).

11. The article was originally published in the *New York World*, probably in November 1903 (sometime before November 23, which was the opening night

of Caruso's *Rigoletto* performance). See "Enrico Caruso in Rigoletto, November 23, 1903," Metropolitan Opera Archives, accessed July 19, 2018, http://archives.metoperafamily.org/Imgs/RigolettoEssay.htm.

12. Pierre V. R. Key and Bruno Zirato, *Enrico Caruso: A Biography* (Little, Brown, 1922), 215.

13. "Where Caruso Sings," *New York Telegraph*, March 6, 1910.

14. "Caruso Carried Away by His Song," *New York Herald*, January 15, 1914.

15. Fischler, "Chili Sauce."

16. Herm Siewert and Gilbert Perry, "That Coon Town Rag" (C. A. Ross Publishing Company, 1913).

17. "£16,000 a Year from Song Writing" [unknown newspaper and date, c. 1911], Scrapbook 1, Box 511, Irving Berlin Collection, Music Division, Library of Congress.

18. Francesco Berger, "A Jazz Band Concert," *Monthly Musical Record*, August 1, 1919.

19. Berger, "Jazz Band Concert."

20. "Calls Ragtime Insanity" [newspaper clipping], October 19, Box 511, Scrapbook 1, Irving Berlin Collection, Music Division, Library of Congress.

21. Eddie Condon, *We Called It Music: A Generation of Jazz* (Da Capo Press, 1992), 107.

22. Condon, *We Called It Music*, 107.

23. Condon, *We Called It Music*, 107.

24. Condon, *We Called It Music*, 109.

25. Condon, *We Called It Music*, 61.

26. Condon, *We Called It Music*, 73.

27. Neil Harris, "John Philip Sousa and the Culture of Reassurance," in *Perspectives on John Philip Sousa*, ed. Jon Newsom (Library of Congress, 1983); Patrick Warfield, *Making the March King: John Philip Sousa's Washington Years, 1854–1893* (University of Illinois Press, 2013); Patrick Warfield, "The Sousa March: From Publication to Performance," in *Six Marches*, by John Philip Sousa (A-R Editions, 2010); Paul E. Bierley, *John Philip Sousa: American Phenomenon*, rev. ed. (Warner Brothers Publications, 2001).

28. *Saginaw Globe*, quoted in Harris, "John Philip Sousa and the Culture of Reassurance."

29. John Philip Sousa, *Marching Along: Recollections of Men, Women and Music* (Hale, Cushman & Flint, 1928), 340.

30. Sousa's argument for the unity of conductor and orchestra echoed Richard Wagner's sentiments on the bond between a composer and the musical performer. Wagner once wrote that in performing a composer's work the musician should "add nothing to it nor take anything away; he is to be *your second self.*" Quoted in Clive Brown: *Classical and Romantic Performing Practice, 1750–1900* (Oxford University Press, 1999), 5.

31. Otis Skinner in a Sousa Band press package, c. 1897, in the Paul Bierley Papers, Sousa Archives Center for American Music, quoted in Warfield, "Sousa March," lii.

32. "Sousa's Band Plays Twice Sunday," clipping labeled *Tribune* (Detroit), April 6, 1899, in HJ8: 243, Sousa Band Press Books, United States Marine Band Library. Quoted in Harris, "John Philip Sousa and the Culture of Reassurance."

33. Irving Berlin, "Why We Love Band Music," *The Billboard* (June 21, 1913), in Box 511 [Scrapbooks], Irving Berlin Collection, Music Division, Library of Congress.

34. Berlin, "Why We Love Band Music."

35. Several aspects of Irving Berlin's description of brass band performances align with Victor Turner's theory of *communitas*. For instance, Berlin's account discusses a mutual resonance between participants and a unifying experience through shared memory, spirit, and emotional release that speak directly to Turner's idea of a shared affective identification that transcends roles and ranks. It also places these encounters in amusement parks, communal settings that were capable of temporarily upending conventional hierarchies in a similar fashion as Turner's liminal settings. See chap. 2 for further discussion on the concept of *communitas*.

36. Nathan Hurwitz, *A History of the American Musical Theatre: No Business Like It* (Routledge, 2014), 76.

37. Alexander Woollcott, *The Story of Irving Berlin* (Da Capo, 1925), 13.

38. Irving Berlin's father could not find work as a synagogue cantor, and therefore he took up sporadic employment at a local kosher meat market. Mary Ellin Barrett, *Irving Berlin: A Daughter's Memoir* (Limelight Editions, 1996), 32.

39. Harry Von Tilzer and Vincent P. Bryan, "It Must Have Been Svengali in Disguise" (Harry Von Tilzer Publishing Co., 1902).

40. Lew Brown (lyrics) and Albert Von Tilzer (composer), "That Hypnotizing Man" (York Music Co., 1911). The song was later recorded by Billy Murray and the American Quartet.

41. Will Dillon and Harry Von Tilzer, "Hip Hip Hypnotize Me" (Harry Von Tilzer Music Publishing Co., 1910).

42. The literary scholar Edmund Wilson interpreted the Svengali character as "a spirit from an alien world who carries with it an uncanny prestige, who may speak in a divine tongue." Edmund Wilson, *Piece of My Mind: Reflections at Sixty* (Farrar, Straus and Giroux, 1956), 105.

43. Dillon and Tilzer, "Hip Hip Hypnotize Me."

44. "Nora Bayes Score as One of Follies," *New York Telegraph*, August 30, 1907.

45. "Bewitching Miss Bayes," *Chicago News*, January 31, 1912; "Great Bill at Majestic," *Chicago News*, January 31, 1912.

46. "B.F. Keith's," *Washington Post*, November 8, 1916; "Nora Bayes Hit of Orpheum Bill," *Brooklyn Eagle*, October 23, 1917; "People of the Stage," *Cincinnati Commercial*, September 10, 1911. See also "Nora Bayes a Hit at New Brighton,"

Brooklyn Eagle, July 17, 1917. All of these sources can be found in Reel 4, Robinson Locke Collection, Billy Rose Theatre Division, New York Public Library for the Performing Arts.

47. Nora Bayes, "Holding My Audience," *Theatre Magazine* (September 1917), 128.

48. Nora Bayes, "Holding My Audience," 128.

49. Nora Bayes, "Why People Enjoy Crying in a Theater," *American Magazine*, April 1918, 33.

50. Kathy J. Ogren, *The Jazz Revolution: Twenties America and the Meaning of Jazz* (Oxford University Press, 1992).

51. James Weldon Johnson, *Along This Way* (Viking Press, [c. 1933] 1968), 328.

52. Marshall Stearns, *Jazz Dance: The Story of American Vernacular Dance* (Da Capo Press, 1968), 111.

53. Cole Porter, Alan Strachan, and Benny Green, *The Mermaid Theatre's Cole: An Entertainment Based on the Words and Music of Cole Porter* (Samuel French, 1981), 54.

54. Norman Mailer, "The White Negro: Superficial Reflections on the Hipster," in *The Portable Beat Reader: Three Commentators on the Beat Generations*, ed. Ann Charters (Viking, 1998), 587.

55. On the phonograph, see especially Andre Millard, *America on Record: A History of Recorded Sound* (Cambridge University Press, 1995); Emily Thompson, "Machines, Music, and the Quest for Fidelity: Marketing the Edison Phonograph in America, 1877–1925," *Musical Quarterly* 79 (Spring 1995): 131–71; Michael Taussig, *Mimesis and Alterity: A Particular History of the Senses* (Routledge, 1993), 193–235; William Howland Kenney, *Recorded Music in American Life: The Phonograph and Popular Memory* (Oxford University Press, 2003).

56. Thompson, "Machines, Music, and the Quest for Fidelity."

57. Schmidt, *Hearing Things*.

58. "The Talking Phonograph," *Scientific American* 22 (December 1877): 385.

59. See Steiner, *Real Presences*.

60. Brian Dolan, *Inventing Entertainment: The Player Piano and the Origins of an American Musical Industry* (Rowman and Littlefield, 2009).

61. J. Hopkins, "A Player-Piano for Natural Musicians," *American Monthly Review of Reviews* 34 (December 1906): 85; J. Alfred Johnstone, "Some Essentials in Fine Piano-Playing: Illustrated by Features in the Art of Mme. Carreno [*sic*]," *Musical Standard*, September 3, 1910: 146.

62. As early as 1895, the Kinetoscope gave way to the Kinetophone, which was outfitted with a phonograph and listening tubes. The recordings included preselected titles from the Edison catalog, including dance tunes and marches. Opportunities for pairing moving pictures with music only expanded with the development of nickelodeons. The equal role played by both visual and audible components was evidenced by the rampant popularity of "illustrated songs." These were shows that

involved the performance of music in conjunction with the projection of still images on glass slides. Often the slides were intended to enhance the musical experience, for instance by including song lyrics that allowed audience members to sing along. The immense popularity of illustrated songs from the 1890s to the 1910s helps signify how important sound and music were in early cinematic spaces. Kathryn Kalinak, *Film Music: A Very Short Introduction* (Oxford University Press, 2010), 33–36.

63. Tom Gunning, "The Cinema of Attractions: Early Film, Its Spectator and the Avant-Garde," *Wide Angle* 8, nos. 3 and 4 (Fall 1986): 64–65.

64. See Gunning, "Cinema of Attractions"; Charles Musser, "American Vitagraph 1897–1901," *Cinema Journal* 22, no. 3 (Spring 1983): 4–46; Charles Musser and Carol Nelson, *High-Class Moving Pictures: Lyman H. Howe and the Forgotten Era of Traveling Exhibition, 1880–1920* (Princeton University Press, 1991).

65. Marshall McLuhan, *Understanding Media: The Extensions of Man* (McGraw-Hill, 1964).

66. Tom Gunning, "Cinema of Attractions," 64–65.

67. Miriam Hansen, *Babel and Babylon: Spectatorship and American Silent Film* (Harvard University Press, 1991), 83.

68. Quoted in Musser and Nelson, *High-Class Moving Pictures*, 66.

69. Quoted in Musser and Nelson, *High-Class Moving Pictures*, 66.

70. Mary Ann Doane, "Technology's Body: Cinematic Vision in Modernity," *differences: A Journal of Feminist Cultural Studies* 5, no. 2 (1993): 15.

71. Kalinak, *Film Music*, 28.

72. Lauren Rabinovitz, "More Than the Movies: A History of the Somatic Visual Culture through Hale's Tours, Imax, and Motion Simulation Rides," in *Memory Bytes: History, Technology, and Digital Culture*, ed. Lauren Rabinovitz and Abraham Geil (Duke University Press, 2004); Lauren Rabinovitz, *For the Love of Pleasure: Women, Movies, and Culture in Turn-of-the-Century Chicago* (Rutgers University Press, 1998).

73. Leon Gurevitch, "The Cinemas of Transactions: The Exchangeable Currency of the Digital Attraction," *Television & New Media* 11, no. 5 (2010): 370.

74. Stephen Bottomore, "The Panicking Audience? Early Cinema and the 'Train Effect,'" *Historical Journal of Film, Radio and Television* 19, no. 2 (1999): 177–216; Ian Christie, *The Last Machine: Early Cinema and the Birth of the Modern World* (BBC-BFI, 1994); David B. Clarke and Marcus A. Doel, "Engineering Space and Time: Moving Pictures and Motionless Trips," *Journal of Historical Geography* 31, no. 1 (2005): 41–60.

75. Hugo Münsterberg, *Psychotherapy* (Moffat, Yard, & Co., 1909), 117; Hugo Münsterberg, *The Photoplay* (Routledge, [1916] 2002), 85, 97.

76. Münsterberg, *Photoplay*, 82.

77. Such a characterization corresponds to what the film scholar Miriam Hansen describes as cinema's own unique "fictional space-time." Miriam Hansen, *Babel and Babylon: Spectatorship and American Silent Film* (Harvard University Press, 1991), 83.

78. "diegesis," in *Oxford Reference*, accessed June 14, 2024, http://www.oxfordreference.com/view/10.1093/oi/authority. 20110803095717289.

79. Annabel J. Cohen, "Music as a Source of Emotion in Film," in *Handbook of Music and Emotion: Theory, Research, and Applications* (Oxford University Press, 2010), 886.

80. Kalinak, *Film Music*, 23.

81. Hanns Eisler and Theodor W. Adorno, *Composing for the Films* (Continuum, [c. 1947] 2005).

82. Kalinak, *Film Music*, 26–27. See also Claudia Gorbman, *Unheard Melodies: Narrative Film Music* (Indiana University Press, 1987). Caryl Flinn elaborates the point, contending that music provides a "fullness of experience" and augments the film's "impression of perfection and integrity." Caryl Flinn, *Strains of Utopia: Gender, Nostalgia, and Hollywood Film Music* (Princeton University Press, 1992), 9.

83. Annabel J. Cohen, "The Functions of Music in Multimedia: A Cognitive Approach," in *Music, Mind, and Science*, ed. S. W. Yi (Seoul National University Press, 1999).

84. Kalinak, *Film Music*, 41.

85. These publications included "Incidental Music for Edison Pictures," *Edison Kinetograms* 1, no. 4 (September 15, 1909); Giuseppi Becce's *Konthek* series published in Berlin (1919–1929); J. S. Zamecnik's *Sam Fox Moving Picture Music* series (1913–1914); Malvin M. Franklin's *Favorite Moving Picture Music Folio*; and Enro Rapee's *Motion Picture Moods for Pianists and Organists* (1924) and *Encyclopedia of Music for Pictures* (1925). Although those who ran and patronized the film world agreed that music was crucial to the cinematic experience, during the early era of film many also complained about the careless choice of compositions or accompanying styles that actually distracted from the storyline. In response to these concerns, many in the film industry set out to improve the coordination between film music and audience reception. According to the film historian Rick Altman, this effort involved a series of decisions and techniques that "concentrated audience attention on identification with the image." This effect was achieved through a variety of methods, including a transition away from lyric-based popular songs and toward instrumental music, and ultimately the commissioning of customized scores for specific movies. Rick Altman, *Silent Film Sound* (Columbia University Press, 2004), 283, 251–58.

86. "At-the-Movies Fun in Your Own Parlor with the Favorite Moving Picture Music Folio," *The Music and Theatre Gossip: A Popular Monthly Magazine of Song, Dance, Concert and Stage* (February 1915), 5. Also see Irving Berlin Collection Scrapbooks, Library of Congress, Box 511, p. 99 of scrapbook.

87. In this usage, the word "literally" comes closer to the definition of "virtually." See "literal, adj. and n." in *OED Online*, accessed September 26, 2016, https://doi.org/10.1093/OED/3009255380.

88. "Feature Films for Feature Music," *Moving Picture World*, April 16, 1910, 591.

89. Some authors avoided allusions to artifice altogether, choosing instead to frame cinematic transport in decidedly real terms. This included the reviewer of D. W. Griffith's 1920 film *Way Down East*, who pointed to the rich musical score, composed by Louis Silvers and William Frederick Peters, as conducive to the effect. The author described the film music as having "touched the heart" in an unforgettable manner, unfolding in a spectacle of pathos and comedy that created a "rapture of transport to pastoral scenes of New England community." "Local Brevities," *The Advertiser* 11, no. 3 (March 19, 1921), 5.

90. "A Cinema Musician, 'Atmosphere,'" *The Strad* (London), March 1926, 17.

91. "A Cinema Musician, 'Atmosphere,'" *The Strad* (London), March 1926, 17.

92. Joseph N. Weber (interview), "Will Machine-Made Music Displace Real Music in Our Theaters?," *Metronome*, September 1928, 50, 102. For another reference to cinematic illusion, see Warren Nolan, "Talking Pictures and the Public," *Transactions of the Society of Motion Picture Engineers* 13, no. 37 (1929): 131–34.

93. Herbert Blumer, *Movies and Conduct* (Macmillan, 1933), 74.

94. Nolan, "Talking Pictures and the Public," 131–34.

95. American Federation of Musicians, "Canned Music on Trial," *Pittsburgh Press*, 1929, Duke University Digital Repository (R0206), accessed November 18, 2023, https://idn.duke.edu/ark:/87924/r4rr1q397.

96. While living in the U.S., Lawrence published a book titled *Studies in Classic American Literature*, which became one of the preeminent books on the topic.

97. Lawrence, *Mornings in Mexico*, 97.

98. Lawrence, *Mornings in Mexico*, 97.

Conclusion

1. Émile Durkheim, *The Elementary Forms of Religious Life*, trans. Joseph Ward Swain (George Allen & Unwin, 1915), 211.

2. Durkheim, *Elementary Forms of Religious Life*, 382.

3. Durkheim, *Division of Labor in Society*, 76.

4. Sawyer concludes that Durkheim approached the collective consciousness as an "emergent" phenomenon. R. Keith Sawyer, "Durkheim's Dilemma: Toward a Sociology of Emergence," *Sociological Theory* 20, no. 2 (July 2002): 227–47.

5. The Austrian psychologist Carl Jung developed a theory of the "collective unconscious" that was in many respects comparable to Durkheim's collective consciousness. It referred to the elements of the unconscious mind that individuals shared in common, and like Durkheim, Jung contended that music and dance, among other activities, could be used to engage with these elements. However, probably on account of his own disciplinary background, Jung's theory seemed to posit, like Freud, that the unconscious was, at bottom, a component of the individual mind and not some integrated entity external to it. In short, he shared little

of Durkheim's ambiguity. Carl G. Jung, *The Portable Jung*, ed. Joseph Campbell (Penguin Classics, 1976).

6. Claude Lévi-Strauss, *Myth and Meaning* (University of Toronto Press, 1978).

7. Claude Lévi-Strauss, *Structural Anthropology*, vol. 2 (Basic Books, 1976), 166.

8. This theory of consumer culture aligns somewhat with the work of other scholars. See, for example, S. J. Levy, "Interpreting Consumer Mythology: A Structural Approach to Consumer Behavior," *Journal of Marketing* 45, no. 3 (1981): 49–61; Pierre McDonagh et al., eds., *Myth and the Market* (University College Dublin, 2014).

9. Lears, for instance, explains the rise of the advertising industry in America as the result of its ability to play with the tension between unreconciled yearnings for authentic experience amid a growing sense of unreality. He demonstrates how advertisers framed consumer goods as capable of fulfilling this longing for authenticity. Ultimately, however, consumers' experiences fell short of their expectations, which reinforced a cycle of consumption. Campbell similarly writes of consumer culture's reliance on unfulfilled promises of authenticity. In *The Romantic Ethic and the Spirit of Modern Consumerism*, he describes the Romantic movement's moral elevation of the imagination as a key driver of consumer culture due to its ability to create pleasurable and convincing fantasies that risked "outperforming" the actual experience of activities and products—a tension that ultimately encouraged people to continue consuming in order to feel (never fully) gratified. The anthropologist Peter Stromberg uses the label "Romantic Realism" to encompass the aesthetic works—the images, stories, and other expressional forms—that encourage consumption by creating this larger-than-life imaginal realm. Other scholars have observed related dynamics motivating non-Western consumption practices. Jean-Marc Philibert, for instance, describes consumption in the Third World as based on a kind of "bait-and-switch" mechanism whereby "individuals purchase objects in order to attain what their image suggests, but there is never enough behind the image. Their desire is forever renewed but never satisfied." See Lears, "From Salvation to Self-Realization"; Lears, *Fables of Abundance*; Campbell, *Romantic Ethic*; Stromberg, *Caught in Play*; see also Jean-Marc Philibert, "Consuming Culture: A Study of Simple Commodity Consumption," in *The Social Economy of Consumption*, ed. Benjamin Orlove and Henry Rutz (University Press of America, 1989), 63.

10. See, for example, Halttunen, *Confidence Men and Painted Women*; Simon During, *Modern Enchantments: The Cultural Power of Secular Magic* (Harvard University Press, 2002); James Cook, *The Arts of Deception: Playing with Fraud in the Age of Barnum* (Harvard University Press, 2001).

11. John M. Andrick, "Futurist Dissonance, Theosophical Transcendence and American Musical Ultra-Modernism, 1909–1930," *International Yearbook of Futurism Studies* 11 (2021): 107–30; Carol J. Oja, *Making Music Modern: New York in the 1920s* (Oxford University Press, 2000); Wilfrid Mellers, *Music in a New Found Land: Themes and Developments in the History of American Music* (Stonehill

Publishing, 1964), chap. 6. These represent just a few of the more noteworthy publications on the topic.

12. See Ian E. Wickramasekera II, "Hypnosis and Transpersonal Psychology: Answering the Call Within," in *The Wiley-Blackwell Handbook of Transpersonal Psychology*, ed. Harris L. Friedman and Glenn Hartelius (John Wiley & Sons, 2013).

Bibliography

Primary Sources

"£16,000 a Year from Song Writing." [Unknown newspaper and date, c. 1911], Scrapbook 1, Box 511, Irving Berlin Collection, Music Division, Library of Congress.

1740 South Carolina Slave Code, Acts of the South Carolina General Assembly, 1740 # 670, South Carolina Department of Archives and History, Columbia, South Carolina. Reproduced in U.S. Department of Education, Teaching American History in South Carolina Program. Accessed November 28, 2023. http://www.teachingushistory.org/ttrove/1740slavecode.htm.

"A Cinema Musician, 'Atmosphere.'" *The Strad* (London), March 1926, 17.

Adams, John Stowell. *The Psalms of Life; a Compilation of Psalms, Hymns, Chants, Anthems, &c., Embodying the Spiritual, Progressive and Reformatory Sentiment of the Present Age.* O. Ditson, 1857.

Alcott, Amos Bronson. *The Journals of Bronson Alcott.* Edited by Odell Shepard. Little, Brown, 1938.

Allen, William Francis, Charles Pickard Ware, and Lucy McKim Garrison. *Slave Songs of the United States.* Peter Smith, (c. 1867) 1951.

American Federation of Musicians. "Canned Music on Trial." *Pittsburgh Press,* 1929. Duke University Digital Repository, (R0206). https://idn.duke.edu/ark:/87924 /r4rr1q397.

"At-the-Movies Fun in Your Own Parlor with the Favorite Moving Picture Music Folio." *Music and Theatre Gossip: A Popular Monthly Magazine of Song, Dance, Concert and Stage* (New York), February 1915, 5.

Barrett, Mary Ellin. *Irving Berlin: A Daughter's Memoir.* Limelight Editions, 1996.

Bayes, Nora. "Holding My Audience." *Theatre Magazine* (September 1917), 128.

Bayes, Nora. "Why People Enjoy Crying in a Theater." *American Magazine,* April 1918, 33–35.

Beard, George M. "Psychology of Spiritism." *North American Review* 129 (1879): 65–80.

Beard, George M. *The Scientific Basis of Delusions: A New Theory of Trance and Its Bearings on Human Testimony.* G.P. Putnam's Sons, 1877.

Berger, Francesco. "A Jazz Band Concert." *Monthly Musical Record* (London), August 1, 1919.

Berlin, Irving. "That Mesmerizing Mendelssohn Tune." Ted Snyder Co., 1909.

Berlin, Irving. "Why We Love Band Music." *The Billboard,* June 21, 1913.

Bernheim, Hippolyte. *Hypnosis and Suggestion in Hypnotherapy.* Aronson, 1884.

"Bewitching Miss Bayes." *Chicago News,* January 31, 1912.

"B.F. Keith's." *Washington Post,* November 8, 1916.

Blumer, Herbert. *Movies and Conduct.* Macmillan, 1933.

Blumhofer, Edith L. *Restoring the Faith: The Assemblies of God, Pentecostalism, and American Culture.* University of Illinois Press, 1993.

Bradford, William. *Of Plymouth Plantation, 1620–1647.* McGraw-Hill, 1981.

Braid, James. *Magic, Witchcraft, Animal Magnetism, Hypnotism, and Electro-Biology.* John Churchill, 1852.

Braid, James. *Neuropnology; or, The Rationale of Nervous Sleep, Considered in Relation with Animal Magnetism.* John Churchill, 1843.

Braid, James. *Observations on Trance or Human Hibernation.* John Churchill, 1850.

Breuer, Josef, and Sigmund Freud, *Studies on Hysteria.* Translated by Nicola Luckhurst. Penguin, 2004.

Britten, Emma Hardinge. *Autobiography of Emma Hardinge Britten.* Edited by Margaret Wilkinson. John Heywood, 1900.

Britten, Emma Hardinge [and Henry Wadsworth Longfellow]. *The Footsteps of Angels; Recitative & Air.* H. Waters, 1856.

Brown, Francis, S. R. Driver, and Charles A. Briggs. *The Brown-Driver-Briggs Hebrew and English Lexicon.* Peabody, MA: Hendrickson Publishers, (c. 1907) 1996.

Brown, Lew (lyrics), and Albert Von Tilzer (composer). "That Hypnotizing Man." York Music Co., 1911.

Brown, William Hill, and Hannah Webster Foster. *The Power of Sympathy* and *The Coquette.* Penguin, 1996.

Brown, William Wells. *My Southern Home, or, The South and Its People.* A.G. Brown, 1880. Accessed November 28, 2023. https://archive.org/details/06248562.4740. emory.edu/page/n81/mode/2up?q=Voudooism.

Bruchman, R. M. *Hopi Ceremonial Snake Dance, Near Winslow, Arizona.* Lithograph Postcard. Winslow, Navajo County, AZ: R.M. Bruchman, Indian Trader, 1915. https://www.terapeak.com/worth/3-near-winslow-arizona-hopi-indian-snake-dance-view-1-c1915-az-litho-postcard/291925805072/.

Bruegel, Pieter, the Elder. *The Fight Between Carnival and Lent.* 1559. Oil on wood panel, 118 x 164 cm, Vienna, Kunsthistorisches Museum. Accessed August 31, 2017. https://upload.wikimedia.org/wikipedia/commons/thumb/1/1a/Pieter_Bruegel_d._%C3%84._066.jpg/800px-Pieter_Bruegel_d._%C3%84._066.jpg.

Buel, James William. *Mysteries and Miseries of America's Great Cities: Embracing New York, Washington City, San Francisco, Salt Lake City, and New Orleans.* A.L. Bancroft & Co., 1883. Accessed November 28, 2023. https://books.google.ca/books?id=rklAAAAAYAAJ.

Burke, Edmund. *A Philosophical Enquiry into the Origin of Our Ideas of the Sublime and the Beautiful.* Oxford University Press, (1757) 1990.

Burton, Robert. *The Anatomy of Melancholy.* Edited by Arthur Richard Shilleto, Arthur Henry Bullen. 3 vols. George Bell and Sons, 1896.

Burwell, Letitia M. *A Girl's Life in Virginia Before the War.* Federick A. Stokes Company, 1895. Electronic ed. Accessed November 28, 2023. https://docsouth.unc.edu/fpn/burwell/burwell.html.

Cable, George Washington. "The Dance in Place Congo." *Century Magazine* 31 (February 1886), 517–32.

"Calls Ragtime Insanity" [newspaper clipping]. October 19, Box 511, Scrapbook 1, Irving Berlin Collection, Music Division, Library of Congress.

Cambrensis, Giraldis. *The Journey Through Wales and the Description of Wales.* Penguin Classics, 1978.

"Caruso Carried Away by His Song." *New York Herald*, January 15, 1914.

Carter, Edward, II, John C. Van Horne, and Lee W. Formwalt, eds. *Journals of Benjamin Henry Latrobe, 1799–1820: From Philadelphia to New Orleans.* Vol. 3. Yale University Press, 1980.

Charcot, Jean-Martin. *Oeuvres completes.* 9 vols. Bureau de Progres Medical, 1886–1893.

Chauncy, Charles. *Enthusiasm Described and Caution'd Against.* Boston, J. Draper, for S. Eliot and J. Blanchard, 1742.

Chauncy, Charles. *Seasonable Thoughts on the State of Religion in New-England.* Rogers and Fowle, 1743.

"Christmas Eve." *Public Ledger* (Philadelphia), December 25, 1844, 2.

"Concert Saloons in New Orleans, Louisiana in 1869." *New Orleans Republican*, December 26, 1869: 1.

"Concerts of the Past Week." *Dwight's Journal of Music* (Boston), February 12, 1853, 149–51.

Condon, Eddie. *We Called it Music: A Generation of Jazz.* Da Capo, 1992.

Copeland, George. "Debussy, the Man I Knew." *Atlantic Monthly* (January 1955): 34–38.

Copeland, George. *Music My Life.* Printed by Monica McCall. Unpublished biography. New York Public Library for the Performing Arts, Music Division, George Copeland Papers. JPB 91–135, Box 2, Folder 19.

Copeland, George. Unpublished biography. New York Public Library for the Performing Arts, Music Division, George Copeland Papers. JPB 91–135, Box 2, Folder 17.

Corning, James Leonard. "The Use of Musical Vibration Before and During Sleep—Supplementary Employment of Chromatoscopic Figures—a Contribution to the Therapeutics of the Emotions." *The Medical Record: A Weekly Journal of Medicine and Surgery* 14 (1899): 79–86.

Couch, R. Randall. "The Public Masked Balls of Antebellum New Orleans: A Custom of Masque Outside the Mardi Gras Tradition." *Louisiana History: The Journal of the Louisiana Historical Association* 35, no. 4 (Autumn 1994): 403–31.

Creecy, James R. *Scenes in the South and Other Miscellaneous Pieces.* Thomas McGill, 1860.

Daily Chronicle (Philadelphia). December 26, 1833.

Darwin, Charles. *The Descent of Man, and Selection in Relation to Sex.* John Murray, 1871.

Darwin, Charles. *The Expression of the Emotions in Man and Animals.* John Murray, 1873.

Darwin, Charles to John Fordyce, May 7, 1879. Letter no. 1204. In *Darwin Correspondence Project.* Accessed July 10, 2017. http://www.darwinproject.ac.uk/DCP-LETT-12041.

Davenport, R. B. *The Deathblow to Spiritualism.* G.W. Dillingham Co., 1897.

Davis, Andrew Jackson. *The Principles of Nature, Her Divine Revelations, and a Voice of Mankind.* S.S. Lyon and Wm. Fishbough, 1847.

Deleuze, J. P. F. *Practical Instruction in Animal Magnetism.* Translated by Thomas C. Hartshorn. D. Appleton & Co., 1843.

Descartes, Rene. *Passions of the Soul.* Translated by Stephen H. Voss. Hackett, 1989.

Desrais, Claude-Louis. *Mesmeric Therapy; A Group of Mesmerised French Patients.* 1778/1784. Oil on canvas, 60.5 x 76.2 cm. London, Wellcome Library, Iconographic Collections 44754i, ICV No. 17651, Photo number: V0017306. Accessed August 31, 2017. https://wellcomeimages.org/indexplus/image/V0017306.html.

Dillon, Will, and Harry Von Tilzer. "Hip Hip Hypnotize Me." Harry Von Tilzer Music Publishing Co., 1910.

Donovan, J. *Music and Action, or, The Elective Affinity Between Rhythm and Pitch.* Kegan Paul, Trench, & Co, 1889.

Douglass, Frederick. *A Narrative of the Life of Frederick Douglass, An American Slave.* The Antislavery Office, 1845.

Du Bois, W. E. B. *The Autobiography of W.E.B. Du Bois: A Soliloquy on Viewing.* International Publishers, 1968.

Du Bois, W. E. B. *The Souls of Black Folk: Essays and Sketches.* A. C. McClurg & Co. 1903.

Durkheim, Émile. *The Division of Labor in Society.* Translated by W. D. Halls. Free Press, 1997.

Durkheim, Émile. *The Elementary Forms of Religious Life.* Translated by Joseph Ward Swain. George Allen & Unwin, 1915.

Dwight, John Sullivan. "Music." In *Aesthetic Papers*, edited by Elizabeth P. Peabody, 25–36. AMS Press, (1849) 1967.

Dwight's Journal of Music, April 9, 1853, 5–6.

Dwight's Journal of Music, February 5, 1853, 141.

"The Early Camp-Meeting Song Writers." *Methodist Quarterly Review* (July 1859): 407.

Edwards, Jonathan. *Sinners in the Hands of an Angry God*. S. Kneeland and T. Green, 1741.

Edwards, Jonathan. *Thoughts on Revival of Religion in New England, 1742*. Dunning and Spalding, 1832.

Edwards, Jonathan. *A Treatise Concerning Religious Affections, in Three Parts*. S. Kneeland and T. Green, 1746; Ann Arbor: Text Creation Partnership, 2011. Accessed November 28, 2023. https://quod.lib.umich.edu/e/evans/N04635.0001.001.

Edwards, Jonathan. *The Works of Jonathan Edwards*. Edited by Edward Hickman, Vol. 1. William Ball, 1819.

Edwards, Jonathan. *The Works of President Edwards, in Four Volumes*, Vol. 1. Leavitt, Trow and Company, 1844.

Emerson, Ralph Waldo. *The Complete Works of Ralph Waldo Emerson, Nature: Addresses and Lectures*. 12 vols. Houghton, Mifflin and Company, 1903.

Emerson, Ralph Waldo. *The Journals and Miscellaneous Notebooks of Ralph Waldo Emerson*. Vol. 5. Edited by Linda Allardt. Belknap Press of Harvard University Press, 1965.

Emerson, Ralph Waldo. *The Letters of Ralph Waldo Emerson*. Vol. 10, *1870–1881*. Edited by Eleanor M. Tilton. Columbia University Press, 1995.

"Enrico Caruso in Rigoletto, November 23, 1903." Metropolitan Opera Archives. Accessed July 19, 2018. http://archives.metoperafamily.org/Imgs/RigolettoEssay.htm.

Faria, Abbé. *Of the Cause of Lucid Sleep or Study of the Nature of Man* [*De la cause du sommeil lucide ou étude de la nature de l'homme*]. Translated by Manoharrai Sardessai. CinnamonTeal Publishing, 2014.

"Feature Films for Feature Music." *Moving Picture World* (New York), April 16, 1910, 591.

Fergusson, Francis. "The Theatre: What Is the Revue?" *The Bookman: A Literary Journal* 72 (1930): 409–11.

Finney, Charles. *How to Experience Revival*. Whitaker House, 2010.

Finney, Charles. "Letters on Revivals: No. 8." *Oberlin Evangelist* (Oberlin, OH) 7 (1845): 75–76.

Finney, Charles Grandison. *Memoirs of Rev. Charles G. Finney*. Applewood Press, (c. 1876) 2009.

Finney, Charles G., and Joshua Leavitt. *Lectures on Revival of Religion*. John P. Jewett & Co., 1858.

"The First Night of 'Fidelio' in America." *The Corsair* (New York), September 14, 1839, 423.

Fischler, H. A. "Chili Sauce: That Tantalizing Rag Time Song." Vandersloot Music Publishing Co., 1910.

Fish, Henry Clay. *The Handbook of Revivals: For the Use of Winners of Souls.* James H. Earle, 1874.

"Fisk Jubilee Singers, ca. 1870s." Howard University, Prints & Photographs Department, Moorland-Spingarn Research Center.

Foxcroft, Thomas. *Some Seasonable Thoughts on Evangelic Preaching, Its Nature, Usefulness, and Obligation.* G. Rogers and D. Fowke, 1740.

"The Freedmen at Port Royal." *North American Review* 101, no. 208 (1865): 1–28. Accessed November 28, 2023. http://www.jstor.org/stable/25107821.

Freud, Sigmund. *Civilization and Its Discontents.* In *The Standard Edition of the Complete Psychological Works of Sigmund Freud,* vol. 21, translated and edited by James Strachey. Hogarth Press, 1964.

Freud, Sigmund. *The Future of an Illusion.* W. W. Norton, 1927.

Freud, Sigmund. *The Interpretation of Dreams.* Macmillan, 1913.

Freud, Sigmund. *New Introductory Lectures on Psychoanalysis.* Translated by James Strachey. W. W. Norton, 1965.

Freud, Sigmund. "The Origin and Development of Psychoanalysis." *American Journal of Psychology* 21, no. 2 (April 1910): 181–218.

Freud, Sigmund. "Recommendations to Physicians Practicing Psychoanalysis." In *The Standard Edition of the Complete Psychological Works of Sigmund Freud,* vol. 12, translated and edited by James Strachey. Hogarth Press, (c. 1912) 1955.

Freud, Sigmund. *Two Encyclopedia Articles,* in *The Standard Edition of the Complete Psychological Works of Sigmund Freud,* vol. 18, translated and edited by James Strachey. Hogarth Press, (c. 1923) 1955.

Garrison, William Lloyd. "Modern Phenomena." *The Liberator* (Boston) 24, no. 9 (March 3, 1854): 34.

Gladden, George. "Is Applause Necessary?" *Music: A Monthly Magazine* 8 (May 1895 to October 1895): 431–36.

Goodspeed, Edgar Johnson. *A Full History of the Wonderful Career of Moody and Sankey in Great Britain and America.* John O. Robinson, 1876.

Gottschalk, Louis Moreau. *Notes of a Pianist: The Chronicle of a New Orleans Music Legend.* Edited by Jeanne Behrend. Princeton University Press, 2006.

"Gottschalk's Concerts." *Dwight's Journal of Music* (Boston) 22, no. 3, October 18, 1862, 230–31.

"Great Bill at Majestic." *Chicago News,* January 31, 1912.

Groos, Karl. *The Play of Man.* Translated by Elizabeth L. Baldwin. Appleton, 1901.

Gurney, E., F. W. H. Myers, and F. Podmore. *Phantasms of the Living.* 2 vols. Society for Psychical Research and Trubner and Co., 1886.

Hall, G. Stanley. *Adolescence: Its Psychology and Its Relations to Physiology, Anthropology, Sociology, Sex, Crime, Religion and Education.* Vol. 1, 265–66. D. Appleton, 1904.

Hand Book of the Carnival. Kain & Co., 1874.

Handy, M. P. "Witchcraft Among the Negroes." *Appletons' Journal: A Magazine of General Literature* 8, no. 194 (December 14, 1872): 666–67. Accessed November 28, 2023. http://quod.lib.umich.edu/m/moajrnl/acw8433.1–08.194/670.

Hardinge, Emma. *Modern American Spiritualism: A Twenty Years' Record of the Communion Between Earth and the World of the Spirits.* Emma Hardinge, 1870.

Harris, Thomas Lake. *Arcana of Christianity: An Unfolding of the Celestial Sense of the Divine World.* Vol. 1. New Church Publishing, 1858.

Harris, Thomas Lake. *The Wisdom of Angels.* New Church Publishing Association, 1857.

Hartley, Florence. *The Ladies' Book of Etiquette and Manual of Politeness.* Lee, Shepard, and Dillingham, 1875.

Harvard College. *Records of the Class, 1883–1908.* Harvard College, 1908.

Haskell, W. G. "The Hymnology of Spiritualism." *Religio-Philosophical Journal* (Chicago), July 28, 1888, 2.

Hastings, Thomas. *Dissertation on Musical Taste.* Mason Brothers, 1853.

Hawthorne, Nathaniel. *The Scarlet Letter.* David Bogue, 1851.

Henck, Esther C. *Spirit Voices: Odes, Dictated by Spirits of the Second Sphere, for the Use of Harmonial Circles.* G. D. Henck, 1854.

Herndon, Richard, and Edwin Bacon, *Men of Progress: One Thousand Biographical Sketches and Portraits of Leaders in Business and Professional Life in the Commonwealth of Massachusetts.* New England Magazine, 1896.

Higginson, Thomas Wentworth. *Army Life in a Black Regiment.* Fields, Osgood and Co. 1870. Accessed November 28, 2023. https://repository.wellesley.edu/object/wellesley30338.

Hoffmann, E. T. A. "Beethoven's Instrumental Music (1813)." In *Strunk's Source Readings in Music History, Revised Edition,* edited by Oliver Strunk, 1193–97. W. W. Norton, 1998.

Hogarth, William. "Hudibras Encounters the Skimmington." 1726. Print, 26.8 x 50.4 cm. The British Museum, London, Museum no: 1847,0508.19. Accessed August 31, 2016. http://www.britishmuseum.org /collectionimages /AN00336/ AN00336768_001_l.jpg.

Home, Daniel Dunglas. *Incidents in My Life.* Carlton, 1863.

Hook, James. "I Leave My Heart with Thee." I & M Paff, 1804.

Hopkins, J. "A Player-Piano for Natural Musicians." *American Monthly Review of Reviews* 34 (December 1906): 85–88.

Houdini, Harry. *A Magician Among the Spirits.* Cambridge University Press, (c. 1924) 2011.

Hume, David "Essay X: Of Superstition and Enthusiasm." In *Essays, Moral, Political, and Literary, Part 1,* edited by Eugene F. Miller, 73–79. Liberty Classics, 1987.

Husson, Henri Marie, and Charles Poyen St Sauveur. *Report on the Magnetical Experiments: Made by the Commission of the Royal Academy of Medicine,* of Paris, Read in the Meetings of June 21 and 28, 1831. D.K. Kitchcock, 1836.

Hutchinson Family. "The Old Granite State." Oliver Ditson, 1843. http://levysheet-music.mse.jhu.edu/catalog/levy:020.102.

Hutchinson Family Singers. 1845. Daguerreotype, 14.4 x 19.7 cm. Metropolitan Museum of Art, Gilman Collection (Acmber: 2005.100.77), New York. Accessed August 31, 2017. http://www.metmuseum.org /art/collection/search/283176.

Hutchinson, Jesse, Jr. "The Hutchinson Family." Letter to the editor. Spiritual Philosopher 1, nos. 11–12 (October 19, 1850): 81–82.

Hutchinson, Jesse, Jr., and E. W. Hazard. "The Case of Judson Hutchinson." Letters to the Editor. Spiritual Philosopher 1, no. 15 (November 9, 1850): 113–14.

Hutchinson, Jesse. "Get Off the Track!" Jesse Hutchinson, 1844.

"Inside Harry Hill's Dance-House." In Matthew Hale Smith, Sunshine and Shadow in New York. J.B. Burr & Co., 1869. New York Public Library, Art and Picture Collection. PC NEW YC-Lif-18 Catalog ID: b17539114 http://digitalcollections.nypl.org/items/510d47e0-d782-a3d9-e040-e00a18064a99.

James, William. A Pluralistic Universe. Harvard University Press, 1977.

James, William. The Principles of Psychology. Henry Holt and Co., 1890.

James, William. "Subjects of Nitrous Oxide." Mind 7 (1882): n.p. Reproduced in http://www.erowid.org /chemicals/nitrous/nitrous_article1.shtml.

James, William. The Varieties of Religious Experience: A Study in Human Nature. Longmans, Green, and Co. 1902.

James, William. The Works of William James: Essays in Radical Empiricism. Edited by Frederick Burkhardt and Fredson Bowers. Harvard University Press 1976.

Johnson, H. Earle. "The Germania Musical Society." Musical Quarterly 39, no. 1 (January 1953): 75–93.

Johnson, James Weldon. Along This Way. Viking, (c. 1933) 1968.

Johnson, Samuel. "No. 89 Tuesday, January 22, 1751." In The Works of Samuel Johnson, LL.D., in Nine Volumes, Volume the Second The Rambler, Volume I. Talboys and Wheeler, 1825.

Johnstone, J. Alfred. "Some Essentials in Fine Piano-Playing: Illustrated by Features in the Art of Mme. Carreno [sic]." Musical Standard (September 3, 1910): 145–47.

Kant, Immanuel. Critique of Judgement. Translated by James Creed Meredith. Clarendon, (1790) 1964.

Kant, Immanuel. Observations on the Feeling of the Beautiful and the Sublime. Translated by John T. Goldthwait. University of California Press, (1764) 1960.

Kilham, Elizabeth. "Sketches in Color: Fourth." Putnam's Magazine of Literature, Science, Art, and National Interests 5, no. 27 (March 1870): 304–11.

King, Edward. The Great South; A Record of Journeys in Louisiana, Texas, the Indian Territory, Missouri, Arkansas, Mississippi, Alabama, Georgia, Florida, South

Carolina, North Carolina, Kentucky, Tennessee, Virginia, West Virginia, and Maryland. American Publish Co., 1875.

Kuhl, Gustav. "The Musical Possibilities of Ragtime." Translated by Gustav Saenger. *Metronome* 19 (March 1903): 11.

Laufeneur, Charles. "Des contractures spontanées et provoquées de la langue chez les hystéro-épileptiques." *Nouvelles Iconographie de la Salpêtrière* 2 (1889): 203–7, plate 34 (located between pages 204 and 205).

Law, William. *Serious Call to a Devout and Holy Life.* 2nd ed. William Innys, 1732.

Lawrence, D. H. *Mornings in Mexico.* Tauris Parke Paperbacks, 2009.

Le Bon, Gustave. *The Crowd: A Study of the Popular Mind.* Macmillan Co., 1896.

Lehmann, Lilli. *My Path Through Life.* G.P. Putnam's Sons, 1914.

Little, Lewis Peyton. *Imprisoned Preachers and Religious Liberty in Virginia: A Narrative Drawn Largely from the Official Records of Virginia Counties, Unpublished Manuscripts, Letters, and Other Original Sources.* J.P. Bell Co., 1938.

Lloyd, Benjamin, ed. *The Primitive Hymns: Spiritual Songs and Sacred Poems.* Published for the Proprietor, (c. 1841) 1858.

"Local Brevities." *The Advertiser* (Boston) 11, no. 3, March 19, 1921, 5.

Lounsbury, Thomas R. ed. *Yale Book of American Verse.* Yale University Press, 1912.

Mace, Thomas. *Musick's Monument.* L. T. Ratcliffe and N. Thompson, for the Author, 1676.

Macmichael, Mary E. "The School-Fellows." *Godey's Lady's Book* 13, no. 2 (August 1836): 67–72.

"Mardi-Gras." *Debow's Review* 6, no. 3 (March 1869), 220–31.

Marsh, J. B. T. *The Story of the Jubilee Singers; With Their Songs.* Rev. ed. Houghton, Mifflin and Company, 1880.

Mason, Lowell. *Carmina Sacra.* J.H. Wilkins & R.B. Carter, 1841.

Mason, Lowell. *Juvenile Lyre, or Hymns and Songs, Religious, Moral, and Cheerful, Set to Appropriate Music.* Richardson, Lord & Holbrook, 1831.

Mason, Lowell. *Manual of the Boston Academy of Music: For Instruction on the Elements of Vocal Music.* 5th ed. J. H. Wilkins & R. B. Carter, 1839.

Mason, Lowell. *The New Carmina Sacra.* Wilkins, Carter, & Co., 1850.

Mather, Cotton. *The Accomplished Singer.* B. Green for S.Gerrish, 1721.

Mather, Cotton. *Diary of Cotton Mather, 1681–1724.* Massachusetts Historical Society, 1911.

Mather, Cotton. *Memorable Providences, Relating to Witchcrafts and Possessions.* Evans Early American Imprint Collection. Accessed June 24, 2024. https://name.umdl.umich.edu/n00392.0001.001.

Mather, Cotton. *The Wonders of the Invisible World, Being an Account of the Tryals of Several Witches Lately Executed in New-England.* John Russel Smith, (1693) 1862. Accessed June 24, 2024. https://doi.org/10.5479/sil.15551.39088001220250.

Mather, Increase. *Remarkable Providences: Illustrative of the Earlier Days of American Colonisation.* Reeves and Turner, 1890.

McCabe, James Dabney. *New York by Sunlight and Gaslight*. Douglass Brothers, 1882.

McGee, John, to Thomas L. Douglas, June 23, 1820 (Letter), *Methodist Magazine* 4 (1821): 191.

M. Carey Thomas Papers. Bryn Mawr College Library, Special Collections. Accessed December 1, 2024. https://digitalcollections.tricolib.brynmawr.edu/collections/m-carey-thomas-papers.

Melville, Herman. *Pierre; or, The Ambiguities*. Harper & Brothers, 1852.

"Mobs in New York." *Niles' Register* (Baltimore), July 19, 1834, 359.

Moody, William R. *The Life of Dwight L. Moody*. Book for the Ages, Ages Software, 1997.

Mooney, James. *The Ghost-Dance Religion and the Sioux Outbreak of 1890*. 14th Annual Report of the Bureau of American Ethnology, part 2. Government Printing Office, 1896.

Moore, Jennie. "Music from Heaven." *The Apostolic Faith* (Los Angeles) 1, no. 8 (May 1907): 3.

Moore, Thomas. "Oh! Why Should the Girl of My Soul Be in Tears." Carr & Schetky, 1809.

Moore, Thomas, and John Stevenson. *A Selection of Popular National Airs*. V. Thurston, 1818.

Moore, Victor. "Music and Drama." *The Record-Herald*, October 2, 1905.

More, Hannah. *The Works of Hannah More*. Vol. 1. S. G. Goodrich, 1827.

Moreau de Saint-Méry, Médéric Louis Élie. *Description of the French Part of Saint Domingue, Volume 1*. Translated by Jonathon B. Schwartz. Bradford Colonial Press, 2018.

The Musical Times (United Kingdom), November 1, 1880, 581.

"Music for Insanity." *New York Daily Tribune*, April 8, 1900, 4.

Münsterberg, Hugo. *The Photoplay: A Psychological Study*. D. Appleton and Co., 1916.

Münsterberg, Hugo. *Psychotherapy*. Moffat, Yard, & Co., 1909.

Myers, Frederic W. H. *Human Personality and Its Survival of Bodily Death*. 2 vols. Longmans, Green, and Co., 1903.

Myers, Frederick W. "The Subliminal Consciousness." *Proceedings of the Society for Psychical Research* 7 (1891–1892): 298–355.

"A New Art—'Silent Music.'" *The Musical Leader* 43 (1922), 515.

"New Scandals Is Striking Success." *Gazette Review* (Minneapolis), 1924. Library of Congress, George and Ira Gershwin Collection, Music Division, Box 72 [Scrapbooks].

New York Herald, October 2, 1865, 7.

Nietzsche, Friedrich. *The Birth of Tragedy*. Translated by Clifton P. Fadiman. Dover, 1995.

Nietzsche, Friedrich. *The Case of Wagner, Nietzsche Contra Wagner, and Selected Aphorisms*. 3rd ed. Translated by Anthony M. Ludovici. T.N. Foulois, 1911, 59–60.

Noble, Charles H. "Gershwin Jazz Numbers Given at the Stadium." *New York Herald Tribune*, July 26, 1927.

Nolan, Warren. "Talking Pictures and the Public." *Transactions of the Society of Motion Picture Engineers* 13, no. 37 (1929): 131–34.

"Nora Bayes a Hit at New Brighton." *Brooklyn Eagle* (New York), July 17, 1917.

"Nora Bayes Hit of Orpheum Bill." *Brooklyn Eagle* (New York), October 23, 1917.

"Nora Bayes Score as One of Follies." *New York Telegraph*, August 30, 1907.

North American (Philadelphia). December 28, 1868.

O'Connell, Frank. "Our London Letter." *Vaudeville News* (New York), June 15, 1923, 7.

Olmsted, Frederick Law. *A Journey in the Seaboard Slave States; With Remarks on Their Economy*. Dix and Edwards, 1856. Electronic ed. Accessed November 28, 2023. https://docsouth.unc.edu/nc/olmsted/olmsted.html.

Packard, J. B. *The Spirit Minstrel; A Collection of Hymns and Music, for the Use of Spiritualists, in Their Circles and Public Meetings*. Bela Marsh, 1853.

Page, John. *A Deed of Gift: To My Dear Son, Captain Matt*. Henry B. Ashmead, (1687) 1856.

Parham, Charles. *A Voice Crying in the Wilderness*. CreateSpace Independent Publishing Platform, (1902) 2012.

Parrish, Lydia. *Slave Songs of the Georgia Sea Islands*. University of Georgia Press, 1992.

Partridge, Pauline. "The Home Set to Music." *Sunset* (November 1924): 68, 75–76.

Payne, Daniel Alexander. *Recollections of Seventy Years*. 2nd ed. Arno Press and the New York Times, (c. 1888) 1968.

Payne, Daniel A., and Charles S. Smith, *Recollections of Seventy Years*. Publishing House of the A.M.E. Sunday School Union, 1888.

Pearson, Elizabeth Ware, ed. *Letters from Port Royal: Sung at the Time of the Civil War*. W.B. Clarke Co., 1906.

Peebles, James Martin. *The Spiritual Harp: A Collection of Vocal Music for the Choir, Congregation, and Social Circle*. W. White, 1868.

"People of the Stage." *Cincinnati Commercial*, September 10, 1911.

Pike, Gustavus. *The Singing Campaign for Ten Thousand Pounds; or, the Jubilee Singers in Great Britain*. American Missionary Society, 1875.

Port-of-Spain Gazette (Trinidad), December 5, 1888.

Rathbun, Valentine. *Some Brief Hints of a Religious Scheme, Taught and Propagated by a Number of Europeans, Living in a Place Called Nisqueunia, in the State of New-York*. Benjamin Edes and Sons, 1782. University of Michigan Library Digital Collections. Accessed December 15, 2024. http://name.umdl.umich.edu/N13973.0001.001.

Reed, Andrew, George Collision, and Robert Winter. *The Ordination Service of the Reverend Andrew Reed*. T. Rutt, 1812.

Reed, Andrew, and James Matheson. *A Narrative of the Visit to the American Churches*. Vol. 1. Jackson and Walford, 1835.

Regnard, Paul. *Les Maladies épidémiques de l'esprit: Sorcellerie, magnétisme, morphinisme, délire des grandeurs* [Epidemic maladies of the spirit: Sorcery, magnetism, morphine addiction, delusions of grandeur]. E. Plon, Nourrit, et cie., 1887.

"Religion in Eighteenth-Century America." *Religion and the Founding of the American Republic*, Library of Congress. Accessed August 18, 2017. https://www.loc.gov/exhibits/religion/rel02.html.

Remington, Frederic. "Ghost Dance of the Oglala Sioux." *Harper's Weekly*, December 1890.

Report of Dr. Benjamin Franklin, and Other Commissioners, charged by the King of France, with the Examination of the Animal Magnetism, as Now Practiced at Paris. Johnson, 1785.

Rider, Alexander, and Hugh Bridgeport. "Camp Meeting." Lithograph, ca. 1832. Harry T. Peters Collection: 19th Century American Lithographs, National Museum of American History, Smithsonian Institution. Accessed August 31, 2017. http://amhistory.si.edu/petersprints/.

Sankey, Ira. *Sankey's Story of the Gospel Hymns and of Sacred Songs and Solos.* Sunday School Times Company, 1906.

Saunders, Charles Francis. *The Indians of the Terraced Houses.* Putnam, 1912.

Schelling, Friedrich. "Ideas for a Philosophy of Nature as Introduction to the Study of this Science [1797]." Translated by Albert Hostadter. In *Philosophy of German Idealism: Fichte, Jacobi, and Schelling*, edited by Ernst Behler and, 167–216. Continuum, 2003.

Schopenhauer, Arthur. "Music as the Cosmic Will Revealed." In *The World as Will and Idea*, vol. 1, translated by R. B. Haldane and J. Kemp. Kegan Paul, Trench, Trübner & Co., 1907.

Seward, Theodore P. *Jubilee Songs: As Sung by the Jubilee Singers.* Bigelow & Main, 1872.

Sharpe, John. "The Negro Plot of 1712." *New York Genealogical and Biographical Record* 21 (1890): 162–63.

Sidis, Boris. *The Psychology of Suggestion: A Research into the Subconscious Nature of Man and Society.* D. Appleton and Co., 1898.

Siewert, Herm, and Gilbert Perry. "That Coon Town Rag." C. A. Ross Publishing Company, 1913.

Smith, Adam. *The Theory of Moral Sentiments.* Edited by Knud Haakonssen. Cambridge University Press, 2002.

Sousa, John Philip. *Marching Along: Recollections of Men, Women and Music.* Hale, Cushman & Flint, 1928.

Spencer, Herbert. "The Origin and Function of Music." *Fraser's Magazine* 56 (October 1857): 396–408.

Spencer, Herbert. *The Principles of Sociology*, Vol. 1. D. Appleton and Co., 1883.

"'Spirits' and Their Manifestations—an Evening's Séance." *Frank Leslie's Illustrated Newspaper* (New York), April 2, 1887.

Squire, Carrie Ransom. *A Genetic Study of Rhythm.* O.B. Wood, 1901.

Stevenson, Robert Louis. *The Works of Robert Louis Stevenson: Memories and Portraits.* Scribner's, 1896.

Stone, Henry Dickinson. *Personal Recollections of the Drama or Theatrical Reminiscences.* Charles van Benthuysen & Sons. 1873.

Strong, George Templeton. *The Diary of George Templeton Strong.* 4 vols. Edited by Allan Nevins and Milton Halsey Thomas. Macmillan, 1952.

Strong, Joseph. "The Duty of Singing, Considered as a Necessary and Useful Part of Christian Worship." Thomas and Samuel Green, 1773.

Sunderland, La Roy. *Book of Psychology.* Stearns & Co., 1853.

Sunderland, La Roy. Letter to the Editor. *The Banner of Light* (Boston), November 13, 1858.

Sunderland, La Roy. *The Trance and Correlative Phenomena.* James Walker, 1868.

Swedenborg, Emanuel. *Heaven and Its Wonders and Hell: From Things Heard and Seen.* Swedenborg Foundation, 2009.

"The Talking Phonograph." *Scientific American* 22 (December 1877): 384–85.

Taylor, Alfred. "Move Along! March Along!" In *Trumpet Notes for the Temperance Battle-Field,* edited by J. N. Stearns and H. P. Main, 92. Royal Templar Book and Pub. House, 1890.

"Tony Pastor's Opera House." *New York Clipper,* July 22, 1865, 120.

"Tony Pastor's Opera House." *New York Clipper,* October 7, 1865, 208.

"Tony's Opera House." *New York Herald,* October 6, 1865, 4.

Towne, Laura M. *The Letters and Diary of Laura M. Towne, Written from the Sea Islands of South Carolina, 1862–1884.* Edited by Rupert Sargent Holland. Riverside Press, 1912. Accessed November 28, 2023. https://babel.hathitrust. org/cgi/pt?id=cool.ark:/13960/t82j7197m&seq=52&q1=%22shout%22.

Trotter, James M. *Music and Some Highly Musical People.* Lee and Shepard Publishers, 1881.

Trowbridge, John Townsend. "Reminiscences of Walt Whitman." *Atlantic Monthly* 89, no. 2 (February 1902): 163–75.

Tufts, James H. "On the Genesis of the Aesthetic Categories." *Philosophical Review* 7, no. 1 (January 1903): 1–15.

Underhill, Ann Leah. *The Missing Link in Modern Spiritualism.* Thomas R. Knox & Co., 1885.

United Artists. *The Thief of Bagdad.* Movie poster, 1924. IMP Awards. http://www. impawards.com/1924/thief _of_bagdad_ver3_xlg.html.

United States Office of Indian Affairs. *Annual Report of the Commissioner of Indian Affairs.* Government Printing Office, 1903.

Van Every, Edward. *Sins of New York as "Exposed" by the Police Gazette.* Frederick A. Stokes, 1930.

Van Vechten, Carl. *The Dance Writings of Carl Van Vechten.* Edited by Paul Padgette. Dance Horizons, 1974.

Von Tilzer, Harry, and Vincent P. Bryan. "It Must Have Been Svengali in Disguise." Harry Von Tilzer Publishing Co., 1902.

"The Voudou or Hoodoo Orgies." *Daily True Delta*, no. 124 (October 21, 1860): 1. Accessed November 28, 2023. https://news.google.com/newspapers?id=2PozAAAAIBAJ&sjid=RyMIAAAAIBAJ&pg=6622%2C1380130.

Wackenroder, Wilhelm Heinrich. *Confessions and Fantasies*. Translated by Mary Hurst Schubert. Pennsylvania State University Press, 1971.

Wagner, Richard. *Tristan und Isolde (Tristan and Isolda): Opera in Three Acts*. Fred Rullman, 1865.

"Waller, Rev. John." In *The Baptist Encyclopaedia*, edited by William Cathcart, D.D., 1205–6. Everts, 1881.

Wallis, John. "XIII. A Letter of Dr. John Wallis, to Mr. Andrew Fletcher; Concerning the Strange Effects Reported of Musick in Former Times, Beyond What is to be Found in Later Ages." In *Philosophical Transactions: Giving some Account of the Present Undertakings, Studies and Labours of the Ingenious, in Considerable Parts of the World*." Vol. 20, edited by Royal Society (Great Britain), 297–303. Royal Society, 1698.

Watson, James Fanning. *Methodist Error*. N.p., 1814.

Watson, John F. *Methodist Error, or Friendly Christian Advice to Those Methodists Who Indulge in Extravagant Religious Emotions and Bodily Exercises*. D. and E. Fenton, 1819.

Watson, John F. "Notitia of Incidents at New Orleans in 1804, 1805." *American Pioneer* 2 (May 1843), 229.

Watts, Isaac. "Thoughts on Poetry and Musick." In *The Grounds and Rules of Musick Explained: or, An Introduction to the Art of Singing by Note*, edited by Thomas Walter. Benjamin Mecom, 1760.

Weber, Joseph N. "Will Machine-Made Music Displace Real Music in Our Theaters? (interview)." *Metronome*, September 1928, 50, 102.

Webster, Noah, Robert Arrowsmith, Harry Thurston Peck. *Webster's New Modern English Dictionary*. Consolidated Book Publishers, 1922.

"Weird Fanaticism Fools Young Girl." *Los Angeles Daily Times*, July 12, 1906.

Wells, S. Y., ed. *Testimonies Concerning the Character and Ministry of Mother Ann Lee and the First Witnesses of the Gospel*. Packard & Van Benthuysen, 1827. Accessed December 12, 2024. https://babel.hathitrust.org/cgi/ssd?id=umn.319510014985649.

Wesley, Charles. *The Early Journal of Charles Wesley*. Charles H. Kelly, 1909.

Wesley, John. "His Journal: Number 1, from October 14, 1735, to February 1, 1738." In *The Works of Reverend John Wesley*. John Jones, 1809.

Wesley, John. *The Journal of John Wesley*. Oxford University Press, 1980.

"Where Caruso Sings." *New York Telegraph*, March 6, 1910.

Whitefield, George. *A Continuation of the Reverend Mr. Whitefield's Journal*. James Hutton, 1740.

Whitman, Walt. *The Complete Writings of Walt Whitman*. 10 vols. Edited by Richard M. Bucke, Thomas B. Harned, and Horace L. Traubel. G.P. Putnam's Sons, 1902.

Whitman, Walt. "Letters from Paumanok." *New York Evening Post*, August 14, 1851, [1].

"Why Jazz Sends Us Back to the Jungle." *Current Opinion* 65 (September 1918), 165.

Wilcox, Ella Wheeler. "The Prelude to 'Tristan und Isolde.'" *Munsey's*, December 1894, 288.

Willard, Frances E. *Glimpses of Fifty Years*. Woman's Temperance Publication Association, 1889.

Woodworth-Etter, Maria. *Signs and Wonders*. Whitaker House, 1997.

Wordsworth, William. *The Miscellaneous Poems of William Wordsworth*. Vol. 2. Longman, Hurst, Rees, Orme, and Brown, 1820.

Wuidar, Laurence. *Fuga Divina: La musique dans l'écrit mystique du Moyen Âge à la première modernité*. Droz, 2021.

Youmans, Letitia. *Campaign Echoes: The Autobiography of Letitia Youmans*. W. Briggs, 1893.

Youngs, Benjamin Seth, et al. *The Testimony of Christ's Second Appearing*. 2nd ed. E. and E. Hosford, State Street, 1810. Accessed December 15, 2024. https://archive.org/details/testimonyofchris1810youn/.

Secondary Sources

Abbott, Lynn, and Doug Seroff. *Out of Sight: The Rise of African American Popular Music, 1889–1895*. University of Mississippi Press, 2002.

Abbs, Peter. "The Development of Autobiography in Western Culture: From Augustine to Rousseau." PhD diss., University of Sussex, 1986.

Abell, Arthur M. *Talks with Great Composers*. Citadel, 1998.

Abrams, M. H. *Natural Supernaturalism: Tradition and Revolution in Romantic Literature*. W. W. Norton, 1971.

Ackerman, Diana. *Deep Play*. Vintage, 2000.

Adorno, Theodor W. *Introduction to the Sociology of Music*. Seabury Press, 1976.

Agnew, Jean-Christophe. *Worlds Apart: The Market and the Theater in Anglo-American Thought, 1550–1750*. Cambridge University Press, 1986.

Albanese, Catherine L. *America Religions and Religion*. 5th ed. Wadsworth, 2012.

Allured, Janet L. "Evaluating a New Orleans Icon: Evidence and Reinterpretation." Review of *The Mysterious Voodoo Queen, Marie Laveaux: A Study of Powerful Female Leadership in Nineteenth-Century New Orleans* by Ina Johanna Fandrich, and *Voodoo Queen: The Spirited Lives of Marie* Laveau, by Martha Ward. *H-Net Reviews* (March 2006). Accessed November 28, 2023. http://www.h-net.org/reviews/showrev.php?id=11484.

Altman, Rick. *Silent Film Sound*. Columbia University Press, 2004.

Andola, John Anthony. "Nathaniel Hawthorne's Use of Mesmerism in Four Major Works." PhD diss., Ball State University, 1977.

Andrews, Edward Deming. *The People Called Shakers: A Search for the Perfect Society*. Dover, 1963.

Andrick, John M. "Futurist Dissonance, Theosophical Transcendence and American Musical Ultra-Modernism, 1909–1930." *International Yearbook of Futurism Studies* 11 (2021): 107–30.

Appleby, Joyce. *Inheriting the Revolution: The First Generation of Americans*. Harvard University Press, 2000.

Arlyck, Kevin. "The 'Code Noir': North American Slavery in Comparative Perspective." *OAH Magazine of History* 17, no. 3 (2003): 39.

Ashby, LeRoy. *With Amusement for All: A History of American Popular Culture Since 1830*. University Press of Kentucky, 2006.

Atkins, Jessica. "Setting the Stage: Dance and Gender in Old-Line New Orleans Carnival Balls, 1870–1920." PhD diss., Florida State University, 2008.

Aveni, John Anthony. "Such Music as Befits the New Order of Things: African American Professional Musicians and the Cultural Identity of a Race, 1880–1920." PhD diss., Rutgers University, 2004.

Bailey, Peter. *Music Hall: The Business of Pleasure*. Open University Press, 1986.

Baker, D. B. *The Oxford Handbook of the History of Psychology: Global Perspectives*. Oxford University Press, 2011.

Bakhtin, Mikhail. *Rabelais and His World*. Translated by Helen Iswolsky. Indiana University Press, 1984.

Ballantine, Christopher. *Music and Its Social Meanings*. Gordon and Breach, 1984.

Balmer, Randall Herbert, ed. *Encyclopedia of Evangelicalism, Revised and Expanded Edition*. Baylor University Press, 2004.

Barfield, Owen. *Saving the Appearances*. Wesleyan University Press, 1988.

Barkan, Elliot Robert, ed. *Immigrants in American History: Arrival, Adaptation, and Integration*. Vol. 1. ABC-CLIO, 2013.

Barker-Benfield, G. J. *Abigail and John Adams: The Americanization of Sensibility*. University of Chicago Press, 2010.

Barker-Benfield, G. J. *The Culture of Sensibility: Sex and Society in Eighteenth-Century Britain*. University of Chicago Press, 1992.

Barresi, John, and Raymond Martin. "History as Prologue: Western Theories of the Self." In *The Oxford Handbook of the Self*, edited by Shaun Gallagher, 33–55. Oxford University Press, 2011.

Bataille, Georges. *Inner Experience*. Translated by Leslie Anne Boldt. State University of New York Press, 1988.

Batis, Emery John. *Saints and Sectaries: Anne Hutchinson and the Antinomian Controversy in the Massachusetts Bay Colony*. University of North Carolina Press, 1962.

Baumeister, Roy F. *Identity: Cultural Change and the Struggle for Self*. Oxford University Press, 1986.

Baxter, Richard. *The Practical Works of Richard Baxter*. Vol. 4. George Virtue, 1838.

Bean, Annemarie, James V. Hatch, and Brooks McNamara. *Inside the Minstrel Mask: Readings in Nineteenth-Century Blackface Minstrelsy*. Wesleyan University Press, 1996.

Bebergal, Peter. *Season of the Witch: How the Occult Saved Rock 'n' Roll*. Penguin, 2014.

Beck, Guy L. *Musicology of Religion: Theories, Methods, and Directions*. State University of New York Press, 2023.

Becker, Judith. *Deep Listeners: Music, Emotion, and Trancing*. Indiana University Press, 2004.

Beckert, Sven, and Julia Rosenbaum, eds. *The American Bourgeoisie: Distinction and Identity in the Nineteenth Century*. Palgrave Macmillan, 2010.

Bell, Daniel. *The Cultural Contradictions of Capitalism*. Basic Books, 1978.

Bellah, Robert. "Civil Religion in America." *Journal of the American Academy of Arts and Sciences* 96, no. 1 (Winter 1967): 1–21.

Bennett, Jane. *The Enchantment of Modern Life: Attachments, Crossings, and Ethics*. Princeton University Press, 2011.

Benson, Bruce Ellis. *Pious Nietzsche: Decadence and Dionysian Faith*. Indiana University Press, 2007.

Berlin, Edward. *Ragtime: A Musical and Cultural History*. Open Road Distribution, 2016.

Berlin, Ira. *Many Thousands Gone: The First Two Centuries of Slavery in North America*. Harvard University Press, 1998.

Berman, Morris. *The Reenchantment of the World*. Cornell University Press, 1981.

Bicknell, Jeanette. *Why Music Moves Us*. Palgrave Macmillan, 2009.

Bierley, Paul E. *John Philip Sousa: American Phenomenon*. Rev. ed. Warner Brothers, 2001.

Blackwell, Albert L. *The Sacred in* Music. Westminster John Knox Press, 1999.

Blesh, Rudi, and Harriet Janis. *They All Played Ragtime: The True Story of an American Music*. Alfred A. Knopf, 1950.

Blum, Edward J. *W. E. B. Du Bois: American Prophet*. University of Pennsylvania Press, 2011.

Bodo, John. *The Protestant Clergy and Public Issues, 1812–1848*. Princeton University Press, 1954.

Boles, John B. *The Great Revival: Beginnings of the Bible Belt*. University of Kentucky Press, 1972.

Bond, Edward L. *Damned Souls in a Tobacco Colony: Religion in Seventeenth-Century Virginia*. Mercer University Press, 2000.

Bottomore, Stephen. "The Panicking Audience? Early Cinema and the 'Train Effect.'" *Historical Journal of Film, Radio and Television* 19, no. 2 (1999): 177–216.

Bottum, Joseph. *An Anxious Age: The Post-Protestant Ethic and the Spirit of America*. Image Books, 2014.

Bourdieu, Pierre. *Distinction: A Social Critique of the Judgment of Taste*. Translated by Richard Nice. Harvard University Press, 1984.

Branch, Lori. *Rituals of Spontaneity: Sentiment and Secularism from Free Prayer to Wordsworth*. Baylor University Press, 2006.

Brands, H. W. *The First American: The Life and Times of Benjamin Franklin*. Doubleday, 2000.

Branham, Robert James, and Stephen J. Hartnett. *Sweet Freedom's Song: "My Country 'Tis of Thee" and Democracy in America.* Oxford University Press, 2002.

Braude, Ann. *Radical Spirits: Spiritualism and Women's Rights in Nineteenth-Century America.* Free Press, 1989.

Brekus, Catherine A. *Strangers and Pilgrims: Female Preaching in America, 1740–1845.* University of North Carolina Press, 1998.

Brennan, Timothy. *Secular Devotion: Afro-Latin Music and Imperial Jazz.* Verso, 2008.

Brissenden, R. F. *Virtue in Distress: Studies in the Novel of Sentiment from Richardson to Sade.* Macmillan, 1974.

Bristol, Michael D. *Carnival and Theatre: Plebeian Culture and the Structure of Authority in Renaissance Britain.* Routledge, 1985.

Brothers, Thomas. *Louis Armstrong's New Orleans.* W. W. Norton, 2006.

Brown, Candy Gunther. *The Word in the World: Evangelical Writing, Publishing, and Reading in America, 1789–1880.* University of North Carolina Press, 2004.

Brown, Clive. *Classical and Romantic Performing Practice, 1750–1900.* Oxford University Press, 1999.

Brown, Frank Burch. "Music." In *The Oxford Handbook of Religion and Emotion,* edited by John Corrigan, 200–222. Oxford University Press, 2008.

Brown, Kenneth O. *Holy Ground: A Study of the American Camp Meeting.* Garland, 1992.

Bruce, Dickson D., Jr., *And They All Sang Hallelujah: Plain-Folk Camp-Meeting Religion, 1800–1845.* University of Tennessee Press, 1973.

Bruce, Dickson D., Jr. "W.E.B. Du Bois and the Idea of Double Consciousness." *American Literature: A Journal of Literary History, Criticism, and Bibliography* 64, no. 2 (1992): 299–309.

Bruce, Neely, and the American Music Group. Vocal performance of "Dead March of the Saloon," by Mary T. Lathrop and William J. Kirkpatrick. *On Temperance Music.* American Music Group Publishing, LP S260–02, vinyl disc, recorded 1982.

Bruce, Steve. *Secularization: In Defence of an Unfashionable Theory.* Oxford University Press, 2011.

Bruhn, Siglind, ed. *Voicing the Ineffable: Musical Representations of Religious Experience.* Pendragon Press, 2002.

Brumm, Ursula. "Passions and Depressions in Early American Puritanism." *La passion dans le monde anglo-américain aux XVIIe et XVIIIe siècles* 7, no. 1 (1978): 85–96.

Burckhardt, Jacob. *The Civilization of the Renaissance in Italy.* Dover, 2012.

Burke, Peter. *Popular Culture in Early Modern Europe.* 3rd ed. Routledge, 2009.

Butler, Jon. *Awash in a Sea of Faith: Christianizing the American People.* Harvard University Press, 1992.

Butler, Jon. "Disquieted History in a Secular Age." In *The Varieties of Secularism in a Secular Age,* edited by Michael Warner, Jonathan Vanantwerpen, and Craig Calhoun, 193–216. Harvard University Press, 2010.

Butsch, Richard. *The Making of American Audiences: From Stage to Television, 1750–1990*. Cambridge University Press, 2000.

Bynum, Caroline Walker. *Jesus as Mother: Studies in the Spirituality of the High Middle Ages*. University of California Press, 1982.

Caillois, Roger. *Man, Play, and Games*. Translated by Meyer Barash. University of Illinois Press, (c. 1958) 2001.

Calhoun, Cheshire, and Robert C. Solomon, eds. *What Is an Emotion: Classical Readings in Philosophical Psychology*. Oxford University Press, 1984.

Campbell, Colin. *The Romantic Ethic and the Spirit of Modern Consumerism*. Blackwell, 1987.

Campbell, Stacey, and Wesley Campbell, *Ecstatic Prophecy*. Chosen Books, 2008.

Carroll, Bret E. *Spiritualism in Antebellum America*. Indiana University Press, 1997.

Carroll, Kenneth L. "Singing in the Spirit in Early Quakerism." *Quaker History* 73, no. 1 (Spring 1984): 1–13.

Carwardine, Richard J. *Evangelicals and Politics in Antebellum America*. Yale University Press, 1993.

Cassam, Quassim. "The Embodied Self." In *The Oxford Handbook of the Self*, edited by Shaun Gallagher, 139–57. Oxford University Press, 2011.

Cavanaugh, William T. "Strange Gods: Idolatry in the Twenty-First Century." *Commonweal*, January 21, 2020. Accessed November 28, 2023. https://www.commonwealmagazine.org/strange-gods.

Cavicchi, Daniel. *Listening and Longing: Music Lovers in the Age of Barnum*. Wesleyan University Press, 2011.

Cazden, Norman, Herbert Haufrecht, and Norman Studer, eds. *Notes and Sources for Folk Songs of the Catskills, Supplement*. Vol. 2. State University of New York Press, 1982.

Chan, Simon. *Pentecostal Theology and the Christian Spiritual Tradition*. Sheffield Academic Press, 2003.

Charters, Samuel. *The Roots of the Blues: An African Search*. Da Capo, 1981.

Chernoff, John Miller. *African Rhythm and African Sensibility*. University of Chicago Press, 1981.

Chernoff, John M. "The Rhythmic Medium in African Music." Papers from the Commonwealth Center for Literary and Cultural Change. *New Literary History* 22, no. 4 (Autumn 1991): 1093–1102.

Chidester, David. *Authentic Fakes: Religion and American Popular Culture*. University of California Press, 2005.

Christie, Ian. *The Last Machine: Early Cinema and the Birth of the Modern World*. BBC-BFI, 1994.

Chudacoff, Howard P., and Judith E. Smith. *The Evolution of American Urban Society*. 4th ed. Prentice-Hall, 1994.

Clark, Elizabeth B. "'The Sacred Rights of the Weak': Pain, Sympathy, and the Culture of Individual Rights in Antebellum America." *Journal of American History* 82, no. 2 (September 1995): 463–93.

Clarke, David B., and Marcus A. Doel. "Engineering Space and Time: Moving Pictures and Motionless Trips." *Journal of Historical Geography* 31, no. 1 (2005): 41–60.

Clough, Patricia. "The Movies and Social Observation: Reading Blumer's *Movies and Conduct*." *Symbolic Interaction* 11, no. 1 (1988): 85–97.

Coale, Samuel Chase. *Mesmerism and Hawthorne: Mediums of American Romance.* University of Alabama Press, 1998.

Coale, Samuel. "The Romance of Mesmerism: Hawthorne's Medium of Romance." In *Nathaniel Hawthorne, Updated Edition*, edited by Harold Bloom, 85–103. Chelsea House, 2009.

Cobussen, Marcel. *The Field of Musical Improvisation.* Leiden University Press, 2017.

Cobussen, Marcel, and Nanette Nielsen. *Music and Ethics.* Routledge, 2011.

Cockrell, Dale. *Demons of Disorder: Early Blackface Minstrels and Their World.* Cambridge University Press, 1997.

Cohen, Annabel J. "The Functions of Music in Multimedia: A Cognitive Approach." In *Music, Mind, and Science*, edited by S. W. Yi, 53–69. Seoul National University Press, 1999.

Cohen, Annabel J. "Music as a Source of Emotion in Film." In *Handbook of Music and Emotion: Theory, Research, and Applications*, edited by Patrik N. Juslin and John Sloboda, 879–908. Oxford University Press, 2010.

Cole, Charles C., Jr. *The Social Ideas of the Northern Evangelists, 1820–1860.* Columbia University Press, 1954.

Coleridge, Samuel Taylor. "Kubla Kahn." In *The Oxford Book of English Verse: 1250–1900*, edited by Arthur Quiller-Couch, 650–51. Clarendon, 1904.

Cook, James. *The Arts of Deception: Playing with Fraud in the Age of Barnum.* Harvard University Press, 2001.

Cook, James W. "Finding Otira: On the Geopolitics of Black Celebrity." *Raritan* 34, no. 2 (Fall 2014): 84–111.

Cooke, Deryck. *The Language of Music.* Oxford University Press, (1959) 1990.

Cooperman, Jessica. "The Great Migration: 1881–1924." In *The Wiley-Blackwell History of Jews and Judaism*, edited by Alan T. Levenson, 831–92. John Wiley & Sons, 2012.

Coudert, Allison. *Religion, Magic, and Science in Early Modern Europe and America.* Praeger, 2011.

Courlander, Harold. *Negro Folk Music, U.S.A.* Columbia University Press, 1963.

Cunningham, Hugh. "Leisure." In *The Working Class England, 1875–1914*, edited by J. Benson, 166–264. Croom Helm, 1985.

Cunningham, Hugh. *Leisure in the Industrial Revolution, c1780–c1880.* Croom Helm, 1980.

Currie, Gregory. *The Nature of Fiction.* Cambridge University Press, 1990.

Cusic, Dan. *Saved by Song: A History of Gospel and Christian Music.* University Press of Mississippi, 2012.

Daniels, Bruce C. *Puritans at Play: Leisure and Recreation in Colonial New England.* Palgrave, 1995.

Darden, Bob. *People Get Ready! A New History of Black Gospel Music.* Continuum, 2006.

Davidson, Cathy N. *Revolution and the Word: The Rise of the Novel in America,* Expanded ed. Oxford University Press, 2004.

Davidson, Robert. *History of the Presbyterian Church in the State of Kentucky.* R Carter, 1847. Accessed November 28, 2023. https://archive.org/details/historyofpresbyt00davi/page/138/.

Davis, Chris. "Before They Were Haitians: Examining Evidence for Kongolese Influence on the Haitian Revolution." *Journal of Haitian Studies* 22, no. 2 (2016): 4–36.

Davis, Lee. *Scandals and Follies: The Rise and Fall of the Great Broadway Revue.* Limelight Editions, 2000.

Davis, Natalie Zemon. *Society and Culture in Early Modern France.* Stanford University Press, 1975.

Dawdy, Shannon Lee. *Building the Devil's Empire: French Colonial New Orleans.* University of Chicago Press, 2008.

Dayton, Donald W. *Theological Roots of Pentecostalism.* Francis Asbury, 1987.

DeNora, Tia. *Beethoven and the Construction of Genius: Musical Politics in Vienna, 1792–1803.* University of California Press, 1997.

Denzin, Norman. *Symbolic Interactionism and Cultural Studies: The Politics of Interpretation.* Blackwell, 1992.

Deveney, John Patrick. *Paschal Beverly Randolph: A Nineteenth-Century Black American Spiritualist, Rosicrucian, and Sex Magician.* State University of New York Pres, 1996.

DiMaggio, Paul. "Cultural Boundaries and Structural Change: The Extension of the High Culture Model to Theater, Opera, and the Dance, 1900–1940." In *Cultural Boundaries and Structural Change: Symbolic Boundaries and the Making of Inequality,* edited by Michèle Lamont and Marcel Fournier, 21–57. University of Chicago Press, 1992.

DiMaggio, Paul J. "Cultural Entrepreneurship in Nineteenth-Century Boston: The Creation of an Organizational Base for High Culture in America." *Media, Culture and Society* 4 (1982): 33–50, 303–22.

Doane, Mary Ann. "Technology's Body: Cinematic Vision in Modernity." *differences: A Journal of Feminist Cultural Studies* 5, no. 2 (1993): 1–23.

Dolan, Brian. *Inventing Entertainment: The Player Piano and the Origins of an American Musical Industry.* Rowman and Littlefield, 2009.

Dooyeweerd, Herman. *De Crisis der Humanistische Staatsleer.* W. Ten Have, 1931.

Dorsett, Lyle W. *A Passion for Souls: The Life of D. L. Moody.* Moody Publishers, 2003.

Douglas, Mary. "The Person in an Enterprise Culture." In *Understanding the Enterprise Culture: Themes in the Work of Mary Douglas,* edited by Shaun Hargreaves Heap and Angus Ross, 41–62. Edinburgh University Press, 1992.

Douglas, Susan J. *Where the Girls Are: Growing Up Female with the Mass Media.* Times Books, 1994.

Downey, James. "The Music of American Revivalism." PhD diss., Tulane University, 1968.

Dronke, Peter. *Poetic Individuality in the Middle Ages.* Oxford University Press, 1970.

Dubois, Laurent. *Avengers of the New World: The Story of the Haitian Revolution.* Belknap Press of Harvard University Press, 2004.

During, Simon. *Modern Enchantments: The Cultural Power of Secular Magic.* Harvard University Press, 2002.

Eagleton, Terry. *Walter Benjamin: or, Towards a Revolutionary Criticism.* New Left Books, 1981.

"Ecstasy." In *Webster's Unabridged Dictionary,* ed. Noah Webster (George and Charles Merriam, 1862), 379. Accessed November 28, 2023. https://ia600307.us.archive.org/27/items/americandiction00webs/americandiction00webs.pdf.

Editors of the American Heritage Dictionaries. *Word Histories and Mysteries: From Abracadabra to Zeus.* Houghton Mifflin, 2004.

Ehrenreich, Barbara. *Dancing in the Streets: A History of Collective Joy.* Metropolitan Books, 2007.

Ehrenreich, Barbara, Elizabeth Hess, and Gloria Jacobs. "Beatlemania: Girls Just Want To Have Fun." In *The Adoring Audience: Fan Culture and Popular Media,* edited by Lisa A. Lewis, 84–105. Routledge, 1992.

Eisler, Hanns, and Theodor W. Adorno. *Composing for the Films.* Continuum, (c. 1947) 2005.

Eliade, Mircea. *Yoga: Immortality and Freedom.* Translated by Willard R. Trask. Princeton University Press, 1969.

Elias, Norbert. *The Civilizing Process, Volume 1: The History of Manners.* Translated by Edmund Jephcott. Pantheon Books, 1982.

Ellis, Clifton. "Dissenting Faith and Domestic Landscape in Eighteenth-Century Virginia." In *Everyday Landscapes: Perspectives in Vernacular Architecture, VII,* edited by Annmarie Adams and Sally McMurry, 23–40. University of Tennessee Press, 1997.

Epstein, Dena J. *Sinful Tunes and Spirituals: Black Folk Music to the Civil War.* University of Illinois Press, 1977.

Epstein, Mark D. "Freud's Influence on Transpersonal Psychology." In *Textbook of Transpersonal Psychiatry and Psychology,* edited by Bruce W. Scotton, Allan B. Chinen, and John R. Battista, 29–38. Basic Books, 1996.

Epstein, Mark D. "On the Neglect of Evenly Suspended Attention." *Journal of Transpersonal Psychology* 16, no. 2 (1984): 193–205.

Erickson, David Allen. "Language, Ineffability and Paradox in Music Philosophy." Master's thesis, Simon Fraser University, 2005.

Erskine, John. *The Philharmonic-Symphony Society of New York: Its First Hundred Years.* Macmillan, 1943.

Erskine, Noel Leo. *Plantation Church: How African American Religion Was Born in Caribbean Slavery*. Oxford University Press, 2014.

Espinosa, Gastón. "Tongues and Healing at the Azusa Street Revival." In *Religions of the United States in Practice*, vol. 2, edited by Colleen McDannell, 216–23. Princeton University Press, 2001.

Eustace, Nicole. *Passion Is the Gale: Emotion, Power, and the Coming of the American Revolution*. University of North Carolina Press, 2011.

Fandrich, Ina Johanna. *The Mysterious Voodoo Queen, Marie Laveaux: A Study of Powerful Female Leadership in Nineteenth-Century New Orleans*. Routledge, 2005.

Fandrich, Ina J. "Yorùbá Influences on Haitian Vodou and New Orleans Voodoo." *Journal of Black Studies* 37, no. 5 (May 2007): 775–91.

Faust, Drew Gilpin. *This Republic of Suffering*. Vintage, 2009.

Ferber, Michael. *Romanticism: A Very Short Introduction*. Oxford University Press, 2010.

Fiedler, Leslie A., and Arthur Zeiger, eds., *O Brave New World: American Literature from 1600 to 1840*. Dell, 1968.

Fields, Armond. *Tony Pastor, Father of Vaudeville*. McFarland & Co., 2007.

Finney, Gretchen L. "Ecstasy and Music in Seventeenth Century England." *Journal of the History of Ideas* 8, no. 2 (April 1947): 153–86.

Finney, Gretchen L. " 'Organical Musick' and Ecstasy." *Journal of the History of Ideas* 8, no. 3 (June 1947): 273–92.

Finseth, Ian Frederick. " 'Liquid Fire Within Me': Language, Self, and Society in Transcendentalism and Early Evangelicalism, 1820–1860." Master's thesis, University of Virginia, 1995.

Fish, Stanley. "Liberalism and Secularism: One and the Same." *New York Times*, September 2, 2007. http://opinionator.blogs.nytimes.com/2007/09/02/liberalism-and-secularism-one-and-the-same/.

Fisher, Burton D., ed. *Wagner's Tristan and Isolde*. Opera Journeys Mini Guides Series. Opera Journeys, 2002.

Flinn, Caryl. *Strains of Utopia: Gender, Nostalgia, and Hollywood Film Music*. Princeton University Press, 1992.

Floyd, Samuel A., Jr. "Ring Shout! Literary Studies, Historical Studies, and Black Music Inquiry." *Black Music Research Journal* 22 (2002): 49–70.

Floyd, Samuel A., Jr. *The Power of Black Music: Interpreting Its History from Africa to the United States*. Oxford University Press, 1995.

Foster, Charles. *An Errand of Mercy: The Evangelical United Front, 1790–1837*. University of North Carolina Press, 1960.

Francis, Richard. *Transcendental Utopias: Individual and Community at Brook Farm, Fruitland, and Walden*. Cornell University Press, 2007.

Frederickson, Donald Laurence. *The Aesthetic of Isolation in Film Theory: Hugo Munsterberg*. Arno Press, 1977.

Frevert, Ute. *Emotions in History: Lost and Found*. Central European University Press, 2011.

Friedmann, Jonathan L., ed. *Music, Theology, and Worship: Selected Writings, 1841–1896.* McFarland & Co., 2011.

Fulop, Timothy E., and Albert J. Raboteau. *African-American Religion: Interpretive Essays in History and Culture.* Taylor and Francis, 2013.

Gabriel, Joseph M. "'Anesthetics and the Chemical Sublime." *Raritan: A Quarterly Review* 30, no. 1 (2010): 69–74.

Gabriel, Ralph H. "Evangelical Religion and Popular Romanticism in Early Nineteenth-Century America." *Church History* 19, no. 1 (March 1950): 34–47.

Gac, Scott. *Singing for Freedom: The Hutchinson Family Singers and the Nineteenth Century.* Yale University Press, 2007.

Gallagher, Shaun, ed. *The Oxford Handbook of the Self.* Oxford University Press, 2011.

Gallo, David A., and Stanley Finger. "The Power of a Musical Instrument: Franklin, the Mozarts, Mesmer, and the Glass Armonica." *History of Psychology* 3, no. 4 (Nov 2000): 326–43.

Geertz, Clifford. *Local Knowledge: Further Essays in Interpretive Anthropology.* 3rd ed. Basic Books, 2000.

Giddens, Anthony. *The Constitution of Society: Outline of the Theory of Structuration.* Polity, 1984.

Giordano, Ralph G. *Social Dancing in America: A History and Reference.* Vol. 1: *Fair Terpsichore to the Ghost Dance, 1607–1900.* Greenwood, 2007.

Glazier, Stephen D. *Encyclopedia of African and African-American Religions.* Routledge, 2001.

Godwin, Joscelyn. *Harmonies of Heaven and Earth.* Inner Traditions, 1978.

Godwin, Joscelyn. *Music, Mysticism, and Magic: A Sourcebook.* Routledge and Kegan Paul, 1986.

Goetz, Stewart, and Charles Taliaferro. *A Brief History of the Soul.* Blackwell, 2011.

Goldsmith, Barbara. *Other Powers: The Age of Suffrage, Spiritualism, and the Scandalous Victoria Woodhull.* Harper, 1999.

Goodman, Glenda. "'The Tears I Shed at the Songs of Thy Church': Seventeenth-Century Musical Piety in the English Atlantic World." *Journal of the American Musicological Society* 65, no. 3 (Fall 2012): 691–725.

Goodman, Russell. "Ralph Waldo Emerson." In *Stanford Encyclopedia of Philosophy.* Stanford University. Article published October 14, 2014. https://plato.stanford. edu/archives /win2014/entries/emerson/.

Gorbman, Claudia. *Unheard Melodies: Narrative Film Music.* Indiana University Press, 1987.

Gordon, Robert Winslow. "Negro 'Shouts' from Georgia." In *Mother Wit from the Laughing Barrel: Readings in the Interpretation of Afro-American Folklore,* edited by Alan Dundes, 445–51. Garland, 1981.

Grabbe, Lester L. *Priests, Prophets, Diviners, Sages: A Socio-Historical Study of Religious Specialists in Ancient Israel.* Trinity Press International, 1995.

Graham, Gordon. *The Re-Enchantment of the Word: Art Versus Religion.* Oxford University Press, 2010.

Gray, Paul. *The Ego and Analysis of Defense.* Jason Aronson, 2005.

Green, Roger J. "1738 John & Charles Wesley Experience Conversions." *Christian History* 28 (1990). http://www.christianitytoday.com/ch/1990/issue28/2844.html.

Greenwood, Andrea, and Mark W. Harris. *An Introduction to the Unitarian and Universalist Traditions.* Cambridge University Press, 2011.

Griffiths, Leslie. "Traditions and Spiritual Guidance: Spirituality and the Hymns of Charles Wesley." *The Way* 31 (1991): 331–40.

Gunning, Tom. "The Cinema of Attractions: Early Film, Its Spectator and the Avant-Garde." *Wide Angle* 8, nos. 3 and 4 (Fall 1986): 63–70.

Gunter, W. Stephen. *The Limits of "Love Divine": John Wesley's Response to Antinomianism and Enthusiasm.* Kingswood Books, 1989.

Gurevich, Aaron. *The Origins of European Individualism.* Translated by Katharine Judelson. Blackwell, 1995.

Gurevitch, Leon. "The Cinemas of Transactions: The Exchangeable Currency of the Digital Attraction." *Television & New Media* 11, no. 5 (2010): 367–85.

Halttunen, Karen. *Confidence Men and Painted Women: A Study of Middle-Class Culture in America, 1830–1870.* Yale University Press, 1982.

Hamburger, Philip. *Separation of Church and State.* Harvard University Press, 2002.

Hamm, Charles. *Music in the New World.* W. W. Norton, 1983.

Hampton, Vinita, and C. J. Wheeler. "The Gallery." *Christian History Magazine* 9, no. 25 (1990): 13.

Hansen, Miriam. *Babel and Babylon: Spectatorship and American Silent Film.* Harvard University Press, 1991.

Hardon, John. *Modern Catholic Dictionary.* Doubleday, 1980.

Harris, Neil. "John Philip Sousa and the Culture of Reassurance." In *Perspectives on John Philip Sousa,* edited by Jon Newsom, 11–40. Library of Congress, 1983.

Hartman, Saidiya. *Scenes of Subjection: Terror, Slavery, and Self-Making in Nineteenth-Century America.* Oxford University Press, 1997.

Harvey, Paul. *Through the Storm, Through the Night: A History of African American Christianity.* Rowman and Littlefield, 2011.

Hatch, Nathan O. *The Democratization of American Christianity.* Yale University Press, 1989.

Hatfield, April Lee. *Atlantic Virginia: Intercolonial Relations in the Seventeenth Century.* University of Pennsylvania Press, 2004.

Hayward, Rhodri. *Resisting History: Religious Transcendence and the Invention of the Unconscious.* Manchester University Press, 2007.

Hazzard-Donald, Katrina. "Hoodoo Religion and American Dance Traditions: Rethinking the Ring Shout." *Journal of Pan African Studies* 4, no. 6 (September 2011): 194–212.

Hazzard-Donald, Katrina. *Mojo Workin': The Old African American Hoodoo System.* University of Illinois Press, 2013.

Hazzard-Gordon, Katrina. "Dancing Under the Lash: Sociocultural Disruption, Continuity, and Synthesis." In *African Dance: An Artistic, Historical, and Philosophical Inquiry,* edited by Kariamu Welsh Asante, 101–30. Africa World Press, 1996.

Heath, Elaine A. "Ecstasy: Mysticism and Mission in the Wesleyan Tradition." Paper presented at the Oxford Institute of Methodist Theological Studies, July 2007.

Hecker, J. F. C. *The Dancing Mania of the Middle* Ages. Translated by B. G. Babington. Franklin, 1970.

Heimer, Alan, and Perry Miller, eds. *The Great Awakening: Documents Illustrating the Crisis and Its Consequences.* Bobbs-Merrill, 1967.

Heitzenrater, Richard P. *Wesley and the People Called Methodists.* 2nd ed. Abington Press, 2013.

Hentoff, Nat, and Albert J. McCarthy, eds. *Jazz: New Perspectives on the History of Jazz by Twelve of the World's Foremost Jazz Critics and Scholars.* Da Capo, 1975.

Herndon, Marcia, and Norma McLeod. *Music as Culture.* Norwood Editions, 1982.

Higgins, Kathleen Marie. *The Music of Our Lives.* Temple University Press, 1991.

Higham, John. "Reorientation of American Culture in the 1890s." In *Origins of Modern Consciousness,* edited by John Weiss, 25–48. Wayne State University Press, 1966.

Hill, Christopher. *Society and Puritanism in Pre-Revolutionary England.* St Martin's, 1997.

Hitchcock, H. Wiley. *Music in the United States: A Historical Introduction.* Prentice-Hall, 1988.

Hittman, Michael, and Don Lynch, eds. *Wovoka and the Ghost Dance.* University of Nebraska Press, 1990.

Hollander, John. *The Untuning of the Sky.* Princeton University Press, 1961.

Holloway, Joseph E. "The Origins of African-American Culture." In *Africanisms in American Culture,* 2nd ed., edited by Joseph E. Holloway, 18–38. Indiana University Press, 2005.

Holman, Clarence Hugh, and William Harmon, *A Handbook to Literature.* 6th ed. Macmillan, 1992.

Horden, Peregrine. "Commentary on Part V, with Notes on Nineteenth-Century America and on Mesmerism and Theosophy." In *Music as Medicine: The History of Music Therapy Since Antiquity,* edited by Peregrine Horden, 315–37. Ashgate, 2000.

Horn, James. "Cavalier Culture? The Social Development of Colonial Virginia." *William and Mary Quarterly* 48, no. 2 (April 1991): 238–45.

Huffmon, H. B. "Company of Prophets: Mari, Assyria, Israel." In *Prophesy in Its Ancient Near Eastern Context.* Society of Biblical Literature, 2000.

Huizinga, Johan. *Homo Ludens: A Study of the Play-Element in Culture.* Routledge & Kegan Paul, 1949.

Hurwitz, Nathan. *A History of the American Musical Theatre: No Business Like It.* Routledge, 2014.

Ingram, Martin. "Ridings, Rough Music and Mocking Rhymes in Early Modern England." In *Popular Culture in Seventeenth-Century England,* edited by Barry Reay, 166–97. Routledge, 1988.

Jackson, Jeffrey H., and Stanley C. Pelkey. *Music and History: Bridging the Disciplines.* University Press of Mississippi, 2005.

Jager, Colin. "After the Secular: The Subject of Romanticism." *Public Culture* 18, no. 2 (Spring 2006): 301–23.

James, Jamie. *The Music of the Spheres: Music, Science, and the Natural Order of the Universe.* Copernicus, 1993.

Jankélévitch, Vladimir. *Music and the Ineffable.* Translated by Carolyn Abbate. Princeton University Press, 2003.

Jarrett, Michael. *Drifting on a Read: Jazz as a Model for Writing.* State University of New York Press, 1999.

Jenkins, Richard. "Disenchantment, Enchantment and Re-Enchantment: Max Weber at the Millennium." *Max Weber Studies* 1, no. 1 (November 2000): 11–32.

Jentz, John. "Artisans, Evangelicals, and the City: A Social History of Abolition and Labor Reform in Jacksonian New York." PhD diss., City University of New York, 1977.

Johnson, Aubrey. *The Vitality of the Individual in the Thought of Ancient Israel.* 2nd ed. Wipf & Stock, (c. 1964) 2006.

Johnson, D. A. " 'Johnson Is Beaten!' A Case of 'Rough Music' at West Bromwich in 1611." *Transactions, Lichfield and South Staffordshire Archaeological and Historical Society* 25 (1983–1984): 31–34.

Johnson, James H. *Listening in Paris: A Cultural History.* University of California Press, 1996.

Johnson, Jerah. "Colonial New Orleans: A Fragment of the Eighteenth-Century French Ethos." In *Creole New Orleans: Race and Americanization,* edited by Arnold R. Hirsh and Joseph Logsdon, 12–47. Louisiana State University Press, 1992.

Johnson, Jerah. *Congo Square in New Orleans.* Louisiana Landmarks Society, 1995.

Johnson, Paul E. *A Shopkeeper's Millennium: Society and Revivals in Rochester, New York, 1815–1837.* Hill and Wang, 2004.

Jones, LeRoi [Amiri Baraka]. *Blues People.* William Morrow, 1963.

Joplin, Scott. *Scott Joplin Complete Piano Works.* Edited by Vera Brodsky Lawrence. New York Public Library, 1981.

Josephson-Storm, Jason A. *The Myth of Disenchantment: Magic, Modernity, and the Birth of the Human Sciences.* University of Chicago Press, 2017.

Joyner, Charles. *Shared Traditions: Southern History and Folk Culture.* University of Illinois Press, 1999.

Jung, Carl G. *The Portable Jung.* Edited by Joseph Campbell. Penguin Classics, 1976.

Kalinak, Kathryn. *Film Music: A Very Short Introduction.* Oxford University Press, 2010.

Karolyi, Otto. *Traditional African and Oriental Music*. Penguin, 1998.

Karush, Matt. "Music in History: Overcoming Historians' Reluctance to Tackle Music as a Source." *OUPblog*, January 15, 2019. Accessed November 28, 2023. https://blog.oup.com/2019/01/musicology-analyzing-music-in-history/.

Kasson, John. *Rudeness and Civility: Civility and Manners in Nineteenth-Century Urban America*. Hill and Wang, 1990.

Kattwinkel, Susan. *Tony Pastor Presents: Afterpieces from the Vaudeville Stage*. Greenwood, 1998.

Keene, James A. *A History of Music Education in the United States*. Glenbridge Publishing, 2010.

Kennaway, James. "Musical Hypnosis: Sound and Selfhood from Mesmerism to Brainwashing." *Social History of Medicine* 25, no. 2 (2012): 271–89.

Kenney, William Howland. *Recorded Music in American Life: The Phonograph and Popular Memory*. Oxford University Press, 2003.

Key, Pierre V. R., and Bruno Zirato. *Enrico Caruso: A Biography*. Little Brown, 1922.

Kidd, Thomas S. *The Great Awakening: The Roots of Evangelical Christianity in Colonial America*. Yale University Press, 2009.

Kim, Sung Ho. "Max Weber." In *Stanford Encyclopedia of Philosophy*. Stanford University, 1997–. Article published July 31, 2012. http://plato.stanford.edu/archives/fall2012 /entries/weber/.

Kimball, Carol. *Song: A Guide to Art Song Style and Literature*. Hal Leonard, 2006.

Klepp, Susan E. "Rough Music on Independence Day: Philadelphia, 1778." In *Riot and Revelry in Early America*, edited by William Pencak, Matthew Dennis, and Simon P. Newman, 156–76. Pennsylvania State University Press, 2002.

Kmen, Henry A. *Music in New Orleans: The Formative Years 1791–1841*. Louisiana State University Press, 1966.

Knoll, Mark. A. *The Civil War as a Theological Crisis*. University of North Carolina Press, 2006.

Knott, Sarah. *Sensibility and the American Revolution*. University of North Carolina Press, 2009.

Knowles, Mark. *Tap Roots: The Early History of Tap Dancing*. Mcfarland and Co, 2002.

Knüppel, Christoph. "Kühl, Gustav: geb. 9.9.1869 Lübeck, gest. 20.10.1906 Berlin; ev.; Lehrer, Schriftsteller, Bibliotheksangestellter." In *Neue Lübecker Lebensläufe*, 357–60. Wachholtz Verlag, 2009.

Koenig, Karl, ed. *Jazz in Print (1859–1929): An Anthology of Selected Readings in Jazz History*. Pendragon Press, 2002.

Koza, Julia Eklund. "Music and the Feminine Sphere: Images of Women as Musicians in 'Godey's Lady's Book' 1830–1877." *Musical Quarterly* 75, no. 2 (Summer 1991): 103–29.

Kristeva, Julia. *La révolution du langage poétique: L'avant-garde à la fin du Xixe siècle, Lautréamont et Mallarmé* [Revolution in poetic language]. Éditions du Seuil, 1974.

Kristeva, Julia. "Word, Dialogue and Novel." In *The Kristeva Reader*, edited by Toril Moi, 34–61. Columbia University Press, 1986.

Kroll-Smith, Jack Stephen. "In Search of Status Power: The Baptist Revival in Colonial Virginia, 1760–1776." PhD diss., University of Pennsylvania, 1982.

Ladurie, Emmanuel Le Roy. *Carnival in Romans*. Translated by Mary Feeney. Braziller, 1979.

Lamothe, Kimerer L. "Enlivening Spirits: Shaker Dance Ritual as Theopraxis." *Théologiques* 25, no. 1 (2017): 103–24.

Landy, Joshua, and Michael Saler, eds. *The Re-Enchantment of the World: Secular Magic in a Rational Age*. Stanford University Press, 2009.

Lanternari, Vittorio. *The Religions of the Oppressed: A Study of Modern Messianic Cults*. Translated by Lisa Sergio. MacGibbon and Kee, 1963.

Lawrence, Vera Brodsky. *Strong on Music: The New York Music Scene in the Days of George Templeton Strong*, vol. 1: *Resonances, 1836–1849*. University of Chicago Press, 1988.

Lears, Jackson. *Fables of Abundance: A Cultural History of Advertising in America*. Basic Books, 1994.

Lears, Jackson. *Rebirth of a Nation: The Making of Modern America, 1877–1920*. HarperCollins, 2009.

Lears, Jackson. *Something for Nothing: Luck in America*. Penguin, 2003.

Lears, T. J. Jackson. "From Salvation to Self-Realization: Advertising and the Therapeutic Roots of the Consumer Culture." In *The Culture of Consumption: Critical Essays in American History, 1880–1980*, edited by Richard Fox and T. J. Jackson Lears, 1–38. Pantheon, 1983.

Lears, T. J. Jackson. *No Place of Grace: Antimodernism and the Transformation of American Culture, 1880–1920*. University of Chicago Press, 1981.

Leathem, Karen Trahan. "A Carnival According to Their Own Desires: Gender and Mardi Gras in New Orleans, 1870–1941." PhD diss., University of North Carolina, 1994.

Lee, Carol. *Ballet in Western Culture: A History of Its Origins and Evolution*. Routledge, 2002.

Legg, Andrew, and Carolyn Paul Harvey, "An Analysis of Performance Practices in African American Gospel Music: Rhythm, Lyric Treatment, and Structures in Improvisation and Accompaniment." *Popular Music* 34, no. 2 (2015): 197–225.

Levine, George. *Darwin Loves You: Natural Selection and the Re-enchantment of the World*. Princeton University Press, 2008.

Levine, Lawrence W. *Black Culture and Black Consciousness: Afro-American Folk Thought from Slavery to Freedom*. Oxford University Press, 1977.

Levine, Lawrence. *Highbrow/Lowbrow: The Emergence of Cultural Hierarchy in America*. Harvard University Press, 1988.

Lévi-Strauss, Claude. *Myth and Meaning*. University of Toronto Press, 1978.

Lévi-Strauss, Claude. *Structural Anthropology*. Vol. 2. Basic Books, 1976.

Levy, S. J. "Interpreting Consumer Mythology: A Structural Approach to Consumer Behavior." *Journal of Marketing* 45, no. 3 (1981): 49–61.

Lewis, Robert M. *From Traveling Show to Vaudeville: Theatrical Spectacle in America, 1830–1910.* Johns Hopkins University Press, 2003.

Lincoln, C. Eric, and Lawrence H. Mamiya. *The Black Church in the African American Experience.* Duke University Press, 1990.

Linkenbach, Antje, and Martin Mulsow. "Introduction: The Dividual Self." In *Religious Individualisation: Historical Dimensions and Comparative Perspectives,* edited by Martin Fuchs, Antje Linkenbach, Martin Mulsow, Bernd-Christian Otto, Rahul Bjørn Parson, and Jörg Rüpke. De Gruyter, 2020.

Locke, Ralph P. "Music Lovers, Patrons, and the 'Sacralization' of Culture in America." *Nineteenth-Century Music* 17, no. 2 (Autumn 1993): 149–73.

Logan, Rayford. *The Negro in American Life and Thought: The Nadir, 1877–1901.* Dial Press, 1954.

Long, Carolyn Morrow. *A New Orleans Voudou Priestess: The Legend and Reality of Marie Laveau.* University of Florida Press, 2007.

Long, Carolyn Morrow. "Perceptions of New Orleans Voodoo: Sin, Fraud, Entertainment, and Religion" *Nova Religio: The Journal of Alternative and Emergent Religions* 6, no. 1 (2002): 86–101.

Long, Kathryn Teresa. *The Revival of 1857–1858: Interpreting an American Religious Awakening.* Oxford University Press, 1998.

Lott, Eric. *Love and Theft: Blackface Minstrelsy and the American Working Class.* Oxford University Press, 1993.

Lowens, Irving. "Writings About Music in the Periodicals of American Transcendentalism, 1835–50." *Journal of American Musicological Society* 10, no. 2 (Summer 1957): 71–85.

Lowerson, John, and John Myerscough. *Time to Spare in Victorian England.* Harvester Press, 1977.

Lundin, Roger. *From Nature to Experience: The American Search for Cultural Authority.* Rowman and Littlefield, 2005.

Lyons-Fontenot, Florence. "Beyond Boundaries: Political Dictates Found in Minstrelsy." PhD diss., Louisiana State University, 2003.

Machado, Maria Helena P. T. *Brazil Through the Eyes of William James: Letters, Diaries, and Drawings, 1865–1866.* Harvard University Press, 2006.

Mailer, Norman. "The White Negro: Superficial Reflections on the Hipster." In *The Portable Beat Reader: Three Commentators on the Beat Generations,* edited by Ann Charters, 582–88. Viking, 1998.

Malcomson, Scott. *One Drop of Blood: The American Misadventure of Race.* Farrar, Straus and Giroux, 2000.

Malinar, Angelika, and Helene Basu. "Ecstasy." In *The Oxford Handbook of Religion and Emotion,* edited by John Corrigan, 241–58. Oxford University Press, 2008.

Mandler, G. *A History of Modern Experimental Psychology: From James and Wundt to Cognitive Science*. MIT Press, 2007.

Marcus, Greil. *Mystery Train: Images of America in Rock 'n' Roll Music*. 6th ed. Plume, 2015.

Marini, Stephen A. *Sacred Song in America: Religion, Music, and Public Culture*. University of Illinois Press, 2010.

Marsh, Christopher. *Music and Society in Early Modern England*. Cambridge University Press, 2010.

Martin, Larry. *The Life and Ministry of William J. Seymour: And a History of the Azusa Street Revival*. Christian Life Books, 1999.

Martin, Raymond, and John Barresi. *The Rise and Fall of Soul and Self: An Intellectual History of Personal Identity*. Columbia University Press, 2006.

Mathews, Donald. "The Second Great Awakening as an Organizing Process, 1780–1830: An Hypothesis." *American Quarterly* 21, no. 1 (Spring 1969): 23–43.

Matt, Susan J., and Peter N. Stearns, eds. *Doing Emotions History*. University of Illinois, 2013.

Maultsby, Portia K. "Africanisms in African-American Music." In *Africanisms in American Culture*, edited by Joseph E. Holloway, 185–210. Indiana University Press, 1990.

Mauss, Marcel. "A Category of the Human Mind: The Notion of Person; The Notion of Self." In *The Category of the Person*, translated by W. D. Halls, edited by M. Carrithers, S. Collins, and S. Lukes, 1–25. Cambridge University Press, 1938.

McCloud, Sean. *Divine Hierarchies: Class in American Religion and Religious Studies*. University of North Carolina, 2009.

McCormick, Steve. "Theosis in Chrysostom and Wesley: An Eastern Paradigm on Faith and Love." *Wesleyan Theological Journal* 26 (1991): 38–103.

McCrone, John. *The Myth of Irrationality: The Science of the Mind from Plato to Star Trek*. Carroll & Graf, 1993.

McDaniel, June. *Lost Ecstasy: Its Decline and Transformation in Religion*. Palgrave Macmillan, 2018.

McDonagh, Pierre, et al., eds. *Myth and the Market*. University College Dublin, 2014.

McGarvie, Mark D. *One Nation Under Law: America's Early National Struggles to Separate Church and State*. Northern Illinois University Press, 2004.

McKay, David P. "Cotton Mather's Unpublished Singing Sermon." *New England Quarterly* 48, no. 3 (September 1975): 410–22.

McLoughlin, William G. *Modern Revivalism: Charles Grandison Finney to Billy Graham*. Ronald Press, 1959.

McLoughlin, William G. *Revivals, Awakenings, and Reform: An Essay on Religion and Social Change in America, 1607–1977*. University of Chicago Press, 1980.

McLuhan, Marshall. *Understanding Media: The Extensions of Man*. McGraw-Hill, 1964.

McNamara, Brooks. *The New York Concert Saloon: The Devil's Own Nights*. Cambridge University Press, 2002.

Mee, Jon. *Romanticism, Enthusiasm, and Regulation: Poetics and the Policing of Culture in the Romantic Period*. Oxford University Press, 2003.

Mellers, Wilfrid. *Music in a New Found Land: Themes and Developments in the History of American Music*. Stonehill Publishing, 1964.

Merleau-Ponty, Maurice. *The Phenomenology of Perception*. Translated by David Landes. Routledge, 2012.

Mesquita, Batja. "Emoting: A Contextualized Process." In *The Mind in Context*, edited by Matja Mesquita, Lisa Feldman Barrett, and Eliot R. Smith, 83–104. Guilford Press, 2010.

Meyer, Leonard. *Emotion and Meaning in Music*. University of Chicago Press, 1956.

Mickey, Sam. "The Rhythm of Spirit Possession: An Entrancing Legacy." *Nomos Journal* (May 14, 2014). Accessed February 18, 2016. http://nomosjournal. org/columns/sounding-sacred/the-rhythm-of-spirit-possession/.

Millard, Andre. *America on Record: A History of Recorded Sound*. Cambridge: Cambridge University Press, 1995.

Miller, Daniel. *Material Culture and Mass Consumption*. Basil Blackwell, 1987.

Miller, Karl Hagstrom. *Segregating Sound: Inventing Folk and Pop Music in the Age of Jim Crow*. Duke University Press Books, 2010.

Miller, Perry. *Errand into the Wilderness*. Belknap Press of Harvard University Press, 1956.

Miller, Perry. *Nature's Nation*. Belknap Press of Harvard University Press, 1967.

Milner, Gabriel. "The Tenor of Belonging: The Fisk Jubilee Singers and the Popular Cultures of Postbellum Citizenship." *Journal of the Gilded Age and Progressive Era* 15, no. 3 (June 2016): 1–19.

Mintz, Steven. *Moralists and Modernizers: America's Pre–Civil War Reformers*. Johns Hopkins University Press, 1995.

Mitchell, Reid. *All on a Mardi Gras Day*. Harvard University Press, 1995.

Modern, John Lardas. *Secularism in Antebellum America*. University of Chicago Press, 2011.

Moore, Henry. *The Life of the Rev. John Wesley, A. M.* Vol. 1. Printed for John Kershaw, 1824.

Moore, R. Laurence. *In Search of White Crows: Spiritualism, Parapsychology, and American Culture*. Oxford University Press, 1977.

Moore, Rebecca. "Angels Among Us in Four San Diego Spiritualist Churches." In *The Spiritualist Movement: Speaking with the Dead in America and Around the World*, vol. 1, edited by Christopher M. Moreman, 161–80. Praeger, 2013.

Moores, D. J. *The Ecstatic Poetic Tradition: A Critical Study from the Ancients Through Rumi, Wordsworth, Whitman, Dickinson, and Tagore*. McFarland & Co., 2014.

Morris, Colin. *The Discovery of the Individual, 1050–1200*. University of Toronto Press, 1987.

Morse, Flo. *The Shakers and the World's People*. University Press of New England, 1980.

Morton, Thomas. *New English Canaan*. Edited by Jack Dempsey. Digital Scanning, 2000.

Munger, Margaret P., ed. *The History of Psychology: Fundamental Questions*. Oxford University Press, 2003.

Music, David W., and Paul Westermeyer. *Church Music in the United States 1760–1901*. MorningStar Music, 2014.

Music, David W. *Hymnology: A Collection of Source Readings*. Scarecrow Press, 1996.

Musser, Charles. "American Vitagraph 1897–1901." *Cinema Journal* 22, no. 3 (Spring 1983): 4–46.

Musser, Charles, and Carol Nelson. *High-Class Moving Pictures: Lyman H. Howe and the Forgotten Era of Traveling Exhibition, 1880–1920*. Princeton University Press, 1991.

Nathan, Hans. *Dan Emmet and the Rise of Early Negro Minstrelsy*. University of Oklahoma Press, 1962.

Needham, Maureen, ed. *I See America Dancing: Selected Readings 1685–2000*. University of Illinois Press, 2002.

Nelson, John K. *A Cheerful and Comfortable Faith: Parishes, Parsons, and Parishioners in Anglican Virginia, 1690–1776*. University of North Carolina Press, 2001.

"New York Slave Rebellion of 1712." *Encyclopedia Britannica*, March 30, 2023. Accessed November 28, 2023. https://www.britannica.com/event/New-York-slave-rebellion-of-1712.

Noon, David Hoogland. "The Evolution of Beasts and Babies: Recapitulation, Instinct, and the Early Discourse on Child Development." *Journal of the History of the Behavioral Sciences* 41, no. 4 (Fall 2005): 367–86.

Nord, David. *Faith in Reading: Religious Publishing and the Birth of Mass Media in America*. Oxford University Press, 2004.

Nussbaum, Martha C. *Upheavals of Thought: The Intelligence of Emotions*. University of Cambridge Press, 2001.

Oatley, Keith. *Emotions: A Brief History*. Wiley-Blackwell, 2004.

O'Brien, Rosary Hartel. "New Orleans Carnival Organizations: Theatre of Prestige." PhD diss., University of California, Los Angeles, 1973.

Ogasapian, John. *Church Music in America, 1620–2000*. Mercer University Press, 2021.

Ogasapian, John. *Music of the Colonial and Revolutionary Era*. Greenwood, 2004.

Ogasapian, John, and N. Lee Orr. *Music of the Gilded Age*. Greenwood, 2007.

Ogren, Kathy J. *The Jazz Revolution: Twenties America and the Meaning of Jazz*. Oxford University Press, 1992.

Oja, Carol J. *Making Music Modern: New York in the 1920s*. Oxford University Press, 2000.

Olsen, Glenn W. *The Turn to Transcendence: The Role of Religion in the Twenty-First Century*. Catholic University of America Press, 2010.

O'Malley, J. Steven. "Pietistic Influence on John Wesley: Wesley and Gerhard Tersteegen." *Wesleyan Theological Journal* 31, no. 2 (Fall 1996): 48–70.

O'Neill, Rosary. *New Orleans Carnival Krewes: The History, Spirit and Secrets of Mardi Gras*. History Press, 2014.

Oriard, Michael. *Sporting with the Gods: The Rhetoric of Play and Game in American Culture*. Cambridge University Press, 1991.

Otto, Rudolf. *The Idea of the Holy: An Inquiry into the Non-rational Factor in the Idea of the Divine and Its Relation to the Rational*. 2nd ed. Oxford University Press, 1936.

Parsons, William B. *The Enigma of the Oceanic Feeling: Revisioning the Psychoanalytic Theory of Mysticism*. Oxford University Press, 1999.

Partridge, Christopher. *The Lyre of Orpheus: Popular Music, the Sacred, and the Profane*. Oxford University Press, 2014.

Paskman, Dailey. *"Gentleman, Be Seated!" A Parade of the American Minstrels*. Clarkson N. Potter, 1976.

Patterson, Daniel. *Gift Drawing and Gift Song: A Study of Two Forms of Shaker Inspiration*. United Society of Shakers, 1983.

Patterson, Daniel W. *The Shaker Spiritual*. Dover, 2000.

Peoples, Gabriel. "A Circular Lineage: The BaKongo Cosmogram and the Ring Shout of the Enslaved Africans and Their Descendants on the Georgian and South Carolinian Sea Islands." Master's thesis, Cornell University, 2008.

Perry, Bliss. *Life and Letters of Henry Lee Higginson*. Atlantic Monthly Press, 1921.

Pestana, Carla Gardina. *The English Atlantic in the Age of Revolution, 1640–1661*. Harvard University Press, 2004.

Pfister, Joel and Nancy Schnog, eds. *Inventing the Psychological: Toward a Cultural History of Emotional Life in America*. Yale University Press, 1997.

Philibert, Jean-Marc. "Consuming Culture: A Study of Simple Commodity Consumption." In *The Social Economy of Consumption*, edited by Benjamin Orlove and Henry Rutz, 59–84. University Press of America, 1989.

Picart, Caroline Joan S. "Nietzsche as Masked Romantic." *Journal of Aesthetics and Art Criticism* 55, no. 3 (Summer 1997): 273–91.

Plamper, Jan. *The History of Emotions: An Introduction*. Translated by Keith Tribe. Oxford University Press, 2015.

Porter, Cole, Alan Strachan, and Benny Green. *The Mermaid Theatre's Cole: An Entertainment Based on the Words and Music of Cole Porter*. Samuel French, 1981.

Poulain, Augustin. "Contemplation." In *The Catholic Encyclopedia*, vol. 4, edited by Charles George Herbermann, 324–29. Robert Appleton Company, 1908. http://oce.catholic.com/index.php?title =Contemplation.

Rabinovitz, Lauren. *For the Love of Pleasure: Women, Movies, and Culture in Turn-of-the-Century*. Rutgers University Press, 1998.

Rabinovitz, Lauren. "More Than the Movies: A History of the Somatic Visual Culture Through Hale's Tours, Imax, and Motion Simulation Rides." In *Memory

Bytes: History, Technology, and Digital Culture, edited by Lauren Rabinovitz and Abraham Geil, 99–125. Duke University Press, 2004.

Raboteau, Albert J. *Canaan Land: A Religious History of African Americans*. Oxford University Press, 1999.

Raboteau, Albert J. *Slave Religion: The "Invisible Institution" in the Antebellum South*. Oxford University Press, 2004.

Radano, Ronald. "Denoting Difference: The Writing of the Slave Spirituals." *Critical Inquiry* 22, no. 3 (Spring 1996): 506–44.

Rasmussen, Daniel. *American Uprising: The Untold Story of America's Largest Slave Revolt*. Harper, 2011.

Rath, Richard. *How Early American Sounded*. Cornell University Press, 2003.

Ratner-Rosenhagen, Jennifer. *American Nietzsche: A History of an Icon and His Ideas*. University of Chicago Press, 2012.

Reddy, William. *The Navigation of Feeling: A Framework for the History of Emotions*. Cambridge University Press, 2001.

Reed, Edward S. *From Soul to Mind: The Emergence of Psychology from Erasmus Darwin to William James*. Yale University Press, 1997.

Reitano, Joanne. *The Restless City: A Short History of New York from Colonial Times to the Present*. 2nd ed. Routledge, 2010.

Reginster, Bernard. *The Affirmation of Life: Nietzsche on Overcoming Nihilism*. Harvard University Press, 2006.

Reynolds, David S. " 'Its Wood Could Only Be American!' Moby-Dick and Antebellum Popular Culture." In *Herman Melville's Moby-Dick*, edited by Harold Bloom, 105–6. Infobase, 2007.

Richards, Graham. "Emotions into Words—or Words into Emotions." In *Representing Emotions: New Connections in the Histories of Art, Music and Medicine*, edited by Helen Hills and Penelope Gouk. Ashgate, 2005.

Rieff, Philip. *The Triumph of the Therapeutic: Uses of Faith After Freud*. Harper and Row, 1966.

Robbinson, Keith. *Nineteenth-Century Britain*. Oxford University Press, 1988.

Roberts, John Storm. *Black Music of Two Worlds: African, Caribbean, Latin, and African American Traditions*. Schirmer Books, 1998.

Roberts, John Storm. *The Latin Tinge: The Impact of Latin American Music on the United States*. Oxford University Press, 1999.

Roberts, Vaughan S., and Clive Marsh. *Personal Jesus: How Popular Music Shapes Our Souls*. Baker Academic, 2012.

Rodriguez, Hector. "The Playful and the Serious: An Approximation to Huizinga's Homo Ludens." *Game Studies* 6, no. 1 (December 2006). http://gamestudies. org/0601 /articles/rodriges.

Roediger, David R. *The Wages of Whiteness: Race and the Making of the American Working Class*. Verso, 1991.

Rosaldo, Renato. "Imperialist Nostalgia." *Representations* 26 (Spring 1989): 107–22.

Rose, Nikolas. "Assembling the Modern Self." In *Rewriting the Self: Histories from the Renaissance to the Present*, edited by Roy Porter, 224–48. Routledge, 1997.

Rosentiel, Tom. "Religion and Secularism: The American Experience." Pew Research Center, December 3, 2007. Accessed November 28, 2023. https://www.pewresearch.org/2007/12/03/religion-and-secularism-the-american-experience/.

Rosenwein, Barbara H. *Generations of Feeling: A History of Emotions, 600–1700*. Cambridge University Press, 2015.

Rouget, Gilbert. *Music and Trance: A Theory of the Relations Between Music and Possession*. University of Chicago Press, 1985.

Rucker, Walter. "Conjure, Magic, and Power: The Influence of Afro-Atlantic Religious Practices on Slave Resistance and Rebellion," *Journal of Black Studies* 32, no. 1 (2001): 84–103.

Ryan, Mary. *Cradle of the Middle Class: The Family in Oneida County, New York, 1790–1865*. Cambridge University Press, 1983.

Sacks, Oliver. *Musicophilia: Tales of Music and the Brain, Revised and Expanded Edition*. Vintage, 2008.

Salen, Katie, and Eric Zimmerman. *Rules of Play: Game Design Fundamentals*. MIT Press, 2004.

Saler, Michael. *As If: Modern Enchantment and the Literary Prehistory of Virtual Reality*. Oxford University Press, 2012.

Samuels, Shirley, ed. *Culture of Sentiment*. Oxford University Press, 1992.

Sanders, Robert Stuart. *Presbyterianism in Paris and Bourbon County, Kentucky, 1786–1961*. Dunne Press, 1961.

Sanjek, David. "They Work Hard for Their Money: The Business of Popular Music." In *American Popular Music: New Approaches to the Twentieth Century*, edited by Rachel Rubin and Jeffrey Paul Melnick, 47–64. University of Massachusetts Press, 2001.

Sanjek, Russell. *American Popular Music and Its Business: The First Four Hundred Years*. Vol. 3, *From 1909 to 1989*. Oxford University Press, 1988.

Sarbanes, Janet. "The Shaker 'Gift' Economy: Charisma, Aesthetic Practice and Utopian Communalism," *Utopian Studies* 20, no. 1 (2009): 121–39.

Sassen, Saskia. "Organized Religions in Our Global Modernity." *Publications of the Modern Language Association of America* 126, no. 2 (2011): 455–59.

Satz, Aura. "Music of Its Own Accord." *Leonardo Music Journal* 20 (2010): 73–78.

Sawyer, R. Keith. "Durkheim's Dilemma: Toward a Sociology of Emergence." *Sociological Theory* 20, no. 2 (July 2002): 227–47.

Scheer, Monique. "Are Emotions a Kind of Practice (and Is That What Makes Them Have a History)? A Bourdieuan Approach to Understanding Emotion." *History and Theory* 51, no. 2 (May 2012): 193–220.

Schmidt, Leigh Eric. *Hearing Things: Religion, Illusion, and the American Enlightenment*. Harvard University Press, 2000.

Scobey, David. "Anatomy of the Promenade: The Politics of Bourgeois Sociability in Nineteenth-Century New York." *Social History* 17, no. 2 (May 1992): 203–27.

Scruton, Roger. "Music and the Transcendental." In *Music and Transcendence*, edited by Ferdia Stone-Davis, 75–84. Routledge, 2015.

S. D., Trav. *No Applause—Just Throw Money: The Book That Made Vaudeville Famous.* Faber and Faber, 2005.

Seigel, Jerrold. *The Idea of the Self: Thought and Experience in Western Europe Since the Seventeenth Century.* Cambridge University Press, 2005.

Seroff, Doug. *Gospel Arts Day Nashville: A Special Commemoration.* Fisk University, Fisk Memorial Chapel (June 18, 1989). https://issuu.com/tnarts/docs/1989_gospel_arts_day_nashville.

Shadle, Karen L. "Singing with Spirit and Understanding: Psalmody as Holistic Practice in Late Eighteenth-Century New England." PhD diss., University of North Carolina at Chapel Hill, 2010.

Sheff, David. *All We Are Saying: The Last Major Interview with John Lennon and Yoko Ono.* St. Martin's, 2000.

Shields, Stephanie A. "The Concept of Self in Emotion Theory." Paper presented at the Annual Convention of the American Psychological Association, Anaheim, CA, August 26–30, 1983.

Shoemaker, Alfred Lewis. *Christmas in Pennsylvania: A Folk-Cultural Study.* Stackpole Books, 1999.

Shortt, S. E. D. "Physicians and Psychics: The Anglo-American Medical Response to Spiritualism, 1870–1890." *Journal of the History of Medicine and Allied Sciences* 39 (1984): 339–55.

Shull, Kristina Karin. "Is the Magic Gone? Weber's 'Disenchantment of the World' and Its Implications for Art in Today's World." *Anamesa* (Fall 2005): 61–73.

Siedentop, Larry. *Inventing the Individual: The Origins of Western Liberalism.* Belknap Press of Harvard University, 2014.

Simonson, Harold P. *Jonathan Edwards: Theologian of the Heart.* Mercer University Press, 1982.

Sluhovsky, Moshe. "Spirit Possession and Other Alterations of Consciousness in the Christian Western Tradition." In *Altering Consciousness: Multidisciplinary Perspectives*, vol. 1., *History, Culture, and the Humanities*, edited by Etzel Cardeña and Michael Winkelman, 73–88. Praeger, 2011.

Small, Christopher. *Musicking: The Meanings of Performing and Listening.* University Press of New England, 1998.

Small, Christopher. *Music of the Common Tongue: Survival and Celebration in Afro-American Music.* Riverrun Press, 1987.

Smith, Christian, ed. *The Secular Revolution: Power, Interests, and Conflict in the Secularization of American Public Life.* University of California Press, 2003.

Snyder, Robert W. *The Voice of the City: Vaudeville and Popular Culture in New York.* Oxford University Press, 1989.

Sobel, Mechal. *Trabelin' On: The Slave Journey to an Afro-Baptist Faith*. Princeton University Press, 1988.

Sorabji, Richard. *Self: Ancient and Modern Insights About Individuality, Life, and Death*. University of Chicago Press, 2006.

Sousa, John Philip. *Six Marches*. Edited by Patrick Warfield. A-R Editions, 2010.

Southern, Eileen. *The Music of Black Americans: A History*. W. W. Norton, 1983.

Southern, R. W. *The Making of the Middle Ages*. Yale University Press, 1992.

Spade, Paul Vincent, and Claude Panaccio. "William of Ockham." In *Stanford Encyclopedia of Philosophy*. Stanford University, 1997–. Article published June 25, 2015. http://plato.stanford.edu/entries/ockham/.

Spencer, Jon Michael. "Musicology as a Theologically Informed Discipline." In *Theomusicology*, edited by Jon Michael Spencer, 36–63. Duke University Press, 1994.

Spencer, Jon Michael. *Theological Music: An Introduction to Theomusicology*. Greenwood, 1991.

Spiro, Lisa. "Reading with a Tender Rapture: Reveries of a Bachelor and the Rhetoric of Detached Intimacy." *Book History* 6 (2003): 57–93.

Stallybrass, Peter, and Allon White. *The Politics and Poetics of Transgression*. Cornell University Press, 1986.

Stauffer, Donald Barlow. "Opera and Opera Singers." In *The Routledge Encyclopedia of Walt Whitman*, edited by J. R. LeMaster and Donald D. Kummings, 484–86. Routledge, 1998.

Stearns, Carol Zisowitz, and Peter N. Stearns. *Anger: The Struggle for Emotional Control in America's History*. University of Chicago Press, 1989.

Stearns, Marshall. *Jazz Dance: The Story of American Vernacular Dance*. Da Capo, 1968.

Stebbins, Emma, ed. *Charlotte Cushman: Her Letters and Memories of Her Life*. Houghton, 1879.

Steel, David Warren. "Sacred Music in Early Winchester." *Connecticut Historical Society Bulletin* 45 (April 1980): 33–44.

Stein, Stephen J. *The Shaker Experience in America: A History of the United Society of Believers*. Yale University Press, 1992.

Steiner, George. *Nostalgia for the Absolute*. CBC Publications, 1974.

Steiner, George. *Real Presences*. University of Chicago Press, 1989.

Stewart, Matthew. *Nature's God: The Heretical Origins of the American Republic*. W. W. Norton, 2014.

Stewart, Steven J. "Skimmington in the Middle and New England Colonies." In *Riot and Revelry in Early America*, edited by William Pencak, Matthew Dennis, and Simon P. Newman, 41–86. Pennsylvania State University Press, 2002.

St. John, Graham. *Global Tribe: Technology, Spirituality and Psytrance*. Equinox, 2012.

St. John, Graham, ed. *Rave Culture and Religion*. Routledge, 2004.

Stock, Brian. *Augustine the Reader: Meditation, Self-Knowledge, and the Ethics of Interpretation*. Belknap Press of Harvard University, 1997.

Stoltzfus, Philip E. *Theology as Performance: Music, Aesthetics and God in Modern Theology.* T & T Clark, 2006.

Stone-Davis, Ferdia J., ed. *Music and Transcendence.* Routledge, 2015.

Storey, John, ed. *Culture Theory and Popular Culture: A Reader.* 4th ed. Routledge, 2008.

Stowe, David W. *How Sweet the Sound: Music in the Spiritual Lives of Americans.* Harvard University Press, 2004.

Stromberg, Peter. *Caught in Play: How Entertainment Works on You.* Stanford University Press, 2009.

Sublette, Ned. *Cuba and Its Music: From the First Drums to the Mambo.* Chicago Review Press, 2007.

Sublette, Ned. *The World That Made New Orleans: From Spanish Silver to Congo Square.* Chicago Review Press, 2009.

Suisman, David. *Selling Sounds: The Commercial Revolution in American Music.* Harvard University Press, 2009.

Sullivan, John Jeremiah. "Talking Drums." *Oxford American* 107 (Winter 2019). Accessed November 28, 2023. https://oxfordamerican.org/magazine/issue-107/talking-drums.

Sutton-Smith, Brian. *The Ambiguity of Play.* Harvard University Press, 2001.

Sylvan, Robin. *Traces of the Spirit: The Religious Dimensions of Popular Music.* New York University Press, 2002.

Sylvan, Robin. *Trance Formation: The Spiritual and Religious Dimensions of Global Rave Culture.* Routledge, 2005.

Synan, Vinson. *The Holiness-Pentecostal Tradition: Charismatic Movements in the Twentieth Century.* W.B. Eerdmans, 1997.

Tallant, Robert. *Mardi Gras . . . as It Was.* Pelican Publishing, 1994.

Tallant, Robert. *Voodoo in New Orleans.* Macmillan, 1962.

Tatar, Maria M. *Spellbound: Studies on Mesmerism and Literature.* Princeton University Press, 1978.

Taussig, Michael. *Mimesis and Alterity: A Particular History of the Senses.* Routledge, 1993.

Taves, Ann. *Fits, Trances, and Visions: Experiencing Religion and Explaining Experience from Wesley to James.* Princeton University Press, 1999.

Tawa, Nicholas E. *From Psalm to Symphony: A History of Music in New England.* Northeastern University Press, 2001.

Tawa, Nicolas E. *Sweet Songs for Gentle Americans: The Parlor Song in America, 1790–1860.* Bowling Green University Popular Press, 1980.

Tawney, R. H. *Religion and the Rise of Capitalism.* Harcourt, Brace, 1926.

Taylor, Charles. *A Secular Age.* Belknap Press of Harvard University Press, 2007.

Taylor, Charles. *Sources of the Self: The Making of the Modern Identity.* Harvard University Press, 1989.

Taylor, Eugene. "William James and Transpersonal Psychiatry." In *Textbook of Transpersonal Psychiatry and Psychology*, edited by Bruce W. Scotton, Allan B. Chinen, and John R. Battista, 21–28. Basic Books, 1996.

Taylor, Gordon Rattray. *The Angel-Makers: A Study in the Psychological Origins of Historical Change, 1750–1850.* Heinemann, 1958.

Taylor, Timothy D. *The Sounds of Capitalism: Advertising, Music, and the Conquest of Culture.* University of Chicago Press, 2012.

Taylor, Timothy D., Mark Katz, and Tony Grajeda, eds. *Music, Sound, and Technology in America: A Documentary History of Early Phonograph, Cinema, and Radio.* Duke University Press, 2012.

Thomas, Kenneth. *The Religious Dancing of American Slaves, 1820–1865: Spiritual Ecstasy at Baptisms, Funerals, and Sunday Meetings.* Edwin Mellen, 2008.

Thompson, E. P. *Customs in Common: Studies in Traditional Popular Culture.* New Press, 1993.

Thompson, Emily. "Machines, Music, and the Quest for Fidelity: Marketing the Edison Phonograph in America, 1877–1925." *Musical Quarterly* 79 (Spring 1995): 131–71.

Thompson, Robert Farris. "An Aesthetic of the Cool." *African Arts* 7, no. 1 (Autumn 1973): 40–43, 64–67, 89–91.

Thompson, Robert Farris. *Flash of the Spirit: African and Afro-American Art and Philosophy.* Vintage, 1984.

Tick, Judith. "Theodore Thomas and His Musical Manifest Destiny." In *Music in the USA: A Documentary Companion*, edited by Judith Tick and Paul Beaudoin, 270–80. Oxford University Press, 2008.

Till, Rupert. *Pop Cult: Religion and Popular Music.* Continuum, 2010.

Toll, Robert C. *Blacking Up: The Minstrel Show in Nineteenth-Century America.* Oxford University Press, 1974.

Torgovnick, Marianna. *Primitive Passions: Men, Women, and the Quest for Ecstasy.* University of Chicago Press, 1997.

Torre, Jose. *The Political Economy of Sentiment: Paper Credit and the Scottish Enlightenment in Early Republic Boston, 1780–1820.* Pickering & Chatto, 2007.

Touchstone, Blake. "Voodoo in New Orleans." *Louisiana History: The Journal of the Louisiana Historical Association* 13, no. 4 (1972): 371–86.

Trautman, Frederick. "New Orleans, the Mississippi, and the Delta Through a German's Eyes: The Travels of Emil Deckert, 1885–1886." *Louisiana History* 25 (1994): 79–98.

Tucker, Susie I. *Enthusiasm: A Study in Semantic Change.* Cambridge University Press, 1972.

Turner, Edith. *Communitas: The Anthropology of Collective Joy.* Palgrave Macmillan, 2012.

Turner, James. *Without God, Without Creed: The Origins of Unbelief in America.* Johns Hopkins University Press, 1986.

Turner, Victor. *Dramas, Fields, and Metaphors: Symbolic Action in Human Society.* Cornell University Press, 1974.

Turner, Victor. "Liminal to Liminoid in Play, Flow, and Ritual: An Essay in Comparative Symbology." *Rice University Studies* 60, no. 3 (1974): 53–92.

Turner, Victor. *The Ritual Process: Structure and Anti-Structure.* Routledge & Kegan Paul, 1969.

Twain, Mark. *Mark Twain's Letters, 1872–1873: Volume 5.* University of California Press, 1997.

Ullman, Walter. *The Individual and Society in the Middle Ages.* Johns Hopkins University Press, 1966.

Underdown, David. *Revel, Riot and Rebellion.* Oxford University Press, 1985.

Ustinova, Yulia. *Caves and the Ancient Greek Mind: Descending Underground in the Search for Ultimate Truth.* Oxford University Press, 2009.

Ustinova, Yulia. "Consciousness Alteration Practices in the West from Prehistory to Late Antiquity." In *Altering Consciousness,* vol. 1, *History, Culture, and the Humanities,* edited by Etzel Cardeña and Michael Winkelman, 45–72. Praeger, 2011.

Van Dyken, Tamara J. "Singing the Gospel: Evangelical Hymnody, Popular Religion, and American Culture; 1870–1940." PhD diss., University of Notre Dame, 2008.

Wacker, Grant. *Heaven Below: Early Pentecostals and American Culture.* Harvard University Press, 2001.

Walker, Sheila S. *Ceremonial Spirit Possession in African and Afro-America: Forms, Meanings, and Functional Significance for Individual and Social Groups.* Brill, 1972.

Waller, John. *The Dancing Plague: The Strange, True Story of an Extraordinary Illness.* Sourcebooks, 2009.

Walser, Richard. "Boston's Reception of the First American Novel." *Early American Literature* 17, no. 1 (Spring 1982): 65–74.

Walton, John K. *The English Seaside Resort.* St. Martin's, 1983.

Walton, Kendall. *Mimesis as Make-Believe.* Harvard University Press, 1990.

Warfield, Patrick. *Making the March King: John Philip Sousa's Washington Years, 1854–1893.* University of Illinois Press, 2013.

Warfield, Patrick. "The Sousa March: From Publication to Performance." In *Six Marches,* by John Philip Sousa. A-R Editions, 2010.

Warner, Michael. "Rethinking Secularism: Was Antebellum America Secular?" In *The Immanent Frame: Secularism, Religion, and the Public Sphere.* Social Science Research Council, October 2, 2012. http://blogs.ssrc.org/tif/2012/10/02 / was-antebellum-america-secular/.

Warner, Michael, Jonathan Van Antwerpen, and Craig Calhoun, eds. *Varieties of Secularism in a Secular Age.* Harvard University Press, 2010.

Warner, Wayne. *Maria Woodworth-Etter: For Such a Time as This.* Bridge-Logos, 2004.

Warren, Jeff R. *Music and Ethical Responsibility*. Cambridge University Press, 2014.

Weber, Max. *From Max Weber*. Edited by H. H. Gerth and C. Wright Mills. Oxford University Press, 1946.

Weber, Max. *The Protestant Ethic and the Spirit of Capitalism*. Translated by Talcott Parsons Max. Routledge, (1930) 2005.

Weber, Max. *The Rational and Social Foundations of Music*. Translated by D. Martindale, J. Riedel, and G. Neuwirth. Southern Illinois University Press, 1958.

Weber, Max. *The Sociology of Religion*. Translated by Talcott Parson. Beacon, (c. 1922) 1993.

Weber, William. "Did People Listen in the 18th Century." *Early Music* 25, no. 4 (November 1997): 678–91.

Webster, Noah. *American Dictionary of the English Language / Webster's Dictionary 1828* [electronic edition]. (MasonSoft Technology, 2022). Accessed November 28, 2023. https://webstersdictionary1828.com.

Wertheimer, Michael. *A Brief History of Psychology*. Psychology Press, 2011.

White, Shane, and Graham White. *The Sounds of Slavery: Discovering African American History Through Songs, Sermons, and Speech*. Beacon, 2005.

Wickramasekera, Ian E., II. "Hypnosis and Transpersonal Psychology: Answering the Call Within." In *The Wiley-Blackwell Handbook of Transpersonal Psychology*, edited by Harris L. Friedman and Glenn Hartelius, 492–511. John Wiley & Sons, 2013.

Wigger, John H. *Taking Heaven by Storm: Methodism and the Rise of Popular Christianity in America*. Oxford University Press, 1998.

Wilentz, Sean. *Chants Democratic: New York City and the Rise of the American Working Class, 1788–1850*. Oxford University Press, 1984.

Wiley, Norbert. "History of the Self: From Primates to Present." *Sociological Perspectives* 37, no. 4 (Winter 1994): 527–45.

Williams, Peter. *J. S. Bach: A Life in Music*. Cambridge University Press, 2007.

Williams, Raymond. *Keywords: A Vocabulary of Culture and Society*. Rev. ed. Oxford University Press, (c. 1976) 1983.

Williams, Raymond. *The Long Revolution*. Chatto and Windus, 1961.

Williams, Raymond. *Marxism and Literature*. Oxford University Press, 1977.

Wilmeth, Don B., and Christopher Bigsby, eds., *The Cambridge History of American Theatre*, Vol. 1: *Beginnings to 1870*. Cambridge University Press, 1998.

Wilson, Edmund. *Piece of My Mind: Reflections at Sixty*. Farrar, Straus and Giroux, 1956.

Winner, Lauren F. *A Cheerful and Comfortable Faith: Anglican Religious Practice in the Elite Households of Eighteenth-Century Virginia*. Yale University Press, 2010.

Wittgenstein, Ludwig. *Philosophical Investigations*. Translated by G. E. M. Anscombe. Macmillan, 1953.

Woodlief, Ann. "Emerson and Thoreau as American Prophets of Eco-Wisdom." Paper presented at the Virginia Humanities Conference, 1990. http://transcendentalism-legacy.tamu.edu/criticism/ecotran.html.

Woollcott, Alexander. *The Story of Irving Berlin*. Da Capo, 1925.

Wright, Walter Francis. *Sensibility in English Prose Fiction, 1760–1814: A Reinterpretation*. Folcroft Press, (1937) 1970.

Wurth, Kiene Brillenburg. *Musically Sublime: Indeterminacy, Infinity, Irresolvability*. Fordham University Press, 2009.

Zellers, Parker. *Tony Pastor: Dean of the Vaudeville Stage*. Eastern Michigan University Press, 1971.

Index